THE MINOR PROPHETS

THE IGNATIUS CATHOLIC STUDY BIBLE

REVISED STANDARD VERSION
SECOND CATHOLIC EDITION

THE MINOR PROPHETS

With Introduction, Commentary, and Notes

by

Scott Hahn and Curtis Mitch

with

Mark Giszczak and David Twellman

and with

Study Questions by

Dennis Walters

IGNATIUS PRESS   SAN FRANCISCO

Original RSV Bible text:
Revised Standard Version, Catholic Edition
Nihil Obstat: Thomas Hanlon, S.T.L., L.S.S., Ph.L.
Imprimatur: + Gordon Joseph Gray
Archbishop of Saint Andrews and Edinburgh
Epiphany, 1966
Imprimatur: +Peter W. Bartholome, D.D.
Bishop of St. Cloud, Minnesota
May 11, 1966

Introduction, commentaries, and notes:
Nihil Obstat: Dr. Ruth Ohm Sutherland, Ph.D., M.T.S.
Imprimatur: + The Most Reverend Salvatore Cordileone
Archbishop of San Francisco
October 3, 2022

Second Catholic Edition approved by the
National Council of the Churches of Christ in the USA

Cover art: *The Prophet Amos* by James Tissot (1836–1902)
The Jewish Museum of New York/A gift of the heirs of Jacob Schiff

Cover design by Riz Boncan Marsella

CONTENTS

INTRODUCTION TO
THE IGNATIUS STUDY BIBLE
by Scott Hahn, Ph.D.

You are approaching the "word of God". This is the title Christians most commonly give to the Bible, and the expression is rich in meaning. It is also the title given to the Second Person of the Blessed Trinity, God the Son. For Jesus Christ became flesh for our salvation, and "the name by which he is called is The Word of God" (Rev 19:13; cf. Jn 1:14).

The word of God is Scripture. The Word of God is Jesus. This close association between God's *written* word and his *eternal* Word is intentional and has been the custom of the Church since the first generation. "All Sacred Scripture is but one book, and this one book is Christ, 'because all divine Scripture speaks of Christ, and all divine Scripture is fulfilled in Christ'[1]" (CCC 134). This does not mean that the Scriptures are divine in the same way that Jesus is divine. They are, rather, divinely inspired and, as such, are unique in world literature, just as the Incarnation of the eternal Word is unique in human history.

Yet we can say that the inspired word resembles the incarnate Word in several important ways. Jesus Christ is the Word of God incarnate. In his humanity, he is like us in all things, except for sin. As a work of man, the Bible is like any other book, except without error. Both Christ and Scripture, says the Second Vatican Council, are given "for the sake of our salvation" (*Dei Verbum* 11), and both give us God's definitive revelation of himself. We cannot, therefore, conceive of one without the other: the Bible without Jesus, or Jesus without the Bible. Each is the interpretive key to the other. And because Christ is the subject of all the Scriptures, St. Jerome insists, "Ignorance of the Scriptures is ignorance of Christ"[2] (CCC 133).

When we approach the Bible, then, we approach Jesus, the Word of God; and in order to encounter Jesus, we must approach him in a prayerful study of the inspired word of God, the Sacred Scriptures.

Inspiration and Inerrancy The Catholic Church makes mighty claims for the Bible, and our acceptance of those claims is essential if we are to read the Scriptures and apply them to our lives as the Church intends. So it is not enough merely to nod at words like "inspired", "unique", or "inerrant". We

have to understand what the Church means by these terms, and we have to make that understanding our own. After all, what we believe about the Bible will inevitably influence the way we read the Bible. The way we read the Bible, in turn, will determine what we "get out" of its sacred pages.

These principles hold true no matter what we read: a news report, a search warrant, an advertisement, a paycheck, a doctor's prescription, an eviction notice. How (or whether) we read these things depends largely upon our preconceived notions about the reliability and authority of their sources—and the potential they have for affecting our lives. In some cases, to misunderstand a document's authority can lead to dire consequences. In others, it can keep us from enjoying rewards that are rightfully ours. In the case of the Bible, both the rewards and the consequences involved take on an ultimate value.

What does the Church mean, then, when she affirms the words of St. Paul: "All Scripture is inspired by God" (2 Tim 3:16)? Since the term "inspired" in this passage could be translated "God-breathed", it follows that God breathed forth his word in the Scriptures as you and I breathe forth air when we speak. This means that God is the primary author of the Bible. He certainly employed human authors in this task as well, but he did not merely assist them while they wrote or subsequently approve what they had written. God the Holy Spirit is the *principal* author of Scripture, while the human writers are *instrumental* authors. These human authors freely wrote everything, and only those things, that God wanted: the word of God in the very words of God. This miracle of dual authorship extends to the whole of Scripture, and to every one of its parts, so that whatever the human authors affirm, God likewise affirms through their words.

The principle of biblical inerrancy follows logically from this principle of divine authorship. After all, God cannot lie, and he cannot make mistakes. Since the Bible is divinely inspired, it must be without error in everything that its divine and human authors affirm to be true. This means that biblical inerrancy is a mystery even broader in scope than infallibility, which guarantees for us that the Church will always teach the truth concerning faith and morals. Of course the mantle of inerrancy likewise covers faith and morals, but it extends even farther to ensure that all the facts and events of salvation history are accurately presented for us in

---

[1] Hugh of St. Victor, *De arca Noe* 2, 8: PL 176, 642: cf. ibid. 2, 9: PL 176, 642–43.
[2] *DV* 25; cf. Phil 3:8 and St. Jerome, *Commentariorum in Isaiam libri xviii*, prol.: PL 24, 17b.

the Scriptures. Inerrancy is our guarantee that the words and deeds of God found in the Bible are unified and true, declaring with one voice the wonders of his saving love.

The guarantee of inerrancy does not mean, however, that the Bible is an all-purpose encyclopedia of information covering every field of study. The Bible is not, for example, a textbook in the empirical sciences, and it should not be treated as one. When biblical authors relate facts of the natural order, we can be sure they are speaking in a purely descriptive and "phenomenological" way, according to the way things appeared to their senses.

Biblical Authority Implicit in these doctrines is God's desire to make himself known to the world and to enter a loving relationship with every man, woman, and child he has created. God gave us the Scriptures not just to inform or motivate us; more than anything he wants to save us. This higher purpose underlies every page of the Bible, indeed every word of it.

In order to reveal himself, God used what theologians call "accommodation". Sometimes the Lord stoops down to communicate by "condescension"—that is, he speaks as humans speak, as if he had the same passions and weakness that we do (for example, God says he was "sorry" that he made man in Genesis 6:6). Other times he communicates by "elevation"—that is, by endowing human words with divine power (for example, through the Prophets). The numerous examples of divine accommodation in the Bible are an expression of God's wise and fatherly ways. For a sensitive father can speak with his children either by condescension, as in baby talk, or by elevation, by bringing a child's understanding up to a more mature level.

God's word is thus saving, fatherly, and personal. Because it speaks directly to us, we must never be indifferent to its content; after all, the word of God is at once the object, cause, and support of our faith. It is, in fact, a test of our faith, since we see in the Scriptures only what faith disposes us to see. If we believe what the Church believes, we will see in Scripture the saving, inerrant, and divinely authored revelation of the Father. If we believe otherwise, we see another book altogether.

This test applies not only to rank-and-file believers but also to the Church's theologians and hierarchy, and even the Magisterium. Vatican II has stressed in recent times that Scripture must be "the very soul of sacred theology" (*Dei Verbum* 24). As Joseph Cardinal Ratzinger, Pope Benedict XVI echoed this powerful teaching with his own, insisting that "the *normative theologians* are the authors of Holy Scripture" (emphasis added). He reminded us that Scripture and the Church's dogmatic teaching are tied tightly together, to the point of being inseparable: "Dogma is by definition nothing other than an interpretation of Scripture." The defined dogmas of our faith, then, encapsulate the Church's infallible interpretation of Scripture, and theology is a further reflection upon that work.

The Senses of Scripture Because the Bible has both divine and human authors, we are required to master a different sort of reading than we are used to. First, we must read Scripture according to its *literal* sense, as we read any other human literature. At this initial stage, we strive to discover the meaning of the words and expressions used by the biblical writers as they were understood in their original setting and by their original recipients. This means, among other things, that we do not interpret everything we read "literalistically", as though Scripture never speaks in a figurative or symbolic way (it often does!). Rather, we read it according to the rules that govern its different literary forms of writing, depending on whether we are reading a narrative, a poem, a letter, a parable, or an apocalyptic vision. The Church calls us to read the divine books in this way to ensure that we understand what the human authors were laboring to explain to God's people.

The literal sense, however, is not the only sense of Scripture, since we interpret its sacred pages according to the *spiritual* senses as well. In this way, we search out what the Holy Spirit is trying to tell us, beyond even what the human authors have consciously asserted. Whereas the literal sense of Scripture describes a historical reality—a fact, precept, or event—the spiritual senses disclose deeper mysteries revealed through the historical realities. What the soul is to the body, the spiritual senses are to the literal. You can distinguish them; but if you try to separate them, death immediately follows. St. Paul was the first to insist upon this and warn of its consequences: "God ... has qualified us to be ministers of a new covenant, not in a written code but in the Spirit; for the written code kills, but the Spirit gives life" (2 Cor 3:5–6).

Catholic tradition recognizes three spiritual senses that stand upon the foundation of the literal sense of Scripture (see CCC 115). **(1)** The first is the *allegorical* sense, which unveils the spiritual and prophetic meaning of biblical history. Allegorical interpretations thus reveal how persons, events, and institutions of Scripture can point beyond themselves toward greater mysteries yet to come (OT) or display the fruits of mysteries already revealed (NT). Christians have often read the Old Testament in this way to discover how the mystery of Christ in the New Covenant was once hidden in the Old and how the full significance of the Old Covenant was finally made manifest in the New. Allegorical significance is likewise latent in the New Testament, especially in the life and deeds of Jesus recorded in the Gospels. Because Christ is the Head of the Church and the source of her spiritual life, what was accomplished in Christ the Head during his earthly life prefigures what he continually produces in his members through grace. The allegorical sense builds up the virtue of faith. **(2)** The second is the *tropological* or *moral* sense, which reveals how the actions of God's people in the Old Testament and the life of Jesus in the New Testament prompt us to form virtuous habits in our own lives. It therefore draws from Scripture warnings against sin and vice as well as inspirations to pursue holiness and purity. The moral sense is intended to build up the virtue of charity. **(3)** The third is the *anagogical* sense, which points upward to heavenly glory. It shows us how countless events in the Bible prefigure our final union with God in eternity and how things that are "seen" on earth are figures of things "unseen" in heaven. Because the anagogical sense leads us to contemplate our destiny, it is meant to build up the virtue of hope. Together with the literal sense, then, these spiritual senses draw out the fullness of what God wants to give us through his Word and as such comprise what ancient tradition has called the "full sense" of Sacred Scripture.

All of this means that the deeds and events of the Bible are charged with meaning beyond what is immediately apparent to the reader. In essence, that meaning is Jesus Christ and the salvation he died to give us. This is especially true of the books of the New Testament, which proclaim Jesus explicitly; but it is also true of the Old Testament, which speaks of Jesus in more hidden and symbolic ways. The human authors of the Old Testament told us as much as they were able, but they could not clearly discern the shape of all future events standing at such a distance. It is the Bible's divine Author, the Holy Spirit, who could and did foretell the saving work of Christ, from the first page of the Book of Genesis onward.

The New Testament did not, therefore, abolish the Old. Rather, the New fulfilled the Old, and in doing so, it lifted the veil that kept hidden the face of the Lord's bride. Once the veil is removed, we suddenly see the world of the Old Covenant charged with grandeur. Water, fire, clouds, gardens, trees, hills, doves, lambs—all of these things are memorable details in the history and poetry of Israel. But now, seen in the light of Jesus Christ, they are much more. For the Christian with eyes to see, water symbolizes the saving power of Baptism; fire, the Holy Spirit; the spotless lamb, Christ crucified; Jerusalem, the city of heavenly glory.

The spiritual reading of Scripture is nothing new. Indeed, the very first Christians read the Bible this way. St. Paul describes Adam as a "type" that prefigured Jesus Christ (Rom 5:14). A "type" is a real person, place, thing, or event in the Old Testament that foreshadows something greater in the New. From this term we get the word "typology", referring to the study of how the Old Testament prefigures Christ (CCC 128–30). Elsewhere St. Paul draws deeper meanings out of the story of Abraham's sons, declaring, "This is an allegory" (Gal 4:24). He is not suggesting that these events of the distant past never really happened; he is saying that the events both happened *and* signified something more glorious yet to come.

The New Testament later describes the Tabernacle of ancient Israel as "a copy and shadow of the heavenly sanctuary" (Heb 8:5) and the Mosaic Law as a "shadow of the good things to come" (Heb 10:1). St. Peter, in turn, notes that Noah and his family were "saved through water" in a way that "corresponds" to sacramental Baptism, which "now saves you" (1 Pet 3:20–21). It is interesting to note that the expression translated as "corresponds" in this verse is a Greek term that denotes the fulfillment or counterpart of an ancient "type".

We need not look to the apostles, however, to justify a spiritual reading of the Bible. After all, Jesus himself read the Old Testament this way. He referred to Jonah (Mt 12:39), Solomon (Mt 12:42), the Temple (Jn 2:19), and the brazen serpent (Jn 3:14) as "signs" that pointed forward to him. We see in Luke's Gospel, as Christ comforted the disciples on the road to Emmaus, that "beginning with Moses and all the prophets, he interpreted to them in all the Scriptures the things concerning himself" (Lk 24:27). It was precisely this extensive spiritual interpretation of the Old Testament that made such an impact on these once-discouraged travelers, causing their hearts to "burn" within them (Lk 24:32).

Criteria for Biblical Interpretation We, too, must learn to discern the "full sense" of Scripture as it includes both the literal and spiritual senses together. Still, this does not mean we should "read into" the Bible meanings that are not really there. Spiritual exegesis is not an unrestrained flight of the imagination. Rather, it is a sacred science that proceeds according to certain principles and stands accountable to sacred tradition, the Magisterium, and the wider community of biblical interpreters (both living and deceased).

In searching out the full sense of a text, we should always avoid the extreme tendency to "over-spiritualize" in a way that minimizes or denies the Bible's literal truth. St. Thomas Aquinas was well aware of this danger and asserted that "all other senses of Sacred Scripture are based on the literal" (*STh* I, 1, 10, *ad* 1, quoted in CCC 116). On the other hand, we should never confine the meaning of a text to the literal, intended sense of its human author, as if the divine Author did not intend the passage to be read in the light of Christ's coming.

Fortunately the Church has given us guidelines in our study of Scripture. The unique character and divine authorship of the Bible call us to read it "in the Spirit" (*Dei Verbum* 12). Vatican II outlines this teaching in a practical way by directing us to read the Scriptures according to three specific criteria:

1. We must "[b]e especially attentive 'to the content and unity of the whole Scripture'" (CCC 112).

2. We must "[r]ead the Scripture within 'the living Tradition of the whole Church'" (CCC 113).

3. We must "[b]e attentive to the analogy of faith" (CCC 114; cf. Rom 12:6).

These criteria protect us from many of the dangers that ensnare readers of the Bible, from the newest inquirer to the most prestigious scholar. Reading Scripture out of context is one such pitfall, and probably the one most difficult to avoid. A memorable cartoon from the 1950s shows a young man poring over the pages of the Bible. He says to his sister: "Don't bother me now; I'm trying to find a Scripture verse to back up one of my preconceived notions." No doubt a biblical text pried from its context can be twisted to say something very different from what its author actually intended.

The Church's criteria guide us here by defining what constitutes the authentic "context" of a given biblical passage. The first criterion directs us to the literary context of every verse, including not only the words and paragraphs that surround it, but also the entire corpus of the biblical author's writings and, indeed, the span of the entire Bible. The *complete* literary context of any Scripture verse includes every text from Genesis to Revelation— because the Bible is a unified book, not just a library of different books. When the Church canonized the Book of Revelation, for example, she recognized it to be incomprehensible apart from the wider context of the entire Bible.

The second criterion places the Bible firmly within the context of a community that treasures a "living tradition". That community is the People of God down through the ages. Christians lived out their faith for well over a millennium before the printing press was invented. For centuries, few believers owned copies of the Gospels, and few people could read anyway. Yet they absorbed the gospel—through the sermons of their bishops and clergy, through prayer and meditation, through Christian art, through liturgical celebrations, and through oral tradition. These were expressions of the one "living tradition", a culture of living faith that stretches from ancient Israel to the contemporary Church. For the early Christians, the gospel could not be understood apart from that tradition. So it is with us. Reverence for the Church's tradition is what protects us from any sort of chronological or cultural provincialism, such as scholarly fads that arise and carry away a generation of interpreters before being dismissed by the next generation.

The third criterion places scriptural texts within the framework of faith. If we believe that the Scriptures are divinely inspired, we must also believe them to be internally coherent and consistent with all the doctrines that Christians believe. Remember, the Church's dogmas (such as the Real Presence, the papacy, the Immaculate Conception) are not something *added* to Scripture; rather, they are the Church's infallible interpretation *of* Scripture.

Using This Study Guide This volume is designed to lead the reader through Scripture according to the Church's guidelines—faithful to the canon, to the tradition, and to the creeds. The Church's interpretive principles have thus shaped the component parts of this book, and they are designed to make the reader's study as effective and rewarding as possible.

Introductions: We have introduced the biblical book with an essay covering issues such as authorship, date of composition, purpose, and leading themes. This background information will assist readers to approach and understand the text on its own terms.

Annotations: The basic notes at the bottom of every page help the user to read the Scriptures with understanding. They by no means exhaust the meaning of the sacred text but provide background material to help the reader make sense of what he reads. Often these notes make explicit what the sacred writers assumed or held to be implicit. They also provide a great deal of historical, cultural, geographical, and theological information pertinent to the inspired narratives—information that can help the reader bridge the distance between the biblical world and his own.

Cross-References: Between the biblical text at the top of each page and the annotations at the bottom, numerous references are listed to point readers to other scriptural passages related to the one being studied. This follow-up is an essential part of any serious study. It is also an excellent way to discover how the content of Scripture "hangs together" in a providential unity. Along with biblical cross-references, the annotations refer to select paragraphs from the *Catechism of the Catholic Church*. These are not doctrinal "proof texts" but are designed to help the reader interpret the Bible in accordance with the mind of the Church. The *Catechism* references listed either handle the biblical text directly or treat a broader doctrinal theme that sheds significant light on that text.

Topical Essays, Word Studies, Charts: These features bring readers to a deeper understanding of select details. The *topical essays* take up major themes and explain them more thoroughly and theologically than the annotations, often relating them to the doctrines of the Church. Occasionally the annotations are supplemented by *word studies* that put readers in touch with the ancient languages of Scripture. These should help readers to understand better and appreciate the inspired terminology that runs throughout the sacred books. Also included are various *charts* that summarize biblical information "at a glance".

Icon Annotations: Three distinctive icons are interspersed throughout the annotations, each one corresponding to one of the Church's three criteria for biblical interpretation. Bullets indicate the passage or passages to which these icons apply.

📖 Notes marked by the book icon relate to the "content and unity" of Scripture, showing how particular passages of the Old Testament illuminate the mysteries of the New. Much of the information in these notes explains the original context of the citations and indicates how and why this has a direct bearing on Christ or the Church. Through these notes, the reader can develop a sensitivity to the beauty and unity of God's saving plan as it stretches across both Testaments.

🕊 Notes marked by the dove icon examine particular passages in light of the Church's "living tradition". Because the Holy Spirit both guides the Magisterium and inspires the spiritual senses of Scripture, these annotations supply information along both of these lines. On the one hand, they refer to the Church's doctrinal teaching as presented by various popes, creeds, and ecumenical councils; on the other, they draw from (and paraphrase) the spiritual interpretations of various Fathers, Doctors, and saints.

🗝 Notes marked by the keys icon pertain to the "analogy of faith". Here we spell out how the mysteries of our faith "unlock" and explain one another. This type of comparison between Christian beliefs displays the coherence and unity of defined dogmas, which are the Church's infallible interpretations of Scripture.

Putting It All in Perspective Perhaps the most important context of all we have saved for last: the interior life of the individual reader. What we get out of the Bible will largely depend on how we approach the Bible. Unless we are living a sustained and disciplined life of prayer, we will never have the reverence, the profound humility, or the grace we need to see the Scriptures for what they really are.

You are approaching the "word of God". But for thousands of years, since before he knit you in your mother's womb, the Word of God has been approaching you.

One Final Note. The volume you hold in your hands is only a small part of a much larger work still in production. Study helps similar to those printed in this booklet are being prepared for *all* the books of the Bible and will appear gradually as they are finished. Our ultimate goal is to publish a single, one-volume Study Bible that will include the entire text of Scripture, along with all the annotations, charts, cross-references, maps, and other features found in the following pages. Individual booklets will be published in the meantime, with the hope that God's people can begin to benefit from this labor before its full completion.

We have included a long list of Study Questions in the back to make this format as useful as possible, not only for individual study, but for group settings and discussions as well. The questions are designed to help readers both "understand" the Bible and "apply" it to their lives. We pray that God will make use of our efforts and yours to help renew the face of the earth! «

INTRODUCTION TO HOSEA

Author and Date The Book of Hosea is mainly a collection of sayings that Jewish and Christian tradition ascribes to the prophet Hosea, who spoke the word of the Lord to the Northern Kingdom of Israel in the eighth century B.C. According to the superscription in 1:1, his prophetic career covered as many as five decades (ca. 760–710 B.C.). This means that he prophesied during a period overlapping the ministries of Isaiah, Amos, and Micah. But unlike these three prophets, who lived in Judah in southern Israel, Hosea was active in northern Israel.

Modern scholarship, without reaching a consensus on matters of detail, broadly accepts that the substance of the book derives from a single author who wrote in northern Israel in the eighth century B.C. Some argue that this original edition of the book was expanded by a later editor in the Southern Kingdom of Judah, at which time references to Judah (1:7, 11; 4:15; 5:5; 6:11; etc.) and its Davidic kings were added to the text (1:1; 3:5). This is a possibility but not a certainty. The hypothesis of a Judean redaction after the time of Hosea rests on evidence that is too limited to support the likelihood of substantial later additions, although minor additions are conceivable. But even granting the traditional view that Hosea uttered all the prophecies contained in the book, the book makes no explicit claim about who was responsible for preserving them in writing. It may well have been Hosea himself, or it may have been one of his disciples, or perhaps some combination of the two. Whatever the case, the content of the book is reliably traced to the preaching of Hosea, and its composition may be dated near the end of the prophet's lifetime. One can reasonably envision the book reaching its final form in the last quarter of the 700s B.C.

Title The book is named after Hosea, the son of Beeri, mentioned in the opening verse. Its Hebrew form, *Hôshēaʿ*, is based on a verb that means "save" or "deliver". This name appears in the Greek Septuagint as the title *Ōsēe*, while the heading is expanded in the Latin Vulgate to *Osee Propheta*, "Hosea the Prophet". English titles for the book follow these ancient traditions.

Place in the Canon Hosea has long been revered as a canonical book of Scripture. In the Jewish Bible, or Tanakh, it stands among the Latter Prophets in a sub-collection of writings known as "the Book of the Twelve". In Christian Bibles, these twelve books are called the Minor Prophets, not because they are less important than Isaiah, Jeremiah, Ezekiel, and Daniel, but because they are comparatively much shorter. Hosea always stands first among the Minor Prophets in ancient Hebrew, Greek, and Latin manuscripts. This is probably because Hosea is one of the oldest books in the collection and is the longest in the collection attributed to a preexilic prophet.

Structure The Book of Hosea has a loose organizational structure. It opens with a superscription that situates the prophet on the timeline of Israel's history (1:1) and closes with a short postscript that appeals to the reader to find wisdom in the teaching of the book (14:9). Between these endpoints, chapters 1 and 3 give an account of Hosea's marriage to a promiscuous woman, chapter 2 presents the Lord speaking to his unfaithful bride Israel, and chapters 4–14 are taken up with prophetic oracles that denounce Israel's sins, warn of judgments that are coming, and occasionally speak of mercy and restoration in a more distant future. This second part of the book, chapters 4–14, is difficult to outline with confidence. Distinct oracles are not always easy to mark off, and the prophet's references to persons and events are often ambiguous and difficult to correlate with what is known of the eighth century B.C. Still, the main distinction between chapters 1–3 and 4–14 is reasonably clear.

The Prophet and His Times Hosea began his prophetic career late in the reign of Jeroboam II, ruler of the Northern Kingdom of Israel from 793 to 753 B.C. It was a time of economic and military strength but also a time of moral decline and religious apostasy. The northern dynasty of Jehu, king of Israel, was founded in 841 B.C. and survived for four generations, as the Lord had promised (2 Kings 10:30). But this dynasty came to an abrupt end in 753 B.C. with the death of Zechariah, son of Jeroboam II, and over the next three decades the Northern Kingdom spiraled into political chaos. Zechariah, who reigned only six months, was assassinated by the rebel Shallum, who succeeded him as king of Israel (752 B.C.). Shallum, in turn, was followed in relatively brisk succession by the last four kings of northern Israel: Menahem, Pekahiah, Pekah, and Hoshea. During this time, the Assyrian Empire was at the height of its power and seeking imperial expansion westward, offering rulers of smaller states such as Israel and Judah the opportunity for peace in exchange for tribute and vassal rule. Because northern Israel, after accepting vassalage for a time, rebelled against its overlord, the Assyrians invaded the land of Israel and dismembered the Northern Kingdom in stages, annexing Galilee, parts of the western coastlands, and the Transjordan territories in the late 730s B.C. (2 Kings 15:29; 1 Chron 5:26), finally destroying the capital city of Samaria in 722 B.C. (2 Kings 17:5–6). These events marked the end of the Northern Kingdom of Israel and the beginning of the Assyrian Exile. From then onward, the northern tribes of Israel were deprived of royal government and thousands were deported to foreign lands, never again to return to the Israelite homeland. The northern tribes, scattered to various locations in the Near East, would become known as the "lost tribes" of Israel.

The Message of the Prophet The Book of Hosea is all about God's covenant with Israel, a dual mystery described as a *marriage* between a Husband and wife (chaps. 1–3) and an *adoption* of sons and daughters by a caring Father (chaps. 1, 11). Both metaphors communicate how the Lord forged a close familial bond with his people, how both parties assumed obligations of love and loyalty toward one another, and how a betrayal of that love inevitably led to painful consequences. The analogy of marriage and family likewise helps the prophet to explain God's tenacious love for his people, a love that never grows cold or weak or disinterested, not even when his people turn their backs on him and go wildly astray. It is because God is a faithful Husband and Father that he will stop at nothing to mend his relationship with unfaithful Israel.

Hosea gives attention to the history of this covenant relationship as well as its present status and its future prospects. **(1)** *Israel of the Past.* As Hosea sees it, Israel became the Lord's bride and son at the time of the Exodus, so that the wilderness period between leaving Egypt and entering the Promised Land could be likened to a honeymoon period for newlyweds (2:14–15) and to a time when God reared young Israel and taught him to walk (11:3). Though not a time of perfect harmony, it was still a time when Israel trusted the Lord and returned his affections. This spiritual situation changed after Israel settled in the land of Canaan (Joshua-Judges), clamored for an earthly king (1 Sam 8), and divided into Northern and Southern Kingdoms in the tenth century B.C. (1 Kings 12). **(2)** *Israel of the Present.* By the time we reach Hosea, who preached mainly to the Northern Kingdom of Israel in the eighth century B.C., things had gone from bad to worse. The northern tribes of Israel had fully embraced the worship of idols fashioned in the images of calves (2:13; 8:5; 11:2; 13:2); they participated in sexual immorality linked to these idol cults (4:13–14); they maintained some level of devotion to the Lord by offering sacrifices to him, but their actions proved to be empty religious rituals without heartfelt commitment (8:13; 9:4–5); the religious leaders of Israel were morally and spiritually corrupt (4:4–10); the royal leaders of Israel put their faith in alliances with nations such as Assyria and Egypt instead of trusting in the Lord (7:11; 8:9–10); the masses were ignorant of God's Law and guilty of violating the Decalogue (4:1–2); and even the Southern Kingdom of Judah was beginning to slide down this same path, although the spiritual crisis in the north was more advanced at this point in history (5:5, 10, 13; 6:4). It was Hosea's prophetic diagnosis that the northern tribes of Israel had ceased to "know" the Lord in any meaningful way (4:1–6; 5:4; 6:6). **(3)** *Israel of the Near Future.* The prophet's outlook for northern Israel was bleak in the short term but bright in the long term. His vision of the near future saw nothing but judgment. Because Israel brazenly rebelled against the covenant, the curses of the covenant were about to go into effect: the northern tribes would not be pitied by the Lord (1:6); they would no longer be called God's people (1:9); and they would either fall by the sword (7:16) or be torn from their homeland and forced to live in exile (5:14; 9:17). Still, this is not a complete renunciation of Israel on God's part. Ultimately, the Lord's judgments were meant to bring his people to repentance, to a reconciliation with their "first husband" (2:7). **(4)** *Israel of the Distant Future.* Hosea's generation had doomed itself to death and deportation by the Assyrians, but hope is held out for future generations of northern Israelites who would be "swallowed up" among the nations (8:8). When the northern tribes finally come to their senses, turning to seek the Lord and his forgiveness (14:1–3), God promises to "heal their faithlessness" (14:4) and to restore his abundant blessings (14:5–8). Hosea sees this as God making a new "covenant" (2:18) in which he espouses Israel as his wife once again (2:14–20) and reinstates his exiled people in the covenant as "Sons of the living God" (1:10). Because rebellious Israel spiritually "died" through the worship of idols (13:1), restored Israel will have to undergo a resurrection to new life (6:1–2; 13:14). Then the whole family of Israel and Judah will be reunited once again (1:11) under the rule of a Davidic king (3:5) and will "know the LORD" like never before (6:3).

This message of judgment followed by mercy is made concrete in Hosea's personal life. On the premise that actions speak louder than words, the Lord instructs Hosea to marry "a wife of harlotry" and to start a family with her (1:2). The prophet then marries a woman named Gomer, and together they have three children, each of whom is given a name that forecasts doom for northern Israel (1:4–9). Almost nothing is known about their married life except that, at some point, Gomer betrayed Hosea by going after other "lovers" (2:5) and made herself an "adulteress" (3:1). Presumably this resulted in a time of separation or divorce, because the Lord later commanded Hosea to "love" her again by taking her back as his wife (3:1–3). The purpose of this action, according to 2:1–13, was to dramatize the Lord's marital relationship with Israel. Gomer represents Israel, whose promiscuous pursuit of pagan idols was a form of spiritual adultery against the Lord, her divine Husband. Yet even her worst infidelities could not undo her Husband's love. Just as Hosea reacquired Gomer as his wife, so the Lord wished to rekindle his romance with Israel by taking her back into the nuptial bonds of a new covenant (2:14–23). By comparing Israel's sin to marital infidelity, the Book of Hosea underscores the depth of betrayal that God's people perpetrate when they forsake him for idols; at the same time, by comparing the plan of salvation to Hosea's reunion with Gomer, it declares that God's merciful love is unconquerable for those who turn back to him.

Christian Perspective The New Testament quotes select passages from the Book of Hosea and develops its vision of God entering a marital covenant with his people. Explicit citations are found in the Gospel of Matthew and in the Letters of Peter and Paul. Matthew cites Hos 11:1, a passage that looks back to Israel's Exodus from Egypt. For the evangelist, the departure of God's son from that land also looks forward to the infant Jesus, God's eternal Son, following the footsteps of his ancestors and fleeing Egypt in order to settle in the Promised Land (Mt 2:15). Later in the Gospel, Jesus cites Hos 6:6 to remind the Pharisees that God puts greater value on mercy than on cultic observances such as sacrifice (Mt 9:13; 12:7). In the epistles, Paul and Peter both reference Hos 2:23 to say that God is fulfilling his pledge to restore northern Israel by bringing the Gentiles to faith in Christ (Rom 9:25; 1 Pet 2:10) and by adopting them as his children (Rom 9:26, referring to Hos 1:10). Some think this is an "accommodated" use of Hosea in a new Christian context, but more likely Peter and Paul viewed the Church's Gentile mission as the unique way that God had chosen to save the northern tribes of Israel after they slowly dissolved into the nations where they had been exiled. Paul also uses the words of Hos 13:14 to speak about the resurrection of the body as God's final triumph over the power of death (1 Cor 15:55). Finally, the nuptial theme that dominates Hos 1–3, where Hosea's marriage and remarriage to an unfaithful wife mirrors the Lord's marriage and remarriage to an unfaithful people—a theme echoed elsewhere in the OT (Is 54:5; 62:4–5; Jer 2:1–7)—lays essential groundwork for NT images of Christ wedded to the Church as his Bride (2 Cor 11:2; Eph 5:22–32) and for the kingdom of God portrayed as a marriage feast (Mt 22:1–14; Rev 19:7–9). Strikingly, Jesus is cast in the role of the God of Israel, the divine Bridegroom, in relation to his covenant people (Mk 2:19–20; Jn 3:29).

OUTLINE OF HOSEA

1. Superscription (1:1)

2. Prophetic Actions: Hosea and His Unfaithful Wife (1:2—3:5)
    A. The Marriage to Gomer, the Names of Her Children (1:2–9)
    B. The Restoration of God's People (1:10—2:1)
    C. The Prophetic Meaning of the Unfaithful Wife (2:2–23)
    D. The Adulteress Redeemed (3:1–5)

3. Prophetic Speeches: God's Judgment on Unfaithful Israel (4:1—14:8)
    A. The Adultery of Israel (4:1—6:3)
    B. The Judgment of Israel (6:4—10:15)
    C. The Lord's Love for Israel (11:1–11)
    D. The Sins of Israel (11:12—12:14)
    E. The Anger of God (13:1–16)
    F. A Plea for Repentance, A Promise of Restoration (14:1–8)

4. Postscript for the Wise (14:9)

THE BOOK OF
HOSEA

1 The word of the LORD that came to Hose′a the son of Bee′ri, in the days of Uzzi′ah, Jo′tham, A′haz, and Hezeki′ah, kings of Judah, and in the days of Jerobo′am the son of Jo′ash, king of Israel.

Hosea Marries a Harlot and Has Children

2 When the LORD first spoke through Hose′a, the LORD said to Hosea, "Go, take to yourself a wife of harlotry and have children of harlotry, for the land commits great harlotry by forsaking the LORD." 3So he went and took Gomer the daughter of Dibla′im, and she conceived and bore him a son.

4 And the LORD said to him, "Call his name Jezre′el; for yet a little while, and I will punish the house of Je′hu for the blood of Jezreel, and I will put an end to the kingdom of the house of Israel. 5And on that day, I will break the bow of Israel in the valley of Jezre′el."

6 She conceived again and bore a daughter. And the LORD said to him, "Call her name Not pitied, for I will no more have pity on the house of Israel, to forgive them at all. 7But I will have pity on the house of Judah, and I will deliver them by the LORD their God; I will not deliver them by bow,

---

1.3, 5. Hos 2.23, 1 Pet 2:10.

1:1 The word of the LORD: Prophetic revelation from God. See essay: *The Word of the LORD.* **Hosea:** The Hebrew name *Hôshēaʿ* is probably an abbreviated form of a name that translates "the LORD has saved". It was a popular name in OT times (e.g., Num 13:8; 2 Kings 15:30; 1 Chron 27:20; Neh 10:23). Like Elijah and Elisha, Hosea was a prophet from northern Israel who lived in the period of the divided monarchy. **Beeri:** Otherwise unknown. **Uzziah, Jotham, Ahaz, and Hezekiah:** Four kings of the Southern Kingdom of Judah who were contemporaries of Hosea. Uzziah's reign ended around 740 B.C., and Hezekiah's reign as co-regent with his father, Ahaz, began around 729 B.C., with his independent reign beginning in 715 B.C. See chart: *Kings of the Divided Monarchy* at 1 Kings 13. **Jeroboam the son of Joash:** Jeroboam II, ruler of the Northern Kingdom of Israel from 793 to 753 B.C. Hosea's ministry probably began in the last decade of Jeroboam's reign.

1:2 a wife of harlotry: Or "a wife of fornication". It is uncertain whether Hosea's wife was guilty of sexual sin before or after they were wedded. Either way, marrying a woman who gave herself to "lovers" (2:5) other than her husband is a prophetic action that symbolizes God's relationship with Israel, his unfaithful bride. The prophets sometimes performed shocking deeds in order to dramatize a spiritual crisis in Israel or announce a coming judgment (Is 20:2–4; Jer 16:1–9; Ezek 4:1–17; 24:15–24). A second issue is whether Hosea's marriage is a historical event, a visionary experience, or a literary allegory. Some scholars, ancient as well as modern, prefer a visionary or allegorical interpretation of 1:2–9 to a historical one, in part because they find it problematic that

God would command his prophet to marry a woman defiled by sexual sin. Nevertheless, the text gives every indication of describing a real-life event of the past. • If God, out of his boundless love in Christ, approaches those who are defiled and uncleansed of sin, then we should not dismiss as unbecoming the account of the blessed Hosea, which beautifully depicts the divine Word having spiritual communion with us while we were still loathsome and polluted (St. Cyril of Alexandria, *Commentary on Hosea* 1, 2–3). Hosea, when he took for himself a wife of fornication or an adulterous woman, was guilty of neither fornication nor adultery, because she was given to him by a command of God, the Author of marriage. This was a case of divine authority being exercised over the divine institution of marriage (St. Thomas Aquinas, *Summa Theologiae* I-II, 100, 8). **great harlotry:** The sexual promiscuity of Hosea's wife symbolizes the religious promiscuity of Israel. The northern tribes had broken faith with the Lord by transgressing his covenant and giving themselves to the worship of other gods (Ex 34:15–16; Deut 31:16). For God's marital relationship with Israel, see Is 54:6; 62:5; Jer 2:2–3; Ezek 16.

1:3–9 Hosea and his wife have three children, two sons and a daughter. They, like Isaiah's children (Is 7:3; 8:3–4), are given names that bear a prophetic message.

1:3 Gomer: She pursued sexual relations with multiple "lovers" (2:5, 7) even after her marriage to Hosea, making herself an "adulteress" (3:1). The marriage of Hosea and Gomer may be dated ca. 760 B.C.

1:4 Jezreel: Hosea's first-born is named after a fertile valley in lower Galilee that witnessed the bloody overthrow of the northern dynasty of Omri (885–841 B.C.) and the founding of the northern dynasty of Jehu in its place (841–753 B.C.). This succession was facilitated by the murders of Jehoram, king of Israel, Ahaziah, king of Judah, and seventy male survivors of King Ahab's line (2 Kings 9–10). The name "Jezreel" thus bears an ominous message: Jehu's dynasty is destined to meet the same horrible fate as Omri's. For a positive significance to the name, see 2:22–23.

1:5 the bow of Israel: A symbol of military strength (1 Sam 2:4).

1:6 Not pitied: Translates the Hebrew expression *lōʾ ruḥāmāh.* It signifies that Israel, bent on pursuing wickedness, can no longer rely on God's compassion but has condemned itself to a severe judgment. This will begin in 753 B.C., when the Northern Kingdom begins its descent into chaos, and will culminate in 722 B.C., when the Assyrians conquer Samaria and take thousands of Israelites into exile.

1:7 the house of Judah: The Davidic dynasty in Jerusalem. It experienced its promised deliverance when the Lord's angel

---

The Books of the Minor Prophets

These twelve are grouped together both in the Hebrew and in the Greek. The only reason for this seems to be that the books happen to be short. They are not "minor" in any other way; their religious value is great. They do not belong to any one historical period, and they range from Amos (eighth century B.C.) to Malachi, Joel, Obadiah, and Jonah (fifth to fourth century B.C.). They are here arranged according to their traditional order in the Hebrew, which is not the same as their historical order. The Latin Vulgate also follows the order of the Hebrew.

Hosea (Osee) preached and prophesied during the century—the eighth—that saw the decline and final destruction of the northern kingdom. It was a period of both moral and material dissolution, and it is this that gives his prophecy its peculiar characteristics. Hosea seems to take occasion of his own unhappy marriage to draw a parallel between it and the relationship between God and his unfaithful spouse Israel. He attacks passionately the moral evils and the injustice of the society in which he lives. Above all, he condemns the idolatry rampant everywhere, as well as the debased Yahweh worship. Israel will be punished, but after repentance the people will be welcomed back to their God.

Israel y Judah 7 2 kingdoms to be conquered

nor by sword, nor by war, nor by horses, nor by horsemen."

8 When she had weaned Not pitied, she conceived and bore a son. [9]And the LORD said, "Call his name Not my people, for you are not my people and I am not your God."[a]

Israel's Restoration

[10][b] Yet the number of the people of Israel shall be like the sand of the sea, which can be neither measured nor numbered; and in the place where it was said to them, "You are not my people," it shall be said to them, "Sons of the living God."

1:10: Rom 9:26.

---

slew thousands of Assyrian soldiers besieging Jerusalem in 701 B.C. (2 Kings 19:32–37).

1:8 weaned: When the child was around three years old (2 Mac 7:27).

1:9 Not my people: Translates the Hebrew expression *lō' 'ammî*. It signifies that northern Israel has broken the covenant so badly that God plans to disown it for a time. Jeremiah

describes this as the Lord giving northern Israel a decree of divorce (Jer 3:6–8). **you are not my people and I am not your God:** A reversal of the covenant formula, which states that God and Israel belong to one another as partners in covenant and thus as members of the same family (Ex 6:7; Lev 26:12; Jer 11:4).

1:10—2:1 Hosea's perspective shifts from the near future (curse and judgment, 1:2–9) to the distant future (blessing and restoration, 1:10–11). The Lord is ready to expel the northern tribes of Israel from the land for their rebellion against the

---

[a] Heb *I am not yours.*
[b] Ch 2:1 in Heb.

The Word of the LORD

The biblical expression "word of the Lord" or "God's word" is a theologically rich indication of God's intention to reveal his purposes to man and to engage him in dialogue. It occurs nearly 400 times in the legal, liturgical, and prophetic portions of the Old Testament, indicating the delivery of a message that God wishes to communicate to man through Israel. The content of the revealed message is announced in formulas such as "Thus says the LORD", "Hear the word of the LORD", and "The word of the LORD which [the prophet] saw". It was typical in Israel that instruction in the *Law* of Moses came from the priest, *counsel* came from the wise man, and a *word* of revelation came from the prophet (Jer 18:18). In this sense, the expression "the word of the LORD" is a fitting introduction to the body of oracles, visions, judgments, and promises given in an individual prophetic book (Jer 1:4; Hos 1:1; Joel 1:1; Mic 1:1; Zeph 1:1; Hag 1:3). The expression "God's word" is sometimes (especially in Ps 119 and the wisdom literature) synonymous with the body of commands, decrees, oracles, and judgments transmitted by the prophets in the texts of Sacred Scripture.

Readers of the Bible in English should be aware that the Hebrew noun meaning "word" (*dābār*) shares a common root with a verb that means "to speak" (frequently vocalized as *dibber*). There is thus a tight connection between the act of speaking and the content of what is spoken. This is quite significant when a word comes from God. When God speaks, his word goes forth in power and brings about what he intends, as in the creation account: when God says, "Let there be ...", the biblical text records that "it was so". The unchallenged power of God's word in Genesis sets the biblical account of creation in sharp contrast to other ancient creation stories in which the world is born out of a titanic struggle among rival gods and goddesses. In Scripture, the word of God is the instrument of his will, bringing new things into existence and causing events to come to pass (see Ps 33:6, 9; Wis 9:1; Is 55:11). The potency of God's word is echoed in praise (Ps 56:10; 119), instruction (Prov 13:13; 30:5), warning (Is 1:10; 66:5; Amos 3:1), judgment (Hos 6:5), and edification (Wis 16:12; Heb 4:12).

Besides its power, God's word is also revered for its permanence and reliability. Created things pass away, but the word of the Lord endures forever (Is 40:7–8; Zech 1:5-6). In contrast to the coming and going of created things over time, God's word stands firm as an unshakeable basis for hope. His word is reliable to sustain human life, which depends not on "bread alone" but on "everything that proceeds out of the mouth of the LORD" (Deut 8:3; Wis 16:26; cf. Mt 4:4; Lk 4:4). The word of the Lord is reliable because it is trustworthy without fail (Ps 33:4; Is 45:23; Heb 5:13).

In the Old Testament, the word of the Lord seems to take on personhood itself. It is said to compel speech (Jer 20:9; Amos 3:8; Jon 1:1; 3:1) and even execute judgment (Wis 18:14–15). This is further developed in the New Testament, where we learn that the Word of God, which brought all things into existence, is not merely a power but a Person—God the Son (Jn 1:1-5, 14). The Word made flesh is the superlative agent of revelation, the One who reveals God the Father to all (Jn 1:18; Heb 1:2).

The analogy between God's word in Scripture and God's Word in the Incarnation is made explicit by the Church: "Indeed the words of God, expressed in the words of men, are in every way like human language, just as the Word of the eternal Father, when he took on himself the flesh of human weakness, became like men" (CCC 101, quoting Vatican II, *Dei Verbum* 13). Finally, the expression "the word of God" is used to describe the totality of Sacred Scripture, Old Testament and New, welcomed by the Church "not as a human word, 'but as what it really is, the word of God'" (CCC 104, quoting Vatican II, *Dei Verbum* 24, citing 1 Thess 2:13).

[11]And the people of Judah and the people of Israel shall be gathered together, and they shall appoint for themselves one head; and they shall go up from the land, for great shall be the day of Jezre′el.

Israel's Infidelity, Punishment, and Redemption

2 [c]Say to your brother,[d] "My people," and to your sister,[e] "She has obtained pity."
[2]"Plead with your mother, plead—
　for she is not my wife,
　and I am not her husband—
that she put away her harlotry from her face,
　and her adultery from between her breasts;
[3]lest I strip her naked
　and make her as in the day she was born,
and make her like a wilderness,
　and set her like a parched land,
　and slay her with thirst.

[4]Upon her children also I will have no pity,
　because they are children of harlotry.
[5]For their mother has played the harlot;
　she that conceived them has acted
　　shamefully.
For she said, 'I will go after my lovers,
　who give me my bread and my water,
　my wool and my flax, my oil and my
　　drink.'
[6]Therefore I will hedge up her[f] way with thorns;
　and I will build a wall against her,
　so that she cannot find her paths.
[7]She shall pursue her lovers,
　but not overtake them;
and she shall seek them,
　but shall not find them.
Then she shall say, 'I will go
　and return to my first husband,
　for it was better with me then than now,'

2:1, 23: Rom 9:25; 1 Pet 2:10.

---

covenant, but after a period of exile, he will reunite them with himself in a renewed covenant. The prophet calls this time of future restoration "the day of Jezreel" (1:11).

1:10 like the sand of the sea: Recalls the Lord's oath to Abraham that his descendants would be too numerous to count (Gen 22:17). **Sons of the living God:** Kinship with God is a grace of the covenant that made the Israelites the Lord's adopted "sons" (Deut 14:1). Restoration to divine sonship implies that God will renew his covenant with the exiled tribes of northern Israel, gathering them back as his children once again. • Paul quotes this verse to claim that God has called both Jews and Gentiles to sonship in Christ (Rom 9:26). Many find it odd that he cites Hosea, since the prophet is speaking neither about the Jews (= the tribes of the Southern Kingdom of Judah) nor about pagan Gentiles (= peoples who are unrelated to Israel) but about the restoration of Israel's ten northern tribes, who were exiled by the Assyrians. Paul, however, has not misread or misapplied the text. He recognizes that the northern tribes, never having returned from exile, lost their Israelite identity over the centuries as they slowly dissolved into the Gentile populations of the world by intermarriage and cultural assimilation. Northern Israel's return to sonship is thus achieved by *Gentiles* coming to faith in Jesus.

1:11 gathered together: For the reunion of Israel and Judah in a future covenant, see also Is 11:11–13; Jer 31:31; Ezek 37:15–28. **one head:** The royal Davidic Messiah (3:5; Ezek 37:24–25). **go up from the land:** Or "go up from the earth", suggesting the Israelites are pictured as plants sprouting up from the ground. Some envision a resurrection of Israel, as in 6:1–2 and Ezek 37:1–14. **Jezreel:** The same location mentioned in 1:5, where the strength of northern Israel was broken. Here the name is given a positive significance, announcing the time of Israel's future restoration.

2:1 your brother ... your sister: Israel and Judah, reunited in the future, will again acknowledge one another as siblings in the family of God (1:11). Despite the chapter division of the RSV2CE, this verse is the conclusion of the restoration oracle in 1:10–11, not the start of a new section. **My people ... She has obtained pity:** A reversal of fortunes following the judgment

foretold in the names of Hosea's son ("Not my people", 1:9) and daughter ("Not pitied", 1:6).

2:2–23 The Lord brings charges against unfaithful Israel, who has committed spiritual adultery by worshiping other gods. Punishments are imposed, but ultimately these are restorative: they are meant, not simply to shame his wayward bride (2:10) and to restrain her wantonness (2:11–13), but to draw her back to her divine Husband (2:7). Even though Israel has sought the pleasures of other gods (the "lovers" of 2:5, 7) and forgotten her Spouse (2:13), God still loves Israel (3:1) and plans to restore their marriage (2:14–23).

2:2 Plead with: Or "make an accusation against" (from the Hebrew verb *rîv*). The prophet contends that Israel's covenant with God has been broken—a grievance that calls for redress. See essay: *Covenant Lawsuit* at Mic 6. **she is not my wife:** God divorces the faithless tribes of northern Israel for a time (as in Jer 3:6–8). They are about to be sent forth from the Promised Land into exile, just as a divorced woman is sent forth from her husband's home with a decree of divorce in hand (Deut 24:1–4). **harlotry ... adultery:** Two ways the Bible speaks about idolatry (Ex 34:14–16). When the Israelites give themselves to the worship of other gods, they defile themselves like a prostitute who gives herself to a client; and every time they do so, they prove unfaithful to the Lord, their divine Spouse, to whom they are joined by a marital covenant (CCC 2380). Use of sexual metaphors for idolatry mirrors the fact that idol worship in the biblical world sometimes involved acts of sexual impurity such as cultic prostitution (see 4:13–14; Ex 32:6; Num 25:1–2).

2:3 lest I strip her naked: Language used in Near Eastern treaties for the curses threatened against a partner who proves disloyal. In such a context, stripping naked refers to plundering and humiliating a rebel nation. It also alludes to an ancient rite of shaming a convicted adulteress (Ezek 16:35–39).

2:5 played the harlot: By worshiping idols. See note on 2:2–23. **my bread ... water ... oil ... drink:** The idolaters of Israel credit Canaanite gods with supplying life's necessary provisions. In reality, it was the Lord who met their needs (2:8).

2:6 I will hedge up her way: An act of restraint, preventing further infidelity (2:7). Israel is like a "stubborn heifer" that is prone to wander off and needs to be restrained (4:16).

2:7 return: The language of repentance. See word study: *Return* at Jer 3:1. **my first husband:** The Lord. Desperation and need will finally draw the sinners of northern Israel away from their lovers (= idols) and back to the one true God.

---

[c] Ch 2:3 in Heb.
[d] Gk: Heb *brothers*.
[e] Gk Vg: Heb *sisters*.
[f] Gk Syr: Heb *your*.

⁸And she did not know
   that it was I who gave her
   the grain, the wine, and the oil,
and who lavished upon her silver
   and gold which they used for Ba'al.
⁹Therefore I will take back
   my grain in its time,
   and my wine in its season;
and I will take away my wool and my flax,
   which were to cover her nakedness.
¹⁰Now I will uncover her lewdness
   in the sight of her lovers,
   and no one shall rescue her out of my hand.
¹¹And I will put an end to all her mirth,
   her feasts, her new moons, her sabbaths,
   and all her appointed feasts.
¹²And I will lay waste her vines and her fig trees,
   of which she said,
'These are my hire,
   which my lovers have given me.'

I will make them a forest,
   and the beasts of the field shall devour
   them.
¹³And I will punish her for the feast days of the
   Ba'als
   when she burned incense to them
and decked herself with her ring and jewelry,
   and went after her lovers,
   and forgot me, says the LORD.

¹⁴"Therefore, behold, I will allure her,
   and bring her into the wilderness,
   and speak tenderly to her.
¹⁵And there I will give her her vineyards,
   and make the Valley of A'chor a door of
   hope.
And there she shall answer as in the days of
   her youth,
   as at the time when she came out of the land
   of Egypt.

2:8 it was I: The Lord—not the storm and fertility god Baal worshiped in Canaan—is the one who waters the earth with rain and causes it to produce abundantly (Deut 11:13–17).

2:9 I will take back my grain: The Northern Kingdom of Israel, which enjoyed great prosperity during the reign of Jeroboam II, is about to suffer a time of adversity and want.

2:10 uncover her lewdness: A public act of shaming. A wordplay may be intended, since the Hebrew verb *gālāh* can mean both "uncover" and "go into exile".

WORD STUDY

Baal (2:8)

Ba'al (Heb.): a noun meaning "lord" or "master". In relation to property and marriage, it carries the sense of "owner" (Ex 21:28) or "husband" (Ex 21:22). The verbal form of the Hebrew root means "to marry" or "rule over". In a cultic context, *Ba'al* is frequently used as a title for Hadad, the storm and fertility god of Canaanite religion. Places where this deity was worshiped often include his name in the location (e.g., Baal-peor, Deut 4:3; Baal-berith, Judg 9:4). This probably indicates that a shrine dedicated to Baal stood at these locations. In Canaanite mythology, Baal bore the epithet "he who rides on the clouds" (a prerogative claimed for the Lord in Ps 68:4; 104:3; Is 19:1). Being a storm god, he was invoked to bring rain after the summer dry season, a key feature of the agricultural cycle in Canaan. Service to this false deity included child sacrifice (Jer 19:5), self-mutilation (1 Kings 18:28), and cultic prostitution (Hos 4:11–14). The OT presents Baal as the Lord's chief rival for the allegiance of his people. The cult of Baal, which ensnared the Israelites at many points in their history, is strongly denounced in historical texts (1 Kings 18:17–46; 2 Kings 1:2–17) and especially in the judgment oracles of the prophets (Jer 2:8; 7:9; 19:5; Hos 2:8, 16; 7:16; 9:10; 13:1; Zeph 1:4).

2:11 feasts … new moons … sabbaths: Holy days of rest and rejoicing in Israel's liturgical calendar (Lev 23:1–44). The Lord is displeased with northern Israel's observance of these sacred times and will put an end to them, enacting one of the curses of the covenant (Lev 26:31). The reason appears to be twofold: the Israelites were guilty of *formalism* (going through the motions of religious rituals without serving the Lord in their hearts, Is 29:13) and *syncretism* (celebrating the Lord's feasts while at the same time participating in the idolatrous "feast days of the Baals", 2:13). Religious tolerance of idol cults violates the exclusivity of the marriage covenant between the Lord and Israel.

2:12 my hire: A harlot's hire (9:1). Unlike the modern practice of prostitution, where sex in exchange for payment is often a brief, onetime event, prostitution in the biblical world sometimes entailed an ongoing relationship of sexual services in exchange for material support (2:5).

2:13 the Baals: Canaanite idols. See word study: *Baal* at 2:8. **forgot me:** When Israel goes after other gods, the Lord is forsaken and forgotten (Deut 32:15–18).

2:14–23 The restoration of Israel after the judgments in 2:2–23. At this time a new "covenant" (2:18) will be established in which God and Israel are reunited in marriage (2:19). • Hosea follows the prophetic timeline of Deuteronomy, which predicts covenant curses of devastation and exile finally giving way to blessings of mercy and healing (Deut 4:27–31; 30:1–10; 32:19–36).

2:14 I will allure her: The language of romantic attraction and courtship. The Lord will heal his broken relationship with Israel by enticing his estranged wife to rekindle their spousal love. **into the wilderness:** The setting of God's original honeymoon with Israel after rescuing the people from slavery in Egypt (13:4–5; Jer 2:2–3). **speak tenderly to her:** Literally, "speak to her heart".

2:15 Valley of Achor: One of the gateways into central Canaan near Jericho. It is infamous as the place where Achan, who disobeyed the law of devoted things and brought trouble (Heb., *ākôr*) on Israel, was stoned to death (Josh 7:1–26). It will be given a new and positive significance when God restores his people. Leading his bride from the wilderness (2:14) through the Valley of Achor implies a reentrance into the Promised Land and thus a new beginning for Israel (cf. Is 65:10). **the days of her youth:** The time of the Exodus. In these early days, when Israel was young, the people feared and believed in the Lord (Ex 4:31; 14:31).

16 "And in that day, says the LORD, you will call me, 'My husband,' and no longer will you call me, 'My Ba′al.' [17] For I will remove the names of the Ba′als from her mouth, and they shall be mentioned by name no more. [18] And I will make for you[g] a covenant on that day with the beasts of the field, the birds of the air, and the creeping things of the ground; and I will abolish[h] the bow, the sword, and war from the land; and I will make you lie down in safety. [19] And I will espouse you for ever; I will espouse you in righteousness and in justice, in steadfast love, and in mercy. [20] I will espouse you in faithfulness; and you shall know the LORD.

[21] "And in that day, says the LORD,
> I will answer the heavens
> and they shall answer the earth;

[22] and the earth shall answer the grain, the wine,
> and the oil,
> and they shall answer Jezre′el;[i]
23   and I will sow him[j] for myself in the land.
> And I will have pity on Not pitied,
> and I will say to Not my people, 'You are my people';
> and he shall say 'You are my God.'"

The Lord's Love for His Unfaithful People

3 And the LORD said to me, "Go again, love a woman who is beloved of a paramour and is an adulteress; even as the LORD loves the people of Israel, though they turn to other gods and love cakes of raisins." [2] So I bought her for fifteen shekels of silver and a homer and a lethech of barley. [3] And I said to her, "You must dwell as mine for many days;

2:16 in that day: A day of prophetic fulfillment. **My husband:** Israel will address God in a way that suggests intimacy and a renewed commitment to the exclusivity of the marriage covenant. **My Baal:** Restored Israel will no longer address the Lord as a harsh master who punishes (Jer 31:31–32) and will no longer call upon the pagan idols of Baal (2:17).

2:18 a covenant: A new covenant of peace, as also foretold by Isaiah (Is 54:10), Jeremiah (Jer 31:31–34), and Ezekiel (Ezek 34:25). God and his people will be reconciled and reunited in marriage, this time with his bride dwelling securely, undisturbed by threats of armies and ravaging animals, in contrast to 2:12 (CCC 2787). **Beasts ... birds ... creeping things:** Three classes of living creatures listed in Gen 1:30.

2:19 I will espouse you: Or "I will betroth you". Betrothal in ancient Israel was not a period of engagement before marriage but the first stage of marriage itself. Betrothed couples, having given their consent to be wedded, were already husband and wife in the eyes of the Mosaic Law, even though they customarily lived apart for a time before cohabitating and initiating marital relations. The new nuptial bond between God and his people will last forever, being characterized by fidelity, loyalty, and mercy beyond that of the original marriage ratified in the Mosaic covenant. • The OT image of God and Israel as husband and wife is taken up in the NT to describe Christ's relationship to the Church as his beloved bride (Mt 25:1–12; Mk 2:19–20; Jn 3:29–30; Eph 5:23–28; 2 Cor 11:2; Rev 19:7–9). This is based, in part, on Hosea's vision of the New Covenant as a marriage between the Lord and his people, with Jesus being the divine Bridegroom. • The bond of love between a husband and wife is an image of the covenant that unites God and his people, and so God's faithful love is presented as a model of the faithful love that should exist between spouses (John Paul II, *Familiaris Consortio* 12). **steadfast love:** The Hebrew *ḥesed* refers to a binding commitment of love and loyalty between partners in a covenant relationship. See word study: *Merciful Love* at Ex 34:7.

2:20 you shall know the LORD: The new covenant of 2:18 will bring Israel into closer communion with the Lord (cf. Jer 31:34). Right knowledge of God, as well as its lack, is a key theme in Hosea (2:8; 4:1, 6; 5:4; 6:3, 6; 8:2; 9:7; 11:3; 13:4; 14:9). In Hebrew, the verb "know" is sometimes a euphemism

for sexual intimacy between a man and a woman (Gen 4:1; Num 31:18; 1 Kings 1:4). See note on 6:3 and word study: *Know* at Judg 19:22.

2:21–23 Israel's restoration signals changes in the names of Hosea's children. The name of his son **Jezreel** (meaning "God will sow") no longer bears a message of doom, as in 1:4, but announces that God will make northern Israel grow and bear fruit again. His daughter **Not pitied** and his younger son **Not my people** will have their names reversed in honor of the blessings to come. • Paul cites 2:23 to indicate that the dispersed tribes of northern Israel, no longer distinguishable from Gentiles, are finally reestablished as God's people when Gentiles accept the gospel (Rom 9:25). Peter likewise draws from this passage when he describes Gentile Christians becoming God's people (1 Pet 2:10). See note on 1:10.

3:1–5 God instructs Hosea to reclaim his adulterous wife—a prophetic action that symbolizes how the Lord will reclaim Israel despite the nation's love affair with idols. Some think Hosea is told to marry, not Gomer, but another loose woman. Marrying a second wife seems unlikely, however, because it disrupts the book's theological message: the Lord does not cast Israel aside only to wed himself to a new people; rather, he takes back his original bride despite her unfaithfulness.

3:1 a paramour: Another man who is not her husband. **as the LORD loves:** God's love for his people is stronger than their infidelity. Even more than a *romantic* love, God's love for his bride is a *redeeming* love that goes to extraordinary lengths to restore their relationship (Jn 3:16; Eph 5:25). Notice that God's love is contrasted with Israel's disordered love for the sensual pleasures associated with idolatry (see 4:11–14). **cakes of raisins:** An ancient delicacy, apparently offered or eaten in honor of the Canaanite goddess Asherah, sometimes addressed as "the queen of heaven" (Jer 7:18; 44:19).

3:2 I bought her: The reason for payment is unclear. She may have been purchased from slavery, or at least from a relationship of dependency on a client (see note on 2:12). Whatever the case, it is a tangible sign of Hosea's desire to rebuild the ruins of his marriage with Gomer. **a homer:** A dry measure roughly equal to six bushels. **a lethech of barley:** An unknown amount. The Greek LXX reads instead "a jug of wine".

3:3 not play the harlot: Hosea will keep his wife from consorting with other men by receiving her back into his home. See note on 2:2. **so will I also be to you:** The couple will not have marital relations for a time, so that living in sexual continence will lead the unfaithful spouse from the vice of adultery to the virtue of chastity. This signifies that Israel, whom Gomer represents, will be weaned from Baalism and converted to monotheism, being devoted to the Lord alone.

---

[g] Heb *them.*
[h] Heb *break.*
[i] That is *God sows.*
[j] Cn: Heb *her.*

you shall not play the harlot, or belong to another man; so will I also be to you." ⁴For the children of Israel shall dwell many days without king or prince, without sacrifice or pillar, without ephod or teraphim. ⁵Afterward the children of Israel shall return and seek the Lᴏʀᴅ their God, and David their king; and they shall come in fear to the Lᴏʀᴅ and to his goodness in the latter days.

God Accuses Israel

4 Hear the word of the Lᴏʀᴅ, O people of Israel;
for the Lᴏʀᴅ has a controversy with the
inhabitants of the land.
There is no faithfulness or kindness,
and no knowledge of God in the land;
²there is swearing, lying, killing, stealing, and
committing adultery;
they break all bounds and murder follows
murder.
³Therefore the land mourns,
and all who dwell in it languish,
and also the beasts of the field,
and the birds of the air;
and even the fish of the sea are taken away.

⁴Yet let no one contend,
and let none accuse,
for with you is my contention, O priest. ᵏ
⁵You shall stumble by day,
the prophet also shall stumble with you by night;
and I will destroy your mother.
⁶My people are destroyed for lack of knowledge;
because you have rejected knowledge,
I reject you from being a priest to me.
And since you have forgotten the law of your God,
I also will forget your children.

⁷The more they increased,
the more they sinned against me;
I will change their glory into shame.
⁸They feed on the sin of my people;
they are greedy for their iniquity.
⁹And it shall be like people, like priest;
I will punish them for their ways,
and repay them for their deeds.
¹⁰They shall eat, but not be satisfied;
they shall play the harlot, but not multiply;
because they have forsaken the Lᴏʀᴅ
to cherish harlotry.

3:4 many days: The long period of exile, when Israel's northern tribes will be captives in foreign lands and deprived of self-government. **without sacrifice:** Exiles will be unable to worship as they did in the land of Israel. The references that follow indicate that northern Israel embraced a syncretistic religion, one that mixed elements of Mosaic worship with Canaanite superstitions. **pillar:** A large stone propped upright in honor of the fertility god Baal (10:1). Israel was forbidden to erect these pillars in the land (Lev 26:1). **ephod:** A multicolored garment worn by Israel's high priest (Ex 28:6–14). Here, however, the word may refer to an object used for pagan divination, as in Judg 17:5; 18:14. **teraphim:** Cultic figurines that served as household gods (Gen 31:19; Ezek 21:21).

3:5 the children of Israel: The northern tribes of Israel in particular. **return:** The language of repentance. See word study: *Return* at Jer 3:1. **seek the Lᴏʀᴅ:** In pursuit of an authentic relationship with the living God (Zech 8:22; Mal 3:1). **David their king:** The time of restoration will see the reunion of Israel and Judah, northern and southern tribes, under a single Davidic king (1:11). This recalls the days of David and Solomon (2 Sam 5:1–5; 1 Kings 4:20) before the northern tribes broke away from Davidic rule and formed a rival government in 930 B.C. (1 Kings 12:1–33). Since the prophesied reunion did not occur before the disappearance of the Davidic monarchy in 586 B.C., the figure of David their king must be the Davidic Messiah foretold by the prophets (Is 9:6–7; 11:1–13; Jer 23:5–6; 30:9; Ezek 34:23–24; 37:24).
• The NT proclaims Jesus as this royal messianic David (Mt 1:1–16; Lk 1:32–33), under whose rule the twelve tribes of Israel are to be reconstituted (Mt 19:28; Lk 22:28–30). The conversion of Samaritans in the early Church also fits into this picture (Jn 4:39; Acts 8:5–8, 14), since these are descendants of the northern Israelites who never went into the Assyrian Exile but intermixed with foreign peoples who were forcibly resettled in central Israel (2 Kings 17:24–34). **fear:** A reverence for God that entails turning away from evil (Ex 20:20; Job 1:1). **the latter days:** Days of prophetic fulfillment. See word study: *The Latter Days* at Is 2:2.

4:1–19 A prophetic lawsuit against northern Israel. Priests, prophets, and people are all alike corrupt, with the failure of Israel's spiritual leaders being a root cause of the prevailing disobedience among the masses (4:1, 4–5). God's shaming judgment is coming to northern Israel as a result (4:7, 19).

4:1 Hear: A summons to attention (also in 5:1). **controversy:** The Hebrew *rîb* refers to a covenant lawsuit brought by God against violators of the Mosaic covenant. See essay: *Covenant Lawsuit* at Mic 6. **kindness:** Israel is lacking in *ḥesed*—the binding commitment of love and loyalty between partners in a covenant relationship. See word study: *Merciful Love* at Ex 34:7. **no knowledge of God:** Knowledge of God and his Law are wrongly withheld from the people by Israel's priests (4:4). Lack of knowledge in Israel points to a breakdown in the covenant relationship.

4:2 swearing, lying, killing, stealing ... adultery: Violations of five of the Ten Commandments, which form the heart of the Mosaic covenant (Ex 20:1–17; Deut 5:6–21). Israelites in Hosea's day were guilty of taking false oaths in the Lord's name, bearing false witness, murderous violence, thievery, and marital infidelity (CCC 2056–63).

4:3 the land mourns: An image of creation suffering the detrimental effects of human sin (Is 24:4–5; Rom 8:19–23).

4:4 O priest: The priests are guilty of forgetting the Law of God (4:6) and neglecting to impart knowledge of it to the people (4:6). In ancient Israel, priests had the duty of teaching the precepts of the Law to the community (Lev 10:11; Deut 33:10).

4:5 stumble: Refers to committing iniquity (14:1), which leads to a fall from "the ways of the Lᴏʀᴅ" (14:9). Moses foresaw that Israel's "foot shall slip" from the path of the covenant, provoking God's vengeance (Deut 32:35). **prophet:** Also targeted for judgment, presumably for failing to preach repentance.

4:6 lack of knowledge: See note on 2:20.

4:8 They feed on the sin: Priests were given a portion of meat from every sin offering (Lev 6:25–30). This could become a self-interested arrangement, since priests would be guaranteed a greater supply of food the more sin flourished among the people. Corrupt priests would be disinclined to preach repentance (cf. 1 Sam 2:12–17).

ᵏCn: Heb uncertain.

¹¹Wine and new wine
  take away the understanding.
¹²My people inquire of a thing of wood,
  and their staff gives them oracles.
For a spirit of harlotry has led them astray,
  and they have left their God to play the harlot.
¹³They sacrifice on the tops of the mountains,
  and make offerings upon the hills,
under oak, poplar, and terebinth,
  because their shade is good.

Therefore your daughters play the harlot,
  and your brides commit adultery.
¹⁴I will not punish your daughters when they play
    the harlot,
  nor your brides when they commit adultery;
for the men themselves go aside with harlots,
  and sacrifice with cult prostitutes,
and a people without understanding shall come
    to ruin.

¹⁵Though you play the harlot, O Israel,
  let not Judah become guilty.
Enter not into Gilgal,
  nor go up to Beth-a'ven,
  and swear not, "As the LORD lives."

¹⁶Like a stubborn heifer,
  Israel is stubborn;
can the LORD now feed them
  like a lamb in a broad pasture?

¹⁷E'phraim is joined to idols,
  let him alone.
¹⁸A band¹ of drunkards, they give themselves
    to harlotry;
  they love shame more than their
    glory.ᵐ
¹⁹A wind has wrapped themⁿ in its wings,
  and they shall be ashamed because of their
  altars.ᵒ

Impending Judgment on Israel and Judah; and a Call to Repentance

5 Hear this, O priests!
  Give heed, O house of Israel!
Listen, O house of the king!
  For the judgment pertains to you;
for you have been a snare at Mizpah,
  and a net spread upon Ta'bor.
²And they have made deep the pit of Shittim;ᵖ
  but I will chastise all of them.

4:11–14 Hosea denounces the paganized worship of northern Israel, which included heavy drinking, offerings to idols, and sexual revelry.

4:11 Wine and new wine: Drunkenness destroys sober thinking about the gravity of sin (4:18).

4:12 a thing of wood: A handmade idol, foolishly consulted for "divine" guidance. **a spirit of harlotry:** A perverse infatuation with idolatry (5:4). See note on 2:2.

4:13 mountains ... terebinth: Refers to idol shrines and sacred groves in northern Israel where Canaanite gods and goddesses were served (Deut 12:2). See word study: *High Places* at 2 Kings 23:5. **brides commit adultery:** Like Hosea's wife, Gomer (3:1).

4:14 play the harlot: Men and woman engaged in sexual relations with priests and priestesses at idol shrines. The point is disputed, but biblical texts read in light of Canaanite mythology suggest to many scholars that this was a fertility rite in which sexual union with a cult prostitute was a way of petitioning gods such as Baal and Asherah to multiply the fruitfulness of one's flocks, fields, and families (cf. 4:10). One reason idolatry is described as harlotry in the Bible is because idol worship often included this type of sexual sin (e.g., Ex 32:6; Num 25:1–2). See essay: *Shun Immorality, Shun Idolatry* at 1 Cor 6. **cult prostitutes:** See note on Deut 23:17.

4:15 let not Judah become guilty: A warning to the Southern Kingdom of Judah not to imitate the idolatry of the Northern Kingdom. **Gilgal:** The location of an unlawful cult shrine (12:11; Amos 5:5). The prophet refers either to the town of Gilgal in the western Jordan valley near Jericho (Josh 4:19) or to the town of Jiljulieh, roughly seven miles north of Bethel in central Israel. **Beth-aven:** Translates "house of iniquity". It is a derogatory slur for the town of Bethel, which translates "house of God" and had been home to a golden calf idol (10:5) ever

since the northern tribes of Israel broke away from the Jerusalem Temple after the death of Solomon (1 Kings 12:25–33). **As the LORD lives:** An oath formula. Invoking the Lord's holy name in the house of an idol is especially sacrilegious—an instance of taking his name "in vain" (Ex 20:7).

4:17 Ephraim: Another name for the Northern Kingdom of Israel. Ephraim was its dominant tribe and the tribe of its first king, Jeroboam I (1 Kings 11:26). The term is used as a name for northern Israel more than 30 times in Hosea.

4:17 joined to idols: Golden calf idols in particular (8:5; 10:5; 13:2; 1 Kings 12:28–29).

4:19 A wind: A gale of divine judgment that will blow the northern tribes of Israel into exile (cf. Ps 1:4; Jer 22:22).

5:1–15 The Lord is ready to pounce on Ephraim (= northern Israel) and drag the people away like a lion seizing its prey (5:14). Judgment on Israel in the north has been a recurring theme in previous chapters, but here the prophet gives a new revelation: God is also preparing to bring judgment on Judah in the south, since they, too, will stumble in sin (5:5, 10, 12). Hosea's warning to Judah in 4:15 evidently went unheeded. On literary grounds, 5:1–7 appears to be distinct from 5:8–15, which is the beginning of a longer oracle that extends to 7:16.

5:1 O priests: An address to the clergy of the Northern Kingdom. See note on 4:4. **O house of Israel:** An address to the people of the Northern Kingdom in general. **O house of the king:** An address to the royal government of the Northern Kingdom, which lasted until the Assyrian conquest of Samaria in 722 B.C. **a snare:** A hunting trap, suggesting the locations mentioned in this verse were cultic sites that ensnared Israelites in idolatry. **Mizpah:** The name of two different towns, one east of the Jordan (Judg 10:17) and another about seven miles north of Jerusalem in Benjaminite territory (1 Sam 7:5). The referent here is uncertain. **Tabor:** A prominent mountain in lower Galilee (Judg 4:6). Christian tradition identifies it as the Mount of Transfiguration (Mt 17:1; Mk 9:2; Lk 9:28).

5:2 pit Dug by hunters to capture large prey. **Shittim:** On the plains of Moab directly northeast of the Dead Sea (Num 33:49). It was once the site of a temple to the Canaanite god Baal (Num 25:1–5; Deut 4:3).

¹Cn: Heb uncertain.
ᵐCn Compare Gk: Heb of this line uncertain.
ⁿHeb *her*.
ᵒGk Syr: Heb *sacrifices*.
ᵖCn: Heb uncertain.

3 I know E'phraim,
and Israel is not hidden from me;
for now, O Ephraim, you have played the harlot,
Israel is defiled.
4 Their deeds do not permit them
to return to their God.
For the spirit of harlotry is within them,
and they know not the LORD.
5 The pride of Israel testifies to his face;
E'phraim[q] shall stumble in his guilt;
Judah also shall stumble with them.
6 With their flocks and herds they shall go
to seek the LORD,
but they will not find him;
he has withdrawn from them.
7 They have dealt faithlessly with the LORD;
for they have borne alien children.
Now the new moon shall devour them with
their fields.

8 Blow the horn in Gib'e-ah,
the trumpet in Ra'mah.
Sound the alarm at Beth-a'ven;
tremble,[r] O Benjamin!
9 E'phraim shall become a desolation
in the day of punishment;
among the tribes of Israel
I declare what is sure.
10 The princes of Judah have become
like those who remove the landmark;
upon them I will pour out
my wrath like water.
11 E'phraim is oppressed, crushed in judgment,
because he was determined to go after
vanity.[s]
12 Therefore I am like a moth to E'phraim,
and like dry rot to the house of Judah.

13 When E'phraim saw his sickness,
and Judah his wound,
then Ephraim went to Assyria,
and sent to the great king.[t]
But he is not able to cure you
or heal your wound.
14 For I will be like a lion to E'phraim,
and like a young lion to the house of
Judah.
I, even I, will tear and go away,
I will carry off, and none shall rescue.
15 I will return again to my place,
until they acknowledge their guilt and seek
my face,
and in their distress they seek me, saying,

6 "Come, let us return to the LORD;
for he has torn, that he may heal us;
he has stricken, and he will bind us up.

5:3 Ephraim: See note on 4:17. **played the harlot:** By worshiping idols. See notes on 2:2 and 4:14. **Israel is defiled:** Like an adulteress (Num 5:20; cf. 6:10).

5:4 spirit of harlotry: A perverse infatuation with idolatry (4:12). **they know not:** See note on 2:20.

5:5 the pride of Israel: The arrogant defiance of God's covenant that was epidemic in northern Israel since its founding (1 Kings 12:16). **stumble:** Refers to committing iniquity (14:1), which leads to a fall from "the ways of the LORD" (14:9). Moses foresaw that Israel's "foot shall slip" from the path of the covenant, provoking God's vengeance (Deut 32:35).

5:6 to seek the LORD: By offering sacrifices.

5:7 alien children: The northern Israelites, having betrayed their divine Father and the responsibilities that come with being his sons and daughters, have lost their right to an inheritance in the Promised Land. In the words of Deuteronomy, "they are no longer his children because of their blemish" (Deut 32:5). **the new moon:** Normally a time for festal celebration (Num 28:11–15).

5:8 Blow the horn: An alarm sounded in the tribal territory of Benjamin, which borders the Northern Kingdom of Israel. When Israel is finally conquered and made an Assyrian territory, Judah will be exposed to hostile nations coming from the north. **Gibe-ah:** About five miles north of Jerusalem. **Ramah:** Another Benjaminite town, just north of Gibe-ah. **Beth-aven:** A derogatory epithet for Bethel, near the border between Benjaminite and Ephraimite territory. See note on 4:15.

5:9 what is sure: God's judgment on the Northern Kingdom is certain.

5:10 remove the landmark: The dishonest practice of stealing a neighbor's property by moving its boundary markers. The Mosaic Law forbids tampering with landmarks (Deut 19:14) and utters a curse on violators (Deut 27:17). Scholars think it likely that Judah claimed territory north of Jerusalem sometime after the Syro-Ephraimite conflict in 735 B.C. (2 Kings 16:1–20). **I will pour out my wrath:** The flood of the Assyrian invasion will sweep down into Judah in 701 B.C. (Is 8:5–8).

5:13 Ephraim went to Assyria: King Menahem of Israel paid tribute to Assyria and made the Northern Kingdom an Assyrian vassal state about 740 B.C. (2 Kings 15:19–20). King Hoshea of Israel did the same about 732 B.C. (2 Kings 17:3). These measures brought temporary relief to Israel but no lasting cure for its ills. **the great king:** Tiglath-pileser III of Assyria, who reigned from 745 to 727 B.C.

5:14 like a lion: See also 13:7–8.

5:15 my place: The lion's den (5:14). **until they acknowledge their guilt:** The northern tribes of Israel will suffer God's chastisement until they come to their senses and confess their sin. **seek my face:** The Lord is said to "hide" his face when he executes judgment on unfaithful Israel (Deut 31:18; 32:20).

6:1–3 A call to repentance. Israel has been mauled to death by the judgments of God (5:13) and is slain by the words of the prophets (6:5). Hosea reveals what is needed for national restoration: if Israel turns back to God in exile, the repentant tribes will be resurrected to new life in God's covenant, becoming sons and daughters once again (1:10). The language of the passage presupposes an ancient belief in bodily resurrection, a topic to which Hosea returns in 13:14. For other references to resurrection in the OT, see Is 26:19, Ezek 37:1–14, Dan 12:2–3, and essay: *Resurrection in the Old Testament* at 2 Mac 7. • The picture of God reviving his people after a time of judgment and death recalls the Song of Moses, where the Lord declares: "I kill and I make alive; I wound and I heal" (Deut 32:39).

6:1 return: The language of repentance and conversion, which are conditions of Israel's recovery. See word study: *Return* at Jer 3:1.

---

[q] Heb *Israel and Ephraim.*
[r] Cn Compare Gk: Heb *after you.*
[s] Gk: Heb a *command.*
[t] Cn: Heb *a king that will contend.*

²After two days he will revive us;
    on the third day he will raise us up,
    that we may live before him.
³Let us know, let us press on to know the LORD;
    his going forth is sure as the dawn;
he will come to us as the showers,
    as the spring rains that water the earth."
⁴What shall I do with you, O E'phraim?
    What shall I do with you, O Judah?
Your love is like a morning cloud,
    like the dew that goes early away.
⁵Therefore I have hewn them by the prophets,
    I have slain them by the words of my
        mouth,
    and my judgment goes forth as the light. ᵘ

⁶For I desire mercy and not sacrifice,
    the knowledge of God, rather than burnt
        offerings.

⁷But at ᵛ Adam they transgressed the covenant;
    there they dealt faithlessly with me.
⁸Gilead is a city of evildoers,
    tracked with blood.
⁹As robbers lie in wait ʷ for a man,
    so the priests are banded together; ˣ
they murder on the way to She'chem,
    yes, they commit villainy.
¹⁰In the house of Israel I have seen a horrible
        thing;
    E'phraim's harlotry is there, Israel is defiled.

6:6: Mt 9:13; 12:7.

6:2 he will revive us: Literally, "he will make us live". **on the third day:** The day before corruption begins. A corpse was thought to decompose in earnest on the fourth day after death (Jn 11:39). • The hope of Israel's resurrection **on the third day** anticipates Jesus' Resurrection "on the third day" (Mt 16:21). As the Messiah, he enters into Israel's suffering and death, fulfills Israel's mission to love the Lord with his whole being, and is raised to new life as a sign of what awaits repentant Israel when it accepts the gospel (Rom 11:15). In this way, Jesus was resurrected "on the third day in accordance with the Scriptures" (1 Cor 15:4; Acts 10:40; CCC 627). See note on Lk 24:46. • The Lord not only heals but revives after two days, and by rising from the lower world on the third day he raises up the entire human race with him (St. Jerome, *Commentary on Hosea* 6, 1–3). Hosea foretold that Christ's Resurrection would occur on the third day in the veiled manner that is appropriate for such a prophecy (St. Augustine, *City of God* 18, 28).

6:3 know the LORD: The prophet urges Israel's exiles to deepen their relationship with God, i.e., to return his spousal love, to recommit themselves to his covenant, and to acknowledge his sovereign lordship over their lives. **the spring rains:** Represent the blessings of God pouring down on his people.

6:4 What shall I do with you: The words of a distraught husband (= the Lord) who is exasperated by the continued betrayal of his wife (= Israel) despite his earnest pleadings. **cloud ... dew:** Israel's commitment to the Lord is fleeting and evaporates quickly (cf. 13:3).

6:5 hewn them by the prophets: Divine oracles of judgment do not fail to accomplish their purpose but put the curses of the covenant into effect (Is 55:11). **the words of my mouth:** For the word of God as a sword of judgment, see Deut 32:41; Wis 18:15–16; Ezek 21:8–17; Heb 4:12. **as the light:** As a word that exposes Israel's wickedness.

6:6 I desire mercy: The Lord wants sincere devotion (Heb., ḥesed) more than animal sacrifices (1 Sam 15:22; Jud 16:16). The contrast between what God desires and what he does not is a Semitic way, not of rejecting sacrificial worship, but of stressing what is more important. Life and liturgy are meant to form a unity, so that love for the Lord is expressed by obedience as well as ritual offerings (CCC 2100). Going through the motions of worship without the heart's adherence to God is hypocrisy (Is 1:11–17; 29:13). The Hebrew term rendered "mercy" occurs six times in Hosea. The RSV2CE variously translates it "steadfast love" (2:19), "kindness" (4:1), "love" (6:4; 12:6), and "mercy" (6:6; 10:12). See word study: *Merciful Love* at Ex 34:7. • Jesus cited Hosea's words against the Pharisees, whose concern for ritual exactness distracted them from the higher priority of sinners repenting and coming back into a loving relationship with the Lord (Mt 9:13). • Christ is our mercy from the Father. His mission is to forgive and remove sins, to justify by faith, to save the lost, and to give proof against death. Knowledge of God is therefore better than sacrifices and burnt offerings when attained in Christ. Through him we have come to know the Father and be adorned with justification by faith (St. Cyril of Alexandria, *Commentary on Hosea* 6, 5–6). We worship God with external sacrifices and offerings, not for his benefit, but for our benefit and for that of our neighbor. God does not need our sacrifices, yet he wishes them to be offered in order to rouse our devotion and to benefit our neighbor. Consequently, mercy, by which we meet the needs of our neighbor, is a sacrifice more acceptable to him (St. Thomas Aquinas, *Summa Theologiae* II-II, 31, 4).

6:7 at Adam: The Hebrew reads "like Adam" (Heb., ke'ādām), suggesting to some scholars that Hosea refers to the first man created by God (Gen 2:7), while the next line uses the adverb "there" (Heb., shām), suggesting to others that Hosea has in view the town of Adam, which stood in the eastern Jordan valley north of Jericho (Josh 3:16). Favoring a reference to the first man: Adam's transgression of the original covenant in Eden (Gen 2:15–17) is clearly indicated in Scripture (Gen 3:17), while nothing is known of an Israelite apostasy or heinous crime at the town of Adam. Favoring a reference to the town: the following verses point to sins committed at various locations in northern Israel (Gilead, 6:8; Shechem, 6:9), and similar statements in Hosea expose the guilt of sinful cities (Gilgal, 9:15; Gibe-ah, 10:9). For the belief that God made a covenant with Adam at creation, see Sir 14:17 and note on Gen 2:15–17. **the covenant:** Israel is guilty of transgressing the Mosaic covenant (8:1).

6:8 Gilead: Ramoth Gilead, a city east of the Jordan River. **tracked with blood:** Bloodshed in Gilead was especially disturbing, since it was set apart as a city of refuge to give safe haven to persons involved in manslaughter (Josh 20:3). See note on Josh 20:1–9.

6:9 Shechem: About 30 miles north of Jerusalem. It was the first capital of the Northern Kingdom of Israel (1 Kings 12:25), and, like Ramoth Gilead in 6:8, it was a city of refuge (Josh 20:7).

6:10 Israel is defiled: Like an adulteress (Num 5:20; cf. 5:3).

ᵘGk Syr: Heb *your judgment goes forth.*
ᵛCn: Heb *like.*
ʷCn: Heb uncertain.
ˣSyr: Heb *a company.*

¹¹For you also, O Judah, a harvest is appointed.
  When I would restore the fortunes of my
    people,

7 ¹when I would heal Israel,
  the corruption of E′phraim is revealed,
    and the wicked deeds of Samar′ia;
  for they deal falsely,
    the thief breaks in,
    and the bandits raid without.
²But they do not consider
    that I remember all their evil works.
  Now their deeds encompass them,
    they are before my face.
³By their wickedness they make the king glad,
    and the princes by their treachery.
⁴They are all adulterers;
    they are like a heated oven,
  whose baker ceases to stir the fire,
    from the kneading of the dough until it is
      leavened.
⁵On the day of our king the princes
    became sick with the heat of wine;
    he stretched out his hand with mockers.
⁶For like an oven their hearts burnʸ with intrigue;
    all night their anger smolders;
    in the morning it blazes like a flaming fire.
⁷All of them are hot as an oven,
    and they devour their rulers.
  All their kings have fallen;
    and none of them calls upon me.

⁸E′phraim mixes himself with the peoples;
    Ephraim is a cake not turned.

⁹Aliens devour his strength,
    and he knows it not;
  gray hairs are sprinkled upon him,
    and he knows it not.
¹⁰The pride of Israel witnesses against him;
    yet they do not return to the LORD their
      God,
    nor seek him, for all this.

¹¹E′phraim is like a dove,
    silly and without sense,
    calling to Egypt, going to Assyria.
¹²As they go, I will spread over them my net;
    I will bring them down like birds of the air;
    I will chastise them for their wicked deeds.ᶻ
¹³Woe to them, for they have strayed from me!
    Destruction to them, for they have rebelled
      against me!
  I would redeem them,
    but they speak lies against me.

¹⁴They do not cry to me from the heart,
    but they wail upon their beds;
  for grain and wine they gash themselves,
    they rebel against me.
¹⁵Although I trained and strengthened their
      arms,
    yet they devise evil against me.
¹⁶They turn to Ba′al;ᵃ
    they are like a treacherous bow,
  their princes shall fall by the sword
    because of the insolence of their tongue.
  This shall be their derision in the land of Egypt.

6:11 a harvest: A time of judgment, when Judah will reap the fruits of its evildoing (Jer 51:33; Joel 3:13).

7:1–16 Hosea continues to rail against the abominations of northern Israel. Deeds singled out for condemnation include thievery (7:1), drunkenness (7:5), political intrigue (7:6), reliance on foreign nations (7:8, 11), and participation in pagan cult practices (7:16). The background is the chaotic period between 753 and 722 B.C., which ended with the fall of the Northern Kingdom of Israel and the exile of the northern tribes to Assyrian lands (2 Kings 15–17).

7:1 Ephraim: See note on 4:17. **Samaria:** Capital of the Northern Kingdom of Israel since the days of King Omri (1 Kings 16:24).

7:4 adulterers: Members of the royal government who pretend to be loyal to the king but treacherously plot against him. **a heated oven:** Represents a smoldering conspiracy that burns low for a time and then blazes up when stoked, resulting in a violent coup (7:6).

7:7 all their kings have fallen: Instability marked the final years of the Northern Kingdom of Israel, which saw the fall of six kings, four of them by assassination, between 753 and 722 B.C.

7:8 mixes himself: Like a baker mixes flour and oil together for a new batch of bread. **with the peoples:** Northern Israel, ceasing to trust in the Lord, sought political alliances with powerful nations such as Assyria and Egypt (7:11; 12:1), only to get burned and become useless like a **cake** of dough

left unturned in a hot oven (7:4–7). Reliance on foreign powers for military help and maintenance of power amounts to spurning the Lord (2 Chron 16:7–8; Is 31:1).

7:9 devour his strength: Israel paid heavy tribute to Assyria (2 Kings 15:19; 17:3). **gray hairs ... he knows it not:** Northern Israel is unaware that its kingdom is growing old and nearing death. Its people thus fail to realize that time is short for turning away from evil.

7:10 The pride of Israel: The arrogant defiance of God's covenant that was epidemic in northern Israel since its founding (5:5; 1 Kings 12:16).

7:11 a dove: Easily captured in a fowler's net (7:12). **Egypt ... Assyria:** See note on 7:8.

7:13 Woe: A cry of lamentation that anticipates a coming calamity (9:12; Num 21:29; Is 3:11).

7:14 not ... from the heart: Israel's devotion to the Lord is shallow and superficial (Is 29:13). **gash themselves:** Self-laceration was an ancient mourning rite (Jer 16:6) and a means of seeking the favor of the Canaanite god Baal in times of drought (1 Kings 18:28). The practice is forbidden in the Mosaic Law (Lev 19:28; Deut 14:1). Again, the northern tribes are accused of following pagan religious practices, as in 2:13; 4:12–14, 17; 10:1, 5–8, etc.

7:16 the land of Egypt: A metaphor for exile, as in 8:13 and 9:3. The scattering of rebellious Israel to distant nations is compared to reversing the Exodus from Egypt, bringing the people from freedom back into slavery (Ex 1:8–14). • Moses declared that when sinful Israel goes into exile, it will be like the people are hauled back "in ships to Egypt" and made "slaves" all over again (Deut 28:68).

ʸ Gk Syr: Heb *brought near.*
ᶻ Cn: Heb *according to the report to their congregation.*
ᵃ Cn: Heb uncertain.

Israel's Apostasy

8 Set the trumpet to your lips,
for[b] a vulture is over the house of the Lord,
because they have broken my covenant,
and transgressed my law.
2To me they cry,
My God, we Israel know you.
3Israel has spurned the good;
the enemy shall pursue him.

4They made kings, but not through me.
They set up princes, but without my
knowledge.
With their silver and gold they made idols
for their own destruction.
5I have[c] spurned your calf, O Samar'ia.
My anger burns against them.
How long will it be
till they are pure 6in Israel?[d]

A workman made it;
it is not God.
The calf of Samar'ia
shall be broken to pieces.[e]

7For they sow the wind,
and they shall reap the whirlwind.

The standing grain has no heads,
it shall yield no meal;
if it were to yield,
aliens would devour it.
8Israel is swallowed up;
already they are among the nations
as a useless vessel.
9For they have gone up to Assyria,
a wild donkey wandering alone;
E'phraim has hired lovers.
10Though they hire allies among the nations,
I will soon gather them up.
And they shall cease[f] for a little while
from anointing[g] king and princes.

11Because E'phraim has multiplied altars for
sinning,
they have become to him altars for sinning.
12Were I to write for him my laws by ten
thousands,
they would be regarded as a strange thing.
13They love sacrifice;[h]
they sacrifice flesh and eat it;
but the Lord has no delight in them.
Now he will remember their iniquity,
and punish their sins;
they shall return to Egypt.

8:1–14 Doom is pronounced on Israel for its many rebellions. Though the northern tribes claim to know God (8:2), they are guilty of staging royal coups (8:4), fabricating idols (8:5–6), seeking alliances with foreign nations (8:9–10), multiplying altars of sin (8:11), and engaging in hypocritical worship (8:13). All of this is tantamount to spurning what is good (8:3) and forgetting the Lord (8:14). Judgment is certain for Israel in the north, and not even Judah in the south will be left unscathed (8:14).

8:1 the trumpet: Used for sounding an alarm. See word study: *Trumpet* at Judg 6:34. **a vulture:** Or "an eagle". Moses used this word (Heb., *nesher*) for an enemy nation that will bring a curse of devastation on the land of Israel (Deut 28:49). **house of the Lord:** Normally this expression refers to the Temple in Jerusalem (as in 9:4). However, some interpret this verse as a reference to the Promised Land, from which the northern tribes will be expelled (as in 9:15). **my covenant:** The Mosaic covenant.

8:3 the enemy: The Assyrians.

8:4 They made kings: The final years of the Northern Kingdom of Israel saw four kings assassinated and the throne seized by four different families. This was the tragic result, not of seeking the Lord's will, but of purely human calculations and power struggles. Moreover, from the perspective of Judah in the south, the northern kings were illegitimate from the start since the Northern Kingdom was founded in opposition to God's anointed kings in Jerusalem—the royal descendants of David (1 Kings 12:19–20). Hosea prophesies that northern

Israel's restoration will include its resubmission to Davidic rule (3:5). See chart: *Kings of the Divided Monarchy* at 1 Kings 12. **they made idols:** Jeroboam I, the first king of northern Israel, forged calf and goat idols (1 Kings 12:28; 2 Chron 11:14–15). Golden calves continued to be venerated by the northern tribes in Hosea's day (8:5; 10:5; 13:2).

8:5 calf, O Samaria: Either a calf idol was worshiped in Samaria, the capital of the Northern Kingdom of Israel at this time, or the word "Samaria" is used to refer to the whole Northern Kingdom. The former is possible, but many scholars adopt the latter position and propose that Hosea is targeting the calf idol in Bethel/Beth-aven (10:5; cf. 1 Kings 12:28).

8:7 sow the wind ... reap the whirlwind: A proverb meaning that Israel will get exactly what its evil works deserve (cf. Gal 6:7). Had Israel sown righteousness, it would have reaped God's mercy (10:12).

8:8 Israel is swallowed up: The exile of Israel's northern tribes and their absorption into foreign nations is so certain that Hosea describes it as an accomplished fact. Indeed, the process had already begun in the late 730s B.C., when the Assyrians deported thousands of Israelites from upper Galilee (2 Kings 15:29) and the Transjordan territories (1 Chron 5:26).

8:9 gone up to Assyria: I.e., to seek political alliances. See note on 5:13. **hired lovers:** Israel made payments of tribute to their Assyrian overlords (8:10; 2 Kings 15:19; 17:3).

8:11 multiplied altars: It is unclear if these are pagan altars dedicated to the fertility god Baal (4:13; 10:1) or altars dedicated to the Lord (1 Kings 19:10). Either way, whether the Israelites were engaged in idolatry or were sacrificing to the Lord at locations outside Jerusalem, they were acting in violation of the covenant, which demands exclusive worship of the Lord in his Temple (Deut 5:6–10; 12:13–14).

8:13 they sacrifice: Perhaps offerings made to idols (see 2:13; 4:13). However, even sacrifices made to the Lord are unacceptable when offered by sinners who are unrepentant (Ps 51:16–17). **return to Egypt:** See note on 7:16.

---

[b]Cn: Heb *as.*
[c]Heb *He has.*
[d]Gk: Heb *for from Israel.*
[e]Or *shall go up in flames.*
[f]Gk: Heb *begin.*
[g]Gk: Heb *burden.*
[h]Cn: Heb uncertain.

¹⁴For Israel has forgotten his Maker,
    and built palaces;
and Judah has multiplied fortified cities;
    but I will send a fire upon his cities,
    and it shall devour his strongholds.

Punishment for Israel's Sin

9 Rejoice not, O Israel!
    Exult notⁱ like the peoples;
for you have played the harlot, forsaking your
    God.
    You have loved a harlot's hire
    upon all threshing floors.
²Threshing floor and winevat shall not feed them,
    and the new wine shall fail them.
³They shall not remain in the land of the Lord;
    but E'phraim shall return to Egypt,
    and they shall eat unclean food in Assyria.

⁴They shall not pour libations of wine to the Lord;
    and they shall not please him with their
    sacrifices.
    Their bread^j shall be like mourners' bread;
    all who eat of it shall be defiled;
for their bread shall be for their hunger only;
    it shall not come to the house of the Lord.

⁵What will you do on the day of appointed festival,
    and on the day of the feast of the Lord?
⁶For behold, they are going to Assyria;^k
    Egypt shall gather them,
    Memphis shall bury them.
Nettles shall possess their precious things of silver;
    thorns shall be in their tents.

⁷The days of punishment have come,
    the days of recompense have come;
    Israel shall know it.
The prophet is a fool,
    the man of the spirit is mad,
    because of your great iniquity
    and great hatred.
⁸The prophet is the watchman of E'phraim,
    the people of my God,
yet a fowler's snare is on all his ways,
    and hatred in the house of his God.
⁹They have deeply corrupted themselves
    as in the days of Gib'e-ah:
he will remember their iniquity,
    he will punish their sins.

¹⁰Like grapes in the wilderness,
    I found Israel.

8:14: Amos 1:4, 7, 10, 12, 14; 2:2, 5.   **9:7:** Lk 21:22.

8:14 fire upon his cities: The Assyrians invaded Judah in 701 B.C., capturing 46 Judean towns and taking thousands into exile, according to the surviving *Annals of Sennacherib*. Jerusalem was spared conquest at this time, however (2 Kings 18–19).

9:1–17 The punishments ready to fall on Israel for its wickedness. Having become "deeply corrupted" (9:9), the northern tribes are about to face "days of recompense" (9:7) that will end with thousands of Israelites dispersed "among the nations" (9:17). The pain of exile will be increased by the death of children at the hands of the ruthless Assyrians (9:12–13, 16).

9:1 played the harlot: By worshiping idols. See note on 2:2. **loved a harlot's hire:** Northern Israelites mistakenly viewed their abundant harvests as provisions of the fertility god Baal in exchange for religious service. In reality, the fruitfulness of the land was the Lord's gift, not Baal's (2:8).

9:2 Threshing floor and winevat: Represent the joyous times of the grain and grape harvests. These will be nothing but a memory when Israel is expelled from its land (9:3).

9:3 Ephraim: Northern Israel. See note on 4:17. **return to Egypt:** See note on 7:16. **unclean food:** Animals forbidden for Israelite consumption by the Mosaic Law (Lev 11:1–47; Deut 14:1–21).

9:4 libations: Drink offerings of wine poured out at the Lord's altar (Ex 29:38–40). **shall not please him:** Obligations of divine worship will be unfulfillable for Israel in exile, where the northern tribes will be cut off from the Lord's Temple and its sacred liturgies. **mourners' bread:** Food shared with a grieving family to console them over the loss of a loved one (Jer 16:7). **shall be defiled:** Exiles will eat the "unclean" food of the Assyrians (9:3; Ezek 4:13).

9:5 the feast of the Lord: The autumn Feast of Booths, also called Tabernacles, which celebrated the end of the harvest season (Lev 23:33–43). Observance of such feasts will be impossible for Israel in exile.

9:6 to Assyria: The Hebrew reads "from destruction", and the Greek LXX reads "from misery". The reference may be to Israel's futile hope that making alliances with stronger nations such as Assyria and Egypt will prevent its destruction. Hosea is adamant that these political efforts will end, not in greater security, but in mass burials. See note on 7:8. **Memphis:** A city in northern Egypt famous for its pyramid tombs. **Nettles … thorns … in their tents:** Indicates that during the Exile, abandoned Israelite homes will fall into ruin and become overgrown with weeds, as will their idol shrines (10:8).

9:7 days of punishment: Literally, "days of visitation". **Israel shall know it:** Ironically, Israel will "know" the Lord's judgment because its claim to "know" him as a faithful covenant partner is false (8:2), a fact noted several times in the book (e.g., 4:1, 6; 5:4). See note on 2:20. **The prophet is a fool:** Northern Israel's insulting view of Hosea. For the perception of prophets as madmen, see also Jer 29:26.

9:8 The prophet is the watchman: Hosea's description of himself, in contrast to 9:7. A true prophet is like a sentinel on a tower or city wall who sounds the alarm when he sees danger approaching (Ezek 3:17; Hab 2:1).

 9:9 the days of Gibe-ah: A time of moral atrocities in Israel. Most notably, wicked men from the tribe of Benjamin raped and abused a helpless woman in Gibe-ah, a town of Benjamin, and as a result, the whole tribe was nearly exterminated by the violent retaliation of the other tribes (see Judg 19–20). This time it is northern Israel that faces armed assault and drastic population reduction for its abominations.

9:10—11:11 Israel is depicted under four images: a cluster of **grapes** (9:10–17), a flourishing **vine** (10:1–10), a trained **heifer** (10:11–15), and a young **child** (11:1–11). All four indicate that God delighted in Israel during its early history, lavishing his people with care and attention.

9:10 Baal-peor: An idol of the fertility god Baal that was venerated at a location northeast of the

---

ⁱ Gk: Heb *to exultation.*
^j Cn: Heb *to them.*
^k Cn: Heb *from destruction.*

Like the first fruit on the fig tree,
　in its first season,
　I saw your fathers.
But they came to Ba'al-pe'or,
　and consecrated themselves to Ba'al,[1]
　and became detestable like the thing they loved.
[11]E'phraim's glory shall fly away like a bird—
　no birth, no pregnancy, no conception!
[12]Even if they bring up children,
　I will bereave them till none is left.
Woe to them
　when I depart from them!
[13]E'phraim's sons, as I have seen, are destined for
　a prey;[m]
　Ephraim must lead forth his sons to slaughter.
[14]Give them, O LORD—
　what will you give?
Give them a miscarrying womb
　and dry breasts.

[15]Every evil of theirs is in Gilgal;
　there I began to hate them.
Because of the wickedness of their deeds
　I will drive them out of my house.
I will love them no more;
　all their princes are rebels.

[16]E'phraim is stricken,
　their root is dried up,
　they shall bear no fruit.

Even though they bring forth,
　I will slay their beloved children.
[17]My God will cast them off,
　because they have not listened to him;
　they shall be wanderers among the
　　nations.

Israel's Sin and Captivity

10 Israel is a luxuriant vine
　that yields its fruit.
The more his fruit increased
　the more altars he built;
as his country improved
　he improved his pillars.
[2]Their heart is false;
　now they must bear their guilt.
The LORD[n] will break down their altars,
　and destroy their pillars.

[3]For now they will say:
　"We have no king,
for we fear not the LORD,
　and a king, what could he do for us?"
[4]They utter mere words;
　with empty oaths they make covenants;
so judgment springs up like poisonous
　weeds
　in the furrows of the field.
[5]The inhabitants of Samar'ia tremble
　for the calf[o] of Beth-a'ven.

Dead Sea. • Israel committed apostasy at Peor in Num 25:1–5. The episode shows that even in the early days of God's relationship with Israel, the people fell headlong into idolatry and sexual impurity, provoking the Lord to anger (Ps 106:28–29). See word study: *Baal* at 2:8. **detestable like the thing they loved:** Israelites became as offensive to God as the idol they worshiped. • Contrary to the claim that the good or evil of an action is not related to its object, a person becomes abominable to God on account of doing evil. The evil of his action is thus related to the evil things that a person loves (St. Thomas Aquinas, *Summa Theologiae* I-II, 18, 2).

9:11 no birth, no pregnancy: Contrary to the meaning of Ephraim's name, which translates "doubly fruitful" (cf. Gen 41:52). Hosea also draws attention to this reversal of meaning in 9:14 and 9:16.

9:12 Woe: A cry of lamentation that anticipates a coming calamity (7:13; Num 21:29; Is 3:11).

9:15 Gilgal: The location of an unlawful cult shrine (12:11; Amos 5:5). See note on 4:15. **I began to hate them:** Another way of saying, as in 9:10, that Israel made itself detestable in God's eyes by worshiping idols. **I will drive them out:** Like a husband who sends his divorced wife out of his home (Deut 24:1). **my house:** This expression refers to the Jerusalem Temple in 9:4, but here the word "house" seems to refer to the Promised Land from which the northern tribes will be expelled (9:17). **love them no more:** Means the northern tribes will become "Not my people", i.e., cut off from the Lord's covenant for a period of time (1:9).

9:17 cast them off: Temporarily, not permanently (1 Sam 12:22; Rom 11:2). **wanderers:** A comparison between Israel and Cain is implied: the northern tribes will be driven from the land to become wanderers among foreign nations (9:15), just as Cain, being guilty of grave sin, was driven from the Lord's presence to be a wanderer in another land (Gen 4:8–14).

10:1 a luxuriant vine: A traditional image of Israel planted and thriving in the Promised Land (Ps 80:8–11; Ezek 19:10–11). Although God blessed his people with prosperity, they misused their abundance to finance the worship of other gods. **altars:** Unlawful altars used for sacrificing to idols (2:13; 4:13) or even to the Lord (9:4). The Torah forbids not only serving idols but sacrificing to the Lord anywhere outside the sacred precincts of his Temple in Jerusalem (Deut 12:10–14). **pillars:** Large stones propped upright in honor of the Canaanite god Baal (10:1). Israel was forbidden to erect these in the land (Lev 26:1).

10:3 for we fear not the LORD: Israel will come to see the error of its ways, but not until judgment falls and the northern monarchy is destroyed in 722 B.C.

10:4 empty oaths: Refers to taking the Lord's name "in vain", which is a violation of the Decalogue (Ex 20:7; Deut 5:11). **covenants:** Formal agreements between two parties that are sealed by verbal or ritual oaths that invoke the Lord's name (Deut 7:12; Ps 89:3; Ezek 17:13–19). See essay: *What Is a Covenant* at Deut 5.

10:5 Samaria: Capital of the Northern Kingdom of Israel since the days of King Omri (1 Kings 16:24). **the calf of Beth-aven:** The golden calf idol stationed in Bethel since the founding of the Northern Kingdom (1 Kings 12:28–29). Hosea foretells its capture by the Assyrians (10:6). **idolatrous priests:** Priests who served the god Baal (Zeph 1:4). **its glory ... departed:** Possibly an allusion to 1 Sam 4:21–22.

---

[1]Heb *shame*.
[m]Cn Compare Gk: Heb uncertain.
[n]Heb *he*.
[o]Gk Syr: Heb *calves*.

Its people shall mourn for it,
    and its idolatrous priests shall wail[p] over it,
    over its glory which has departed from it.
⁶Yes, the thing itself shall be carried to Assyria,
    as tribute to the great king.[q]
E'phraim shall be put to shame,
    and Israel shall be ashamed of his idol.[r]

⁷Samar'ia's king shall perish,
    like a chip on the face of the waters.
⁸The high places of A'ven, the sin of Israel,
    shall be destroyed.
Thorn and thistle shall grow up
    on their altars;
and they shall say to the mountains, Cover us,
    and to the hills, Fall upon us.

⁹From the days of Gib'e-ah, you have sinned, O
    Israel;
there they have continued.
    Shall not war overtake them in Gibe-ah?
¹⁰I will come[s] against the wayward people to
    chastise them;
and nations shall be gathered against them
when they are chastised[t] for their double
    iniquity.

¹¹E'phraim was a trained heifer
    that loved to thresh,
    and I spared her fair neck;

but I will put Ephraim to the yoke,
    Judah must plow,
    Jacob must harrow for himself.
¹²Sow for yourselves righteousness,
    reap the fruit[u] of mercy;
    break up your fallow ground,
for it is the time to seek the Lord,
    that he may come and rain salvation upon you.

¹³You have plowed iniquity,
    you have reaped injustice,
    you have eaten the fruit of lies.
Because you have trusted in your chariots[v]
    and in the multitude of your warriors,
¹⁴therefore the tumult of war shall arise among
    your people,
    and all your fortresses shall be destroyed,
as Shal'man destroyed Beth-ar'bel on the day of
    battle;
    mothers were dashed in pieces with their
    children.
¹⁵Thus it shall be done to you, O house of Israel,[w]
    because of your great wickedness.
In the storm[x] the king of Israel
    shall be utterly cut off.

God's Compassion Despite Israel's Unfaithfulness

11 When Israel was a child, I loved him,
    and out of Egypt I called my son.

10:8: Lk 23:30; Rev 6:16.   **10:12:** 2 Cor 9:10.   **11:1:** Mt 2:15.

10:7 Samaria's king shall perish: Hoshea, the last of the northern kings of Israel, was imprisoned by the Assyrians before the fall of Samaria in 722 B.C. (2 Kings 17:4–6). **like a chip:** Like a twig or splinter of wood carried off by the current of a river or stream.

10:8 high places: Unlawful cultic shrines. See word study: *High Places* at 2 Kings 23:5. **Aven:** The Hebrew word for "iniquity". Some see a reference to the town of Bethel, which Hosea calls Beth-aven (4:15; 10:5). **Thorn and thistle shall grow:** The idol shrines in northern Israel will be abandoned and overgrown. **Cover us ... Fall upon us:** The cries of people overwhelmed with suffering. They beg for instant death and burial. • Jesus cites these words in a prediction of doom on Jerusalem, telling the women who weep over his Passion that days are coming for the city that will cause many to plead for an end to their agony (Lk 23:30). A similar scene appears in Revelation: when the sixth seal is broken, people hide in caves from the wrath of the Lamb and bid the mountains, "Fall on us" (Rev 6:16).

10:9 the days of Gibe-ah: See note on 9:9.

10:11 heifer: Or "female calf". **to thresh:** Oxen were used to tread upon wheat and barley stalks on platforms called

threshing floors. The process separated edible grains from their useless husks. It was not a particularly laborious task for the animal, which was even allowed to eat freely as it worked (Deut 25:4). Hosea insists that these days of ease are over. Israel and Judah, because of their sin, will now bear the **yoke** of God's chastisement and be forced to **plow** the hard ground (10:11; 11:7).

10:12 time to seek the Lord: The exiles of Israel are invited to turn to God in their suffering, confident that he wants to show them compassion and to restore his blessings (Deut 30:1–6).

10:13 plowed ... reaped: See note on 8:7. **trusted in your chariots:** The folly of thinking that military might can protect northern Israel from the consequences of its iniquity (cf. Is 31:1–3).

10:14 as Shalman destroyed Beth-arbel: The person, place, and incident are all unknown outside this verse, though they must have been familiar to Hosea's audience. **dashed in pieces:** Near Eastern warfare was a merciless affair that sanctioned brutal attacks even on women and children (2 Kings 8:12; Is 13:16; Nahum 3:10).

11:1–11 Images of God as the loving Father of his people. With tender affection, he comforted, fed, and taught young Israel to walk (11:3–4). Most of all, his fatherly care was shown by calling the people out of Egypt (11:1). But like many adolescents, Israel grew stubborn and disobedient along the way (11:2), and so God had to discipline his people with a yoke of servitude among the nations (11:5–7). Even then, the Lord never ceased to love his rebellious son but showed him compassion (11:8–9) and announced plans for his restoration (11:10–11). Jesus told a similar story about the merciful Fatherhood of God in the parable of the Prodigal Son (Lk 15:11–32; CCC 218–19, 370). See note on Wis 14:3.

---

[p] Cn: Heb *exult.*
[q] Cn: Heb a *king that will contend.*
[r] Cn: Heb *counsel.*
[s] Cn Compare Gk: Heb *in my desire.*
[t] Gk: Heb *bound.*
[u] Gk: Heb *according to.*
[v] Gk: Heb *way.*
[w] Gk: Heb *O Bethel.*
[x] Cn: Heb *dawn.*

²The more I ʸ called them,
  the more they went from me; ᶻ
  they kept sacrificing to the Ba'als,
    and burning incense to idols.

³Yet it was I who taught E'phraim to walk,
  I took them up in my ᵃ arms;
  but they did not know that I healed them.
⁴I led them with cords of compassion, ᵇ
  with the bands of love,
  and I became to them as one
    who raises an infant to his cheeks,
    and I bent down to them and fed them.

⁵They shall return to the land of Egypt,
  and Assyria shall be their king,
  because they have refused to return to
    me.
⁶The sword shall rage against their cities,
  consume the bars of their gates,
  and devour them in their fortresses. ᶜ
⁷My people are bent on turning away from
    me; ᵈ
  so they are appointed to the yoke,
    and none shall remove it.

⁸How can I give you up, O E'phraim!
  How can I hand you over, O Israel!
  How can I make you like Admah!
    How can I treat you like Zeboi'im!
  My heart recoils within me,
    my compassion grows warm and tender.
⁹I will not execute my fierce anger,
  I will not again destroy E'phraim;
  for I am God and not man,
    the Holy One in your midst,
    and I will not come to destroy. ᵉ

¹⁰They shall go after the LORD,
  he will roar like a lion;
  yes, he will roar,
    and his sons shall come trembling from the
      west;
¹¹they shall come trembling like birds from Egypt,
  and like doves from the land of Assyria;
  and I will return them to their homes, says the
    LORD.
¹² ᶠ E'phraim has encompassed me with lies,
  and the house of Israel with deceit;
  but Judah is still known by ᵍ God,
    and is faithful to the Holy One.

📖 **11:1 When ... a child:** A flashback to the beginning of God's relationship with Israel at the time of the Exodus. **I loved him:** The basis of Israel's divine election (Deut 7:6-8). **out of Egypt:** The deliverance of Israel from slavery, which is likened to the adoption of an infant nation. **my son:** The Lord demanded that Pharaoh release the Israelites from bondage, since they were his "first-born son" (Ex 4:22; CCC 441). • In the Gospel of Matthew, the Holy Family's flight to Egypt set the stage for another fulfillment of this Scripture: God would again call his Son, the infant Jesus, out of Egypt and back to the land of Israel (Mt 2:15). The idea is that Jesus, as the Messiah, relives the history of his people—only now with perfect obedience—in order to fulfill God's saving mission for Israel and the world.

11:2 the Baals: See word study: *Baal* at 2:8.

11:3 I healed: In the sense of "I nursed back to health" (6:1; 7:1; Ex 15:26).

🕊 **11:4 I bent down to them and fed them:** An allusion to the manna in the wilderness (Ex 16:4-35; Ps 78:23-25). • This prefigures how the Lord came down, leaving the kingdom of heaven and taking the form of a man, that he might eat with them as a companion at table and might give them his body as food (St. Jerome, *Commentary on Hosea* 11, 3-4).

11:5 return to ... Egypt: A reference to exile. See note on 7:16.

11:6 The sword: The Assyrian army, which will conquer northern Israel in 722 B.C.

11:7 the yoke: Represents exile and foreign domination (Deut 28:48). See note on 10:11.

11:8 Admah ... Zeboiim: Cities near the Dead Sea (Gen 14:2) that were completely destroyed by the Lord along with Sodom and Gomorrah (Deut 29:23; cf. Gen 19:24-25). The point here is one of contrast: the northern tribes of Israel deserve the same extreme punishment, but God says he will *not* annihilate them as he did the wicked cities of old.

11:9 I am God and not man: Unlike men, who show no restraint when thrown into a violent rage, the Lord tempers his wrath with mercy. Here God will stop short of obliterating Israel's northern tribes by leaving a remnant that escapes destruction and eventually returns to him (11:10-11). In strict theological terms, God is unchangeable and has no emotions. Biblical descriptions of God being moved by emotions are called anthropopathisms—figures of speech that show God is a personal Being but should not be taken literally. See notes on Gen 6:6 and Lam 2:1. **the Holy One:** See note on Is 1:4.

11:10-11 A prophecy of restoration, offering a message of hope in the midst of judgment on northern Israel. For the eventual recovery of the northern tribes, see 1:10-11; Is 27:12-13; Jer 50:17-20.

11:10-11 like a lion: No longer the devouring lion of 5:14, the Lord will roar again in the future to summon the exiles back to himself. **trembling:** Or "hurrying". **like birds ... doves:** Creatures that can travel long distances quickly.

11:12—13:16 Formal charges are brought against Israel and Judah in a covenant lawsuit.

📖 **11:12 deceit:** The same word is translated "guile" in Gen 27:35, describing how Jacob tricked his father into giving him the blessing meant for his brother Esau. For allusions to Jacob in this section, see note on 12:2-6. **still known by God:** Or "still walks with God", meaning the Southern Kingdom of Judah continues to live in covenant with the Lord. The Northern Kingdom of Israel, by contrast, lived in constant rebellion against the institutions established by the Lord such as the Davidic monarchy and the Jerusalem Temple (1 Kings 12:19-20). Judah will eventually commit apostasy and face judgment as well (5:5, 12, 14; 6:11; 8:14; 12:2). **the Holy One:** See note on Is 1:4.

ʸ Gk: Heb *they*.
ᶻ Gk: Heb *them*.
ᵃ Gk Syr Vg: Heb *his*.
ᵇ Heb *man*.
ᶜ Cn: Heb *counsels*.
ᵈ The meaning of the Hebrew is uncertain.
ᵉ Cn: Heb *into the city*.
ᶠ Ch 12:1 in Heb.
ᵍ Cn Compare Gk: Heb *roams with*.

The Long History of Israel's Rebellion

12 E′phraim herds the wind,
    and pursues the east wind all day long;
they multiply falsehood and violence;
    they make a bargain with Assyria,
    and oil is carried to Egypt.

2 The LORD has an indictment against Judah,
    and will punish Jacob according to his ways,
    and repay him according to his deeds.
3 In the womb he took his brother by the heel,
    and in his manhood he strove with God.
4 He strove with the angel and prevailed,
    he wept and sought his favor.
  He met God at Bethel,
    and there God spoke with him[h]—
5 the LORD LORD the God of hosts,
    the LORD is his name:
6 "So you, by the help of your God, return,
    hold fast to love and justice,
    and wait continually for your God."

7 A trader, in whose hands are false balances,
    he loves to oppress.
8 E′phraim has said, "Ah, but I am rich,
    I have gained wealth for myself";
but all his riches can never offset[i]
    the guilt he has incurred.

9 I am the LORD your God
    from the land of Egypt;
I will again make you dwell in tents,
    as in the days of the appointed feast.

10 I spoke to the prophets;
    it was I who multiplied visions,
    and through the prophets gave parables.
11 If there is iniquity in Gilead
    they shall surely come to nothing;
if in Gilgal they sacrifice bulls,
    their altars also shall be like stone heaps
    on the furrows of the field.
12 (Jacob fled to the land of Ar′am,
    there Israel did service for a wife,
    and for a wife he herded sheep.)
13 By a prophet the LORD brought Israel up from
        Egypt,
    and by a prophet he was preserved.
14 E′phraim has given bitter provocation;
    so his LORD will leave his bloodguilt upon
        him,
    and will turn back upon him his reproaches.

God the Savior and Judge of Israel

13 When E′phraim spoke, men trembled;
    he was exalted in Israel;
    but he incurred guilt through Ba′al and died.

12:8: Rev 3:17.

12:1 herds the wind: An utterly futile pursuit (Eccles 1:14; 2:11). **they make a bargain:** Literally, "they cut a covenant". **Assyria ... Egypt:** Treaty alliances with these mighty nations are denounced as acts of betrayal against the Lord, in whom God's people should have placed their trust for safety and security (7:8–13; 8:9–10).

12:2–6 The personal history of Jacob foreshadows the national history of Israel; the family of twelve tribes descended from him. Hosea recalls **(1)** the day of Jacob's birth, when he grasped the **heel** of his twin brother, Esau, prefiguring how he would supplant his brother as the recipient of his father's blessing (Gen 25:24–26); **(2)** the night when Jacob, as an adult, **strove** with an angel of God and earned the name Israel, meaning "he who strives with God" (Gen 32:22–30); and **(3)** the night when God appeared to him in a dream at **Bethel** and promised to bring him back to the land of Israel after a time of flight and exile (Gen 28:10–19). The implied message: the people of Israel, after a history of deceit and selfish pursuits, will be forced into exile, but eventually the Lord will bring them back in his mercy. See note on 11:12.

12:2 indictment: See essay: *Covenant Lawsuit* at Mic 6. **against Judah:** The Southern Kingdom of Judah, though not yet at the advanced stage of rebellion seen in northern Israel (11:12), will eventually have to answer for its sins as well (5:5, 12, 14; 6:11; 8:14).

12:4 the angel: Appeared as a man (Gen 32:24). **he wept:** Either because of the injury he suffered (Gen 32:25) or because of the intensity of his plea for God's blessing (Gen 32:26).

12:5 LORD ... of hosts: A title for the Lord as commander of the armies of angels (Josh 5:14) and the military forces of Israel (1 Sam 17:45). **his name:** See note on Ex 3:15.

12:6 return: The language of repentance. See word study: *Return* at Jer 3:1. **love and justice:** The path that Israel is advised to take.

12:7 false balances: Dishonest business practices that are forbidden by the Torah (Lev 19:36) and other passages of Scripture (Prov 11:1; Ezek 45:10; Amos 8:5; Mic 6:11).

12:9 I am the LORD your God from the land of Egypt: The Greek LXX reads: "I, the Lord your God, led you up from the land of Egypt." **the appointed feast:** The autumn Feast of Booths, also called Tabernacles. During the seven days of the feast, the people of Israel dwelt in small huts called "booths" (Lev 23:39–43).

12:10 visions: E.g., Dan 7:1–14. **parables:** E.g., 2 Sam 12:1–4.

12:11 Gilead: East of the Jordan River. **Gilgal:** The location of an unlawful cult shrine (12:11; Amos 5:5). See note on 4:15.

12:12 Jacob fled: Summarizes the story of Gen 29, where Jacob escaped the wrath of Esau by fleeing to Laban, his kinsman in Paddan-Aram (eastern Syria), and working for the hand of Laban's daughters, Rachel and Leah, in marriage.

12:13 a prophet: Moses, the greatest prophet in Israel's early history (Deut 34:10–11).

13:1–16 Northern Israel has condemned itself to suffer God's just punishment.

13:1 exalted: Ephraim was the largest and strongest of the northern tribes of Israel, thanks in part to Jacob's blessing of extraordinary fruitfulness pronounced on his father, Joseph (Gen 49:22–26). Jeroboam I, the first king of northern Israel, was also from the tribe of Ephraim (1 Kings 11:26). **Baal:** See word study: *Baal* at 2:8. **died:** Spiritual or covenantal death, caused by violation of the Torah's prohibition to worship gods other than the Lord (Deut 30:15–20). Israel's restoration after judgment is thus envisioned as a resurrection from the dead (13:14). Ironically, the god Baal was believed to confer the gifts of fertility that produce and support life.

---

h Gk Syr: Heb *us*.
i Cn Compare Gk: Heb obscure.

²And now they sin more and more,
 and make for themselves molten images,
idols skilfully made of their silver,
 all of them the work of craftsmen.
Sacrifice to these, they say.ʲ
 Men kiss calves!
³Therefore they shall be like the morning mist
 or like the dew that goes early away,
like the chaff that swirls from the threshing
   floor
 or like smoke from a window.

⁴I am the Lord your God
 from the land of Egypt;
you know no God but me,
 and besides me there is no savior.
⁵It was I who knew you in the wilderness,
 in the land of drought;
⁶but when they had fedᵏ to the full,
 they were filled, and their heart was lifted up;
 therefore they forgot me.
⁷So I will be to them like a lion,
 like a leopard I will lurk beside the way.
⁸I will fall upon them like a bear robbed of her
   cubs,
 I will tear open their breast,
and there I will devour them like a lion,
 as a wild beast would tear them.

⁹I will destroy you, O Israel;
 whoˡ can help you?
¹⁰Whereᵐ now is your king, to save you;
 where are allⁿ your princes,ᵒ to defend youᵖ—
those of whom you said,
 "Give me a king and princes"?
¹¹I have given you kings in my anger,
 and I have taken them away in my wrath.
¹²The iniquity of E′phraim is bound up,
 his sin is kept in store.
¹³The pangs of childbirth come for him,
 but he is an unwise son;
for now he does not present himself
 at the mouth of the womb.

¹⁴Shall I ransom them from the power of Sheol?
 Shall I redeem them from Death?
O Death, whereᑫ are your plagues?
 O Sheol, whereᑫ is your destruction?
 Compassion is hidden from my eyes.

¹⁵Though he may flourish as the reed plant,ʳ
 the east wind, the wind of the Lord, shall come,
 rising from the wilderness;
and his fountain shall dry up,
 his spring shall be parched;
it shall strip his treasury
 of every precious thing.

13:14: 1 Cor 15:55.

13:2 the work of craftsmen: Idols are not actual gods but merely human creations (Ps 135:15–18; Is 40:19–20; Jer 10:1–10). **Men kiss calves:** The veneration of calf idols, such as those in Dan and Bethel (1 Kings 12:28–29). Bulls, which signify strength and fertility, often represented gods in the iconography of the ancient Near East. Here they seem to represent Baal, whose image was kissed (1 Kings 19:18).

13:3 chaff: The useless husks that are blown away by the wind when grains are processed on a threshing floor (Ps 1:4; Mt 3:12).

13:4 I am the Lord ... Egypt: See note on 12:9. **know:** For the theme of knowledge in Hosea, see notes on 2:20 and 6:3. **besides me there is no savior:** Israel will not be saved from catastrophe by its kings (13:10) or its alliances with powerful nations (14:3). Passages such as Deut 32:39 may lie in the background.

13:5–6 The story of Israel in the wilderness parallels part of the Song of Moses in Deut 32:10–18.

13:7–8 A frightening picture of divine judgment similar to 5:14 and Jer 5:6.

13:11 kings in my anger: The founding of the Northern Kingdom of Israel was a divine concession to sin. God allowed it but did not fully approve of it (1 Sam 8:4–12; 10:17–19). He had intended all twelve tribes to live under the rule of a Davidic king in Jerusalem (as under David and Solomon, 2 Sam 5:1–5; 1 Kings 4:25).

13:13 The pangs of childbirth: The painful onset of judgment (Jer 6:24; Is 13:8; Mt 24:8). **unwise son ... of the womb:** Ephraim, who refuses to repent, is like a breeched baby who refuses to be born. In the ancient world, this typically resulted in death.

13:14 Shall I ransom...? Shall I redeem: The Hebrew can also be translated, not as questions, but as statements about the future, as in the Greek LXX and the Latin Vulgate. Literally, these lines read: "From the hand of Sheol I will ransom them, from death I will redeem them." The passage, which promises hope and restoration after a time of judgment, amounts to a resurrection prophecy (6:1–2; Is 26:19; Dan 12:2–3). **Sheol:** Hebrew name for the netherworld of the dead. See word study: *Sheol* at Num 16:30. **O Death, where are your plagues?:** Death and its power are taunted like defeated enemies. Others interpret these questions as invitations for death to work its lethal power against Israel. • Paul cites a Greek version of this passage in 1 Cor 15:55, where he sees its fulfillment in the resurrection of the saints, whose bodies will rise immortal and imperishable, no longer subject to death's power. According to this reading, Hosea announces the final defeat of death. • The Lord delivered and redeemed all in the suffering of the Cross and the shedding of his blood when his soul descended to the realm of the dead and his flesh did not see corruption. To death and its realm, he said: "O death, I will be your death" (St. Jerome, *Commentary on Hosea* 13, 14–15). **destruction:** Or possibly "sting", as in the Greek LXX. **Compassion:** Alternatively, the noun may refer to "a change of mind".

13:15 he: Ephraim, that is, the Northern Kingdom of Israel (13:1). **the east wind:** A gale of divine judgment representing Assyrian invaders (Is 27:8; Jer 18:17).

ʲ Gk: Heb *to these they say sacrifices of.*
ᵏ Cn: Heb *according to their pasture.*
ˡ Gk Syr: Heb *for in me.*
ᵐ Gk Syr Vg: Heb *I will be.*
ⁿ Cn: Heb *in all.*
ᵒ Cn: Heb *cities.*
ᵖ Cn Compare Gk: Heb *and your judges.*
ᑫ Gk Syr: Heb *I will be.*
ʳ Cn: Heb *among brothers.*

16 s Samar′ia shall bear her guilt,
  because she has rebelled against her God;
they shall fall by the sword,
  their little ones shall be dashed in pieces,
  and their pregnant women ripped open.

A Plea for Repentance and a Promise

14 Return, O Israel, to the LORD your God,
  for you have stumbled because of your
    iniquity.
2 Take with you words
  and return to the LORD;
say to him,
  "Take away all iniquity;
accept that which is good
  and we will render
  the fruit t of our lips.
3 Assyria shall not save us,
  we will not ride upon horses;
and we will say no more, 'Our God,'
  to the work of our hands.
In you the orphan finds mercy."

4 I will heal their faithlessness;
  I will love them freely,
  for my anger has turned from them.

5 I will be as the dew to Israel;
  he shall blossom as the lily,
  he shall strike root as the poplar; u
6 his shoots shall spread out;
  his beauty shall be like the olive,
  and his fragrance like Lebanon.
7 They shall return and dwell beneath my v
    shadow,
  they shall flourish as a garden; w
they shall blossom as the vine,
  their fragrance shall be like the wine of
    Lebanon.
8 O E′phraim, what have I to do with idols?
  It is I who answer and look after you. x
I am like an evergreen cypress,
  from me comes your fruit.

9 Whoever is wise, let him understand these
    things;
  whoever is discerning, let him know them;
for the ways of the LORD are right,
  and the upright walk in them,
  but transgressors stumble in them.

14:2: Heb 13:15.   **14:9:** Acts 13:10.

13:16 Samaria: Capital of the Northern Kingdom since the days of King Omri (1 Kings 16:24). **shall fall by the sword:** The Assyrian conquest of Samaria in 722 B.C. is foretold (2 Kings 17:6). **dashed in pieces:** See note on 10:14.

14:1–9 Hosea's final plea for repentance is addressed to Israel of the future. Judgment and exile are already certain for the prophet's own generation (5:14), but later generations will confess their guilt and seek the Lord (5:15; Deut 30:1–3).

14:1 you have stumbled: By committing iniquity (5:5), which leads to a fall from "the ways of the LORD" (14:9). Moses foresaw that God would have to judge his people because Israel's "foot shall slip" from the path of the covenant (Deut 32:35). The Greek LXX says that Israel "became weak/ill" because of its sin (cf. 5:13).

14:2 words: The prayer of penitent faith that follows in quotation marks (14:2b–3). **Take away all iniquity:** A prayer inspired by the revelation at Mt. Sinai that the Lord forgives "iniquity and transgression and sin" (Ex 34:7). **the fruit of our lips:** Translates the Greek LXX rather than the Hebrew, which reads "the bulls of our lips" (perhaps referring to bull sacrifices promised to the Lord by a vow). Either way, the reference is to giving God praise and thanksgiving. • The same expression is used in Heb 13:15, where believers are encouraged to offer "a sacrifice of praise to God, that is, the fruit of lips that acknowledge his name". • The voice is used in prayer as though in payment of a debt, so that man might serve God with all he possesses from God. He thus prays, not only with his mind, but also with his body. This is especially so when prayer is considered an act of satis-

faction, as in Hosea (St. Thomas Aquinas, *Summa Theologiae* II–II, 83, 12).

14:3 Assyria shall not save: A renunciation of the political alliances that northern Israel's kings had made with the Assyrians (2 Kings 15:19–20; 17:3). **we will say no more:** A renunciation of idolatry and a recommitment to the Lord as the one true God. **the work of our hands:** Manufactured idols (Ps 115:4; Wis 13:10; Mic 5:13). **In you:** In the Lord, who has a special love for orphans (Ps 146:9; Sir 35:14; Jas 1:27).

14:4–8 The restoration that will follow genuine repentance. Thanks to the Lord's healing love, Israel will flourish again like a beautiful flower, a hearty tree, and a productive grapevine. All will be a work of God's grace, even the **fruit** that his people will bear (cf. Jn 15:4–5).

14:4 I will heal their faithlessness: By transforming the hearts of his people, enabling them to love the Lord and obey his covenant. • Scripture speaks of this in various ways: God, in his compassion, will circumcise their hearts (Deut 30:6), write his Law on their hearts (Jer 31:33), and give them a new heart and a new Spirit (Ezek 36:26). **I will love them freely:** The same divine love that underlies Israel's election as a chosen people (Deut 7:6–8) underlies its future restoration (Jer 31:3; Rom 11:28–29). God's persistent love for his people was earlier symbolized by Hosea reclaiming his unfaithful wife (3:1) (CCC 218–20).

14:6 the olive: A tree that flourishes in Israel (Ps 52:8). **Lebanon:** Directly north of Israel and famous for its towering, aromatic cedars (Song 4:11).

14:8 evergreen cypress: Symbolizes life that endures through all seasons. **fruit:** Probably a wordplay on the name Ephraim, which means something like "doubly fruitful" (cf. Gen 41:52).

14:9 Whoever is wise: A closing appeal, written in the style of a biblical wisdom saying, for hearers (and readers) to discern the way of the Lord and to follow it carefully, lest they repeat the mistakes of the Northern Kingdom of Israel and stumble in sin (14:1; cf. Ps 107:43).

---

s Ch 14:1 in Heb.
t Gk Syr: Heb *bulls.*
u Cn: Heb *Lebanon.*
v Heb *his.*
w Cn: Heb *they shall grow grain.*
x Heb *him.*

STUDY QUESTIONS
Hosea

Chapter 1

For understanding

1. **Topical Essay: The Word of the Lord.** Indicating as it does the delivery of a message that God wishes to communicate to man through Israel, how is the content of the revealed message announced, and by whom? Because there is a tight connection between the act of speaking and the content of what is spoken, how is this quite significant when a word comes from God? Besides its power, for what is God's word also revered? In the Old Testament, how does the word of the Lord seem to take on personhood itself, and how is this further developed in the New Testament? How is the analogy between God's word in Scripture and God's Word in the Incarnation made explicit by the Church?
2. **1:2.** Whether Hosea's wife was guilty of sexual sin before or after they were wedded, what kind of action was marrying a woman who gave herself to "lovers" other than her husband, and what did it symbolize? Why did prophets sometimes perform shocking deeds? How do some scholars, ancient as well as modern, prefer to view Hosea's marriage? Nevertheless, what indication does the text give? How do St. Cyril of Alexandria and St. Thomas Aquinas view this issue? As for her great harlotry, what does the sexual promiscuity of Hosea's wife symbolize?
3. **1:10—2:1.** To what does Hosea's perspective shift in these verses? What is the Lord ready to do in the near term, and what will he do after a period of exile? What does the prophet call this time of future restoration?
4. **1:10.** What oath does "like the sand of the sea" recall? If kinship with God is a grace of the covenant that made the Israelites the Lord's adopted "sons", what does the restoration of divine sonship imply? What does Paul quote this verse to claim? Why do many find it odd that he cites Hosea? If Paul, however, has not misread or misapplied the text, what does he recognize about the northern tribes? How is northern Israel's return to sonship thus achieved?

For application

1. **1:2-3.** What are the limits of your willingness to obey the Lord? While he would never direct you to do anything immoral, if he asked you to do something that appeared imprudent, controversial, or foolish, how would you decide whether or not to obey?
2. **1:4.** The *Catechism* describes one's name as "the icon of the person" (CCC 2158). What does that mean to you? What is the significance of your own name? If you were to name a child, what sort of name would you select, and why?
3. **1:6.** Hosea named his children for a prophetic purpose, even though the name might later prove an embarrassment for the child. Since the name of a person is a "sign of the dignity of the one who bears it" (CCC 2158), why give a child a name that invites disrespect or ridicule? What sort of name should Christians avoid giving their children (CCC 2156)?

Chapter 2

For understanding

1. **2:2-23.** On what grounds does the Lord bring charges against unfaithful Israel? What does it mean that the punishments imposed are restorative? Even though Israel has sought the pleasures of other gods (the "lovers" of 2:5, 7) and forgotten her Spouse, what does God plan to do and why?
2. **2:2.** What does the prophet contend has happened to Israel's covenant with God? What does it mean that God divorces the faithless tribes of northern Israel for a time? How is the Israelites giving of themselves to the worship of other gods like harlotry and adultery? To what fact does the use of sexual metaphors for idolatry provide a mirror?
3. **Word Study: Baal (2:8).** As a noun, what does *ba'al* mean? In relation to property and marriage, what sense does it carry? What does the verbal form of the Hebrew root mean? In a cultic context, for whom is the title *Ba'al* frequently used? In Canaanite mythology, what epithet did Baal bear? Being a storm god, for what was he invoked? What did service to this false deity include? How does the OT present Baal? In what ways is the cult of Baal, which ensnared the Israelites at many points in their history, strongly denounced?
4. **2:19.** How is betrothal in ancient Israel unlike the period of engagement before marriage? What were betrothed couples, having given their consent to be wedded, in the eyes of the Mosaic Law, considered to be even though they customarily lived apart for a time before cohabiting and initiating marital relations? What will characterize the new nuptial bond between God and his people? How is the OT image of God and Israel as husband and wife taken up in the NT? Upon what, in part, is this based? To what does the Hebrew *ḥesed* refer?
5. **2:21-23.** How does Israel's restoration affect the names of Hosea's children? What message does the name of his son Jezreel (meaning "God will sow") announce? What will happen to the names of his daughter Not pitied and his younger son Not my people? What does Paul cite 2:23 to indicate? What does Peter likewise draw from this passage?

For application

1. **2:6-13.** What is "tough love"? What is the point of making the life of a problem child difficult for a time? How has the Lord used "tough love" to shape up your spiritual life?
2. **2:11.** The note for this verse alludes to the problem of formalism in Israelite worship—that is, going through the motions of religion without serving the Lord in their hearts. How does this observation apply to the way some Christians celebrate feasts like Christmas and Easter? How do some popular customs obscure or obfuscate what these feasts are all about?
3. **2:14.** Why would a person go, as Jesus did, into a waterless desert to seek the Lord? What advantage would such a hostile environment provide? As an image of spiritual purgation, have spiritual deserts—times of dryness or God's seeming absence—ever actually served to draw you toward him? If so, in what way?
4. **2:15.** Think back to a time when you had a conversion experience or a major turning toward the Lord. What happened then? How did it affect your spiritual life? How has your relationship with the Lord developed since then; that is, how have you either grown or fallen back? If you need a renewal of faith, how will you go about obtaining it?

Study Questions

Chapter 3

For understanding

1. **3:1–5.** What does God instruct Hosea to do, and what action does it symbolize? While some think Hosea is told to marry, not Gomer, but another loose woman, why does his marrying a second wife seem unlikely?
2. **3:1.** Who is Hosea's wife's paramour? What kind of love is God's love for his people? With what is God's love contrasted? What is a raisin cake, and to whom was it offered?
3. **3:3.** How will Hosea keep his wife from consorting with other men? Why will the couple not have marital relations for a time? What does this signify about Israel, whom Gomer represents?
4. **3:5.** Who are "the children of Israel"? Why will they seek the Lord? What will the time of restoration see, and what days will it recall? Since the prophesied reunion did not occur before the disappearance of the Davidic monarchy in 586 B.C., who must the figure of David their king be? Who does the NT proclaim him to be? How does the conversion of Samaritans in the early Church fit into this picture? With what kind of fear are the children of Israel to come to the Lord? What are the "latter days"?

For application

1. **3:1.** Adultery within a marriage does not invalidate the marriage covenant, though it may prompt a separation. What trial does the Lord's command to "love a woman who is beloved of a paramour" mean for the aggrieved spouse? According to the note for this verse, what kind of love would attempt restoration of the marriage?
2. **3:2.** Reclaiming a wandering spouse is not as simple as paying money, but it demonstrates the need to do something concrete. How does one restore trust and fidelity in a broken marriage? What are the options if the spouse refuses to reconcile (cf. CCC 1649–51)?
3. **3:3.** The note for this verse refers to the virtue of chastity. How is chastity to be practiced within a marriage? How do the vows recited at the wedding ceremony suggest ways to practice marital chastity?

Chapter 4

For understanding

1. **4:1–19.** What process do these verses initiate? What is the root cause of the corruption of the priests, prophets, and people? What is coming to northern Israel as a result?
2. **4:8.** What were priests given with every sin offering? How could this become a self-interested arrangement? What would corrupt priests be disinclined to do?
3. **4:14.** What did men and women do with priests and priestesses at idol shrines? Though the point is disputed, what do biblical texts read in light of Canaanite mythology suggest to many scholars? What is one reason idolatry is described as harlotry in the Bible?
4. **4:15.** What warning is the prophet giving the Southern Kingdom of Judah? As the location of an unlawful cult shrine, to which town of Gilgal is the prophet referring? How does "Beth-aven" translate? For what town is it a derogatory slur? As an oath formula, what is wrong with invoking the Lord's holy name in the house of an idol?

For application

1. **4:1–3.** How do environmental problems result from the sins listed in verse 2? How would knowledge of God work to correct such problems?
2. **4:4–6.** How would you rate the level of knowledge of the faith in your parish? What types of catechetical programs are available there for both children and adults? How often do the clergy in your parish (priests and deacons) actually teach catechism? What catechetical responsibilities do they delegate to others? What should they retain for themselves?
3. **4:12.** According to the note for this verse, a "spirit of harlotry" is a "perverse infatuation with idolatry". How does that infatuation manifest itself in our modern era? How might that spirit infect even baptized Christians?
4. **4:14.** As head of his wife and family, what responsibility does the husband have for the spiritual welfare of the household (cf. Eph 5:23–28)? If the men leave that responsibility to their wives and do nothing themselves, how likely is it that the children, especially boys, will retain the faith when they become adults?

Chapter 5

For understanding

1. **5:1–15.** What is the Lord ready to do to Ephraim (= northern Israel)? While judgment on Israel in the north has been a recurring theme in previous chapters, what new revelation does the prophet give here? How did Judah respond to Hosea's warning in 4:15?
2. **5:1.** What three groups is the prophet addressing in this verse? What does the mention of a hunting trap suggest about the locations mentioned in this verse? To what towns does the name "Mizpah" refer? What is "Tabor", and how does Christian tradition identify it?
3. **5:7.** Why does the prophet call the Northern Israelites "alien children"? In the words of Deuteronomy, why are they no longer God's children? What time does the new moon normally indicate?
4. **5:10.** How is the dishonest practice of stealing a neighbor's property done? How does the Mosaic Law address this problem? What territory do scholars think it likely that Judah was claiming? How will the Lord pour out his wrath on Judah?

For application

1. **5:4.** What kind of deed would not permit one to return to God? How can a "spirit of harlotry" reinforce such a deed? What deed would be necessary to enable a return to God after all?
2. **5:5.** How are pride and arrogance related? How are they different? What obstacles do these vices place in the way of effective repentance? What is their antidote?

3. **5:12.** What does a moth do to clothes? What does dry rot do to wood? How do these figures describe the state of a soul habituated to patterns of sin?

Chapter 6

For understanding
1. **6:1–3.** What has happened to Israel, who is being called to repentance? What does Hosea reveal is needed for national restoration? What ancient belief does the language of the passage presuppose? What song does the picture of God reviving his people after a time of judgment and death recall?
2. **6:2.** Why is the third day after death significant? When was a corpse thought to decompose in earnest? What does the hope of Israel's resurrection "on the third day" anticipate? As the Messiah, how does Jesus fulfill this hope? According to St. Jerome, how does the Lord not only heal but revive the entire human race? According to St. Augustine, when did Hosea foretell that Christ's Resurrection would occur?
3. **6:6.** What does the Lord want more than animal sacrifices? What is the contrast between what God does and does not desire a Semitic way of stressing? How are life and liturgy meant to form a unity? Why did Jesus cite Hosea's words against the Pharisees? According to St. Cyril of Alexandria, how is knowledge of God better than sacrifices and burnt offerings when attained in Christ? According to St. Thomas Aquinas, although God does not need external sacrifices, why does he wish them to be offered?
4. **6:8.** Where is Ramoth Gilead? Why was bloodshed in Gilead especially disturbing?

For application
1. **6:4.** If you make New Year's resolutions, how many of them do you keep? If, during your morning prayer, you resolve to do a religious act such as to pray a daily Rosary, how long does the resolution last? How like wishful thinking is your determination to know the Lord?
2. **6:5.** How many examples can you think of for words or expressions that actually change reality (e.g., "You're fired!")? Which words in the liturgy have the same effect? For what does the symbolism of a sharp sword coming from the mouth of the rider in Rev 19:15 stand?
3. **6:6.** In the play *Fiddler on the Roof*, when his wife protests that she prepares his food and mends his clothes, Tevye repeatedly asks, "But do you love me?" How might his question address the tendency to substitute doing things for God in place of loving him? How can serving God from a sense of obligation be transformed into a service of love?

Chapter 7

For understanding
1. **7:1–16.** Of the abominations of northern Israel that Hosea continues to rail against, which are the deeds singled out for condemnation? What period is the background of these evils, and with what did it end?
2. **7:8.** How does Ephraim mix himself with the peoples, and with what result? To what does reliance on foreign powers for military help and maintenance of power amount?
3. **7:14.** What is Israel's devotion to the Lord like? For what was self-laceration used? What did the Mosaic Law say about it?
4. **7:16.** To what is the scattering of rebellious Israel to distant nations compared? What did Moses declare that, when sinful Israel went into exile, life would be like?

For Application
1. **7:1–7.** What sorts of moral corruption lead to the fall of a nation? How do these vices sap the nation's moral strength? How do such considerations apply to the moral health of our country?
2. **7:8.** If, according to the note for this verse, the alliances of Israel with Assyria and Egypt amount to spurning the Lord, what do modern alliances mean for us? What modern nation would rely on the Lord in preference to forming military alliances? What does the answer say about where we place our faith?
3. **7:9.** How would military alliances with foreign countries actually threaten the security of ancient Israel? What, for example, would be the interests of Assyria and Egypt in making an alliance with a small nation like Israel? How do the alliances we make potentially threaten our own national security?

Chapter 8

For understanding
1. **8:1–14.** Why is doom pronounced on Israel? Though the northern tribes claim to know God, of what are they guilty? If judgment is certain for Israel in the north, what will happen to Judah in the south?
2. **8:4.** What did the final years of the Northern Kingdom of Israel see with regard to its kings? If this was not the tragic result of seeking the Lord's will, of what was it a result? From the perspective of Judah in the south, why were the northern kings illegitimate from the start? What does Hosea prophesy that northern Israel's restoration will include? Who forged calf and goat idols for northern Israel?
3. **8:7.** What does this proverb mean that Israel will get? Had Israel sown righteousness, what would it have reaped?
4. **8:8.** Why does Hosea describe the exile of Israel's northern tribes and their absorption into foreign nations as an accomplished fact? Indeed, when did the process begin?

For application
1. **8:1.** When you see vultures circling overhead, for what do you think are they looking? What does the image of the vulture suggest about the condition of ancient Israel? What are some indications that a person's spiritual life is nearly dead?

2. **8:2.** Jesus warned that some who say to him "Lord, Lord" will hear him reply to them, "I never knew you" (Mt 7:22–23). How does Jesus recognize those who are genuine disciples?
3. **8:6.** Is the destruction of idols that Hosea threatens here nothing more than iconoclastic vandalism? How is destruction of idols different from the defacement of statues and images of Jesus and the saints (CCC 2129, 2132)?
4. **8:13.** What sorts of prayer is the Lord most likely to answer? What sorts is he more likely to ignore?

Chapter 9

For understanding
1. **9:1–17.** What do these verses describe? Having become "deeply corrupted", what are the northern tribes about to face? How will the pain of exile be increased?
2. **9:4.** What are libations? How will the obligations of divine worship be unfulfillable for Israel in exile? What is mourner's bread? What will the exiles have to eat?
3. **9:8.** How does Hosea describe himself? What is a true prophet like?
4. **9:10.** What is Baal-peor? What does the apostasy that Israel committed at Peor in Num 25:1–5 show? How offensive to God did Israel become? Contrary to the claim that the good or evil of an action is not related to its object, how does a person become abominable to God? According to Thomas Aquinas, to what is the evil of his action thus related?

For application
1. **9:1.** Our nation is accustomed to abundant harvests. To what do we attribute them? What do we do with them? According to the note for this verse, who deserves the thanks for them?
2. **9:3.** The Mosaic Law distinguished between clean and unclean foods because the Israelites were to be holy as God is holy (Lev 11:44–45). How would being forced to eat unclean food in Assyria have made them unholy or defiled? What did Jesus say defiles a person (Mt 15:16–18)?
3. **9:8.** The note for this verse refers to the prophet's duty as a watchman in times of danger. Who are the prophetic watchmen in today's Church? If clergy have the threefold office of priest, prophet, and king, what should their prophetic role be? What of the prophetic role of the laity?
4. **9:15.** For certain grave sins, the Church attaches the canonical penalty of excommunication. What is its purpose? What is the excommunicated person not allowed to do (CCC 1463)? What concern should the Church have for the excommunicated person? Under what conditions would this person be received back?

Chapter 10

For understanding
1. **10:1.** What is a traditional image for Israel? Although God blessed his people with prosperity, how did they misuse their abundance? Besides forbidding the service of idols, what else does the Torah forbid? What are the pillars mentioned here, and what was Israel forbidden to do with them?
2. **10:8.** What are high places? What does the Hebrew word "Aven" mean? To what town do some see a reference? What will happen to the idol shrines of northern Israel? Overwhelmed with suffering, for what will the people beg? When Jesus cites these words in a prediction of doom on Jerusalem, what is he telling the women who weep over his Passion? Where does a similar scene appear in Revelation?
3. **10:11.** How were oxen used in threshing grain? What did the process do? Because it was not a particularly laborious task for the animal, what could it do freely? Since these days of ease are over, what does Hosea insist that Israel and Judah, because of their sin, will do?

For application
1. **10:1.** In Deuteronomy, Moses warns the people of the pitfalls of material prosperity (Deut 8:11–17). Why would prosperity tempt the chosen people to forget their God? How has our enjoyment of material prosperity drawn us away from him?
2. **10:4.** Suppose a couple at a wedding ceremony were to treat the marriage vows as a mere formula and the ceremony as just a hoop to jump through. What poisonous weeds are likely to sprout in that relationship? How might that marriage come under judgment?
3. **10:8.** What is the most frightening experience you can remember, especially if you thought your life was in danger? To where did you want to fly, or where did you wish to hide? What, if any, thoughts about God came to mind then? What impact did the experience have on your later life?
4. **10:12.** What is fallow ground? How would a farmer prepare it for sowing? How does Hosea's metaphor apply to seeking the Lord?

Chapter 11

For understanding
1. **11:1–11.** With what do these verses deal? With tender affection, what did God do for Israel? But like many adolescents, when Israel grew stubborn and disobedient along the way, what did God have to do? Even then, what was God's attitude toward his rebellious son? In which of his parables did Jesus tell a similar story about the merciful Fatherhood of God?
2. **11:8.** What are "Admah" and "Zeboiim"? What is the point here?
3. **11:9.** Unlike men, who show no restraint when thrown into a violent rage, how does the Lord temper his wrath? How will God stop short of obliterating Israel's northern tribes? Since, in strict theological terms, God is unchangeable and has no emotions, what are biblical descriptions of God being moved by emotions called, and how should they be taken?

For application

1. **11:1.** Through the Gospel, God calls each of us out of our own personal Egypt, our own "house of bondage". If you have had an experience that led you to conversion, from what were you led out? If you cannot recall a distinct conversion experience, how have you grown more and more detached from sin, especially the sins of your youth? Either way, into what relationship with himself has the Lord led you?
2. **11:3.** The expression "teach ... how to walk" can have multiple meanings. How do toddlers learn to walk? What is the role of the parents in this process? How does God teach us to walk? What is our role in this?
3. **11:7.** At certain points in their lives, usually during adolescence, children rebel against their parents. Why do they rebel? How can parents affirm their authority without alienating their children? If the rebellion becomes obstinate to the point of breaking off relations with the family, what should loving parents do?
4. **11:9.** The note for this verse reminds readers that God has no emotions, yet Scripture proclaims his compassion. When did the incarnate Son of God show emotion? How did he demonstrate compassion? How has this divine compassion manifested itself in your life?

Chapter 12

For understanding

1. **12:1.** To what does herding the wind amount? What are treaty alliances with Egypt and Assyria denounced as?
2. **12:2-6.** As Hosea recalls it, how does the personal history of Jacob foreshadow the national history of Israel? What is the implied message?
3. **12:7.** To what do false balances refer?
4. **12:9.** How does the Greek LXX read for this verse? What is "the appointed feast"? What do the people of Israel do during this feast?

For application

1. **12:3.** In some ways, the spiritual life can be described as a continual striving with God. What is this wrestling match all about? Just as Jacob refused to give up the fight until God blessed him (Gen 32:26), how determined are you to cling to God until he blesses you?
2. **12:6.** Psalm 27 encourages us to "wait for the LORD; be strong, and let your heart take courage; yes, wait for the LORD." Why does waiting for the Lord require strength and courage? With what obstacles do we contend? Whose help do we need?
3. **12:9.** What was the point of dwelling in makeshift booths for a week during the Feast of Tabernacles? How does the symbolism of that activity contrast with the false confidence in riches of the previous verse? On whom must we depend for everything we have?
4. **12:13.** Read the note for this verse. What does a prophet do? In what way was Moses a prophet? Why is Jesus referred to in the NT as a prophet (e.g., Lk 24:19; Jn 9:17)? As a member of the Body of Christ, what makes you a prophet?

Chapter 13

For understanding

1. **13:1.** What accounts in part for Ephraim becoming the largest and strongest of the northern tribes of Israel? From which tribe was Jeroboam I, the first king of northern Israel? What kind of death did Ephraim die? How is Israel's restoration after judgment thus envisioned? Ironically, what gifts was the god Baal believed to confer?
2. **13:2.** If idols are not actually gods, what are they? To what does men kissing calves refer? Why did bulls represent gods in the iconography of the ancient Near East? Which one do they seem to represent here?
3. **13:13.** What do the pangs of childbirth represent? To what is Ephraim, who refuses to repent, compared? In the ancient world, in what did this typically result?
4. **13:14.** How can the Hebrew also be translated? Literally, how do these lines read? To what does this passage, which promises hope and restoration after a time of judgment, amount? What forces are taunted like defeated enemies? How do others interpret these questions? Citing a Greek version of this passage in 1 Cor 15:55, in terms of what does Paul see its fulfillment? According to this reading, what does Hosea announce? According to St. Jerome, how did Jesus bring about the death of death and its realm?

For application

1. **13:1-2.** What happens spiritually to the person who commits mortal sin (CCC 1856-61)? How is the condition of that person exacerbated by repeated mortal sin? What makes repentance so difficult in that latter case?
2. **13:4.** In Acts 4, Peter testifies before the Sanhedrin that "there is salvation in no one else [than Jesus], for there is no other name under heaven ... by which we must be saved" (Acts 4:12). Why do people take offense at a statement like this? Despite their objections, why does the Church insist that Jesus is the only savior? What does the Church teach about the salvific effectiveness of other religions (CCC 842-45)?
3. **13:14.** What thought have you given to the prospect of your own death? How confident are you in the mercy of God at that moment? What hope do you derive from the Christian belief in the resurrection of the dead?

Chapter 14

For understanding

1. **14:1-9.** To whom is Hosea's final plea for repentance addressed? Since judgment and exile are already certain for the prophet's own generation, what about later generations?

Study Questions

2. **14:2.** By what is the prayer of penitent faith that follows in quotation marks inspired? This verse translates the Greek LXX rather than the Hebrew. How does the Hebrew read? Either way, to what does the text refer? In Heb 13:15, what kind of sacrifice are believers encouraged to offer? According to St. Thomas Aquinas, how is the voice to be considered an act of satisfaction in prayer?
3. **14:4.** How will the Lord heal Israel's faithlessness? In what various ways does Scripture speak of this? What does the same divine love that underlies Israel's election as a chosen people also underlie? How was God's persistent love for his people earlier symbolized by Hosea?
4. **14:9.** What does the closing appeal, written in the style of a biblical wisdom saying, urge hearers (and readers) to do? Why?

For application

1. **14:2.** In your private prayer, how often do you pray aloud? What are some advantages of praying spontaneously and vocally? If you have ever overheard someone praying aloud, what was your impression? How, for example, might overhearing someone pray aloud encourage you in your prayer?
2. **14:3.** Why do spiritual writers, such as John of the Cross, stress the need for detachment from material things? What is the spiritual danger in having material resources? Ultimately, where should one's resources lie?
3. **14:5–7.** Healthy plants, such as the lily, often emit a pleasant fragrance. What is the "odor of sanctity"? What sort of fragrance does holiness produce?

INTRODUCTION TO JOEL

Author and Date Little is known with certainty about the origins of the Book of Joel. The superscription states that its message was given to "Joel, the son of Pethuel" (1:1), but no further information about him or his father is given in the OT. Internal evidence indicates that Joel, like many of Israel's prophets, was a passionate preacher of repentance, and it appears that he addressed his message to Judah and Jerusalem in southern Israel. Beyond that, our curiosity is left unsatisfied.

The Book of Joel also contains minimal clues about the time of its composition. Scholars have proposed dates for the book as early as the ninth century B.C. and as late as the second century B.C., with most estimates falling somewhere between these endpoints. Some commentators, noting that Joel stands in the Hebrew Bible between two eighth-century prophets, Hosea and Amos, contend that ancient Jewish scribes identified Joel as a figure of the eighth century as well. Probably the strongest case for a date in the eighth century B.C. situates the book during the early years of Jehoash, king of Judah, who was a minor when he came to the throne in 835 B.C. Most commentators, however, place the book in postexilic Judah near the end of the fifth century B.C. Observations bearing on the date of the book include the following. **(1)** The Jerusalem Temple was operational in Joel's day (1:9, 13), which means he must have delivered his oracles either before the Babylonian Exile or afterward, but not in the decades when the sanctuary lay in ruins between 586 and 515 B.C. **(2)** The prophet delivers God's promise to restore the fortunes of Judah and Jerusalem and to judge the Gentile nations who scattered his people to foreign lands (3:1–2). This information suggests a setting after the sixth century B.C., when Israel's conquest and captivity by the Assyrians and Babylonians were both events of the past. **(3)** The prophet addresses "the elders" of his people (1:14; 2:16) but has no word of exhortation for kings or royal officials. Failure to mention the monarchies of Israel or Judah fits comfortably in a postexilic context after the disappearance of Israel's Northern and Southern Kingdoms in 722 and 586, respectively. **(4)** In contrast to Hosea and Amos, Joel never denounces idolatry or religious syncretism among the people, even though he preaches the need for repentance in the strongest terms. This fits readily with a historical context for Joel's ministry after the Babylonian Exile, when idol worship was far less a problem than in earlier times. **(5)** Reference is made to hostile neighbors selling captives from Judah as slaves to "the Greeks" (3:6). Such a scenario would not have been impossible in the preexilic period, but the

Greeks rose to greater prominence as traders in the Mediterranean world in the postexilic period. Taken together, these factors weigh in favor of a postexilic date for the book, perhaps around 400 B.C., although this is merely a tentative proposal based on limited and sometimes ambiguous evidence.

Title The book is named after Joel, the son of Pethuel, mentioned in the opening verse. Its Hebrew form, *Yôʾēl*, means "the LORD is God." This name appears in the Greek Septuagint as the title *Iōēl*, while the heading is expanded in the Latin Vulgate to *Ioel Propheta*, "Joel the Prophet". English titles for the book follow these ancient traditions.

Place in the Canon Joel has long been revered as a canonical book of Scripture. In the Jewish Bible, or Tanakh, it stands among the Latter Prophets in a sub-collection of writings known as "the Book of the Twelve". In Christian Bibles, these twelve books are called the Minor Prophets, not because they are less important than Isaiah, Jeremiah, Ezekiel, and Daniel, but because they are comparatively much shorter. In the Hebrew Bible as well as the Latin Vulgate, Joel stands second among the Minor Prophets between Hosea and Amos. This is also its position in English Bibles. In the Greek Septuagint, it stands fourth in the collection of Minor Prophets after Hosea, Amos, and Micah.

Structure The Book of Joel divides into two major parts, following a short superscription (1:1). **(1)** The first part of the book deals with a present crisis. The prophet laments a recent plague of locusts (1:2–20), which he views as a foretaste of the coming "day of the LORD" (2:1–11). The devastation caused to fields and orchards by swarms of these ravenous insects is an invitation to seek the Lord with fasting, tears, and prayer (2:12–17). **(2)** The second part of the book looks to the immediate and distant future. If the people of Judah repent, God promises to restrain his judgment on Judah and to restore his blessings on the land (2:18–27). And beyond the horizons of Joel's day lies the eschatological fulfillment of God's plans. Events to come include an outpouring of God's Spirit on his people (2:28–29), the salvation of a faithful remnant in Zion (2:30–32), and a day of harvest when the Lord judges all nations (3:1–15). The book concludes with a vision of the Lord dwelling securely with his people in an undefiled Jerusalem (3:16–21).

The Message of the Prophet The theme that ties together the oracles of the Book of Joel is "the day of the LORD", which is mentioned five times in three chapters (1:15; 2:1, 11, 31; 3:14). As elsewhere in the prophetic books of Scripture, this is a day of divine reckoning for Israel and the Gentiles. It is a day when God intervenes powerfully in history to hold people and nations accountable for their evildoing. Joel thus describes it as a day of "destruction" that comes "from the Almighty" (1:15) and as a day of "darkness and gloom" (2:2) that most cannot hope to "endure" (2:11). But thankfully the day of the Lord does not come without warning. Joel's task as a prophet is to alert the people of Judah that an apocalyptic day of justice is drawing "near" (2:1), and so his announcement is coupled with strenuous appeals for the community to fast and mourn and to return to the Lord in their hearts (1:14; 2:12–16). It is implied that only if the people repent quickly and wholeheartedly can the approaching judgment be halted and the people be spared another calamity. Evidently the people of Judah respond to the prophet's urgent call for reform, for the Lord assures them of his "pity" (2:18) and promises to reverse the devastation caused by the locust invasion (2:19–26). The restoration of his blessing will be a sign that the Lord is "in the midst of Israel" and that his people will never again be "put to shame" in this way (2:27).

References to the day of the Lord point to an escalating severity of judgment. On the one hand, the day of the Lord that threatened to strike Judah was anticipated by the locust plague, which gave the people a taste of the affliction that could become much worse if the prophet's call to repentance went unheeded. This is made clear in 2:1–11, where the invaders ready to swarm Judah are described in terms of the locust invasion of 1:1–20. On the other hand, the day of the Lord in Joel's time is a small-scale version of the final "day of the LORD" at the end of history (3:14). The prophet foresees a day when the Lord will gather all the nations to a war of judgment to receive from his hand the wages of their wickedness (3:1–16). The enormity of this day is indicated by the apocalyptic signs of total darkness and cosmic trembling (3:15–16). Theologically, these oracles confirm the Lord's sovereignty over all nations, who stand accountable to him for their deeds, as well as over the heavens and the earth, which display an array of signs and wonders according to his will.

That said, the prospect of God's intervention in history is not all gloom and doom. Joel also sees the Spirit of God pouring down on the whole community of his people, male and female, young and old, giving them gifts of prophecy, visions, and dreams (2:28–29). This comes with the promise that "all who call upon the name of the LORD shall be delivered" (2:32) from the awesome "day of the LORD" awaited at the end (2:31). A picture of what this will look like is painted in 3:17–21. All the nations who have been hostile to God's people will be judged for their evil, while "those whom the LORD calls" (2:32) will dwell with him on the holy height of Zion, the eschatological Jerusalem, forever protected from enemy threats and forever refreshed by a fountain of blessing flowing from the Lord's Temple. This is the bright side of the day of the Lord, who makes himself a "refuge" for his faithful ones (3:16). Theologically, this theme throws light on the Lord's bountiful goodness. He responds to genuine repentance with "pity" (2:18), and he delivers those who invoke his name for salvation (2:32). When all is said and done, he will forever be their God and they will be his people (2:27).

Christian Perspective The Book of Joel is referenced several times in the New Testament. Best known is Peter's quotation of 2:28–32 on the day of Pentecost, where Joel's vision of God's Spirit pouring out upon his people is fulfilled in the Holy Spirit's descent upon the earliest Christian community (Acts 2:17–21), an event marking the founding of the Church by signs of heavenly fire and inspired speech (Acts 2:3–4). Later, in the Book of Romans, Paul cites 2:32a to announce that Jesus is the divine "Lord" whose name is called upon for salvation, and he applies Joel's universal language of "all" who invoke the Lord to Gentiles as well as to Jews (Rom 10:13). Other borrowings from Joel appear in the Book of Revelation. The plague of infernal locusts unleashed by the fifth trumpet uses imagery from the prophet's description of the locusts that afflicted Judah in his own day (compare 1:6 with Rev 9:8, and 2:4 with Rev 9:7). So too, the climactic events of world history in Rev 20–22, which describe the gathering of armies for battle, the Last Judgment, and the unveiling of the new Jerusalem in heaven, is based in part on 3:1–21, the book's concluding vision of war and judgment on the nations and salvation for the Lord's people in a future Jerusalem. Finally, Joel's appeal for conversion and fasting makes the message of the book particularly suited to penitential seasons such as Lent. Indeed, the prophet's call for community repentance in 2:12–18 is read in the Church's liturgy on Ash Wednesday.

OUTLINE OF JOEL

1. Superscription (1:1)

2. The Call to Repentance (1:2–2:17)
    A. The Devastation of the Locusts (1:2–20)
    B. The Day of the Lord Approaches (2:1–11)
    C. The Summons to Weeping and Penance (2:12–17)

3. The Coming Restoration (2:18–3:21)
    A. The Restoration of Divine Blessing (2:18–27)
    B. The Outpouring of the Spirit (2:28–29)
    C. The Remnant of Mount Zion (2:30–32)
    D. The Lord Judges All Nations (3:1–15)
    E. The Lord Dwells with the Redeemed in Zion (3:16–21)

THE BOOK OF

JOEL

Lament and Call to Repentance

1 The word of the LORD that came to Joel, the son of Pethu'el:

²Hear this, you aged men,
   give ear, all inhabitants of the land!
 Has such a thing happened in your days,
   or in the days of your fathers?
³Tell your children of it,
   and let your children tell their children,
   and their children another generation.

⁴What the cutting locust left,
   the swarming locust has eaten.
 What the swarming locust left,
   the hopping locust has eaten,
 and what the hopping locust left,
   the destroying locust has eaten.

⁵Awake, you drunkards, and weep;
   and wail, all you drinkers of wine,
 because of the sweet wine,
   for it is cut off from your mouth.
⁶For a nation has come up against my land,
   powerful and without number;
 its teeth are lions' teeth,
   and it has the fangs of a lioness.
⁷It has laid waste my vines,
   and splintered my fig trees;
 it has stripped off their bark and thrown it
   down;
   their branches are made white.
⁸Lament like a virgin clothed with sackcloth
   for the bridegroom of her youth.
⁹The cereal offering and the drink offering are
   cut off
   from the house of the LORD.

1:6: Rev 9:8.

1:1 The word of the LORD: Prophetic revelation from God. See essay: *The Word of the Lord* at Hos 1. **Joel:** Almost nothing is known about him except that his name means "the LORD is God." The references to "my vines" and "my fig trees" in 1:7 may indicate that he was an orchard farmer. Unlike other superscriptions that appear in the Bible's prophetic books, this one fails to situate Joel within a specific historical context by synchronizing his ministry with the kings of Israel or Judah (e.g., Is 1:1; Jer 1:1–3; Ezek 1:1–3; Hos 1:1; Amos 1:1). See introduction: *Author and Date.* **Pethuel:** Otherwise unknown.

1:2–12 Locusts had recently devastated the countryside of Judah. An entire harvest of fields, orchards, and vineyards had been devoured by the insects (1:10–12), a crisis made worse by wildfires and a shortage of rainfall (1:19–20). Joel views this calamity as an advance warning: unless the people of Judah repent of their sins, a more severe judgment will come on "the day of the LORD" (1:15). The prophet's description of the devastation is thus followed by urgent appeals for reform (1:13–20).

1:2 Hear this: A call to attention and decisive action. **aged men:** As distinct from "young men" (2:28). Some envision the prophet addressing community leaders or "elders", as in 1:14 and 2:16.

1:4 locust ... locust ... locust: Locusts in multiple waves and staggering numbers devoured the growth of the land like a massive army laying waste to everything in its path (cf. Judg 6:5; Jer 46:23; Nahum 3:15). Joel views this natural disaster as a divine judgment, although specific violations of the covenant are not mentioned in the book. • Destruction of crops by locusts is one of the curses of the Mosaic Law on those who disobey the covenant (Deut 28:38).

It also recalls the eighth plague of the Exodus, when locusts swarmed the land of Egypt and devoured all of its plants and trees (Ex 10:12–15).

1:5 you drunkards: The people of Judah, who need to sober up and cease their reckless indulgence in sin before the Lord brings "destruction" on them (1:15). **Wine ... cut off:** Because local vineyards are ravaged and withered (1:12).

1:6 a nation: The locust hordes are likened to foreign invaders. **my land:** The land of Judah in southern Israel, where the Jerusalem Temple is located (1:14; 2:1). **lions' teeth:** Represent the locusts' capacity to devour and destroy. • The Book of Revelation, drawing from this passage, describes a plague of demonic locusts with "lions' teeth" that are summoned to torture those who are not marked as God's servants (Rev 9:8). • Unless we put to death our inordinate passions by receiving the precious Blood of Christ, listening attentively to the Scriptures, and giving alms, they will kill us in the life to come. These passions are cruel and insatiable and never stop devouring us. Their teeth are lions' teeth, or rather more fierce. For the lion leaves its victim's carcass once it is satisfied, but these passions are never satisfied and never leave us (St. John Chrysostom, *Homilies on Matthew* 4, 17).

1:7 vines ... fig trees: Traditional symbols of security and prosperity in Israel (1 Kings 4:25; Mic 4:4; Zech 3:10). These idyllic conditions have been shattered by the locust plague.

1:8 a virgin: The land of Judah is compared to a young, betrothed bride who is suddenly widowed and unable to support herself. Betrothed women in Israel remained virgins for a period of time before they lived with their husbands and began to have marital relations (Deut 22:23–24). **sackcloth:** A coarse fabric spun from goat hair and worn in times of grief (Gen 37:34). Sackcloth was also worn as an expression of penance and supplication to God (1 Kings 21:27; Jon 3:5).

1:9 cereal offering ... drink offering: The food shortage in Judah disrupted the daily Temple services in Jerusalem. Besides the threat of hunger facing the people, supplies were lacking for the twice-daily lamb sacrifices, which included a flour-and-oil offering and a libation of wine every morning and evening (Ex 29:38–41; Num 28:3–8). Failure to worship the

---

Joel prophesied about four centuries later than Hosea, during the postexilic period. He foretells a plague of locusts as punishment and speaks threateningly of the "day of the LORD"; but then at once declares the Lord to be merciful and kind to those who repent. Toward the end of chapter 2 the style becomes apocalyptic and he speaks of the outpouring of the Spirit upon the people in the Messianic age. This was fulfilled (Acts 2:16–21) at Pentecost.

The priests mourn,
 the ministers of the Lord.
¹⁰The fields are laid waste,
 the ground mourns;
because the grain is destroyed,
 the wine fails,
 the oil languishes.

¹¹Be confounded, O tillers of the soil,
 wail, O vinedressers,
for the wheat and the barley;
 because the harvest of the field has perished.
¹²The vine withers,
 the fig tree languishes.
Pomegranate, palm, and apple,
 all the trees of the field are withered;
and gladness fails
 from the sons of men.

¹³Put on sackcloth and lament, O priests,
 wail, O ministers of the altar.
Go in, pass the night in sackcloth,
 O ministers of my God!
Because cereal offering and drink offering
 are withheld from the house of your God.

¹⁴Sanctify a fast,
 call a solemn assembly.
Gather the elders
 and all the inhabitants of the land
to the house of the Lord your God;
 and cry to the Lord.

¹⁵Alas for the day!
 For the day of the Lord is near,
 and as destruction from the Almighty it
  comes.
¹⁶Is not the food cut off
 before our eyes,
joy and gladness
 from the house of our God?

¹⁷The seed shrivels under the clods,ᵃ
 the storehouses are desolate;
the granaries are ruined
 because the grain has failed.
¹⁸How the beasts groan!
 The herds of cattle are perplexed
because there is no pasture for them;
 even the flocks of sheep are dismayed.

Lord as mandated in the Torah could only make Judah's situation more desperate, thus adding greater urgency to Joel's call for repentance. **the house of the Lord:** Probably the Second Temple, completed in 515 B.C. If, however, Joel lived in the preexilic period, then his reference is to Solomon's Temple, which stood from ca. 960 to 586 B.C.

1:10 oil languishes: Because the local olive groves have been stripped bare and left to wither (1:12).

1:11 wheat ... barley: Harvested in the springtime.

1:13 priests: Descendants of Aaron serving the altar in Jerusalem (Ex 40:12–15). **sackcloth:** See note on 1:8. **Cereal ... drink:** See note on 1:9.

 1:14 fast: Abstaining from food is a way of seeking God and his favor. Among its aims and benefits, fasting can express sorrow for sin and dependence on God; it can subdue the cravings of the flesh and detach a person from the pleasures of the world, freeing the heart to serve God; and it can be an offering to God to grant a specific request made by the penitent. Joel calls for a special day of supplication to the Lord, with prayers made more fervent by community fasting (2:12; Jer 36:9). There were also days of prescribed fasting in Israel such as the Day of Atonement (Lev 16:29) and the Feast of Purim (Esther 9:31–32). • Jesus affirms the importance of fasting as a spiritual practice among Christians, even as he criticizes those who make a show of it for selfish reasons (Mt 6:16–18). • The Catholic Church commends fasting as an act of religion. Fasting is required before receiving Holy Communion and as preparation for liturgical feasts such as Easter (CCC 1387, 1969, 2043). • Devout fasting is valuable for gaining God's mercy and strengthening human weakness. We know this from the teaching of the holy prophets, who are adamant that divine justice aroused by wickedness cannot be placated except by fasting. For this reason, we must heed Joel's exhortation in our own times as well (St. Leo the Great, *Sermons* 88, 1). **solemn assembly:** The people of Judah are summoned for prayer and penance in the Temple (cf. Neh 9:1–2). **elders:** Community leaders.

1:16 food ... joy: Summarizes how the locust plague caused an agricultural crisis (1:10) as well as a liturgical crisis (1:9, 13).

WORD STUDY

The Day of the Lord (1:15)

Yôm Yhwh (Heb.): a traditional concept in the OT and the unifying theme of the Book of Joel (Joel 2:1, 11, 31; 3:14). The day of the Lord is a day of judgment when God comes to settle accounts with Israel and the nations. It will melt the hearts of all (Is 13:6–16) because it comes as a day of darkness, doom, and distress (Jer 46:10; Ezek 30:3; Amos 5:18–20; Zeph 1:14–16). On this day the Lord will bring low all that is proud and lifted up against him (Is 2:11–22). He will battle against nations who assault and exploit his people (Obad 1:15), bring healing and blessing to all who repent (Mal 4:1–6), and manifest his divine kingship over the world (Zech 14:1–9). The history of Israel is punctuated with days of the Lord that are "near" the times of their first hearers (Joel 2:1; 3:14; Zeph 1:14). Ultimately, these days of judgment within history are a foreshadowing of the final Day of Judgment at the end of history. This prophetic theme appears in the NT as "the day of the Lord Jesus" (1 Cor 5:5; 2 Cor 1:14). On this day, which will come like a thief in the night (1 Thess 5:2), all people and nations will stand before the judgment seat of Christ (2 Cor 5:10), whom God has appointed to judge the world (Acts 17:31) (CCC 678–82). See also note on Is 2:12.

ᵃ Heb uncertain.

¹⁹Unto you, O LORD, I cry.
  For fire has devoured
    the pastures of the wilderness,
  and flame has burned
    all the trees of the field.
²⁰Even the wild beasts cry to you
    because the water brooks are dried up,
  and fire has devoured
    the pastures of the wilderness.

The Day of the Lord Is Coming

2 Blow the trumpet in Zion;
  sound the alarm on my holy mountain!
Let all the inhabitants of the land tremble,
  for the day of the LORD is coming, it is near,
²a day of darkness and gloom,
  a day of clouds and thick darkness!
Like blackness there is spread upon the
    mountains
  a great and powerful people;
their like has never been from of old,
  nor will be again after them
  through the years of all generations.

³Fire devours before them,
  and behind them a flame burns.
The land is like the garden of Eden before them,
  but after them a desolate wilderness,
  and nothing escapes them.

⁴Their appearance is like the appearance of
    horses,
  and like war horses they run.
⁵As with the rumbling of chariots,
  they leap on the tops of the mountains,
like the crackling of a flame of fire
  devouring the stubble,
like a powerful army
  drawn up for battle.

⁶Before them peoples are in anguish,
  all faces grow pale.
⁷Like warriors they charge,
  like soldiers they scale the wall.
They march each on his way,
  they do not swerveᵇ from their paths.
⁸They do not jostle one another,
  each marches in his path;
they burst through the weapons
  and are not halted.
⁹They leap upon the city,
  they run upon the walls;
they climb up into the houses,
  they enter through the windows like a thief.

¹⁰The earth quakes before them,
  the heavens tremble.
The sun and the moon are darkened,
  and the stars withdraw their shining.

2:4-5: Rev 9:7, 9. **2:10:** Rev 9:2.

1:19 fire has devoured: Either a literal reference to wildfires or poetical language for the scorching effect of unusually dry conditions.

1:20 brooks are dried up: Drought and thirst are added to the problems of crop destruction and hunger.

2:1-11 Judah and Jerusalem, already devastated by locusts, face the prospect of an even more terrible judgment on the approaching "day of the LORD" (2:1). The precise nature of the threat is disputed: either **(1)** Joel envisions another *locust plague*, which he compares to an invading army, or **(2)** Joel envisions an *actual army* marching on Judah, which he compares to the land being overrun by locusts. Either way, the Lord is behind the coming chastisement, its destructive forces being "his army" (2:11). Literarily, this section is noted for its apocalyptic images and themes, which paint a picture of cosmic upheaval, celestial signs, and divine judgment. The apocalyptic literary form appears elsewhere in the OT (Is 24–27; Daniel; Zechariah), in ancient Jewish texts outside the Bible (*1 Enoch; Assumption of Moses*), and in the NT (Mk 13:1–37; 2 Thess 2:3–12; Book of Revelation).

2:1 Blow the trumpet: Like a watchman on a city wall who sounds the alarm when enemies approach (Ezek 33:2–3). See word study: *Trumpet* at Judg 6:34. **Zion:** The mountain height of Jerusalem. See note on 2 Sam 5:7. **holy:** The elevation is sanctified by the Lord's presence in his Temple. **the day of the LORD:** See word study: *The Day of the LORD* at 1:15.

2:2 darkness and gloom: Traditionally associated with the day of the Lord (Amos 5:20; Zeph 1:14–15). **people:** Either foreign invaders or locusts personified as invaders (1:6).

Identifying an actual military threat to Judah is difficult, owing to uncertainties about Joel's historical time period. Possibilities include the Assyrian invasion of 701 B.C. or the Babylonian invasions of 597 or 586 B.C. See note on 2:1–11 and introduction: *Author and Date*.

2:3 the garden of Eden: The place of original blessedness, lush with well-watered trees and abundant food (Gen 2:8–10; 13:10). The land of Judah is similarly blessed with fruitfulness, yet the Lord's judgment will leave it a ravaged wasteland. For this imagery in reverse, see Is 51:3 and Ezek 36:35.

2:4 horses: Horses and locusts are sometimes compared (Job 39:20; Jer 51:27; Rev 9:7). **like war horses:** Said to favor the view that Joel envisions a locust invasion, whose noisy approach is compared to a cavalry thundering into battle.

2:7 Like warriors: Said to favor the view that Joel envisions a locust invasion, which is compared to soldiers swarming a city. **scale the wall:** No defensive barriers will be able to protect Judah against the coming assault.

2:10–11 Apocalyptic scenes of cosmic disturbance make the day of the LORD a frightful prospect for Judah. See word study: *The Day of the LORD* at 1:15. • Earthquake, darkness, and hearing the Lord's voice recall the theophany on Mt. Sinai, when God first made his power and glory manifest to Israel (Ex 19:16-19; Deut 4:11). This awesome display was meant to induce the people to a reverent fear of (respect for) the Lord and to a firm commitment to his covenant (Ex 20:18-20; Deut 5:10).

2:10 sun ... moon ... stars: A blackout in the heavens is typical apocalyptic imagery (2:31; Is 13:10; Ezek 32:7-8; Amos 8:9; Mt 24:29; Rev 6:12; 8:12). • A locust plague followed by total darkness recalls the sequence of the eighth and ninth plagues on Egypt, when locusts invaded the land, followed by three days of oppressive gloom (Ex 10:1-29).

ᵇGk Syr Vg: Heb *take a pledge*.

¹¹The Lord utters his voice
    before his army,
for his host is exceedingly great;
    he that executes his word is powerful.
    For the day of the Lord is great and very
        awesome;
    who can endure it?

¹²"Yet even now," says the Lord,
    "return to me with all your heart,
with fasting, with weeping, and with mourning;
¹³   and tear your hearts and not your garments."
    Return to the Lord, your God,
        for he is gracious and merciful,
    slow to anger, and abounding in mercy,
        and repents of evil.
¹⁴Who knows whether he will not turn and repent,
        and leave a blessing behind him,
    a cereal offering and a drink offering
        for the Lord, your God?

¹⁵Blow the trumpet in Zion;
    sanctify a fast;
call a solemn assembly;
¹⁶   gather the people.
    Sanctify the congregation;
        assemble the elders;

gather the children,
    even nursing infants.
Let the bridegroom leave his room,
    and the bride her chamber.

¹⁷Between the vestibule and the altar
    let the priests, the ministers of the Lord, weep
and say, "Spare your people, O Lord,
    and make not your heritage a reproach,
    a byword among the nations.
Why should they say among the peoples,
    'Where is their God?'"

¹⁸Then the Lord became jealous for his land,
    and had pity on his people.
¹⁹The Lord answered and said to his people,
    "Behold, I am sending to you
        grain, wine, and oil,
        and you will be satisfied;
and I will no more make you
    a reproach among the nations.

²⁰"I will remove the northerner far from you,
    and drive him into a parched and desolate
        land,
his front into the eastern sea,
    and his rear into the western sea;

2:11: Rev 6:17.

2:11 who can endure it?: Similar questions are asked in Nahum 1:6 and Mal 3:2.

2:12-18 Joel calls for a national act of repentance in which everyone participates, even infants, children, and newly married couples (2:16). These verses, which call God's people to contrition and conversion, are read on Ash Wednesday to set the tone for the penitential season of Lent (CCC 1430). • Our Savior exhorts us through the prophet and shows us how to return to him. Note carefully that Lent signifies life in the present world, while Easter is a figure of eternal happiness. Just as we observe Lent with a kind of sadness before rejoicing at Easter, so we should do penance in this life that we might be forgiven of our sins and come to eternal joy (St. Caesarius of Arles, *Sermons* 198, 1).

2:12 even now: Judah's judgment is conditional rather than inevitable. If the community recommits itself to God and his covenant, the dreadful "day of the Lord" can be averted (2:1). The urgency of Joel's appeal suggests the time for amendment is short. **return:** The language of repentance. See word study: *Return* at Jer 3:1. **with all your heart:** Moses prescribed wholehearted conversion as the path to Israel's restoration (Deut 4:29; 30:2). **fasting:** See note on 1:14. **mourning:** A penitential act of lamenting sin (Ezra 10:1-2).

2:13 tear your hearts: An appeal for genuine contrition. Outward signs of repentance are meaningless unless they mirror the inward acts of the heart. **not your garments:** Tearing one's garments is a response to extreme distress or grief (Gen 37:34; 44:13). **gracious and merciful:** The unchanging attributes of God revealed to Moses on Mt. Sinai (Ex 34:6-7). This revelation of the divine character came in the aftermath of Israel's apostasy in worshiping the golden calf (Ex 32:1-6), at which time God postponed "the day" of his judgment on their sin (Ex 32:34). **repents of evil:** Not moral evil, which God never commits, but the suffering that he brings as chastisement. In this context, God has the sovereign authority to call off the attack on Judah, thus allowing more time for the people to change

their ways (Jon 4:2). For descriptions of God acting in a human way, see notes on Gen 6:6 and 1 Sam 15:29.

2:14 Who knows ...? : Indicates that Judah's future is uncertain (2 Sam 12:22). Whether the people will face divine judgment or experience divine mercy depends on the people's response to the prophet's call for immediate reform (cf. Amos 5:15). **cereal offering ... drink offering:** See note on 1:9.

2:15 Blow the trumpet in Zion: See note on 2:1. **fast:** See note on 1:14.

2:16 Sanctify the congregation: Probably envisions rituals undertaken as preparation for a spiritual encounter with God (see Ex 19:14-15). **the elders:** Judah's community leaders.

2:17 the vestibule and the altar: Priests ministered in the open court between the bronze altar of sacrifice and the porched entrance to the Temple building (Ezek 8:16). **Spare your people:** The priests are intercessors mediating between God and Judah through prayer. **Where is their God?:** The prospect of Judah's punishment raises a concern for the Lord's reputation, i.e., onlookers could wrongly conclude that God is not loyal to his people but abandons them to suffering (cf. Ex 32:12; Ps 79:10).

2:18-27 The divine restoration of Judah. In response to their repentance, the Lord promises to drive away the locusts (2:20), to bring abundant rain (2:23), to make the land green (2:21-23), to produce a plentiful harvest (2:24), and to satisfy his people with food (2:19, 26). These events taken together will show that the Lord is "in the midst of Israel" (2:27).

2:18 jealous: Or "zealous". See note on Zech 8:2.

2:19 grain, wine, and oil: Barley, wheat, grapes, and olives were among the main crops harvested in Judah. All were devastated by the locusts (1:10).

2:20 the northerner: Said to favor the view that Joel envisions a human army attacking Judah, since invasions of the land of Israel often came from the north (Is 14:31; Jer 6:22-23; Ezek 38:14-16). **eastern sea:** The Dead Sea. **western sea:** The Mediterranean Sea.

the stench and foul smell of him will rise,
    for he has done great things.

²¹"Fear not, O land;
    be glad and rejoice,
    for the Lord has done great things!
²²Fear not, you beasts of the field,
    for the pastures of the wilderness are green;
    the tree bears its fruit,
    the fig tree and vine give their full yield.

²³"Be glad, O sons of Zion,
    and rejoice in the Lord, your God;
    for he has given the early rain for your vindication,
    he has poured down for you abundant rain,
    the early and the latter rain, as before.

²⁴"The threshing floors shall be full of grain,
    the vats shall overflow with wine and oil.
²⁵I will restore to you the years
    which the swarming locust has eaten,
    the hopper, the destroyer, and the cutter,
    my great army, which I sent among you.

²⁶"You shall eat in plenty and be satisfied,
    and praise the name of the Lord your God,
    who has dealt wondrously with you.

And my people shall never again be put to
    shame.
²⁷You shall know that I am in the midst of Israel,
    and that I, the Lord, am your God and there is
    none else.
And my people shall never again be put to
    shame.

²⁸ᶜ"And it shall come to pass afterward,
    that I will pour out my spirit on all flesh;
your sons and your daughters shall prophesy,
    your old men shall dream dreams,
    and your young men shall see visions.
²⁹Even upon the menservants and maidservants
    in those days, I will pour out my spirit.

Portents in Heaven and Judgment of the Nations

30 "And I will give signs in the heavens and on the earth, blood and fire and columns of smoke. ³¹The sun shall be turned to darkness, and the moon to blood, before the great and awesome day of the Lord comes. ³²And it shall come to pass that all who call upon the name of the Lord shall be delivered; for in Mount Zion and in Jerusalem there shall be those who escape, as the Lord has said, and among the survivors shall be those whom the Lord calls.

2:28-32: Acts 2:17–21. **2:31:** Rev 6:12. **2:32:** Rom 10:13.

2:21 be glad and rejoice: A reversal of 1:10, which describes the land mourning.

2:22 Fear not: A reversal of 1:20, which describes the beasts crying out for lack of food and water.

2:23 sons of Zion: The residents of Jerusalem. **the early rain for your vindication:** Probably the fall rains that come in October/November. Another possible translation is: "the teacher of righteousness", which was adopted as a title by a priestly leader of the Jewish community at Qumran. He is mentioned more than a dozen times in the Dead Sea Scrolls. **the latter rain:** The spring showers that come to Israel in March/April.

2:24 threshing floors: Broad platforms, usually on windy hilltops, where grains were separated from their husks in preparation for storage. **vats:** Stone troughs that collected juice or oil when grapes and olives were pressed out (3:13).

2:25 the years: Either rhetorical exaggeration or an indication that locusts ravaged Judah for more than one harvest season. **my great army:** The locust hordes. See note on 1:4.

2:27 there is none else: An affirmation of monotheism, the belief that only one God exists (Deut 4:35, 39; Is 45:5-6). **my people:** Echoes the covenant formula, reaffirming that God and Israel are bound to one another in a kinship or family relationship (Lev 26:12).

2:28-32 These final verses, which follow the numbering of the Latin Vulgate, correspond to 3:1-5 in the Hebrew text and in some modern English translations (e.g., NABRE). The prophecy looks forward to a time "afterward" (2:28) and "in those days" (2:29), an unspecified future following the restoration of Judah in 2:18-27. • Peter quotes from this prophecy to explain the sign of miraculous speech at the first Christian Pentecost (Acts 2:17-21). This and other wonders, which accompanied the birth of the Church, verified the descent of the Holy Spirit—a gift now given when believers invoke the name of the Lord Jesus in Baptism (Acts 2:38; 1 Cor 6:11). These verses are a reading option for the Vigil Mass for the Solemnity of Pentecost (CCC 715, 1287).

2:28 pour out my spirit: The mighty presence of God will descend upon his people, making them all recipients of divine revelation. The Spirit of the Lord, here and elsewhere in the prophets, is implicitly compared to water being poured from a vessel (Is 32:15; 44:3; Ezek 39:29). Pouring down rains upon the earth, just mentioned in 2:23, seems to be in mind. • The event will fulfill Moses' wish in Num 11:29 that all of God's people—not just a select few—would receive the Spirit and become prophets. **all flesh:** All men and women, regardless of age or social status. • The expression "I will pour out" indicates a lavish gift. For God does not give the Spirit by measure, but the Father has given everything into the hands of his Son, including the power to confer the Holy Spirit on whomever he wills (St. Cyril of Jerusalem, *Catechesis* 17, 19). **your daughters shall prophesy:** Manifest in the early Church in the four daughters of Philip the evangelist who prophesied (Acts 21:9). **dreams ... visions:** Channels of divine revelation (Num 12:6; Is 1:1; Dan 2:1-45).

2:30 blood ... fire ... smoke: Evokes memories of God descending on Mt. Sinai in fire and smoke (Ex 19: 17-18) while the Israelites offered blood sacrifices at the foot of the mountain to ratify the Mosaic covenant (Ex 24:5-8). During NT times, the Jewish Feast of Pentecost celebrated the giving of the Torah at Sinai. See note on 2:28-32.

2:31 sun ... darkness: Portents in the heavens. See note on 2:10. **the moon to blood:** Or the moon will appear to turn blood-red. The image suggests a lunar eclipse, which can give the moon a reddened appearance, or perhaps smoke or dust in the atmosphere, which can have the same effect. **day of the Lord:** See word study: *The Day of the Lord* at 1:15.

2:32 call upon: In prayer and worship (Gen 12:8; 1 Kings 18:24; Ps 116:17). **the name of the Lord:** Yhwh, probably pronounced "Yahweh", although always

---

ᶜCh 3:1 in Heb.

49

3 [d]"For behold, in those days and at that time, when I restore the fortunes of Judah and Jerusalem, [2]I will gather all the nations and bring them down to the valley of Jehosh'aphat, and I will enter into judgment with them there, on account of my people and my heritage Israel, because they have scattered them among the nations, and have divided up my land, [3]and have cast lots for my people, and have given a boy for a harlot, and have sold a girl for wine, and have drunk it.

4 "What are you to me, O Tyre and Si'don, and all the regions of Philis'tia? Are you paying me back for something? If you are paying me back, I will repay your deed upon your own head swiftly and speedily. [5]For you have taken my silver and my gold, and have carried my rich treasures into your temples.[e] [6]You have sold the people of Judah and Jerusalem to the Greeks, removing them far from their own border. [7]But now I will stir them up from the place to which you have sold them, and I will repay your deed upon your own head. [8]I will sell your sons and your daughters into the hand of the sons of Judah, and they will sell them to the Sabe'ans, to a nation far off; for the LORD has spoken."

[9]Proclaim this among the nations:
Prepare war,
    stir up the mighty men.
Let all the men of war draw near,
    let them come up.
[10]Beat your plowshares into swords,
    and your pruning hooks into spears;
    let the weak say, "I am a warrior."

[11]Hasten and come,
    all you nations round about,
    gather yourselves there.
Bring down your warriors, O LORD.

3:4–8: Is 23; Ezek 26:1–28:19; Amos 1:9–10; Zech 9:3–4; Ezek 28:20–26; Zech 9:2; Is 14:29–31; Jer 47; Ezek 25:15–17; Amos 1:6–8; Zeph 2:4–7; Zech 9:5–7. **3:10:** Is 2:4; Mic 4:3.

---

translated "the LORD" in the RSV2CE. This name, revealed to Moses at the burning bush (Ex 3:14), has the power to save because it bears the divine presence within it (CCC 206-9). • Paul, who quotes from Joel's prophecy, identifies Jesus as the divine "Lord" who is called upon for salvation (Rom 10:13); he further applies its promise to **all** who invoke his name, Gentiles as well as Jews (Rom 10:12). • The apostle cited this testimony to show that the prophets foretold all nations believing in God. It used to be that only the people of Israel called on the name of God, the maker of heaven and earth, while the rest of the nations invoked idols that cannot hear or speak. But when the fullness of time had come, then was fulfilled the prophecy that everyone who calls on the name of the Lord will be saved (St. Augustine, *Sermons* 56, 1). **Mount Zion:** See note on 2:1. **those who escape:** The remnant chosen by grace (Rom 11:5) to escape the judgments of the day of the Lord (2:1, 11, 31). • Whoever calls on the Lord's name following his Resurrection comes to salvation. The beginning of those who are saved in Zion and Jerusalem are the remnant, that is, those who believed from the Jewish people (St. Jerome, *Commentary on Joel* 2, 32).

3:1-21 The final chapter, which follows the numbering of the Latin Vulgate, corresponds to 4:1–21 in the Hebrew text and in some modern English translations (e.g., NABRE).

3:1-16 The Lord summons all nations to a **war** of divine **judgment**. It will be a day of vindication for Israel and a day of vengeance on enemies who scattered the covenant people into exile, sold them into slavery, and seized parts of their land (3:2-3). The defeat of the nations is assured, since there can be no victory against the God of Israel.

3:1 those days ... that time: A future time of fulfillment. Jeremiah uses this expression in his prophecies of the messianic age, when David's royal heir will come (Jer 33:15-16) and a new covenant of forgiveness will be ratified (Jer 50:4-5, 20). **I restore the fortunes:** As foreseen by Moses (Deut 30:3). **Judah and Jerusalem:** Joel appears to be speaking after a series of Babylonian invasions in the early sixth century left the city destroyed and led thousands into exile (2 Kings 24:14-16; 25:11).

3:2 valley of Jehoshaphat: Location unknown. It is sometimes identified with the Kidron Valley, the ravine

directly east of Jerusalem, but since the name Jehoshaphat translates "the LORD has judged", the reference is more likely to a place of judgment in general, without reference to the geography of Israel. Joel also calls it "the valley of decision" (3:14). The vision is often read in Christian tradition as a prophecy of the Last Judgment. • After the history of the world comes to an end, all men will rise again, and when the archangel's trumpet sounds, they will appear in the valley of Jehoshaphat. The righteous will rise with glorified and luminous bodies, the wicked with frightful and hideous bodies (St. Francis de Sales, *Introduction to the Devout Life* 1, 14). **scattered:** The language of deportation and exile (Deut 28:64; 30:3).

3:3 cast lots for my people: Also noted in Nahum 3:10. **for a harlot ... for wine:** Evil is added to evil when profits from child slave trade are spent on sinful indulgences.

3:4 Tyre and Sidon: Cities along the Mediterranean coast of Phoenicia, north of Israel. **Philistia:** The coastal strip of southwest Israel. The Philistines, longstanding enemies of Israel, handed God's people over to the Edomites (Amos 1:6-8), as did the people of Tyre (Amos 1:9-10). For God's intention to punish Tyre, Sidon, and Philistia for their hostilities toward Israel, see also Jer 47:4.

3:5 my silver and my gold: The plundering of sacred vessels from the Jerusalem Temple appears to be in view (2 Kings 24:13; 25:13-16). **into your temples:** As indicated in Dan 1:2.

3:6 the Greeks: Known in the Bible as the people of Javan (Gen 10:2; Is 66:19). For their involvement in Mediterranean slave trade, see Ezek 27:13.

3:7 I will stir: Or "I will rouse". **from the place:** Implies a regathering of Israel from the lands of exile (Deut 30:3-4).

3:8 I will sell your sons: The nations will suffer as they have made Israel to suffer, as Moses prophesied (Deut 30:7). **the Sabeans:** Traders from southern Arabia (modern Yemen).

3:9 Prepare: The same Hebrew expression is translated "sanctify" in 1:14 and 2:15-16.

3:10 Beat ... into swords ... into spears: Reshaping farm implements into weapons of war is a reversal of Isaiah's and Micah's visions of peace (Is 2:4; Mic 4:3). **the weak:** Even persons unsuited for armed conflict are mustered for battle.

3:11 your warriors, O LORD: The holy angels (Josh 5:14), who come with the Lord when he judges the world (Zech 14:5; Mt 13:49-50; 16:27; 2 Thess 1:7).

---

[a] Ch 4:1 in Heb.
[e] Or *palaces*.

¹²Let the nations bestir themselves,
    and come up to the valley of
       Jehosh'aphat;
    for there I will sit to judge
      all the nations round about.

¹³Put in the sickle,
    for the harvest is ripe.
Go in, tread,
    for the wine press is full.
The vats overflow,
    for their wickedness is great.

¹⁴Multitudes, multitudes,
    in the valley of decision!
For the day of the Lord is near
    in the valley of decision.
¹⁵The sun and the moon are darkened,
    and the stars withdraw their shining.

¹⁶And the Lord roars from Zion,
    and utters his voice from Jerusalem,
    and the heavens and the earth shake.
But the Lord is a refuge to his people,
    a stronghold to the people of Israel.

3:13: Mk 4:29; Rev 14:15, 18, 19. **3:16:** Amos 1:2.

3:12 there I will sit to judge: See note on 3:2.

3:13 the harvest: A prophetic image of judgment (Hos 6:11). The separation of the righteous and the wicked is likened to a farmer separating grains from their husks after ripe stalks have been sickled and gathered from the fields (Ps 1:4–6; Mt 13:36–42; Rev 14:15–16). **the wine press:** Another image of judgment (Is 63:2–6). Clusters of grapes were trampled by foot and their juices collected in stone vats (2:24).

3:14 the day of the Lord: See note on 1:15.

3:15 sun ... moon ... darkened: See note on 2:10.

3:16 the Lord roars from Zion: Also stated in Amos 1:2 (cf. Jer 25:30). According to some scholars, the appearance of the same expression at the end of Joel and at the beginning of Amos may have influenced the decision of Jewish scribes to place Joel before Amos in the arrangement of the Hebrew Bible. **his voice:** Likened to booming thunder, which makes the world tremble (cf. Ps 29:3–9). **refuge:** A place of protection (Is 25:4).

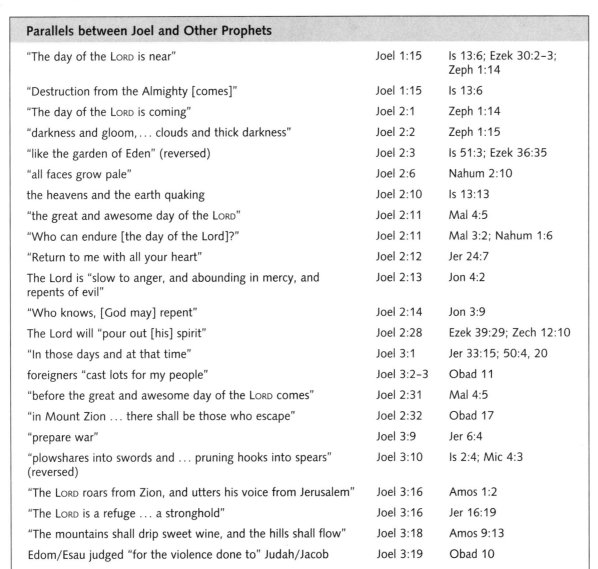

Parallels between Joel and Other Prophets		
"The day of the Lord is near"	Joel 1:15	Is 13:6; Ezek 30:2-3; Zeph 1:14
"Destruction from the Almighty [comes]"	Joel 1:15	Is 13:6
"The day of the Lord is coming"	Joel 2:1	Zeph 1:14
"darkness and gloom, ... clouds and thick darkness"	Joel 2:2	Zeph 1:15
"like the garden of Eden" (reversed)	Joel 2:3	Is 51:3; Ezek 36:35
"all faces grow pale"	Joel 2:6	Nahum 2:10
the heavens and the earth quaking	Joel 2:10	Is 13:13
"the great and awesome day of the Lord"	Joel 2:11	Mal 4:5
"Who can endure [the day of the Lord]?"	Joel 2:11	Mal 3:2; Nahum 1:6
"Return to me with all your heart"	Joel 2:12	Jer 24:7
The Lord is "slow to anger, and abounding in mercy, and repents of evil"	Joel 2:13	Jon 4:2
"Who knows, [God may] repent"	Joel 2:14	Jon 3:9
The Lord will "pour out [his] spirit"	Joel 2:28	Ezek 39:29; Zech 12:10
"In those days and at that time"	Joel 3:1	Jer 33:15; 50:4, 20
foreigners "cast lots for my people"	Joel 3:2-3	Obad 11
"before the great and awesome day of the Lord comes"	Joel 2:31	Mal 4:5
"in Mount Zion ... there shall be those who escape"	Joel 2:32	Obad 17
"prepare war"	Joel 3:9	Jer 6:4
"plowshares into swords and ... pruning hooks into spears" (reversed)	Joel 3:10	Is 2:4; Mic 4:3
"The Lord roars from Zion, and utters his voice from Jerusalem"	Joel 3:16	Amos 1:2
"The Lord is a refuge ... a stronghold"	Joel 3:16	Jer 16:19
"The mountains shall drip sweet wine, and the hills shall flow"	Joel 3:18	Amos 9:13
Edom/Esau judged "for the violence done to" Judah/Jacob	Joel 3:19	Obad 10

¹⁷"So you shall know that I am the Lᴏʀᴅ your God,
　who dwell in Zion, my holy mountain.
And Jerusalem shall be holy
　　and strangers shall never again pass through
　　　it.

¹⁸"And in that day
　the mountains shall drip sweet wine,
　　and the hills shall flow with milk,
　and all the stream beds of Judah
　　shall flow with water;
　and a fountain shall come forth from the house of
　　　the Lᴏʀᴅ
　　and water the valley of Shittim.

¹⁹"Egypt shall become a desolation
　and E'dom a desolate wilderness,
　for the violence done to the people of Judah,
　　because they have shed innocent blood in their
　　　land.
²⁰But Judah shall be inhabited for ever,
　and Jerusalem to all generations.
²¹I will avenge their blood, and I will not clear the
　　　guilty,ᵍ
　for the Lᴏʀᴅ dwells in Zion."

3:18: Ezek 47:1–12; Amos 9:13; Zech 14:8; Rev 22:1.

3:17–21 Judah and Jerusalem after the great war of judgment. Once the nations are punished for their crimes, God's persecuted people will finally have peace. The Lord will inhabit Zion forever, his people will dwell with him forever, and threats of violence will be banished forever. • Beginning in the NT, Christian tradition reads oracles about the future Jerusalem as prophecies about the heavenly Jerusalem (Gal 4:26–27; Heb 12:22). The final visions of Joel underlie the final visions of the Book of Revelation, where the Last Judgment is followed by the Lord dwelling with his people in the new Jerusalem that comes down from heaven (Rev 20–22). • Those who fight against Zion will come to utter ruin. However, the place that is neither conquered nor burned is the spiritual and heavenly Jerusalem, the Zion above, the lovely city whose artisan and builder is God. May we come there through Christ, in whom glory is given to the Father with the Holy Spirit (St. Cyril of Alexandria, *Commentary on Joel* 3, 19–21).

3:17 I am the Lᴏʀᴅ your God: The Lord made similar statements to Abraham, after he guided him to the land of Canaan (Gen 15:7), and to the people of Israel, after he saved them from Egypt (Ex 20:2). **Zion:** The mountain height of Jerusalem, where the Lord dwells in his Temple (Ps 48:1–2; 76:1–2). **Jerusalem shall be holy:** The city will be re-consecrated as a holy place after its devastation and defilement by the foreign armies of Babylon in 586 B.C. **never again:** God will protect the city from enemy invasion in the future.

3:18 wine … milk: Abundant wine is the sign of a bountiful harvest (Amos 9:13), and abundant milk a sign of prospering of flocks and herds (Ex 3:8). **flow with water:** A sign of plentiful rainfall. **a fountain:** Parallels the vision of Ezekiel, who saw a river of water flowing from the side of the Temple and bringing life to the barren wilderness all the way to the Dead Sea (Ezek 47:1–12; cf. Zech 14:8; Rev 22:1–2). **the valley of Shittim:** Translates "the valley of acacias". Since these trees grow in arid regions, the reference may be to the lower Jordan valley. An area directly northeast of the Dead Sea is called Shittim in Num 25:1.

3:19 Egypt … Edom: Judah's enemies to the south will be made desolate. The Egyptian forces of Pharaoh Neco fought with Judah in Josiah's day (2 Kings 23:29), and the Edomites treacherously raided Judah after its conquest by the Babylonians (Is 34:5–15; Ezek 35:1–15; Obad 1–16).

3:21 the Lᴏʀᴅ dwells in Zion: Peacefully, sovereignly, and eternally, making Jerusalem forever secure. See note on 3:17–21.

ᵍGk Syr: Heb *I will hold innocent their blood which I have not held innocent.*

STUDY QUESTIONS
Joel

Chapter 1

For understanding
1. **1:2–12.** What had recently devastated the countryside of Judah? What had been devoured, and what made the crisis worse? How does Joel view this calamity? What thus follows the prophet's description of the devastation?
2. **1:6.** To what are the locust hordes likened? What image represents the locusts' capacity to devour and destroy? What does the Book of Revelation, drawing from this passage, describe? According to St. John Chrysostom, what will kill us in the life to come? How are these things more fierce than lions' teeth?
3. **1:9.** What did the food shortage in Judah disrupt? Besides the threat of hunger facing the people, what supplies were lacking? What would failure to worship the Lord as mandated in the Torah cause? To what is "the house of the Lord" probably referred here?
4. **1:14.** What are the aims and benefits of abstaining from food? For what special day does Joel call? What are the days of prescribed fasting? Although Jesus affirms the importance of fasting, what does he criticize about it? When is fasting commended by the Catholic Church? When is it required? According to St. Leo the Great, for what is devout fasting valuable, and how do we know this?
5. **Word Study: The Day of the Lord (1:15).** As a traditional concept in the OT and the unifying theme of the Book of Joel, what is the "day of the Lord"? Why does it melt the hearts of all? What will happen on the day of the Lord? What do the days of the Lord that punctuate the history of Israel ultimately foreshadow? How does this prophetic theme appear in the NT? What will happen on this day?

For application
1. **1:2–4.** What stories of hard times have your grandparents or older relatives passed down in your family? In your experience, what sorts of economic or material disaster would you want to tell your descendants about? Why do families pass such stories down from one generation to the next?
2. **1:13.** What is sackcloth, and why would one wear it at a time of tribulation or mourning? In stories of the saints, why do some of them wear uncomfortable clothing like hair shirts even when times are good? What would prompt you to consider wearing such garments?
3. **1:14.** Most Christian communions require periods of fasting, especially before major feasts or holy days. What purposes do such periods serve? In your Catholic ritual church (e.g., Roman, Byzantine, Maronite, etc.), what are the major periods of fasting? What guidelines or regulations govern such fasts?
4. **1:19–20.** Joel imagines not only people but also animals praying for relief from natural disasters such as wildfires and pest infestations. About which environmental crises are you most concerned? What recourse to prayer do you have in the face of such conditions?

Chapter 2

For understanding
1. **2:1–11.** What do Judah and Jerusalem, already devastated by locusts, face, and why is its precise nature disputed? Either way, who is behind the coming chastisement? For what is this section of the book noted, literarily? Where else does the apocalyptic literary form appear in the OT and the NT?
2. **2:12–18.** Who is to participate in the national act of repentance for which Joel calls? When are these verses, which call God's people to contrition and conversion, read and for what purpose? What are we to note carefully about Lent and Easter? Just as we observe Lent with a kind of sadness before rejoicing at Easter, why should we do penance in this life, according to St. Caesarius of Arles?
3. **2:13.** What makes outward signs of repentance meaningful? To what is tearing one's garments a response? When were the unchanging attributes of God, his graciousness and mercy, revealed, and to whom? What did God postpone in the aftermath of Israel's apostasy in worshiping the golden calf? Of what kind of evil does this verse say God repents? In this context, what does God have the sovereign authority to do?
4. **2:28.** On whom will the mighty presence of God descend, and what will it make of them? To what is the Spirit of the Lord implicitly compared? What wish of Moses will this event fulfill? According to St. Cyril of Jerusalem, how does God give the Spirit? How was prophecy manifested in the early Church among women? What do dreams and visions serve as?
5. **2:32.** What power does the name YHWH, revealed to Moses in the burning bush, have the power to do, and why? To whom does Paul, who quotes from Joel's prophecy, apply this promise? According to St. Augustine, why did the apostle cite this testimony? What happens to those who call on the Lord's name following his Resurrection? Who are the "remnant" who will be saved?

For application
1. **2:1–11.** The "day of the Lord" is mentioned twice in these verses. What kind of "day of the Lord" does our civilization face? What kind of imagery would you use to describe it? How dire is it? What role do you think the Lord plays in it?
2. **2:12–13.** Read the notes for these two verses. What moral responsibility do we have for the environmental crises we face? What acts of repentance can we make that would appeal to God's mercy to avert these chastisements?
3. **2:15–16.** What is your practice with respect to fasting? If you never or seldom fast, why do you avoid doing it? Do you fast mainly at liturgically mandated times, or do you fast privately? If you fast regularly, what motivates you?
4. **2:28–29.** Joel prophesies that the Holy Spirit will be poured out on everyone. In Christian sacramental experience, when does that outpouring typically occur? How might the outpouring of the Spirit occur outside of reception of the sacraments? What indications would you expect to see that such an outpouring has occurred?

Chapter 3

For understanding
1. **3:1–16.** To what kind of war does the Lord summon all nations? For whom will it be a day of vindication? Why is the defeat of the nations assured?
2. **3:2.** With what valley is the valley of Jehoshaphat sometimes identified? Since the name Jehoshaphat translates "the Lord has judged", what reference is more likely? How is the vision often read in Christian tradition? According to St. Francis de Sales, what will happen after the history of the world comes to an end?
3. **3:13.** Of what is the harvest a prophetic image? To what is the separation of the righteous and the wicked likened? Since the wine press is another image of judgment, what happens to clusters of grapes?
4. **3:17–21.** With what do these verses deal? What will happen once the nations are punished for their crimes? Beginning in the NT, how does Christian tradition read oracles about the future Jerusalem? How do the final visions of Joel underlie the final visions of the Book of Revelation? According to St. Cyril of Alexandria, although those who fight against Zion will come to utter ruin, which place will be neither conquered nor burned?

For application
1. **3:2–3.** Why is human trafficking so heinous a crime? How serious a problem is it in our own country? Compare these verses with the Judgment of the Nations parable in Matthew 25. Even if you are not involved in actively combating human trafficking, what corporal or spiritual works of mercy can you do to aid its victims?
2. **3:10.** Read the note for this verse. In what kind of warfare are Christians engaged? Though military imagery in spiritual matters is sometimes alien to the modern mind, why is it critical that you consider yourself a warrior? According to Eph 6:10ff., what weapons do you have?
3. **3:13.** If you are a farmer or a gardener, how do you know when the produce you planted is ripe for harvest? What conditions does Joel see that indicate the time is right for judgment? What conditions exist in our own time that suggest a time for judgment may be imminent? With whom would judgment begin (see 1 Pet 4:17)?

INTRODUCTION TO AMOS

Author and Date The Book of Amos is a collection of sayings and visions that both Jewish and Christian tradition ascribe to Amos, a prophet from Judah in southern Israel who spoke the word of the Lord to the Northern Kingdom of Israel in the eighth century B.C. This tradition is based on the opening verse, which traces the origin of the book to "Amos, who was among the shepherds of Tekoa" (1:1). The superscription further indicates that he ministered as a prophet during the reigns of King Uzziah of Judah (792–740 B.C.) and King Jeroboam II of Israel (793–753 B.C.). This historical window can be narrowed to the late 760s if estimates are correct that the earthquake mentioned in 1:1 occurred around 760 B.C. On this chronology, Amos would be an older contemporary of the prophets Hosea, Isaiah, and Micah.

Recent scholarship, without forming a consensus on matters of detail, broadly agrees that the substance of the book originated with Amos, although it remains an open question whether the prophet penned it himself, collaborated with a scribe, or left it to disciples to write down and assemble his oracles into a single volume. Scholars have singled out a few passages that may come from the hand of an editor, such as the superscription in 1:1 and the account of Amos' confrontation with Amaziah in 7:10–17, both of which are written in the third person (he, him, his) rather than the first person (I, me, my). Some argue that other passages such as God's promise to restore Israel and rebuild the kingdom of David in 9:11–15 were added to the Book of Amos long after the prophet's lifetime, perhaps as late as the sixth century B.C. This is not impossible, but neither is it demanded by the evidence. Nothing in the text of Amos strictly requires dates of composition and editing after the prophet's own generation, and so one can estimate a date around 750 B.C. for the final edition of the book.

Title The book is named after Amos, who is identified without reference to his lineage in the opening verse. Its Hebrew form, ʿĀmôs, seems to mean "one who bears a burden". The name appears in the Greek Septuagint as the title Amōs, while this heading is expanded in the Latin Vulgate to *Amos Propheta*, "Amos the Prophet". English titles for the book follow these ancient traditions.

Place in the Canon Amos has long been revered as a canonical book of Scripture. In the Jewish Bible, or Tanakh, it stands among the Latter Prophets in a sub-collection of writings known as "the Book of the Twelve". In Christian Bibles, these twelve books are called the Minor Prophets, not because they are less important than Isaiah, Jeremiah, Ezekiel, and Daniel, but because they are comparatively shorter. In the Hebrew Bible as well as in the Latin Vulgate, Amos stands third among the Minor Prophets between Joel and Obadiah. This is also its position in English Bibles. In the Greek Septuagint, it stands in second place between Hosea and Micah.

Structure The Book of Amos opens with a short superscription (1:1–2) and closes with a promise of restoration (9:11–15). Between these endpoints, a threefold structure is discernible: **(1)** chapters 1–2 feature eight oracles directed against foreign nations bordering the land of Israel, culminating with prophetic indictments against Judah and Israel; **(2)** chapters 3–6 consist of three sermons preached against the Northern Kingdom of Israel, each beginning with the announcement "Hear this word" (3:1; 4:1; 5:1); **(3)** chapters 7–9 recount five visions that Amos received from the Lord, with a biographical account of Amos in Bethel placed in the middle (7:10–17). See *Outline*.

Literary Features The Book of Amos is a work of literary art that employs a variety of rhetorical forms and devices to convey its message. Picturesque images from daily life and arresting turns of phrase have made it one of the most memorable prophetic books of Scripture. It is true that Amos himself may have been only modestly educated; but there is little doubt that he was an unusually gifted communicator. He was adept at using similes and metaphors, sarcasm and irony, refrains and rhetorical questions. Other literary forms in the book include numerical proverbs (1:3, 6, 9, 11, 13; 2:1, 4, 6), hymn fragments (4:13; 5:8–9; 9:5–6), woe oracles (5:18; 6:1, 4), judgment speeches (3:1–15; 4:1–13; 5:1–24), vision reports (7:1–3, 4–6, 7–9; 8:1–3; 9:1–10), a historical report (7:10–17), and a closing oracle of salvation (9:11–15).

The Prophet and His Times Amos was a shepherd from Tekoa in the hill country of Judah as well as an orchard worker who dressed fig trees called sycamores (1:1; 7:14–15). By his own admission, he was not a member of a prophetical guild or otherwise trained to be a prophet (7:14), yet the Lord called him to speak words of prophecy and judgment to the Northern Kingdom of Israel (7:15). He appears to have preached at Bethel in central Israel (3:14; 7:13) and possibly in the northern capital of Samaria as well (3:9; 4:1; 6:1). Some scholars envision Amos as a man of wealth and prominent social status. This is based in part on the word "shepherd" in 1:1, which could suggest, in view of related terms in other Semitic languages, that he was a commercial sheep breeder or perhaps a sanctuary employee. These hypotheses remain speculative, however, and the book overall points to a man of humble origins and occupation—a man that most would assume to be unqualified to speak in the Lord's name. Amos stands in the company of OT figures such as Jacob, Moses, and David as shepherds chosen by God to fulfill his purposes in history.

In Amos' day, both Israel in the north and Judah in the south enjoyed a time of economic prosperity, territorial expansion, and military strength. Not since the golden age of Solomon had the covenant people attained such stability. But this silver age of Israelite history was not to last. The rise in material wealth and comfort was matched by a rise in moral corruption, religious hypocrisy, and a false sense of security, especially among the wealthy elite. Nobles, judges, and merchants lived luxuriously while the poor and peasant classes were trampled underfoot. Northern Israel was guilty of maintaining the externals of religion without the ethics of religion. Amos was tasked with denouncing this spiritual decline and warning the Northern Kingdom of the tragic consequences of unrepentance. Assyria—at the moment distracted with other matters—would soon gather its strength and send its conquering armies into Syria-Palestine. Within a few decades of Amos' preaching, Assyrian hordes would overrun the lands of northern Israel and overthrow its kingdom entirely in 722 B.C.

The Message of the Prophet Amos holds the distinction of being the first of Israel's writing prophets. Other prophets preceded him, such as Elijah and Elisha, but he is the first to leave a record of his sayings for future generations. He was soon followed by the prophet Hosea, who likewise addressed the Northern Kingdom of Israel and left behind a book of prophecies in his name. Moreover, it is remarkable that Amos' oracles were ever preserved for later readers, since unlike other prophets of Israel whose careers extended over many years and sometimes decades, Amos appears to have carried out his mission within a narrow window of time, perhaps less than a year.

The heart of Amos' message clusters around three main themes: social injustice, vain worship, and the approach of divine judgment. The first two are condemned, and the third is the dire consequence of Israel's failure to repent. All three themes are intertwined throughout the book.

(1) *Social Injustice.* The Lord sent Amos to denounce the oppression of the poor and powerless in northern Israel. Although the Mosaic Law called the covenant people to care for persons in poverty and to safeguard their dignity and their interests, Israel's ruling elite was guilty of "trampling" upon

them like dirt (2:7; 5:11; 8:4). Wealthy rulers cared nothing for their needy subjects but reveled in a life of self-indulgence at their expense (6:4–6). Sins that are targeted for rebuke include violence and robbery (3:10), opposition to the truth (5:10), disregard for the prophets (2:12), sexual impurity (2:7), extortion of wine and wheat from farmers (2:8; 5:11), denying justice in court with bribes (5:12), and defrauding buyers in the market by rigging scales in favor of money-hungry merchants (8:5–6). Amos raises his voice in protest against these social evils and calls for a river of justice and righteousness to flow through the land (5:24). His appeal is for immediate repentance and reform: "Hate evil, and love good, and establish justice in the gate" (5:15).

(2) *Vain Worship.* The Lord also sent Amos to denounce the religious ritualism of northern Israel. Despite lavish living and callous abuse of the poor, the audience addressed by the prophet still performed the outward rites of worship. The feasts and solemn assemblies of the Lord continued to be observed, and the sacrifices mandated by the Torah continued to be offered (5:21–22). Yet none of this religiosity was acceptable to God. The Lord "hated" Israel's worship (5:21) precisely because Israel "hated" those who decried their sins (5:10). These Israelites gave all the show of covenant faithfulness without its moral substance. When serving God is reduced to a series of motions that are disconnected from serving our neighbor, the result is a religious hypocrisy that is offensive to the Lord. Idolatry was likewise a corruptive factor in northern Israel's worship (5:26), especially since Amos preached at the Bethel sanctuary, which featured one of the golden calves made by Jeroboam I (1 Kings 12:28–29).

(3) *Approaching Judgment.* Finally, the Lord sent Amos to announce that God's judgment was headed for northern Israel. One finds occasional calls for repentance, in which the northern tribes are urged to "seek" the Lord (5:4, 6) and choose "good" over evil (5:14–15). But overall, the tone of the book is dominated by the sense that disaster—the final "end" of the Northern Kingdom of Israel—was at hand (8:2). This tragic outcome was guaranteed because Israel refused to listen to the truth (5:10) and declined to turn back to the Lord, even when he sent chastisements to invite their return (4:6–11). Defiant refusal of the covenant triggers the curses of the covenant, and these are backed by the Lord's oath to hold Israel fully accountable for its evil (4:2; 6:8; 8:7). Amos speaks of this time of divine reckoning as "the day of the LORD", which some of his hearers supposed would be a day of light and blessing for Israel but which the prophet foresees as dreadful darkness and woe (5:18–20; 6:1, 4). The Northern Kingdom of Israel was about to suffer a complete military conquest at the hands of the Assyrians (3:11; 4:2–3; 5:3; 6:7; 7:17), and many of those who survived would be driven into the lands of exile (4:2–3; 5:27; 6:7; 7:11, 17). Israel, in other words, would be reduced to a tiny remnant of its former self (3:12; 5:3, 15). Even still, a glimmer of hope beyond the coming judgment remains. In the concluding oracle of the book, Amos delivers the Lord's promise to rebuild the ancient kingdom of David and to restore its former glory as an empire that unifies the whole family of Israel and brings the nations under its rule (9:11–12). This implies, as other OT prophecies attest, that the northern tribes of Israel will be restored and reunited with the southern tribes of Judah under the headship of a Davidic Messiah (cf. Is 11:10–16; Ezek 34:23–24; 37:15–28; Hos 1:10–11; 3:5).

Christian Perspective There are two places in the New Testament, both in the Book of Acts, where the prophecies of Amos are cited in a Christian context. The first appears in Acts 7:42–43, where Stephen, the Church's first martyr, cites a Greek translation of Amos 5:25–27 in his prophetic critique of unbelieving Jews. He insinuates that Israel's long history of idolatry, beginning in the days of Moses and continuing into the days of Amos, is mirrored in his own day as those who reject Jesus as God's Messiah make the Jerusalem Temple into a new kind of idol. The second appears in Acts 15:16–18, where James, the first bishop of Jerusalem after the apostles, sees the conversion of the first Gentiles as an act of God, whose acceptance of peoples outside the family of Israel is a fulfillment of Amos 9:11–12. According to this prophecy, the Lord had promised to rebuild David's kingdom in messianic times and to extend its reign over the nations. Other uses of Amos in the New Testament appear to be more implicit than explicit, e.g., Matthew's account of the Crucifixion in Mt 27:45–54 evokes key details from Amos 8:9–10, and James' denunciation of the rich who oppress the righteous has affinities with Amos 2:6–8; 3:9–10; 4:1; 5:12.

OUTLINE OF AMOS

1. Superscription (1:1–2)

2. Eight Oracles against the Nations and Israel (1:3—2:16)
A. Oracle against Damascus (1:3–5)
B. Oracle against Gaza (1:6–8)
C. Oracle against Tyre (1:9–10)
D. Oracle against Edom (1:11–12)
E. Oracle against Ammon (1:13–15)
F. Oracle against Moab (2:1–3)
G. Oracle against Judah (2:4–5)
H. Oracle against Israel (2:6–16)

3. Three Declarations of Judgment against Israel (3:1—6:14)
A. Sinful Israel Faces Conquest (3:1–15)
B. Unrepentant Israel Faces a Just God (4:1–13)
C. Complacent Israel Faces Desolation (5:1—6:14)

4. Five Prophetic Visions (7:1—9:10)
A. Vision 1: The Locust Plague (7:1–3)
B. Vision 2: The Devouring Fire (7:4–6)
C. Vision 3: The Plumb Line (7:7–9)
D. Historical Report: Amos and Amaziah (7:10–17)
E. Vision 4: The Basket of Summer Fruit (8:1–14)
F. Vision 5: The Lord at the Altar (9:1–10)

4. Promise of Restoration (9:11–15)

Isreal North
Judah South

THE BOOK OF

AMOS

Judgment on Israel's Neighbors

1 The words of Amos, who was among the shepherds of Teko'a, which he saw concerning Israel
in the days of Uzzi'ah king of Judah and in the days
of Jerobo'am the son of Jo'ash, king of Israel, two
years[a] before the earthquake. 2And he said:
"The LORD roars from Zion,
and utters his voice from Jerusalem;
the pastures of the shepherds mourn,
and the top of Carmel withers."
3Thus says the LORD:
"For three transgressions of Damascus,
and for four, I will not revoke the punishment;[b]
because they have threshed Gilead
with threshing sledges of iron.
4So I will send a fire upon the house of Haz'ael,
and it shall devour the strongholds of
Benha'dad.
5I will break the bar of Damascus,
and cut off the inhabitants from the Valley of
A'ven,[c]

1:2: Joel 3:16. **1:3–5:** Is 17:1–3; Jer 49:23–27; Zech 9:1.

1:1 The words: The oracles of the book, originally spoken by the prophet in the eighth century B.C. and now preserved in writing. **Amos:** The Hebrew *'Āmôs* seems to mean "one who bears a burden". The lack of any reference to his father's name may imply that he came from a family of low social standing. Amos is not to be confused with Amoz, the father of the prophet Isaiah (Is 1:1). **shepherds:** Not the typical word for keepers of flocks but one that may mean "sheep breeders" in light of a cognate term in Ugaritic. It is not clear, however, that Amos was a well-to-do businessman; he claims only to have been a herdsman who followed flocks when the Lord called him to be a prophet (7:14–15). **Tekoa:** A town five miles south of Bethlehem in the highlands of Judah (2 Chron 11:5–6). **he saw:** God delivers messages to the prophets in visual as well as verbal ways (Is 1:1; Ezek 7:26). Amos received at least five visions (7:1–3, 4–6, 7–9, 8:1–14; 9:1–10). **Uzziah:** Reigned over the Southern Kingdom of Judah from 792 to 740 B.C. **Jeroboam:** Reigned over the Northern Kingdom of Israel from 793 to 753 B.C. **the earthquake:** Archaeological findings at Hazor point to seismic activity in Israel during the reign of Jeroboam II. It is estimated to have occurred ca. 760 B.C. Amos' audience would have seen it as confirmation of his message that the Lord was about to "shake" the Northern Kingdom of Israel (9:1, 9; cf. 8:8). The same earthquake is remembered in Zech 14:5.

1:2 The LORD roars: Like a lion declaring its kingship and striking fear into the hearts of hearers (3:8; Hos 5:14). This same expression appears in Joel 3:16, leading some to claim that Jewish scribes placed Amos directly after Joel in the canon of Scripture because of this literary connection. **Zion:** Jerusalem. The Lord's voice goes forth from his Temple (Is 66:6; Jer 25:30). **Carmel:** A fertile mountain in northwest Israel (south of modern Haifa).

1:3—2:16 Oracles against the nations. Six are prophecies of judgment against nations that border the land of Israel on the north (Syrians, 1:3–5), northwest (Tyrians, 1:9–10), southwest (Philistines, 1:6–8), southeast (Edomites, 1:11–12), and east (Ammonites, 1:13–15; Moabites, 2:1–3). These neighboring states are charged with crimes against humanity and with acts of rebellion against authority. The latter is related to David subduing these nations, placing them under his rule, and making them part of Israel's multinational empire during the time of the United Monarchy (2 Sam 8:1–12; 1 Kings 4:21). Rejection of this arrangement is a rebellion against the Lord's design for David's royal heirs (Ps 2:2–3, 10–11). The final two oracles are spoken against the covenant people, the Southern Kingdom of Judah (2:4–5) and Northern Kingdom of Israel (2:6–16), who are charged with transgressing the Mosaic Law and oppressing the poor (2:4–8). See essay: *Oracles against the Nations in the Minor Prophets.*

1:3 transgressions: The Hebrew refers to "rebellions" (as in 1 Kings 12:19; 2 Kings 1:1). **and for four:** Successive numbers in parallel lines of poetry is a formula used repeatedly in Amos 1–2 and in wisdom sayings in the Bible (Prov 6:16; 30:18, 21). It is a type of progressive parallelism that puts the rhetorical emphasis on the higher digit. Here the number four is "the final straw"—the point when God's patience runs out and his decree of judgment becomes fixed. **Damascus:** Capital of one of the Aramean kingdoms of Syria, about 60 miles northeast of the Sea of Galilee. **Gilead:** A region east of the Jordan belonging to Israel but controlled at various times by the Syrians (2 Kings 10:32–33). **threshing sledges:** Sleds with studded undersides that were pulled over barley and wheat to separate edible grains from their husks, called chaff (Is 41:15). Threshing is an image of conquest also in 2 Kings 13:7 and Mic 4:13.

1:4 Hazael ... Benhadad: Two Syrian/Aramean kings who harassed northern Israel (2 Kings 13:3). **fire:** Signifies divine judgment. Damascus would fall to Assyrian conquerors in 732 B.C.

1:5 Valley of Aven: Translates "valley of disaster". Some think the Biq'ah Valley in Lebanon is meant. **Beth-eden**: Translates "house of pleasure". Beth-eden is a region on the upper Euphrates, 200 miles northeast of Damascus. **Kir:** Somewhere in Mesopotamia. The Syrians/Arameans had originally come from Kir, according to 9:7, and the Assyrians would exile them back to Kir, according to 2 Kings 16:9.

Amos was a shepherd of Judah called suddenly by God to denounce social corruption and injustice in the northern kingdom during the reign of Jeroboam II (eighth century B.C.). It was a time of great material luxury and worldly splendor, and the pastoral origins of the prophet contrasted strongly with the sophisticated decadence which, together with the people's infidelity, he denounced. He foretells the "day of the LORD," a time of punishment for men's sins, but holds out a hope of God's mercy to "the remnant of Joseph" (5:15). Some of the prophecies are probably of a later age.

[a] Or *during two years.*
[b] Heb *cause it to return.*
[c] Or *On.*

and him that holds the scepter from Beth-e'den;
   and the people of Syria shall go into exile to
     Kir,"

                   says the LORD.

⁶Thus says the LORD:
  "For three transgressions of Gaza,
    and for four, I will not revoke the punishment;**ᵇ**
  because they carried into exile a whole people
    to deliver them up to E'dom.
⁷So I will send a fire upon the wall of Gaza,
    and it shall devour her strongholds.

⁸I will cut off the inhabitants from Ash'dod,
    and him that holds the scepter from Ash'kelon;
  I will turn my hand against Ek'ron;
    and the remnant of the Philis'tines shall perish,"
               says the Lord GOD.

⁹Thus says the LORD:
  "For three transgressions of Tyre,
    and for four, I will not revoke the punishment;**ᵇ**
  because they delivered up a whole people to E'dom,
    and did not remember the covenant of
    brotherhood.

1:6–8: Is 14:29–31; Jer 47; Ezek 25:15–17; Joel 3:4–8; Zeph 2:4–7; Zech 9:5–7.
1:9–10: Is 23; Ezek 26:1—28:19; Joel 3:4–8; Zech 9:3–4.

1:6 transgressions: See note on 1:3. **Gaza:** A Philistine city on the Mediterranean coast west of Judah. It was part of a league of cities in this area that included Ashdod, Ashkelon, Ekron, and Gath (1:8; 6:2; Zeph 2:4). **and for four:** See note on 1:3. **deliver them up:** The Philistines sold captives to Edomite slave traders (1:9), perhaps after making raids in southern Israel (see 2 Chron 21:16–17; 28:18).
1:7 fire: Signifies divine judgment. The Philistine cities would fall to various Assyrian conquerors in the last decades of the eighth century B.C.

1:8 my hand: A representation of God's power (Ex 3:20). **the remnant:** The survivors. **GOD:** Spelled with capital letters when it translates the Hebrew consonants Yʜᴡʜ, referring to "Yahweh", but supplied with the vowels of *'Elōhîm*, meaning "God". This occurs multiple times in Amos (3:5, 8, 11, 13; 4:2, 5, etc.).
1:9 transgressions: See note on 1:3. **Tyre:** A Phoenician coastal city northwest of Israel. **and for four:** See note on 1:3. **they delivered up:** The Tyrians sold captives to Edomite slave traders (1:6). **covenant of brotherhood:** An international alliance between Tyre and an unnamed treaty partner. Covenants of this type, ratified for purposes of trade or national defense, made the parties equivalent to kinsmen who were bound by obligations of loyalty toward one another. Solomon made such a treaty with the king of Tyre in 1 Kings 5:12.

ᵇ Heb *cause it to return.*

Oracles against the Nations in the Minor Prophets

One often finds in the biblical prophets declarations of judgment against nations other than Israel. They are spoken in the name of the Lord against Assyria, Babylonia, Philistia, Egypt, Phoenicia, Edom, Moab, Ammon, Cush, and Aram, among others. The Major Prophets develop this theme in places such as Is 13–23, Jer 46–51, and Ezek 25–32. But the Minor Prophets also announce God's displeasure with specific Gentile nations. Sometimes whole books are devoted to this (Obadiah, Nahum), but more often we find collections of oracles within books that warn of divine judgment on peoples of the biblical world (Joel 3:1–16; Amos 1:3—2:16; Mic 5:5–6; Hab 2:4–20; Zeph 2:4–15; Zech 9:1–8; Mal 1:2–5). A superficial reading of these passages might lead us to think that the Lord had no interest in the behavior of other nations unless they were guilty of mistreating Israel. But this assessment is not quite accurate. Gentile nations *are* faulted when they have wronged the covenant people, but they are *also* charged with sin in general.

The prophetic "oracles against the nations" show us a God whose concern for righteousness is universal. His vision is not restricted to making sure that Israel is protected from the domination of other peoples. Nor is he narrowly focused on making sure that peoples of the world pay for their crimes against Israel. The God of Sacred Scripture is the Creator of all nations, and he wants to be the Savior of all nations. In the first place, he established creation as a witness to himself and to his glory (Ps 19:1–4; Wis 13:5; Acts 14:15–17). This witness includes a basic moral perception of his righteous decrees, which he implants in the conscience of every human being (Rom 1:32). The Lord would have no grounds for judging the nations or holding them accountable for transgressions if this were not so. In addition, God chose the descendants of Abraham, Isaac, and Jacob to be his instrument for blessing and redeeming the entire human race that turned away from him (Gen 12:3; 22:16–18). Israel, in other words, had a mission to be a living example of God's wisdom and to be righteous before the onlooking world (Deut 4:5–8)—a mission to be a light shining out in the darkness (Is 42:6) so that God's salvation could reach the ends of the earth (Is 49:6). This anticipates the mystery of Christ, whereby the Gentiles become "fellow heirs, members of the same body, and partakers of the promise in Christ Jesus through the gospel" (Eph 3:6).

Prophetic "oracles against the nations" must not be taken, then, as a form of ethnic or national prejudice on the part of Israel, its prophets, or its God. Rather, they establish the theological claim that God's love for humanity is universal, as is his concern for righteousness. His election of the one nation of Israel is part of a saving plan to gather all nations into the messianic kingdom of God.

The transgressions #s are a literary device to give that intent

¹⁰So I will send a fire upon the wall of Tyre,
  and it shall devour her strongholds."

¹¹Thus says the LORD:
  "For three transgressions of E'dom,
    and for four, I will not revoke the punishment;**b**
  because he pursued his brother with the sword,
    and cast off all pity,
  and his anger tore perpetually,
    and he kept his wrath **d** for ever.
¹²So I will send a fire upon Te'man,
  and it shall devour the strongholds of Bozrah."

¹³Thus says the LORD:
  "For three transgressions of the Am'monites,
    and for four, I will not revoke the punishment;**b**
  because they have ripped up women with child in
    Gilead,
    that they might enlarge their border.
¹⁴So I will kindle a fire in the wall of Rabbah,
  and it shall devour her strongholds,
  with shouting in the day of battle,
  with a tempest in the day of the whirlwind;
¹⁵and their king shall go into exile,
  he and his princes together,"
                    says the LORD.

Judgment on Israel, Judah, and the Nations

2 Thus says the LORD:
  "For three transgressions of Moab,
    and for four, I will not revoke the punishment;**e**
  because he burned to lime
    the bones of the king of E'dom.
²So I will send a fire upon Moab,
  and it shall devour the strongholds of
    Ker'ioth,
  and Moab shall die amid uproar,
    amid shouting and the sound of the trumpet;
³I will cut off the ruler from its midst,
  and will slay all its princes with him,"
                    says the LORD.

⁴Thus says the LORD:
  "For three transgressions of Judah,
    and for four, I will not revoke the punishment;**e**
  because they have rejected the law of the LORD,
    and have not kept his statutes,
  but their lies have led them astray,
    after which their fathers walked.
⁵So I will send a fire upon Judah,
  and it shall devour the strongholds of
    Jerusalem."

1:11–12: Is 34; 63:1–6; Jer 49:7–22; Ezek 25:12–14; 35; Obad; Mal 1:2–5.   **1:13–15:** Jer 49:1–6; Ezek 21:28–32; 25:1–7; Zeph 2:8–11.
2:1–3: Is 15–16; 25:10–12; Jer 48; Ezek 25:8–11; Zeph 2:8–11.

1:10 fire: Signifies divine judgment. Tyre would be besieged and attacked many times before its destruction by Alexander the Great in 332 B.C.

1:11 transgressions: See note on 1:3. **Edom:** A small kingdom that occupied the rugged highlands south of the Dead Sea. Apparently it was a leader in the regional slave trade (1:6, 9). For the history of animosity between Israel and Edom, see Introduction to Obadiah: *Historical Background*. **and for four:** See note on 1:3. **his brother:** Either a treaty partner (1:9) or a reference to Judah/Israel, since Scripture identifies Isaac's twin sons, Jacob and Esau, as the progenitors of the Israelites and the Edomites (Gen 25:23–26).

1:12 fire: Signifies divine judgment. Edom would fall to the Babylonians about 552 B.C., and the surviving population would be displaced from their native land by the Nabateans in the 400s B.C. **Teman ... Bozrah:** Two leading Edomite cities (Is 34:6; Jer 49:7; Obad 9).

1:13 transgressions: See note on 1:3. **Ammonites:** Ammon was a small kingdom east of the Jordan. Scripture identifies the Ammonites as descendants of Abraham's nephew, Lot (Gen 19:30–38). **and for four:** See note on 1:3. **ripped up women:** The barbaric practice of tearing unborn babies from the wombs of pregnant women. This wartime tactic, also attested in ancient Near Eastern literature outside the Bible, not only terrorized an enemy's civilian population but aimed to destroy its next generation of warriors (2 Kings 8:12; Hos 13:16). **Gilead:** Israelite territory east of the Jordan that bordered the land of Ammon. • By her confession, the Church is a witness to the truth and is thus represented by Gilead, which is interpreted to mean "heap of witness". Souls are with child when they conceive a right understanding of God's word and give birth to it in good works. False teachers, however, use the sword of error to slay the minds of the faithful and to cleave open those who are pregnant with the word. In this way they extend their reputation for knowledge (St. Gregory the Great, *Pastoral Care* 3, 24).

1:14 fire: Signifies divine judgment. Ammon would fall to the Babylonians in the early sixth century B.C. **Rabbah:** Capital of Ammon. The city of Amman in modern Jordan marks its ancient location.

2:1 transgressions: See note on 1:3. **Moab:** A small kingdom directly east of the Dead Sea. Scripture identifies the Moabites as descendants of Abraham's nephew, Lot (Gen 19:30–38). **and for four:** See note on 1:3. **burned ... bones:** An act of desecration against the remains of an entombed Edomite king (2 Kings 23:15–16).

2:2 fire: Signifies divine judgment. Moab would fall to the Babylonians in the early sixth century B.C. **Kerioth:** A leading Moabite city (Jer 48:24). **sound of the trumpet:** An alarm of war. See word study: *Trumpet* at Judg 6:34.

2:4 transgressions: See note on 1:3. **Judah:** The kingdom of Judah, northern Israel's southern neighbor. It was ruled by the royal descendants of David in Jerusalem. **and for four:** See note on 1:3. **the law of the LORD:** The people of Judah are charged with violating the commandments of the Torah and thus breaking the Mosaic covenant. **their lies:** Probably their idols, which are false gods (Is 44:20; Jer 16:19–20; Rom 1:25). The worship of idols is prohibited by the first of the Ten Commandments (Ex 20:3–6).

2:5 fire: Signifies divine judgment. Judah's kingdom fell to the Babylonians when Jerusalem was destroyed in 586 B.C. (2 Kings 25:1–12).

---

b Heb *cause it to return.*
d Gk Syr Vg: Heb *his wrath kept.*
e Heb *cause it to return.*

⁶Thus says the LORD:
"For three transgressions of Israel,
   and for four, I will not revoke the punishment;ᵉ
because they sell the righteous for silver,
   and the needy for a pair of shoes—
⁷they that trample the head of the poor into the
      dust of the earth,
   and turn aside the way of the afflicted;
a man and his father go in to the same maiden,
   so that my holy name is profaned;
⁸they lay themselves down beside every altar
   upon garments taken in pledge;
and in the house of their God they drink
   the wine of those who have been fined.

⁹"Yet I destroyed the Am'orite before them,
   whose height was like the height of the
      cedars,
   and who was as strong as the oaks;
I destroyed his fruit above,
   and his roots beneath.
¹⁰Also I brought you up out of the land of
      Egypt,
   and led you forty years in the wilderness,
   to possess the land of the Am'orite.

¹¹And I raised up some of your sons for prophets,
   and some of your young men for Naz'irites.
   Is it not indeed so, O people of Israel?"
                                        says the LORD.

¹²"But you made the Naz'irites drink wine, ~~law cannot drink wine~~
   and commanded the prophets,
   saying, 'You shall not prophesy.'

¹³"Behold, I will press you down in your place,
   as a cart full of sheaves presses down.
¹⁴Flight shall perish from the swift,
   and the strong shall not retain his strength,
   nor shall the mighty save his life;
¹⁵he who handles the bow shall not stand,
   and he who is swift of foot shall not save himself,
   nor shall he who rides the horse save his life;
¹⁶and he who is stout of heart among the mighty
   shall flee away naked in that day,"
                                        says the LORD.

Israel's Transgression and Punishment

3 Hear this word that the LORD has spoken against you, O sons of Israel, against the whole family which I brought up out of the land of Egypt:

2:6–16 The last and longest oracle of judgment denounces the sins of Israel. Rhetorically, this climax comes as a bombshell. Amos' original audience, the northern Israelites, would have found satisfaction in the litany of prophecies announcing God's punishment on its neighbors (1:3—2:5). But the sequence of divine rebukes, moving from neighboring pagans (Syria, Philistia, Tyre) to neighboring cousins (Edom, Ammon, Moab) to neighboring brothers (Judah) was designed to produce a growing unease in northern Israelite readers as the noose tightened around them. The prophet's harshest words of condemnation are reserved for Israel's northern tribes.

2:6 transgressions: See note on 1:3. **Israel:** The Northern Kingdom of Israel, which separated itself from Judah and Jerusalem after Solomon's death in 930 B.C. (1 Kings 12:19–33). **and for four:** See note on 1:3. **sell the righteous ... the needy:** The powerful of Israel oppressed and took advantage of the devout and poor among them. Amos is one of the most outspoken critics of social injustice in the Bible (3:9–15; 4:1–3; 5:10–15, 24; 6:4–7; 8:4–6).

2:7 trample: Amos' graphic way of describing the ruthless exploitation of people in poverty (5:11; 8:4). **go in to the same maiden:** An act of sexual impurity and possibly worse, e.g., the young woman may have been a cult prostitute who had relations with father and son in an idolatrous rite, or she may have been a poor slave girl who was taken advantage of or raped by men of the same powerful family.

2:8 beside every altar: Suggests a setting in outdoor cultic shrines (cf. Hos 4:13–14). Sacrificial altars outside the Temple in Jerusalem were illegal according to the Torah (Deut 12:1–14). **garments taken in pledge:** A form of collateral given by the poor when they borrowed from a lender. The Mosaic Law stipulates that an article of clothing given as a pledge must be returned before sundown, lest the borrower be without coverings for the night (Ex 22:26–27; Deut 24:10–13; CCC 2401). **the house of their God:** An allusion to Bethel, which translates "house of God". Bethel was one of the sites in northern Israel

where a golden calf shrine was established (1 Kings 12:28–29; Hos 10:5). Sacrificial banquets were often held in religious sanctuaries. **those who have been fined:** Wine was taken from the common people either as a tax or under the pretense of a payment required for some legal infraction.

📖 **2:9 I destroyed the Amorite:** Refers to the conquest of Canaan, a land once occupied by peoples such as the Amorites (Josh 5:1). The Lord, to whom the land belongs (Lev 25:23), gave it as a gift to the descendants of Abraham (Josh 24:8–13). The point here and in the next verse is that Israel had every reason to be grateful to God rather than rebellious.

📖 **2:10 I brought you up:** Refers to Israel's epic departure from Egypt, which was the Lord's gift of freedom to his people (Ex 20:2; Deut 5:6).

📖 **2:11 prophets:** Persons called by God to speak his words to his people (Deut 18:18). Northern Israel was guilty of silencing these messengers who condemned sin and called for repentance (2:12). **Nazirites:** Persons consecrated to God by a vow to abstain from cutting the hair, contact with the dead, and consuming anything made from grapes (Num 6:1–21). Northern Israel was guilty of making Nazirites drink wine and thus violate their vow (2:12).

2:13–16 An announcement of the coming judgment: Israel will face invasion from a superior military force that will wipe out its archers, foot soldiers, and cavalry, causing even its most heroic warriors to flee in fear. Historically, this was carried out by the Assyrians between 734 and 722 B.C. (2 Kings 15:29; 17:5–6; 1 Chron 5:26).

2:13 I will press you down: I.e., under the crushing weight of divine judgment.

2:16 naked: Unarmed and vulnerable. **that day:** The great and terrible "day of the LORD" when northern Israel will face the darkness of its demise (5:18–20).

3:1—6:14 Three judgment speeches against the sins of the Northern Kingdom of Israel. Each begins with the same summons to attention: "Hear this word" (3:1; 4:1; 5:1).

3:1 the whole family: Amos addresses all twelve tribes of Israel inclusively, although his indictment targets the Northern Kingdom of Israel specifically (see 3:9, 12). The purpose of·

ᵉ Heb *cause it to return.*

2"You only have I known
of all the families of the earth;
therefore I will punish you
for all your iniquities.

3"Do two walk together,
unless they have made an appointment?
4Does a lion roar in the forest,
when he has no prey?
Does a young lion cry out from his den,
if he has taken nothing?
5Does a bird fall in a snare on the earth,
when there is no trap for it?
Does a snare spring up from the ground,
when it has taken nothing?
6Is a trumpet blown in a city,
and the people are not afraid?
Does evil befall a city,
unless the LORD has done it?
7Surely the Lord GOD does nothing,
without revealing his secret
to his servants the prophets.
8The lion has roared;
who will not fear?

The Lord GOD has spoken;
who can but prophesy?"

9Proclaim to the strongholds in Assyria, f
and to the strongholds in the land of
Egypt,
and say, "Assemble yourselves upon the
mountains of Samar′ia,
and see the great tumults within her,
and the oppressions in her midst."
10"They do not know how to do right," says
the LORD,
"those who store up violence and robbery
in their strongholds."
11Therefore thus says the Lord GOD:
"An adversary shall surround the land,
and bring down your defenses from you,
and your strongholds shall be plundered."

12 Thus says the LORD: "As the shepherd rescues
from the mouth of the lion two legs, or a piece of
an ear, so shall the people of Israel who dwell in
Samar′ia be rescued, with the corner of a couch and
part g of a bed."

3:7: Rev 10:7.

---

speaking to the whole covenant community is to give warning to the Judahites of the Southern Kingdom, who are also guilty of covenant violation (2:4) and who are about to witness the devastating consequences of rebellion by their northern kinsmen.

3:2 You only have I known: Points to Israel's special relationship with the Lord. By an act of divine love, God chose the people of Israel (Deut 7:6) as his treasured possession (Ex 19:5) to be a living witness to his wisdom, goodness, and righteousness before the eyes of the onlooking world (Deut 4:5–8; Is 49:6). Israel's election is not just a privilege, however; it comes with the responsibility to keep his covenant. When Israel fails in national obedience, as in Amos' day, it is held to account for its iniquities and must face the curses of the covenant (Deut 28:15–68) as the Lord's corrective discipline (Deut 8:5; Prov 3:11–12). In the words of Jesus: "Every one to whom much is given, of him will much be required" (Lk 12:48).

3:3–8 Rhetorical questions anticipating negative answers. The sequence builds to a crescendo in 3:8, where the prophet implies that fear of the Lord and immediate repentance are the proper responses to prophecies of doom. Images of lions feasting on prey, hunters taking game, and trumpets sounding the alarm of war reinforce the message that northern Israel is in grave danger.

3:6 evil: The Hebrew *rā'āh* here means "disaster" or "calamity". **unless the LORD has done it?:** Not a general statement that God is the cause of every misfortune that cities face. The point is rather that God sends or allows chastisements, often by means of foreign invaders, upon cities (and nations) that forsake his covenant and brazenly commit sin (Deut 28:49–57). Amos wants Israel to understand that its rebellion is the reason for its coming downfall. • Evil has two meanings. Sometimes it means what is evil by nature, and sometimes it means what is evil to us, such as tribulation and distress. The latter seem to be evil since they cause us pain, but in fact they are good, because for those who understand

them they are a means of conversion and salvation (St. John of Damascus, *Orthodox Faith* 4, 19). • God is the author of evil in the sense of imposing a penalty, but not the author of evil in the sense of committing a fault (St. Thomas Aquinas, *Summa Theologiae* 1, 49, 2).

3:7 secret: The mystery of God's plan for judgment and redemption. This plan is disclosed in partial ways and in gradual stages to the prophets, but its full revelation awaits the coming of God's Son as the Messiah (Heb 1:1–2). The prophets possessed divine *insight* into the meaning of contemporary events and divine *foresight* into the course of events coming in the future.

3:8 The lion has roared: An image of the Lord repeated from 1:2. Northern Israel should be afraid of being his prey (Hos 5:14). **who can but prophesy?:** Prophets sometimes had an irresistible urge to speak the message that God had entrusted to them (Num 22:38; Jer 20:9).

3:9 Assyria: The wording of the Greek LXX. The Hebrew text, which reads "Ashdod" instead of Assyria, is suspected by many of being corrupt, i.e., the word seems to have been miscopied by a scribe writing out the book by hand. Regardless of which word is original, the point is the same: even pagan nations outside the Mosaic covenant can testify to the internal corruption of Israel. **Samaria:** Nearly 40 miles north of Jerusalem in central Canaan. It had been the capital of the Northern Kingdom of Israel since the days of King Omri (1 Kings 16:24).

3:10 violence and robbery: Disregard for God's Law led to a serious breakdown in social order.

3:11 An adversary: The Assyrians, who will serve as the rod of God's wrath to chastise his people (Is 10:5). They will enact the Lord's judgments by conquering northern Israel in stages between 734 and 722 B.C. (2 Kings 15:29; 17:5–6; 1 Chron 5:26).

3:12 two legs ... piece of an ear: Barely anything will escape or be salvaged after the Lord, like a lion, sets upon his prey and drags it away (Hos 5:14). The point here: what is left of Israel after divine judgment will be nothing but a bare reminder of what the Northern Kingdom used to be. In other words, only a "remnant" or small portion will escape destruction (5:15; 9:8; Is 10:20–22).

---

f Gk: Heb *Ashdod.*
g The meaning of the Hebrew word is uncertain.

¹³"Hear, and testify against the house of Jacob,"
  says the Lord GOD, the God of hosts,
¹⁴"that on the day I punish Israel for his
    transgressions,
  I will punish the altars of Bethel,
  and the horns of the altar shall be cut off
  and fall to the ground.
¹⁵I will strike the winter house with the summer
    house;
  and the houses of ivory shall perish,
  and the great houses ʰ shall come to an end,"
                              says the LORD.

Punishments of Israel

4 "Hear this word, you cows of Bashan,
  who are in the mountain of Samar′ia,
who oppress the poor, who crush the needy,
  who say to their husbands, 'Bring, that we
    may drink!'
²The Lord GOD has sworn by his holiness
  that, behold, the days are coming upon
    you,
  when they shall take you away with hooks,
  even the last of you with fishhooks.
³And you shall go out through the breaches,
  every one straight before her;
  and you shall be cast forth into Har′mon,"
                              says the LORD.

⁴"Come to Bethel, and transgress;
  to Gilgal, and multiply transgression;
  bring your sacrifices every morning,
    your tithes every three days;
⁵offer a sacrifice of thanksgiving of that which is
    leavened,
  and proclaim freewill offerings, publish
    them;
  for so you love to do, O people of Israel!"
                              says the Lord GOD.

⁶"I gave you cleanness of teeth in all your cities,
  and lack of bread in all your places,
  yet you did not return to me,"
                              says the LORD.

⁷"And I also withheld the rain from you
  when there were yet three months to the
    harvest;
  I would send rain upon one city,
  and send no rain upon another city;
  one field would be rained upon,
  and the field on which it did not rain
    withered;
⁸so two or three cities wandered to one city
  to drink water, and were not satisfied;
  yet you did not return to me,"
                              says the LORD.

3:13 the house of Jacob: The tribal family of Israel, descended from Abraham's grandson Jacob (Gen 49:1–27; Ex 1:1–4).
3:14 Bethel: Ten miles north of Jerusalem near the lower boundary of the Northern Kingdom of Israel. It was a place of worship in patriarchal times (Gen 28:18–22; 35:6–7), a temporary site of the Tabernacle in the time of the judges (Judg 20:26–28), and established by Jeroboam I, the first king of northern Israel, as the location of a golden calf shrine (1 Kings 12:28–29). The **altars of Bethel** would have functioned as part of the idolatrous calf cult (1 Kings 12:29). Amos views Bethel as a place where people "transgress" the covenant (4:4) and declares that it will "come to nothing" (5:5). **the horns:** Many altars in biblical Israel had horn-like projections rising from their top four corners (Ex 27:1–2; 1 Kings 2:28).
3:15 winter house ... summer house: A merism meaning "every house". **houses of ivory:** Archaeology has uncovered evidence from ancient Samaria showing that homes of the wealthy were decorated with ivory inlay (cf. 1 Kings 22:39).
4:1 Hear this word: See note on 3:1–6:14. **cows of Bashan:** An insulting description of the wealthy matrons of Samaria, who were as pampered and well-fed as the cattle that grazed on the fertile hills of Bashan, east of the Sea of Galilee. The prophet implies they are fattening themselves for slaughter (Jas 5:5). **Samaria:** Capital of northern Israel. See note on 3:9. **oppress the poor:** Samaria's affluent women reveled in luxuries furnished by unjustly obtained wealth. This holds true whether they participated directly in the extortion of others or simply encouraged their powerful husbands to fleece the less fortunate. **that we may drink:** I.e., wines taken from the common people (2:8).
4:2 GOD has sworn: A divine oath to bring northern Israel to judgment for its mass defection from the covenant. It is

also mentioned in 6:8 and 8:7. **take you away:** They will be dragged from the city either as corpses of the slain or as captives exiled to distant lands. For other prophecies of exile in the book, see 5:5, 27; 6:7; 7:11, 17; 9:4.
4:3 the breaches: Openings made in the wall of a conquered city. **Harmon:** Or, possibly, "Mount Mon". Its location is unknown.
4:4–5 Prophetic sarcasm. Northern Israel is encouraged to continue in sin by continuing to sacrifice. Its worship is unacceptable to God because it is *insincere* (devoid of inner devotion), *illegal* (done in opposition to the Jerusalem Temple), and *idolatrous* (defiled by the veneration of graven images and false gods). See note on 1 Kings 12:28.
4:4 Bethel: See note on 3:14. **Gilgal:** The location of an unlawful religious shrine (5:5; Hos 12:11). Amos refers either to the town of Gilgal in the western Jordan valley near Jericho (Josh 4:19) or to the town of Jiljulieh, roughly seven miles north of Bethel in central Israel.
4:5 sacrifice of thanksgiving: A special kind of peace offering made in gratitude to God. See notes on Lev 7:12 and Ps 50:14. **so you love to do:** Amos witnessed a religious fervor in northern Israel, but it was more concerned with the outward display of ritual than with putting faith and justice into action in daily life (5:21–24).
4:6–11 Five instances in which the Lord chastised sinful Israel. These were not signs of rejection but appeals for repentance. Divine discipline is meant to be restorative, creating an opportunity for people to renounce their sins and recommit themselves to God. Tragically, these warnings went unheeded, as indicated by the refrain "yet you did not return to me" (4:6, 8, 9, 10, 11). See note on Lev 26:14–39.
4:6 cleanness of teeth: Due to a food shortage.
4:7 withheld the rain: Causing a drought and threatening the next year's harvest. **rain ... no rain:** The Lord's discipline was mercifully restrained, affecting some cities but not others.

ʰ Or *many houses.*

9"I struck you with blight and mildew;
    I laid waste[i] your gardens and your vineyards;
    your fig trees and your olive trees the locust
        devoured;
yet you did not return to me,"
                    says the LORD.

10"I sent among you a pestilence after the manner
    of Egypt;
    I slew your young men with the sword;
I carried away your horses;[j]
    and I made the stench of your camp go up into
        your nostrils;
yet you did not return to me,"
                    says the LORD.

11"I overthrew some of you,
    as when God overthrew Sodom and
      Gomor'rah,
    and you were as a brand plucked out of the
      burning;
yet you did not return to me,"
                    says the LORD.

12"Therefore thus I will do to you, O Israel;
    because I will do this to you,
    prepare to meet your God, O Israel!"

13For behold, he who forms the mountains, and
    creates the wind,
    and declares to man what is his thought;
who makes the morning darkness,
    and treads on the heights of the earth—
the LORD, the God of hosts, is his name!

A Lamentation for Israel's Sins

5 Hear this word which I take up over you in lamentation, O house of Israel:
2"Fallen, no more to rise,
    is the virgin Israel;
forsaken on her land,
    with none to raise her up."

3For thus says the Lord GOD:
"The city that went forth a thousand
    shall have a hundred left,
and that which went forth a hundred
    shall have ten left
    to the house of Israel."

4For thus says the LORD to the house of Israel:
"Seek me and live;
5   but do not seek Bethel,
and do not enter into Gilgal
    or cross over to Be'er-she'ba;
for Gilgal shall surely go into exile,
    and Bethel shall come to nothing."

6Seek the LORD and live,
    lest he break out like fire in the house of
      Joseph,
    and it devour, with none to quench it for
      Bethel,
7O you who turn justice to wormwood,
    and cast down righteousness to the earth!

8He who made the Pleiades and Orion,
    and turns deep darkness into the morning,
    and darkens the day into night,

4:9 blight ... locust: Caused crop damage in vineyards and orchards.

4:10 pestilence: The plagues described in Ex 7–12 that forced Pharaoh to release Israel from bondage. **slew ... carried away:** The Lord allowed raids in northern Israel that left some dead and others robbed of livestock.

4:11 Sodom and Gomorrah: Wicked cities that God destroyed with fire and brimstone in the time of Abraham (Gen 19:24-25). **a brand plucked:** A narrow escape from annihilation. The rescue of Lot and his family from Sodom in the nick of time may be in mind (Gen 19:15-23).

4:12 prepare to meet your God: A terrifying announcement of divine confrontation. God is coming as Judge and Enforcer of the covenant to visit stubborn Israel with its curses, the most severe of which is foreign invasion and exile from the land (Deut 28:62-68).

4:13 forms ... creates ... declares: The Lord is supremely qualified to bring Israel (and all peoples) to justice because he is the all-powerful and all-knowing Creator of the universe. **the God of hosts:** A title for the Lord as commander of the heavenly armies of angels (Josh 5:14).

5:1 Hear this word: See note on 3:1—6:14.

5:2 Fallen: Israel's downfall is so certain that Amos speaks as if it had already happened, even though he is prophesying

the future (Is 21:9; Jer 51:8). **the virgin Israel:** An image of northern Israel, portrayed as a young maiden who was ready for marriage and motherhood before she tragically lost her life.

5:3 a hundred left ... ten left: The small remnant that survives after Israel has been decimated by war (3:12; 5:15).

5:4 Seek me: An appeal to be reconciled to God. Practically speaking, this was a call to prayer, fasting, and a renewed commitment to his covenant. See word study: *Sought* at 2 Chron 1:5. **live:** Ongoing life in the Promised Land depends on keeping the Lord's commandments (Lev 18:5; Deut 4:1; 30:16).

5:5 Bethel ... Gilgal: Centers of false worship in northern Israel. See notes on 3:14 and 4:4. **Beer-sheba:** The site of an unlawful shrine or high place in southern Judah (2 Kings 23:8).

5:6 fire: Signifies divine judgment (1:4, 7, 10, 14, etc.). **house of Joseph:** Another name for the Northern Kingdom of Israel (Ps 78:67). Its two dominant tribes, Ephraim and Manasseh, were sons of the patriarch Joseph (Gen 41:50-52).

5:7 wormwood: A plant with an exceedingly bitter taste (6:12; Prov 5:4; Lam 3:15).

5:8 Pleiades and Orion: Constellations related to the changing of the seasons. Luminaries in the day and night sky bear witness to the glory of the Creator (Gen 1:14; Ps 19:1-4). Israel was forbidden to worship the heavenly bodies (Deut 4:19), although violations occurred in biblical history (5:26; 2 Kings 23:5; Ezek 8:16). **the LORD:** YHWH, probably pronounced "Yahweh". See note on Ex 3:15.

---

[i] Cn: Heb *the multitude of.*
[j] Heb *with the captivity of your horses.*

who calls for the waters of the sea,
    and pours them out upon the surface of the earth,
the LORD is his name,
  ⁹who makes destruction flash forth against the
      strong,
    so that destruction comes upon the fortress.

¹⁰They hate him who reproves in the gate,
    and they abhor him who speaks the truth.
¹¹Therefore because you trample upon the poor
    and take from him exactions of wheat,
you have built houses of hewn stone,
    but you shall not dwell in them;
you have planted pleasant vineyards,
    but you shall not drink their wine.
¹²For I know how many are your transgressions,
    and how great are your sins—
you who afflict the righteous, who take a bribe,
    and turn aside the needy in the gate.
¹³Therefore he who is prudent will keep silent in
      such a time;
    for it is an evil time.

¹⁴Seek good, and not evil,
    that you may live;
and so the LORD, the God of hosts, will be with you,
    as you have said.
¹⁵Hate evil, and love good,
    and establish justice in the gate;
it may be that the LORD, the God of hosts,
    will be gracious to the remnant of Joseph.

¹⁶Therefore thus says the LORD, the God of hosts,
    the Lord:
"In all the squares there shall be wailing;
    and in all the streets they shall say, 'Alas!
      alas!'
They shall call the farmers to mourning
    and to wailing those who are skilled in
      lamentation,
¹⁷and in all vineyards there shall be wailing,
    for I will pass through the midst of you,"
                  says the LORD.

¹⁸Woe to you who desire the day of the LORD!
    Why would you have the day of the LORD?
It is darkness, and not light;
¹⁹   as if a man fled from a lion,
    and a bear met him;
or went into the house and leaned with his hand
      against the wall,
    and a serpent bit him.
²⁰Is not the day of the LORD darkness, and not light,
    and gloom with no brightness in it?

²¹"I hate, I despise your feasts,
    and I take no delight in your solemn
      assemblies.
²²Even though you offer me your burnt offerings
    and cereal offerings,
    I will not accept them,
and the peace offerings of your fatted beasts
    I will not look upon.

5:10 him who reproves: A prophet such as Amos, who issued calls for repentance in a public place.

5:11 trample: Amos' graphic way of describing the ruthless exploitation of people in poverty (2:7; 8:4). **houses of hewn stone:** Expensive homes built by the ruling class with resources gained from extorting others. **you shall not dwell in them:** Because invaders will kill or take captive the rich and powerful of the land, leaving their homes abandoned (Hos 9:6).

5:12 who take a bribe: Judges whose impartial concern for justice has been compromised by money or some other incentive to rule against the righteous. In the words of the Torah: "a bribe blinds the eyes of the wise and subverts the cause of the righteous" (Deut 16:19). **the gate:** Where city elders resolved legal disputes (Deut 21:19; 22:15; 25:7). It was supposed to be a place where justice prevailed for all (5:15).

5:13 silent: Evil had become so prevalent that people thought it wise *not* to speak out against injustice, lest they become targets of it as well.

5:14 Seek good: Equivalent to seeking the Lord (5:6). • We must hurry to him who is Goodness itself. He is the patience of Israel and the one calling you to repent, so that you might avoid judgment and receive forgiveness of sins. He is the one of whom the prophet Amos speaks (St. Ambrose, *Letters* 79).

5:15 it may be: Amos holds out hope that God, being gracious, will lessen Israel's sentence of judgment if repentance begins immediately. **the remnant:** The survivors. See note on 3:12. **Joseph:** See note on 5:6.

5:18 Woe: An anguished cry that introduces three funeral laments (5:18; 6:1, 4). These dirges serve as announcements of doom, warning Israel that its death and burial approaches (Is 10:5; Nahum 3:1; Zech 11:17). See word study: *Woe* at Is

28:1. **the day of the LORD:** A day of cataclysmic judgment when God holds a nation accountable for its evildoing. Northern Israelites wrongly supposed that, because the Lord was "with" his people (5:14), divine retribution would fall on their enemies, leaving Israel untouched and vindicated. Amos had to disabuse Israel of this dangerous misunderstanding. The covenant people are not exempt from the dreaded day of the Lord; in fact, they make themselves its target when they defy its demands and refuse to repent. The illustrations in 5:19 teach that this coming judgment is inescapable. Amos is the first of Israel's prophets to mention the "day of the LORD". See note on Is 2:12 and word study: *The Day of the LORD* at Joel 1:15.

5:21-24 A scathing critique of northern Israel's worship. The oracle is not an attack on ritual or sacrificial worship per se since the Mosaic covenant called God's people to serve him in such ways (Lev 1–7). The real problem is that liturgy has been disconnected from morality. Going through the motions of religious ritual without observance of its ethical demands is rank hypocrisy that offends the Lord and makes even sacred actions empty and vain (Is 1:11-17; Jer 6:20; Mic 6:6-8). According to Scripture, there are several things more pleasing to God than ritual sacrifice, e.g., obedience (1 Sam 15:22), contrition (Ps 51:16-17), mercy (Hos 6:6), fear of the Lord (Jud 16:16), and the double love of God and neighbor (Mk 12:32-33) (CCC 2100).

5:21 hate: The same verb used in 5:10, 15. The repetition points to a direct connection between Israel's hatred of social justice and God's hatred of Israel's sacrificial worship.

5:22 you offer me: Not all of northern Israel's worship was idolatrous, but it was blatantly syncretistic, combining worship of the true God with the worship of false gods (cf. Hos 2:11-13). **burnt offerings:** See note on Lev 1:3-17. **cereal**

²³Take away from me the noise of your songs;
  to the melody of your harps I will not listen.
✗²⁴But let justice roll down like waters,
  and righteousness like an ever-flowing stream.

25 "Did you bring to me sacrifices and offerings the forty years in the wilderness, O house of Israel? ²⁶You shall take up Sakkuth your king, and Kai'wan your star-god, your images,ᵏ which you made for yourselves; ²⁷therefore I will take you into exile beyond Damascus," says the Lord, whose name is the God of hosts.

Punishment of Complacency and Pride

6 "Woe to those who are at ease in Zion,
  and to those who feel secure on the mountain
    of Samar'ia,
the notable men of the first of the nations,
  to whom the house of Israel come!
²Pass over to Cal'neh, and see;
  and from there go to Ha'math the great;
  then go down to Gath of the Philis'tines.

Are they better than these kingdoms?
  Or is their territory greater than your
    territory,
³O you who put far away the evil day,
  and bring near the seat of violence?

⁴"Woe to those who lie upon beds of ivory,
  and stretch themselves upon their
    couches,
and eat lambs from the flock,
  and calves from the midst of the stall;
⁵who sing idle songs to the sound of the harp,
  and like David invent for themselves
    instruments of music;
⁶who drink wine in bowls,
  and anoint themselves with the finest oils,
  but are not grieved over the ruin of Joseph!
⁷Therefore they shall now be the first of those to
    go into exile,
  and the revelry of those who stretch
    themselves shall pass away."

5:25–27: Acts 7:42–43.

---

offerings: See note on Lev 2:1–16. **peace offerings:** See note on Lev 3:1–17.

5:24 justice: The Hebrew *mishpaṭ* means a fair and unprejudiced application of the Mosaic Law to the entire covenant community, regardless of one's wealth or social standing. Amos is calling Israelites to defend the rights of the poor, to reject bribes that deny them justice, to stop seizing others' resources, and to cease gouging buyers in the marketplace (5:11–12; cf. 2:6–7; 4:1; 8:4–6) (CCC 1435; 2208; 2443–47). **righteousness:** A standard met by faithful adherence to the Lord's commandments (Deut 6:25; Lk 1:6). See word study: *Righteous* at Neh 9:8.

📖 **5:25 Did you bring me …?:** The answer is yes, but Israel's sacrifices in the wilderness did not have their intended effect of drawing God's people away from idolatry, a sin they succumbed to multiple times after leaving Egypt (Ex 32:6; Lev 17:7; Num 25:1–2). In Moses' time as in Amos' time, sacrificial worship and grievous sins against the covenant existed side by side. See essay: *Sacrifice in the Old Testament* at Lev 7. **forty years:** The time Israel spent wandering in the wilderness after leaving Egypt (2:10; Deut 8:2).

📖 **5:26 Sakkuth … Kaiwan:** Two Mesopotamian astral deities, rendered *Sikkût* and *Kiyyûn* in Hebrew. The former refers to the god Ninurta and the second is a name for the planet Saturn. These idols, venerated in northern Israel, will be unable to save their devotees from the destruction and exile that are coming; indeed, their images will go into captivity with them (cf. Is 46:1–2; Jer 48:7). • Stephen quotes a Greek version of this passage in a speech in Jerusalem before his martyrdom (Acts 7:42–43). The names of the deities appear differently in the translation he cites, but the rhetorical purpose is the same—to link Israel's history of idolatry in the past with contemporary sins of false worship. Stephen faults his Jewish hearers with making an idol of the Temple.

5:27 exile: The Assyrian exile of the northern tribes of Israel (2 Kings 15:29; 17:6). **beyond Damascus:** The Syrian city of Damascus lies directly between northern Israel and Assyria on a northeast trajectory.

6:1 Woe: See note on 5:18. **those who are at ease:** People deluded by a false sense of security despite the evildoing that thrives in their midst (2:4, 6–8). **Zion:** The mountain height of Jerusalem, the capital of the Southern Kingdom of Judah. **Samaria:** Capital of the Northern Kingdom of Israel. See note on 3:9. **notable men:** Amos targets the leading male citizens of Samaria, mirroring how he prophesied against its leading women in 4:1–3. **first of the nations:** Echoes the belief that Israel is God's "first-born" son (Ex 4:22) and "the chief of the nations" (Jer 31:7).

6:2 Calneh … Hamath … Gath: Calneh and Hamath were in Syria, north of Israel, and Gath was one of the five leading cites of the Philistines along the coastal strip west of Judah (1:6–8). Zion and Samaria are no more invincible than these other cities in the region, which were eventually overrun by the Assyrians.

6:3 the evil day: The day of the Lord's judgment (5:18). **seat of violence:** Seats of authority where corrupt judges made rulings that were demeaning and abusive to the poor (5:12).

6:4–7 Doom is pronounced on the wealthy aristocrats of Israel. They delighted in all the pleasures that money could buy, and yet they gave no thought to the misery they had brought upon others. Distracted by a life of self-indulgence, they were oblivious to the dreadful judgments that were headed their way. Amos warns that they shall be "the first of those to go into exile" (6:7).

6:4 Woe: See note on 5:18. **beds of ivory:** Luxury beds with ivory inlay (3:15).

📖 **6:5 David:** Remembered in Scripture as a gifted songwriter and musician (1 Sam 16:14–23). His mention implies a contrast: while David devoted his artistic talents to composing psalms of prayer and praise to the Lord (2 Sam 23:1), the banquet musicians in Amos' day merely provided entertainment for an elite crowd of partygoers.

6:6 anoint: The application of olive oil to the skin, often the forehead (Ps 23:5; Mt 6:17). **the ruin of Joseph:** Preoccupied with gratifying their desires, aristocrats were unbothered by the corruption and social injustice that prevailed in northern Israel. See note on 5:6.

ᵏHeb *your images, your star-god.*

[8]The Lord God has sworn by himself
(says the Lord, the God of hosts):
"I abhor the pride of Jacob,
and hate his strongholds;
and I will deliver up the city and all that is in it."

Oppression and Devastation to Come

9 And if ten men remain in one house, they shall die. [10]And when a man's kinsman, he who burns him,[1] shall take him up to bring the bones out of the house, and shall say to him who is in the innermost parts of the house, "Is there still any one with you?" he shall say, "No"; and he shall say, "Hush! We must not mention the name of the Lord."

[11]For behold, the Lord commands,
and the great house shall be struck down into fragments,
and the little house into bits.
[12]Do horses run upon rocks?
Does one plow the sea with oxen?
But you have turned justice into poison
and the fruit of righteousness into wormwood—
[13]you who rejoice in Lo-de'bar,[n]
who say, "Have we not by our own strength
taken Karna'im[o] for ourselves?"

[14]"For behold, I will raise up against you a nation,
O house of Israel," says the Lord, the God of hosts;
"and they shall oppress you from the entrance of Ha'math
to the Brook of the Ar'abah."

Locusts and Fire

7 Thus the Lord God showed me: behold, he was forming locusts in the beginning of the shooting up of the latter growth; and behold, it was the latter growth after the king's mowings. [2]When they had finished eating the grass of the land, I said,
"O Lord God, forgive, I beg you!
How can Jacob stand?
He is so small!"
[3]The Lord repented concerning this;
"It shall not be," said the Lord.

4 Thus the Lord God showed me: behold, the Lord God was calling for a judgment by fire, and it devoured the great deep and was eating up the land. [5]Then I said,
"O Lord God, cease, I beg you!
How can Jacob stand?
He is so small!"

6:8 God has sworn: A divine oath to bring northern Israel to judgment for its mass defection from the covenant. It is also mentioned in 4:2 and 8:7. by himself: Because there is no one greater by whom he could swear (Heb 6:13; cf. Gen 22:16; Is 45:23). pride: Arrogance has brought the Lord's punishment on many nations (e.g., Is 14:3-15; 16:6-14; Ezek 28:1-10). See note on Prov 16:18.

6:9-10 A segment of prose in the midst of poetic oracles. It envisions the horrors that survivors in Israel will face in the aftermath of conquest. Recognizing that the Lord brought death and devastation to the nation, they fear to rouse his anger again by speaking his name.

6:12 Do horses ... Does one plow: Common sense recognizes these scenarios as absurd, yet Israel's high society failed to grasp how their recklessness endangered the Northern Kingdom. upon rocks: Either jagged rocks or rock cliffs are meant. justice ... righteousness: See note on 5:24. wormwood: A plant with an exceedingly bitter taste (5:7; Prov 5:4; Lam 3:15).

6:13 Lo-debar ... Karnaim: Towns east of the Jordan River that were recently reclaimed by northern Israel when King Jeroboam II enlarged its borders (2 Kings 14:25). Israelites viewed this recovery as proof of their political and military strength. Amos points out, however, that two minor victories pale in comparison to the massive defeat that will sweep over the whole land of Israel (6:14).

6:14 a nation: Assyria. Hamath ... Brook of the Arabah: The northern and southern boundaries of the Promised Land (Num 34:5, 8). Hamath is identified with Lebweh, north of Damascus, and the Brook of the Arabah, also called the Brook of Egypt, is a wadi or seasonal watercourse that flows across the top of the Sinai Peninsula into the Mediterranean (Josh 15:4). Assyrian invaders will wreak havoc throughout the land, capturing northern Israel's territories (ca. 734-732 B.C.),

conquering its capital of Samaria (722 B.C.), and causing mass destruction in southern Israel as well (701 B.C.). See notes on 2 Kings 15:29, 17:1-41, and Is 1:7-9.

7:1—9:10 Five prophetic visions given to Amos. Each begins with an image of divine judgment and includes a prayer or dialogue between the Lord and his prophet. The first two highlight God's mercy, while the final three underscore his justice. A short narrative about Amos in Bethel stands between visions three and four (7:10-17).

7:1-3 In the first vision, Amos sees locusts devouring the green growth of northern Israel and destroying its spring harvest (7:1). The prophet cries out for mercy on Israel's behalf (7:2) and the Lord relents (7:3).

7:1 locusts: Hordes of these ravenous insects can ruin the farmlands and orchards of an entire region. Destruction of crops by a plague of locusts is one of the curses of the Mosaic Law upon those who defiantly transgress the covenant (Deut 28:38). For other instances of divine judgment by locusts, see Ex 10:12-15 and Joel 1:2-12. the king's mowings: Implies that the first portion of the harvest in northern Israel was collected to support the royal household (cf. 1 Kings 4:7).

7:2 forgive, I beg you: An instance of prophetic intercession, in which a covenant mediator pleads for God to stay or remove the hand of his judgment from Israel (Ex 32:31-32; Num 14:13-19; Dan 9:1-19; CCC 2584, 2634-36). Jacob: Israel (Gen 32:28).

7:3 The Lord repented: I.e., he withheld punishment by an act of mercy. The language of repentance applied to God has nothing to do with the Almighty ceasing from moral evil, since he is all-good and incapable of sinning as men do (Num 23:19). Scripture often describes the Lord in human terms in order to make his actions comprehensible to human minds. See notes on Gen 6:6 and 1 Sam 15:29.

7:4-6 In the second vision, Amos sees a raging fire devouring the sea and land (7:4). The prophet cries out for mercy (7:5), and again the Lord relents (7:6).

7:4 the great deep: The primordial ocean that engulfed the world in the beginning (Gen 1:2; Ps 104:6).

---

[1]Or *who makes a burning for him.*
[n]Or *a thing of nought.*
[o]Or *horns.*

⁶The LORD repented concerning this;
  "This also shall not be," said the Lord GOD.

The Plumb Line

7 He showed me: behold, the Lord was standing beside a wall built with a plumb line, with a plumb line in his hand. ⁸And the LORD said to me, "Amos, what do you see?" And I said, "A plumb line." Then the Lord said,

  "Behold, I am setting a plumb line
    in the midst of my people Israel;
    I will never again pass by them;
  ⁹the high places of Isaac shall be made desolate,
    and the sanctuaries of Israel shall be laid waste,
    and I will rise against the house of Jerobo'am
      with the sword."

Amaziah's Complaint

10 Then Amazi'ah the priest of Bethel sent to Jerobo'am king of Israel, saying, "Amos has conspired against you in the midst of the house of Israel; the land is not able to bear all his words. ¹¹For thus Amos has said,

  'Jerobo'am shall die by the sword,
    and Israel must go into exile away from his
      land.'"

¹²And Amazi'ah said to Amos, "O seer, go, flee away to the land of Judah, and eat bread there, and prophesy there; ¹³but never again prophesy at Bethel, for it is the king's sanctuary, and it is a temple of the kingdom."

Amos' Reply

14 Then Amos answered Amazi'ah, "I am no prophet, nor a prophet's son;ᴾ but I am a herdsman, and a dresser of sycamore trees, ¹⁵and the LORD took me from following the flock, and the LORD said to me, 'Go, prophesy to my people Israel.'
¹⁶Now therefore hear the word of the LORD.

  You say, 'Do not prophesy against Israel,
    and do not preach against the house of
      Isaac.'
¹⁷Therefore thus says the LORD:
  'Your wife shall be a harlot in the city,
    and your sons and your daughters shall fall
      by the sword,
    and your land shall be parceled out by
      line;
  you yourself shall die in an unclean land,
    and Israel shall surely go into exile away from
      its land.'"

7:7–9 In the third vision, Amos sees a plumb line, indicating that northern Israel, when measured by the standard of God's justice, is as crooked as a wall that is about to collapse. The prophet does not intercede for Israel after this vision, suggesting he has come to realize that judgment is both deserved and destined to come. As indicated in 4:6-13, punishment comes when opportunities for repentance are squandered.

7:7 plumb line: A mason's line, weighted on one end, that was used to determine the vertical alignment of a wall. If the plumb line revealed structural unsoundness such as bulging, bowing, or leaning, the wall was torn down (2 Kings 21:13; Lam 2:8).

7:9 high places: Illicit sanctuaries. See word study: *High Places* at 2 Kings 23:5. **house of Jeroboam:** The royal family of Jeroboam II, ruler of the Northern Kingdom of Israel from 793 to 753 B.C. **sword:** Jeroboam II's son Zechariah was slain in 752 B.C. (2 Kings 15:8-10).

7:10–17 A narrative interlude about Amos' confrontation with the priest Amaziah in Bethel. Amaziah falsely accuses Amos of treachery against northern Israel's king and demands that he return to his native Judah in the south (7:10-13). Amos insists that he is not a prophet by trade, but one uniquely called by God with a message for northern Israel (7:14-17). The story is placed here for thematic reasons: Amos announced the demise of Jeroboam's house in 7:9, and this is the cause of Amaziah's ire according to 7:11. The account also supplies the backstory for Amos' oracle against Amaziah in 7:17.

7:10 the priest: Amaziah is the chief priest of the Bethel shrine, where a golden calf image was venerated (1 Kings 12:28-29; Hos 10:5). **Bethel:** See note on 3:14. **conspired against you:** A distortion of the truth, as if Amos were part of a plot to assassinate the king. **the land is not able to bear:** Ironically, it is not the preaching of Amos that threatens the land but the judgments of the Lord, which can both devour the land (7:1-2, 4) and remove the northern tribes from it (7:11).

7:11 into exile: The Assyrian Exile, accomplished by several deportations between 734 and 722 B.C. During these years, Israel's northern tribes were dispersed as captives into distant lands, never again to return to home (2 Kings 15:29; 17:6; 1 Chron 5:26). Amos foretells the Assyrian Exile of northern Israel several times in the book (4:2-3; 5:5, 27; 6:7; 7:17). • Israel's dispersion and exile from the Promised Land is the climactic curse of the Mosaic covenant (Deut 28:63-68).

7:12 seer: An archaic name for a prophet (1 Sam 9:9).

7:13 the king's sanctuary: The calf shrine in Bethel was sanctioned by Jeroboam II and possibly funded with a royal endowment. **the kingdom:** The Northern Kingdom of Israel.

7:14 I am no prophet: Amos denies that he is a prophet by profession, i.e., one who speaks oracles in exchange for payments of money or food (1 Sam 9:7; Mic 3:5). He thus counters Amaziah's insinuation that financial opportunity is the motive behind his ministry. On the contrary, he is already making a living as a keeper of livestock and a seasonal orchard worker. Amos' words are not a denial that God called him to prophesy for a time. See note on 1:1. **nor a prophet's son:** Amos denies being a member of a prophetic guild, where students of a senior prophet were called his "sons". See note on 2 Kings 2:3. **sycamore trees:** A species of fig tree. Dressing sycamores meant that cuts were made in the ripening figs so that they might become sweet. These trees grew in low-lying regions such as Jericho and the Shephelah but not in Amos' home of Tekoa (1:1), implying the prophet divided his time, working at different times of the year as a shepherd in the highlands of Judah and as a sycamore dresser in the lowlands of Judah.

7:15 Go, prophesy: Amos was commanded to speak God's word, regardless of opposition from godless or uncomprehending men (Acts 5:29).

7:17 Your wife ... sons ... land: Amaziah and his family will suffer bitterly for his opposition to God's messenger. These hardships will come when Assyria conquers and exiles northern Israel. **harlot:** Amaziah's wife will face such desperation that she will resort to prostitution to support herself after losing her husband, children, and family property. **into exile:** See note on 7:11.

ᴾ Or *one of the sons of the prophets.*

The Basket of Summer Fruit

8 Thus the Lord GOD showed me: behold, a basket of summer fruit.[q] [2]And he said, "Amos, what do you see?" And I said, "A basket of summer fruit."[q] Then the LORD said to me,

"The end[r] has come upon my people Israel;
  I will never again pass by them.
[3]The songs of the temple[s] shall become wailings
    in that day,"

says the Lord GOD;

"the dead bodies shall be many;
  in every place they shall be cast out in silence."[t]

[4]Hear this, you who trample upon the needy,
  and bring the poor of the land to an end,
[5]saying, "When will the new moon be over,
    that we may sell grain?
And the sabbath,
    that we may offer wheat for sale,
that we may make the ephah small and the
    shekel great,
  and deal deceitfully with false balances,

[6]that we may buy the poor for silver
  and the needy for a pair of sandals,
  and sell the refuse of the wheat?"

[7]The LORD has sworn by the pride of Jacob:
  "Surely I will never forget any of their deeds.
[8]Shall not the land tremble on this account,
  and every one mourn who dwells in it,
  and all of it rise like the Nile,
    and be tossed about and sink again, like the
      Nile of Egypt?"

[9]"And on that day," says the Lord GOD,
  "I will make the sun go down at noon,
  and darken the earth in broad daylight.
[10]I will turn your feasts into mourning,
  and all your songs into lamentation;
I will bring sackcloth upon all loins,
  and baldness on every head;
I will make it like the mourning for an only
    son,
  and the end of it like a bitter day.

8:1–3 In the fourth vision, Amos sees a basket of summer fruit and learns that northern Israel's end is at hand. This is indicated by wordplay and symbolic association. **(1)** The Hebrew term *qayiṣ*, translated "summer fruit" (8:1), resembles the sound of the word *qēṣ*, meaning "end" (8:2). **(2)** Summer fruits such as figs, grapes, and pomegranates were ready for picking in late August and September, at the end of the harvest season. The image symbolizes that Israel's time of growth is now over; the nation is ripe for a harvest of judgment. For the harvest as an image of divine reckoning, see Hos 6:11; Joel 3:13; Mt 13:39; Rev 14:15.

8:3 songs of the temple: Unclear whether this refers to liturgical music or to the music of the licentious banquets described in 6:4–7. The latter seems more likely (understanding that the word "temple" can also mean "palace"). Either way, the sounds of celebration will soon become lamentation. **dead bodies ... in every place:** Corpses will be strewn throughout northern Israel after the Assyrian conquest.

8:4–6 Amos decries the greed, dishonesty, callousness, and hypocrisy of wealthy merchants. They are so desirous of gain that they defraud buyers in the marketplace and take advantage of the poor, all the while following impatiently the outward observances of the Mosaic Law. See note on 5:21–24.

8:4 trample: Amos' graphic way of describing the ruthless exploitation of people in poverty (2:7; 5:11) (CCC 2449). **Bring ... to an end:** Extorting the poor in the food market can only weaken their health and hasten their death, making those responsible guilty of grave offenses (CCC 2269).

8:5 new moon ... sabbath: Holy days of the Mosaic liturgical calendar. Conducting business was forbidden on the weekly Sabbath according to the Torah (Lev 23:3) and on the monthly New Moon feast according to tradition (Num 28:11–15). **ephah:** A dry measure slightly more than half a bushel. **shekel:** A coin weighing about 11 grams. **false balances:** A marketplace scam of tilting scales in favor of the seller and against the buyer. The Torah demands "just balances" (Lev 19:36), and Proverbs warns that false balances are "an abomination to the LORD" (Prov 11:1). • According to Catholic teaching, business fraud and price gouging are violations of the seventh commandment, "You shall not steal" (CCC 2409).

8:6 buy the poor: A reference to debt slavery, in which persons facing extreme financial hardship could sell themselves into servitude as a means of survival and debt repayment. **sell the refuse:** Grains were measured and sold while mixed with useless chaff, thus cheating the customer.

8:7–14 God's wrath will come upon northern Israel as an earthquake (8:8), an eclipse (8:9), a famine of the word of God (8:11), and a drought (8:13).

8:7 The LORD has sworn: A divine oath to bring northern Israel to judgment for its mass defection from the covenant. It is also mentioned in 4:2 and 6:8.

8:8 Shall not the land tremble: God also promises to shake the house of Israel in 9:1 and 9:9. The earthquake that occurred two years after Amos spoke was probably viewed as a sign that his words were divinely inspired (1:1). **like the Nile:** Egypt's great river undergoes a yearly inundation, cresting in late summer and reaching its lowest level in late spring. Destruction caused by mass flooding is in view.

8:9 that day: The great and terrible "day of the LORD" when northern Israel will face the darkness of its demise (5:18–20). **make the sun go down:** A solar eclipse at midday when the sun shines brightest. • Amos' vision stands behind the Gospel accounts of the Crucifixion, which describe darkness at noon, an earthquake, and mourning for the death of God's only Son (compare 8:8–10 with Mt 27:45, 51, 54; Lk 23:44–45, 48). • The one who spoke these words clearly announced the darkening of the sun that took place at Jesus' Crucifixion from the sixth hour onward (St. Irenaeus, *Against Heresies* 4, 33, 12). • When they gave the Lord of all over to Crucifixion, the sun went down, and the light became dark. This signified the spiritual darkening of the souls who had crucified him (St. Cyril of Alexandria, *Commentary on Amos* 8, 9).

8:10 feasts into mourning: See note on Tob 2:6. **sackcloth:** A coarse fabric spun from goat hair and worn in times of grief (Gen 37:34).

---

[q] Heb *qayits*.
[r] Heb *qets*.
[s] or *palace*.
[t] or *be silent!*

11"Behold, the days are coming," says the Lord
  God,
  "when I will send a famine on the land;
not a famine of bread, nor a thirst for water,
  but of hearing the words of the Lord.
12They shall wander from sea to sea,
  and from north to east;
they shall run back and forth, to seek the word of
  the Lord,
  but they shall not find it.

13"In that day the fair virgins and the young men
  shall faint for thirst.
14Those who swear by Ash′imah of Samar′ia,
  and say, 'As your god lives, O Dan,'
and, 'As the way of Be′er-she′ba lives,'
  they shall fall, and never rise again."

Destruction, Captivity, and Restoration

9 I saw the Lord standing beside[u] the altar, and
  he said:
  "Strike the capitals until the thresholds shake,
  and shatter them on the heads of all the people;[v]
and what are left of them I will slay with the
  sword;
  not one of them shall flee away,
  not one of them shall escape.

2"Though they dig into Sheol,
  from there shall my hand take them;
though they climb up to heaven,
  from there I will bring them down.
3Though they hide themselves on the top of
  Carmel,
  from there I will search out and take them;

and though they hide from my sight at the
  bottom of the sea,
  there I will command the serpent, and it shall
  bite them.
4And though they go into captivity before their
  enemies,
  there I will command the sword, and it shall
  slay them;
and I will set my eyes upon them for evil and not
  for good."

5The Lord, God of hosts,
  he who touches the earth and it melts,
  and all who dwell in it mourn,
and all of it rises like the Nile,
  and sinks again, like the Nile of Egypt;
6who builds his upper chambers in the heavens,
  and founds his vault upon the earth;
who calls for the waters of the sea,
  and pours them out upon the surface of the
  earth—
  the Lord is his name.

7"Are you not like the Ethiopians to me,
  O people of Israel?" says the Lord.
"Did I not bring up Israel from the land of Egypt,
  and the Philis′tines from Caphtor and the
  Syrians from Kir?
8Behold, the eyes of the Lord God are upon the
  sinful kingdom,
  and I will destroy it from the surface of the
  ground;
except that I will not utterly destroy the house
  of Jacob,"
  says the Lord.

8:11 not a famine of bread: Scarcity of the word of God is the just punishment for rejecting the word of God. Amos appears to say that rebellious Israel, crushed and driven into exile by the Assyrians, will soon be deprived of prophetic instruction. The idea is that man "lives" not by bread alone but by obedience to the Lord's word (Deut 8:3).

8:13 virgins ... young men: Even the strong and youthful of Israel's next generation will perish.

8:14 Ashimah: A goddess worshiped in Hamath, Syria, and in Samaria, the capital of northern Israel (2 Kings 17:30). It is also possible to translate Ashimah as "guilt", indicating that Samaria's idol was a cause of great iniquity. **Dan:** Home to a golden calf shrine in northern Israel (1 Kings 12:28–29). **Beersheba:** The site of an unlawful shrine or high place in southern Judah (2 Kings 23:8).

9:1–10 In the fifth vision, Amos sees the Lord standing beside an altar and hears him pronouncing a final sentence of doom on northern Israel. He learns that none will escape the coming disaster (9:2–4), and not even Israel's election as God's chosen people will afford the northern tribes protection (9:7). The only glimmer of hope is that God will stop short of wiping out the entire population of Israel when he destroys their kingdom (9:8). A hymn extolling the Lord's power forms an interlude to the divine speech (9:5–6).

9:1 the altar: Probably the main altar in the sanctuary at Bethel (3:14), which Amos foretold would "come to nothing" (5:5). Judgment is envisioned as a temple with pillars collapsing on worshipers and killing them (cf. Judg 16:23–30). This appears to be the result of God "shaking" northern Israel with an earthquake (8:8; 9:9).

9:2 Sheol: Hebrew name for the netherworld of the dead. See word study: *Sheol* at Num 16:30.

9:3 Carmel: A fertile mountain in northwest Israel (south of modern Haifa). **the serpent:** A multiheaded sea dragon, called Leviathan, that represents the forces of evil and chaos in Semitic mythology (Ps 74:14; Is 27:1). See word study: *Leviathan* at Job 41:1.

9:4 evil: See note on 3:6.

9:5 God: See note on 1:8. **hosts:** See note on 4:13. **like the Nile:** See note on 8:8.

9:7 Are you not like: A rhetorical question indicating that God has been gracious to nations other than Israel. Even the Exodus from Egypt is not without parallel in the historical migrations of other peoples of the biblical world. **Ethiopians:** The Nubians, who dwelt south of Egypt near the sources of the Nile River. **Philistines:** Enemies of Israel who occupied the southwest coast of Canaan. **Caphtor:** The island of Crete (Jer 47:4). **Syrians:** Arameans. **Kir:** Somewhere in Mesopotamia (2 Kings 16:9).

9:8 I will not utterly destroy: God will leave a remnant of survivors. See note on 3:12.

---

[u] Or *upon*.
[v] Heb *all of them*.

⁹"For behold, I will command,
  and shake the house of Israel among all the
    nations
as one shakes with a sieve,
  but no pebble shall fall upon the earth.
¹⁰All the sinners of my people shall die by the
    sword,
  who say, 'Evil shall not overtake or meet us.'

¹¹"In that day I will raise up
  the booth of David that is fallen
and repair its breaches,
  and raise up its ruins,
  and rebuild it as in the days of old;
¹²that they may possess the remnant of E'dom
  and all the nations who are called by my name,"
  says the LORD who does this.

¹³"Behold, the days are coming," says the LORD,
  "when the plowman shall overtake the reaper
    and the treader of grapes him who sows the
      seed;
the mountains shall drip sweet wine,
  and all the hills shall flow with it.
¹⁴I will restore the fortunes of my people Israel,
  and they shall rebuild the ruined cities and
    inhabit them;
they shall plant vineyards and drink their wine,
  and they shall make gardens and eat their
    fruit.
¹⁵I will plant them upon their land,
  and they shall never again be plucked up
  out of the land which I have given them,"
                                                says the LORD your God.

9:9 a sieve: Used to sift the Northern Kingdom of Israel, separating those to be slain by the sword from those destined for exile (cf. Sir 27:4).

9:10 Evil shall not overtake: The self-incriminating words of the wicked.

9:11–15 The book concludes with an oracle of restoration. The Lord declares his intention to rebuild David's fallen kingdom (9:11–12) and to restore the fortunes of Israel's scattered exiles (9:13–15). This comes as welcome news at the end of a book dominated by oracles of condemnation. Many scholars attribute these final verses, not to Amos, but to an editor of the sixth century B.C. This hypothesis is not impossible, but the case is less than convincing. Other scholars have identified verbal and thematic links between 9:11–15 and oracles of the book that date to the time of Amos in the eighth century B.C.

9:11 booth of David: The kingdom of David, pictured as a small shelter or hut (Heb., *sukkāh*). The Greek LXX translates *skēnē*, "tent" (cf. Is 16:5). **fallen:** Not that David's royal house had ceased to exist, since his descendants continued to rule the Southern Kingdom of Judah in Amos' day, but that it had fallen from its former glory and had ceased to be what God intended. The Lord willed that David and his successors would unite all twelve tribes of Israel under one rule (2 Sam 5:1–5) and extend Israel's dominion over other nations as well (2 Sam 8:1–15; Ps 2:8; 72:8–11). This arrangement held firm during the reigns of David and Solomon (1 Kings 4:21) but fell apart after the northern tribes broke away from Davidic rule in 930 B.C., which began the period of the divided monarchy (1 Kings 12:1–20). From Amos' perspective in the eighth century B.C., the kingdom of David had already fallen into disrepair, even though a small part of David's kingdom survived in Judah. The destruction and exile of northern Israel added a note of finality to the kingdom's fallenness. It created a dire situation that only God could repair. For a future reunion of Israel and Judah, see Is 11:13–14; Ezek 37:15–28; Hos 1:11. **rebuild:** Israel's messianic hope was not simply that God would send a new Davidic king (Hos 3:5) but that he would rebuild the Davidic kingdom (Mk 11:10). **the days of old:** The future kingdom is modeled on the united monarchy of David and Solomon. • Amos 9:11–12 is quoted at the Council of Jerusalem. On the premise that Jesus is the messianic heir of David (Acts 2:30–36), the apostles see the upbuilding of the Church as the rebuilding of David's kingdom, which not only unites the believers of Israel around the Davidic Messiah but gathers Gentiles into his kingdom as well (Acts 15:16–18). See essay: *Kingdom Restoration* at Acts 15.

9:12 the remnant of Edom: Surviving descendants of Jacob's brother, Esau, identified in Genesis as Edomites (Gen 25:23). They inhabited the highlands south of the Dead Sea for much of biblical history. David had incorporated the Edomites into his kingdom (2 Sam 8:13–14). The Greek LXX translates "the remnant of men", reading the Hebrew letters '-d-m as the word *'ādām* ("mankind") rather than *'edōm* ("Edom"). **all the nations:** Belong to the Lord. Israel is God's special possession, but not his only possession, since "all the earth" is his (Ex 19:5).

9:13 plowman ... reaper ... treader: Signs of an extremely bountiful harvest season that stretches into the next plowing and sowing season. Grains were harvested in April and May, and vintage crops in August and September, whereas plowing and seed planting were done in November/December. **drip sweet wine:** Points to a superabundant harvest of grapes. Mountains flowing with wine is a sign of the messianic blessings to come (Joel 3:18), as is the feast with fine wine that Isaiah foresees on Mt. Zion (Is 25:6–8).

9:14 rebuild ... inhabit ... plant ... drink: A point-by-point reversal of 5:11. For similar scenes of starting a new life after exile, see Is 65:21 and Ezek 28:26.

9:15 I will plant them: Like a healthy vine that takes deep root (Ps 80:8–9). For God's promise to plant Israel in a place that is secure and undisturbed, see 2 Sam 7:10.

STUDY QUESTIONS
Amos

Chapter 1

For understanding

1. **1:3—2:16.** Against which specific nations are these oracles directed? With what crimes are these neighboring nations charged? To what is the latter crime related? Against whom are the final two oracles spoken, and with what are they charged?

2. **1:3.** To what does the Hebrew of this verse refer? As a type of progressive parallelism using successive numbers in parallel lines of poetry, where is the rhetorical emphasis placed? To what does the number four refer here? Where is Damascus in relation to the Sea of Galilee? Where is Gilead? What are threshing sledges, and of what is threshing an image?

3. **Essay: Oracles against the Nations in the Minor Prophets.** Since the Minor Prophets often announce God's displeasure with specific Gentile nations, how might a superficial reading of these passages lead to an inaccurate assessment; in other words, for what are these nations actually faulted? How do these prophetic "oracles against the nations" show us a God whose concern for righteousness is universal? What theological claim, then, do these prophetic "oracles against the nations" establish?

4. **1:13.** Where was Ammon, and how does Scripture identify the Ammonites? In what does the barbaric practice of "ripping up women" consist, and what was the purpose of this wartime tactic? According to St. Gregory the Great, how is the Church as a witness to the truth represented by Gilead in the face of false teachers?

For application

1. **1:3.** Threshing is sometimes used as an analogy for spiritual purification. Based on the physical process of threshing grain, what is supposed to happen spiritually? How has the threshing action of the Holy Spirit taken place in your spiritual life?

2. **1:6-8.** The note for v. 6 refers to the ancient slave trade. How is slavery practiced today? How endemic is it in our own country? How would you recognize that a person you meet is actually in bondage to someone else, and what might you do about it?

3. **1:13.** In the comment by Pope St. Gregory the Great, quoted in the note for this verse, the pope describes how false teachers cut out the conception of truth from the minds of the faithful. How does false propaganda try to convince people that its message is true? For example, how would an attorney for a clearly guilty defendant try to "frame the narrative" in his client's favor? How does a person interested in the truth counter such tactics?

Chapter 2

For understanding

1. **2:6-16.** Why does this last and longest oracle of judgment come upon Israel as a rhetorical bombshell? What was the sequence of divine rebukes, moving from neighboring pagans (Syria, Philistia, Tyre) to neighboring cousins (Edom, Ammon, Moab) to neighboring brothers (Judah), designed to produce?

2. **2:8.** What setting does "beside every altar" suggest? Of what are "garments taken in pledge" a form? Why does the Mosaic Law stipulate that an article of clothing given as a pledge must be returned before sundown? Why does Amos allude here to Bethel, which translates "house of God"? Why was wine taken from the common people?

3. **2:11.** Who become prophets? Of what was northern Israel guilty concerning them? Who are Nazirites? Of what was northern Israel guilty in their regard?

4. **2:13-16.** What does this announcement of the coming judgment say Israel will face? Historically, when was this carried out?

For application

1. **2:4.** What makes lies so malicious? How do lies work so as to lead hearers astray? How much of the truth needs to be contained in a lie so as to convince the hearer?

2. **2:6.** What would you call the practice of raising the price of a product seen as necessary for life, such as a medication, to where buyers can only pay for it with difficulty? What are some motives behind this form of extortion? Which commandment does it violate?

3. **2:12.** What happens within a community of strict observance when, either in response to complaints or out of an ideology, the leadership begins to relax the rules? How long will that community continue to respect the original rule? What often happens when the Church relaxes disciplines such as fasting or attendance at liturgy? What happens to virtue when its practice is no longer seen as necessary?

Chapter 3

For understanding

1. **3:1.** Although his indictment targets the Northern Kingdom of Israel specifically, to whom does Amos address himself inclusively? What is the purpose of speaking to the whole covenant community?

2. **3:2.** How does this oracle point to Israel's special relationship with the Lord? While Israel's election is not just a privilege, with what responsibility does it come? When Israel fails in national obedience, as in Amos' day, what must it face? How do the words of Jesus apply here?

3. **3:6.** What does the Hebrew *rā'āh* mean here? If Amos is not making a general statement that God is the cause of every misfortune that cities face, what is his point? What does Amos want Israel to understand? According to St. John of Damascus, what two meanings does evil have? Why does the second of these two seem to be evil when, in fact, it is good? According to St. Thomas Aquinas, in what sense is God the author of evil?

Study Questions

4.   **3:14.** Where is Bethel? For what was it known? What would the altars of Bethel have functioned as? How does Amos view Bethel? What feature did many altars in biblical Israel have?

For Application
1.   **3:2.** The note for this verse refers to the responsibilities Israel had to keep the covenant. What rights does a person have who has been validly baptized? What responsibilities go along with those rights?
2.   **3:6.** Sin has consequences, some of which may be years in coming. What consequences might reasonably be expected from certain addictions, such as to alcohol, drugs, or pornography? How might their consequences affect persons not directly involved in those addictions? What role does God have in causing such consequences?
3.   **3:8.** What is the role of a prophet? How does one distinguish a true prophet from a false one? If a prophet is proved to be true, why is he so often disbelieved?
4.   **3:14.** If the horn signifies strength or power, and four of them are placed on an altar of sacrifice, what is the significance of having them cut off? For a Christian, who provides the "horn of salvation"?

Chapter 4

For understanding
1.   **4:1.** Why are the wealthy matrons of Samaria compared to well-fed cattle? What is the prophet implying? What is Samaria? How does Amos describe Samaria's affluent women as reveling in luxuries furnished by unjustly obtained wealth? What were they accused of drinking?
2.   **4:4–5.** How does the prophet employ sarcasm in these verses? Why is northern Israel's worship unacceptable to God?
3.   **4:6–11.** In what way are the five instances in which the Lord chastised sinful Israel in these verses not signs of rejection but appeals for repentance? What was the refrain that indicates that these warnings tragically went unheeded?
4.   **4:12.** What is so terrifying about the announcement of divine confrontation here?

For application
1.   **4:1.** In our culture, who are the poor and needy? How are the wealthy pampered at their expense? What moral judgment attaches to the wealthy who claim to be unaware of the needy in their midst or who believe that the poor are responsible for their own poverty?
2.   **4:5.** What are some examples of false spirituality in our time? What does a person mean who claims to be spiritual but not religious? Bearing in mind Amos' sarcasm in this verse, what encouragement if any should be given to those who pursue "non-religious" spirituality?
3.   **4:6–11.** Read the note for these verses. Has the Lord ever used hard times and negative experiences as a way of getting you to pay attention to him? If so, how long did it take you to realize his purpose in these events? When was your moment of turning?
4.   **4:12.** How prepared are you to meet your God? What form should your preparation take? For example, what relationships should you repair, what offenses should you forgive, what goods or even attitudes should you eliminate?

Chapter 5

For understanding
1.   **5:8.** To what are the constellations Pleiades and Orion related? To what do the luminaries in the day and night sky bear witness, and what was Israel forbidden to do toward them?
2.   **5:12.** What makes taking a bribe immoral for judges? In the words of the Torah, what does a bribe do? What was the importance of the city gate?
3.   **5:18.** What purpose do the three funeral dirges introduced here serve? What is "the day of the LORD"? What did the northern Israelites wrongly suppose? Not exempted from the dreaded day of the Lord, when do the covenant people make themselves a target? Who is the first of Israel's prophets to mention the "day of the LORD"?
4.   **5:21–24.** With what are these verses concerned? If this oracle is not an attack on ritual or sacrificial worship per se, what is the real problem? According to Scripture, what things are more pleasing to God than ritual sacrifice?
5.   **5:26.** What are Sakkuth and Kaiwan? To what do they refer? What will these idols, venerated in northern Israel, be powerless to do? Though the names of the deities appear differently in the Greek version the deacon Stephen cites before his martyrdom, how is his rhetorical purpose the same as that of Amos'? With what does Stephen fault his Jewish hearers?

For application
1.   **5:4.** According to the note for this verse, what is included in the call to seek the Lord? How often do you seek him this way?
2.   **5:10.** When you were a child, how did you respond emotionally to your parents' corrections? As an adult, how do you regard a peer who corrects you, especially on a moral issue? Why is correction so hard to take and so easy to avoid?
3.   **5:13.** In an age where anything posted on social media is seen by the world, what often happens to a person who states a moral opinion on the Internet? What does prudence counsel when responses are hostile or inflammatory?
4.   **5:14–15.** In an age when good and evil are reversed, where evil is considered good and good evil (cf. Is 5:20), how does one distinguish right from wrong? What does the person who seeks the true good become for the age in which he lives?

Chapter 6

For understanding
1.   **6:4–7.** Why is doom pronounced on the wealthy aristocrats of Israel? Distracted by a life of self-indulgence, to what were they oblivious? Of what does Amos warn them?
2.   **6:5.** How is David remembered in Scripture? What contrast does his mention imply?

74

3. **6:13.** What were Lo-debar and Karnaim? While Israelites viewed this recovery of territory as proof of their political and military strength, to what does Amos point?
4. **6:14.** As the northern and southern boundaries of the Promised Land, with what modern city is Hamath identified, and where is the Brook of the Arabah? How will the Assyrian invaders wreak havoc throughout the land?

For application
1. **6:1.** Why do some say that a totalitarian regime, like that of Communist Russia, cannot take over this country? What explains their confidence that such a thing is impossible? How confident are you in the inviolability of our country?
2. **6:3.** What is a Ponzi scheme? How long do those who organize and recruit "investors" hope their pyramid scheme will last? What happens to everyone involved on the day of reckoning when the scheme disintegrates?
3. **6:6.** Assuming you live a fairly comfortable life, what thought have you given to the homeless and hungry of your own environment? Assuming you live a virtuous life, what grief have you felt over the moral disintegration of the country? To what concrete actions have your thoughts and feelings led you?

Chapter 7

For understanding
1. **7:3.** What does it mean to say that "the LORD repented"? Why does the language of repentance applied to God have nothing to do with the Almighty ceasing from moral evil? Why does Scripture often describe the Lord in human terms?
2. **7:7-9.** What does Amos' third vision of the plumb line indicate regarding northern Israel? Because the prophet does not intercede for Israel after this vision, what does this suggest that he realizes? As indicated earlier, when does punishment come?
3. **7:10-17.** In this narrative interlude, of what has Amaziah falsely accused Amos? What does Amos insist about himself? Why is this story placed here?
4. **7:14.** What does Amos' denial that he is a prophet by profession mean? How does he thus counter Amaziah's insinuation that financial opportunity is the motive behind his ministry? Why does he deny that he is a prophet's son? What is involved in dressing sycamores? What does the fact that trees grew in low-lying regions such as Jericho and the Shephelah but not in Amos' home of Tekoa imply about how the prophet divided his time?

For application
1. **7:2-6.** What is your experience of intercessory prayer? For whom or what do you typically intercede? According to 1 Jn 5:14-15, when is intercessory prayer most effective?
2. **7:7-9.** Read the note for these verses. If you were to intercede regularly for the resolution of a difficult situation, what conditions might prompt you to stop praying for it? How long would you persevere in praying for the conversion of a person who shows no signs of changing?
3. **7:12-13.** How welcome is the Christian gospel in today's public square? What penalties have some businesses and universities imposed on Christian employees and faculty members whose comments cross their "core values"? How confident are you that your own Christian beliefs are safe from attack?
4. **7:15.** What should hinder you from witnessing to your faith in the public square? What mandate do you have to do so (Mt 28:19-20)?

Chapter 8

For understanding
1. **8:1-3.** In his fourth vision of the basket of summer fruit, what does Amos learn? How is this indicated through the wordplay and symbolic association? What does the harvesting of summer fruits symbolize about Israel's time of growth?
2. **8:5.** How important are the new moon and the Sabbath? When was conducting business forbidden? What is an ephah? A shekel? What are false balances? What do the Torah and the Book of Proverbs say about balances? According to Catholic teaching, which commandment do business fraud and price gouging violate?
3. **8:9.** What is "that day"? How does the sun go down at noon? What Gospel account does Amos' vision stand behind? According to St. Irenaeus, what did the one who spoke these words clearly announce? According to St. Cyril of Alexandria, what did the darkening of the sun at the Crucifixion signify?
4. **8:11.** For what is a famine of the word of God a just punishment? What does Amos appear to say about rebellious Israel? What is the idea behind this?

For application
1. **8:4-6.** What are some economic opportunities that are either denied to or restricted for certain racial, ethnic, or religious minorities? Who manipulates the law to give the appearance of legality to these restrictions? How might these injustices have affected you or your family?
2. **8:9.** What is the modern attitude toward a total eclipse of the sun? What are some differences between our view of such events and the view suggested in this verse? If moderns do not regard eclipses as omens of divine judgment, what *would* become such an omen for us?
3. **8:11-12.** What famine of hearing the words of the Lord does our culture experience today? How is it manifested? What may be the causes of such a famine?

Chapter 9

For understanding
1. **9:1-10.** In his fifth vision, what does Amos see the Lord doing and hear him saying? What does he learn about the coming disaster? What is the only glimmer of hope? What forms an interlude to the divine speech?

2. **9:11–15.** How does the book conclude? What does the Lord declare as his intention? To whom do many scholars attribute these final verses? What do other scholars find that dates the book to the time of Amos in the eighth century B.C.?
3. **9:11.** What is the "booth" of David? What does it mean that the booth of David has fallen? What did the Lord will that David and his successors would do? How long did this arrangement actually hold, and when did it fall apart? From Amos' perspective in the eighth century B.C., what had already happened to the kingdom of David? What did the destruction and exile of northern Israel create? What was Israel's messianic hope? On what is the future kingdom modeled? On what premise do the apostles see the upbuilding of the Church as the rebuilding of David's kingdom?
4. **9:13.** Of what are the visions of the plowman, the reaper, and the treader of grapes the signs? When were grains and vintage crops harvested and plowing and seed planting done? Of what are mountains flowing with wine a sign?

For application
1. **9:2–3.** According to Ps 139, how far does God's knowledge of you extend? If you wished to hide from him because of your sins, how would you do it? With what invitation to the Lord does the psalm end, and how might it apply to you?
2. **9:9.** Why would a gardener shake a substance such as rocky soil through a sieve? When a marriage is shaken as with a sieve, what ideally should remain and what should fall away? How might the Lord be shaking the Church in these days, and what hope should come from that process?
3. **9:11.** Read the note for this verse, particularly the last two sentences. Has the upbuilding of the Church completed the rebuilding of the Davidic kingdom? If not, what remains to be done?
4. **9:14.** How does this verse affect your vision of what heaven is like? If a person is judged on the basis of his works, what works are most suited to the attainment of heaven? How will heaven include enjoyment of the fruit of those works?

INTRODUCTION TO OBADIAH

Author and Date Nothing certain is known about the prophet who received the "vision" recounted in this book. The superscription in 1:1 provides no biographical information that would help readers to identify Obadiah beyond his name; nor does it provide historical background that would help to place him on the timeline of Old Testament events. Jewish tradition describes Obadiah as a disciple of the prophet Elijah (*Lives of the Prophets* 9, 2) and identifies him with the royal steward in 1 Kings 18:1–16 who served under King Ahab of Israel in the ninth century B.C. (Babylonian Talmud, *Sanhedrin* 39b). These ancient traditions are not historically impossible, given that a man named Obadiah appears as a prominent figure in 1 Kings 18, but neither are they probable on this basis. Obadiah was a popular name in biblical times. At least twelve different individuals, spread out over several centuries of Israel's history, bear this name in the Old Testament.

Some modern scholars have dated the Book of Obadiah in the ninth century B.C., proposing that Edom's revolt from the rule of King Jehoram of Judah about 845 B.C. is the historical situation that called forth the oracles of the book (2 Chron 21:8–10). This view has a measure of plausibility when we consider that hordes of Philistines and Arabs invaded the land of Judah and plundered Jerusalem in the aftermath of Edom regaining its independence (2 Chron 21:16–17). But while one can recognize broad similarities between these events and the circumstances described in Obadiah, the parallels fall short of a tight fit, not least because the Bible preserves no memory of Edom participating in the Philistine-Arab assault at this time. Yet the prophet charges the Edomites with multiple counts of violence and theft against Judah and Jerusalem at a time when foreigners brought ruin upon the covenant people and their capital city. These circumstances, described in Obadiah 10–14, suggest to most biblical scholars that the prophet delivered his message after Babylonian invaders ravaged the land of Judah, laid waste to the city and Temple of Jerusalem, and took thousands into exile in 586 B.C. This is precisely the time, according to other passages of Scripture, when the Edomites took advantage of Judah's distress. Not only did they fail to help Judah in its time of extreme need, but they even took delight in the razing of Jerusalem (Ps 137:7) and handed fleeing Judahites over to the sword (Ezek 35:1–15). For these acts of treachery, the Lord promised to bring stern punishment on Edom: the decimation of its population, the destruction of its cities, and the desolation of its territory (see Jer 49:7–22; Lam 4:21–22; Ezek 25:12–14). Obadiah's oracles thus align with other prophecies delivered at roughly the same time by Jeremiah and Ezekiel, who denounced Edom for its evildoing and encouraged God's people with the hope of vindication. In view of this shared prophetic outlook, scholars often date the Book of Obadiah in the sixth century B.C., either soon after the fall of Jerusalem, when Edom's malice was felt most acutely by Jewish survivors, or several decades later, when outrage against Edom remained strong among Jewish exiles returning from Babylon.

Title The book is named after Obadiah, mentioned in the opening verse. Its Hebrew form, ʿŌbadyāh, means "worshiper of the LORD" or possibly "servant of the LORD". The prophet's name appears in the Greek Septuagint in the title *Abdios*, while this heading was expanded in the Latin Vulgate to *Abdias Propheta*, "Obadiah the Prophet". English titles for the book follow these ancient traditions.

Place in the Canon Obadiah has long been revered as a canonical book of Scripture. In the Jewish Bible, or Tanakh, it stands among the Latter Prophets in a sub-collection of writings known as "the Book of the Twelve". In Christian Bibles, these twelve books are called the Minor Prophets, not because they are less important than Isaiah, Jeremiah, Ezekiel, and Daniel, but because they are comparatively much shorter. In ancient Hebrew and Latin manuscripts, Obadiah stands between Amos and Jonah. Some speculate that Obadiah, which deals with the judgment of Edom, was placed immediately after Amos because the final chapter of that book touches upon the theme of Israel possessing "the remnant of Edom" (Amos 9:12). In ancient Greek manuscripts, Obadiah stands fifth among the Minor Prophets between Joel and Jonah.

Structure The Book of Obadiah has five basic parts. **(1)** Verse 1a is a superscription that introduces the book and names the prophet. **(2)** Verse 1b–c forms a short introduction in which the nations are called to rise up against Edom. **(3)** Verses 2–9 announce that God is about to humiliate Edom for its arrogant sins. **(4)** Verses 10–14 bring charges against the Edomites for crimes committed against the people of Judah in their time of distress. **(5)** Verses 15–21 widen the focus from Edom's judgment to God's judgment on all nations on the day of the LORD, when both Israel and Edom will be under the rule of his kingdom.

Historical Background Obadiah's message is directed against Edom, a small nation that occupied the rugged highlands south of the Dead Sea. Israel had a long and hostile relationship with these southern neighbors. Scripture traces its beginning to the fraternal rivalry between Isaac's sons, Jacob and Esau (Gen 25–33), which foreshowed the conflict between their future descendants, the Israelites and the Edomites (Gen 25:23). Examples of mutual animosity appear throughout the OT. For instance, at the time of the Exodus, as the Israelites were journeying through the wilderness to the Promised Land, the Edomites refused them passage through their territory, even though they were kin (Num 20:14–21). Later, when Saul became king, he fought against the Edomites (1 Sam 14:47); and when David was subduing threats on Israel's borders, he made Edom a vassal state subjected to Israelite rule (2 Sam 8:13–14). This appears to have lasted until Edom revolted during the reign of King Jehoram (2 Kings 8:20–22). Subsequently we hear of Judah slaying thousands of Edomites (2 Chron 25:11–13) and of Edom launching raids and taking captives from Judah (2 Chron 28:17). This antagonistic history reached an ugly climax when the Edomites celebrated the destruction of Judah and Jerusalem in 586 B.C. They declined to intervene on Judah's behalf and even took advantage of Judah's weakness in the aftermath. These are the troubling events that stand in the background of Obadiah's prophecy.

Message of the Prophet The Book of Obadiah records a single oracle delivered by a single prophet against a single people—the Edomites. Having only twenty-one verses, it is the shortest book of the Old Testament. It is also one of the sternest. Obadiah sugarcoats none of the consequences that Edom's sins deserve. The judgments of God, put into motion by peoples summoned to make war on Edom (2), will bring this proud and treacherous nation low (2–3). The punishments to come are tailored to fit Edom's crimes: "As you have done, it shall be done to you" is the standard of justice the prophet announces (15).

What exactly did Edom do to merit such severity from God? When Babylonian forces under the command of Nebuchadnezzar marched against Judah and Jerusalem in 586 B.C., bringing catastrophe to southern Israel on an unprecedented scale, the Edomites stood by and refused to come to Judah's aid (1). Even worse, they "gloated" over its demise (12), perpetrated "violence" against it (10), pillaged its land of "goods" (13), and "delivered up" its survivors to enslavement and death (14). The Edomites, being evil opportunists, acted like vultures picking clean the remains of a carcass left by an animal of prey. But their acts of omission and commission are even more grave in view of Edom's fraternal relationship with Israel/Judah. Their crimes were committed against a "brother" in need (10, 12). Obadiah's message of doom announces that God will hold Edom fully responsible for its unbrotherly acts of cruelty and spite.

At one level, announcing God's judgment on Edom might be expected to bring some comfort to the people of Judah who suffered at its hands. It confirms their belief that the Lord does not overlook the wrongs done to his people or fail to hold wrongdoers accountable. But this is not the only silver lining of the prophet's message for Israel. More than just retribution, Obadiah envisions a great reversal. Just as Israel was humbled and Edom exalted at the time of the Babylonian invasion, so the coming "day of the LORD" (15) will see Israel exalted again and Edom humbled to become "small among the nations" (2, 4). Israel's exiles will return home from Babylon and Assyria and repossess the full extent of the Promised Land, including territories lost to foreign powers over the centuries (17–20). So, while the outlook for Edom is grim, the prospects for Israel are glorious. Mt. Zion will again be made holy as the sacred center of the Lord's "kingdom" (21).

Though short, the Book of Obadiah boldly reaffirms essential truths about the God of the Bible. The Lord is no mere national deity with a limited reach or influence; he is the sovereign Master of human history and of the fate of all nations. He has the power to prosper the afflicted or to afflict the prosperous, to lift up the weak or to bring down the strong. Edom is a case in point, with its humiliation serving as a lesson for other nations who would dare to harm or exploit God's people. Also, far from acting according to whim or personal preference, the God of Israel sustains a total commitment to justice by enforcing the world's moral laws. Entire peoples, nations, and empires of the world stand accountable to him for their actions. None go unnoticed by the Lord; none escape the consequences of evildoing; and none who seek his mercy and grace will be put to shame in the end.

Christian Perspective The New Testament never quotes directly from the Book of Obadiah, although it gives some attention to its themes. In the Gospel of Matthew, Herod the Great is a man of Edomite descent who destroys the infant boys of Bethlehem in the hope of killing Jesus, the newborn King of the Jews (Mt 2:16). His fury and bloodshed mirror the long history of animosity between Edom and Judah. In the Letter to the Romans, Paul cites words of the prophet Malachi that have a close affinity with Obadiah's message: "Jacob I loved, but Esau I hated" (Rom 9:13). The apostle's point is that salvation history is shaped by the elective will of God, who chose Israel—not Edom—to accomplish his plan of redemption for the world. Lastly, Obadiah's closing statement, "the kingdom shall be the LORD's" (21), is a prophetic hope that Jesus reignites when he announces that the kingdom of God is near (Mk 1:14–15).

OUTLINE OF OBADIAH

1. Superscription (1a)

2. The Divine Summons to War (1b-c)

3. The Divine Judgment of Edom (2–9)

4. The Dishonorable Crimes of Edom (10–14)

5. The Day of the Lord for Edom and Israel (15–21)

THE BOOK OF

OBADIAH

Edom Will Be Brought Low and Israel Triumph

¹The vision of Obadi′ah.

Thus says the Lord God concerning E′dom:
We have heard tidings from the Lord,
  and a messenger has been sent among the
    nations:
"Rise up! let us rise against her for battle!"
²Behold, I will make you small among the nations,
  you shall be utterly despised.
³The pride of your heart has deceived you,
  you who live in the clefts of the rock,ᵃ
  whose dwelling is high,
who say in your heart,
  "Who will bring me down to the ground?"
⁴Though you soar aloft like the eagle,
  though your nest is set among the stars,
  from there I will bring you down,
              says the Lord.

⁵If thieves came to you,
  if plunderers by night—
  how you have been destroyed!—
  would they not steal only enough for
    themselves?
If grape gatherers came to you,
  would they not leave gleanings?
⁶How Esau has been pillaged,
  his treasures sought out!
⁷All your allies have deceived you,
  they have driven you to the border;
  your confederates have prevailed against you;
  your trusted friends have set a trap under you—
  there is no understanding of it.
⁸Will I not on that day, says the Lord,
  destroy the wise men out of E′dom,
  and understanding out of Mount Esau?
⁹And your mighty men shall be dismayed, O
    Te′man,

1–21: Is 34; 63:1–6; Jer 49:7–22; Ezek 25:12–14; 35; Amos 1:11–12; Mal 1:2–5.

1–16 Obadiah's tirade against Edom is related to Jer 49:7–22. The exact nature of the relationship between these two writings remains unclear, however. It could be **(1)** that Obadiah drew upon Jeremiah, **(2)** that Jeremiah drew upon Obadiah, or **(3)** that both prophets drew upon a single ancient source that is no longer known to us. Compare, e.g., verses 1–4 with Jer 49:14–16, verses 5–6 with Jer 49:9–10, verse 8 with Jer 49:7, and verse 16 with Jer 49:12.
1 vision: The prophetic message recorded in the book. The Lord sometimes communicated with the prophets in visual as well as verbal ways (see Is 1:1; Nahum 1:1; Hab 2:2). **Obadiah:** The name in Hebrew translates "worshiper of the Lord" or "servant of the Lord". Nothing more is known about this prophet, not even the century in which he lived, although evidence within the book suggests that he delivered his message in Judah in the sixth century B.C. See introduction: *Author and Date*. **Thus says the Lord God:** The words of the book in verses 2–21 are delivered through the prophet but ultimately come from God, who inspired his speech. **Edom:** A small state directly south of the Dead Sea. The Bible identifies the Edomites as the descendants of Esau, the brother of Jacob (Gen 25:25–26). The name Edom is related to the Hebrew words for "reddish" (′ādōm or ′admônî). In Hellenistic times, which include the NT period, the territory of Edom became known as Idumea. For Israel's many conflicts with Edom, see introduction: *Historical Background*. **We have heard tidings:** The speakers are unidentified. They seem to be the nations recruited to make war on Edom. The Greek LXX is singular: "I have heard tidings", as in Jer 49:14. **a messenger:** Some identify this figure as Obadiah.

2 despised: Fitting punishment for Edom/Esau, who "despised" his birthright in Gen 25:34.
3 pride: A dangerous and deceptive sin. Perched high in their mountain strongholds, the Edomites boast that no one can threaten their security, deluding themselves into thinking they are beyond harm's reach. They forget that the Lord is higher than all and that he thrusts down the arrogant from their lofty thrones (Prov 15:25; Is 2:12–17; 14:12–15; Ezek 28:1–8; Lk 1:52). **rock:** The Hebrew is *sela*'—probably an allusion to the Edomite capital named Sela.
4 I will bring you down: Edom was conquered and claimed by the Babylonians about 552 B.C., displaced from their ancestral territory by the Nabateans in the 400s B.C., and forced to be circumcised and observe the Jewish way of life under the Maccabees in the 200s B.C. (Josephus, *Antiquities* 13, 257). • Lucifer, who formerly rose in the morning, is fallen, and he who was brought up in paradise deserved to hear the Lord's sentence: "Though you be as high as an eagle, and your nest be set among the stars, from there I will bring you down" (St. Jerome, *Letters* 22, 4).
5–7 Obadiah is so certain that Edom will be **destroyed** and **pillaged** and **deceived** in the coming days that he speaks as if these events had already occurred (= the so-called "prophetic perfect" tense).
5 thieves ... gatherers: Neither one can take everything without leaving something behind. By contrast, when the Lord brings plundering armies against Edom, they will leave nothing remaining. • For ancient prophecies that Israel will dispossess Edom, see Num 24:18 and Amos 9:12.
6 Esau: Twin brother of Jacob (Gen 25:24–26) and forefather of the Edomites (Gen 36:1–43).
7 no understanding: Ironically, the Edomites are duped and misled by the scheming of their allies, even though they were renowned in biblical times for their "wise men" (8; Jer 49:7).
8 that day: The "day of the Lord" mentioned in verse 15. **Mount Esau:** The mountainous region of Edom, also called Seir (Deut 2:5). It is the target of the Lord's judgment (9), just as Mt. Zion will be the center of the Lord's restoration of his people (17).

The book of Obadiah (Abdias) is so short that it is difficult to be certain of its date and character. It is a tirade against the people of Edom, who are told not to exult over the misfortune of Jerusalem, for they shall be utterly destroyed, while a remnant from Israel shall survive. It seems to apply to the situation of the postexilic period when the surrounding nations, including Edom, had partly occupied the vacant territory of Judah.
ᵃ Or *Sela*.

81

Obadiah

so that every man from Mount Esau will be
　　cut off by slaughter.
¹⁰For the violence done to your brother Jacob,
　　shame shall cover you,
　　and you shall be cut off for ever.
¹¹On the day that you stood aloof,
　　on the day that strangers carried off his wealth,
　and foreigners entered his gates
　　'and cast lots for Jerusalem,
　　you were like one of them.
¹²But you should not have gloated over the day of
　　your brother
　　in the day of his misfortune;
　you should not have rejoiced over the people of
　　Judah
　　in the day of their ruin;
　you should not have boasted
　　in the day of distress.
¹³You should not have entered the gate of my
　　people
　　in the day of his calamity;
　you should not have gloated over his disaster
　　in the day of his calamity;
　you should not have looted his goods
　　in the day of his calamity.

¹⁴You should not have stood at the parting of the
　　ways
　　to cut off his fugitives;
　you should not have delivered up his survivors
　　in the day of distress.
¹⁵For the day of the LORD is near upon all the
　　nations.
　As you have done, it shall be done to you,
　　your deeds shall return on your own head.
¹⁶For as you have drunk upon my holy mountain,
　　all the nations round about shall drink;
　they shall drink, and stagger,ᵇ
　　and shall be as though they had not been.
¹⁷But in Mount Zion there shall be those that
　　escape,
　　and it shall be holy;
　and the house of Jacob shall possess their own
　　possessions.
¹⁸The house of Jacob shall be a fire,
　　and the house of Joseph a flame,
　　and the house of Esau stubble;
　they shall burn them and consume them,
　　and there shall be no survivor to the house of
　　Esau;
　　　　　for the LORD has spoken.

---

9 mighty men: Warriors. **Teman:** A prominent Edomite city, named after one of Esau's grandsons (Gen 36:9–11). **cut off:** Or "cut down". The punishment is fitting since Edom "cut off" Judah's fugitives (14).

10–14 The Edomites are indicted for hostilities against Judah. They are charged with violence against Judah's citizens (10), with doing nothing to help Judah's distress (11), with rejoicing over Judah's demise (12), with looting Judah's goods (13), and with handing Judah's survivors over to be executed or enslaved (14). This treachery is all the more inexcusable because it betrays the obligations of loyalty to family, Jacob/Israel being Edom's "brother" (10, 12; Deut 2:4, 8).

11 you stood aloof: I.e., you stood aside, refusing to help your kinsmen when Babylonian armies ravaged Judah and Jerusalem in 586 B.C.

13 entered the gate ... looted his goods: Suggests the Edomites conducted raids in Judah after the Babylonian invasion, profiting from the nation's ruin. It appears that Edom also seized territory in southern Judah at this time.

15 the day of the LORD: An approaching day of judgment when God will right the wrongs of history and gives the nations what they deserve. The wicked, including the Edomites, will face God's vengeance, while his afflicted people will be blessed and restored. At another level, Edom exemplifies every hostile nation that persecutes the covenant people, so that its downfall serves as a warning to all other nations who are tempted to follow its example. In rabbinic Judaism, Edom became a cipher for the Romans. See word study: *The Day of the LORD* at Joel 1:15. **As you have done:** The Lord's punitive justice is a proportionate justice, i.e., the guilty are made to suffer the same adversities that they themselves have inflicted upon others (cf. Jer 51:49). The Edomites will be cut

down, plundered, and put to shame (2, 6, 9), just as they have done to the Judahites (13–14).

16 you have drunk: The disasters that befell Judah when it drank the wine of God's punishment are also in store for wicked nations (Jer 25:15–29). For the image of God's judgment as an intoxicating drink that leads one to stagger and fall, see Is 51:17–23; Lam 4:21; Ezek 23:31–35; Hab 2:15–16; Rev 14:10; 16:19. **my holy mountain:** Mt. Zion, crowned with the city of Jerusalem and chosen by the Lord as his hallowed dwelling (Ps 76:2; 78:68).

17–21 Obadiah prophesies Edom's demise alongside Israel's restoration from exile (cf. Lam 4:22). Key events include the resanctification of Jerusalem (17), the preservation of survivors in Judah (17), the return of a remnant of Israelites from captivity (20), the restoration of the full Promised Land, including territories that were taken from Israel over the centuries (19–20), and a reestablishment of the Lord's rule over Edom (21).

17 those that escape: A remnant of survivors called by the Lord, as in Joel 2:32. **shall be holy:** A reversal of Jerusalem's defilement by the Babylonians in 586 B.C. The destroyed Temple would be rebuilt by 515 B.C. **the house of Jacob:** The whole family of Israel. See note on verse 20. • If Edom is a figure for the Gentiles, we can see a prophecy about Christ. Those who are saved on Mt. Zion are believers from Judea, especially the apostles, and it was foretold that in Judea there would be salvation and a holy place, which is Christ Jesus. Mt. Esau, on the other hand, is Edom, which signifies the Church of the Gentiles. It is made a kingdom for the Lord through the preaching of the gospel (St. Augustine, *City of God* 18, 31).

18 Joseph: The favored son of Jacob whose descendants, the tribes of Ephraim and Manasseh, were once the strongest group in the family of Israel. **no survivor:** Overstated for rhetorical effect, but a prediction of severe judgment all the same. For Edom's humiliations, see note on 4. **Esau:** See note on 6.

ᵇCn: Heb *swallow.*

82

¹⁹Those of the Neg′eb shall possess Mount Esau,
and those of the Shephe′lah the land of the
Philis′tines;
they shall possess the land of E′phraim and the
land of Samar′ia
and Benjamin shall possess Gilead.
²⁰The exiles in Ha′lah^c who are of the people of
Israel
shall possess^d Phoeni′cia as far as Zar′ephath;

and the exiles of Jerusalem who are in Sephar′ad
shall possess the cities of the Neg′eb.
²¹Saviors shall go up to Mount Zion
to rule Mount Esau;
and the kingdom shall be the Lord.

---

19 Negeb: The arid region stretching across the deep south of Judah. Its inhabitants will expand their territory eastward to include Edomite lands south of the Dead Sea. **Shephelah:** The low hills of western Israel, between the coastal plain and the central hill country. Its inhabitants will expand their territory to include Philistine lands in southwest Canaan. **Ephraim:** The central highlands of Canaan. The time of restoration will see Israelites reclaiming its northern lands, taken from Israel since the fall of **Samaria** to Assyrian conquerors in 722 B.C. **Gilead:** The territory east of the Jordan. It was taken from Israel with the Assyrian invasions of 734–732 B.C. See note on Is 9:1.

20 Halah: The Hebrew is unclear at this point. Many think the reference is to Halahhu, a region northeast of Nineveh on the Tigris River. Captives from the northern tribes of Israel were exiled to "Halah" in 722 B.C. and never returned (2 Kings 17:6). The implication is that northern exiles will return from distant lands to expand their territory into **Phoenicia**. The northern limit of Canaan was the Phoenician city of Sidon, according to Gen 10:19. **Zarephath:** A coastal city south of Sidon (cf. 1 Kings 17:8–24). **Sepharad:** Sometimes identified as Spain (Iberian peninsula) or as Sardis (western Turkey). More likely the reference is to Saparda, a region northwest of Media since captives from Israel's northern tribes were exiled to various "cities of the Medes" (2 Kings 17:6). If this is correct, Obadiah envisions a reunion of all Israel—not only southern Judahites returning from Babylon but also northern Israelites from the Assyrian exile. For other prophets who foresee a restoration of the exiled tribes of northern Israel and their reunion with a remnant of Judah, see Is 27:12–13; Jer 50:17–20; Ezek 37:15–28; Hos 1:10–11. For the NT fulfillment of these hopes, see essay: *The Salvation of All Israel* at Rom 11.

21 Saviors: Or "deliverers". The word is used elsewhere to describe the biblical judges, who delivered God's people from oppressors and brought them a new era of peace (Judg 3:9, 15). The prophet seems to envision leaders in Israel who oversee the work of restoration and guide the covenant people to fulfill the Lord's purposes. Jesus' apostles continue this work in the NT age. **the kingdom:** The Lord's kingship over Israel, rejected by the people before the founding of the monarchy (1 Sam 8:7), will be reaffirmed when God shepherds his people (Ezek 34:15) through the Davidic Messiah (Ezek 34:23–24).

^c Cn: Heb *this army*.
^d Cn: Heb *which*.

STUDY QUESTIONS
Obadiah

For understanding

1. **1:** How did the Lord sometimes communicate with the prophets? How does Obadiah's name translate in Hebrew? What is known about this prophet? Although the words of the book in vv. 2–21 are delivered through the prophet, from where do they ultimately come? Where is Edom, and how does the Bible identify the Edomites? To what Hebrew words is the name Edom related? In Hellenistic times, which includes the NT period, how did the territory of Edom become known? Who do the unidentified speakers seem to be?

2. **3:** Perched high in their mountain strongholds, of what do the Edomites boast? What do they forget? To what is the Hebrew word for "rock" probably an allusion?

3. **10–14:** In general, for what are the Edomites indicted? Specifically, with what are they charged? Why is this treachery all the more inexcusable?

4. **15:** What is "the day of the LORD"? What will the wicked, including the Edomites, face, and what will happen to the Lord's afflicted people? At another level, what does Edom exemplify, and what purpose will its downfall serve? In Rabbinic Judaism, what does Edom become? In what way is the Lord's punitive justice a proportionate justice?

5. **17:** Who are "those that escape"? How shall Jerusalem's defilement by the Babylonians in 586 B.C. be reversed? According to St. Augustine, if Edom is a figure for the Gentiles, how can we see a prophecy about Christ?

For application

1. **3:** We are often encouraged to take pride in things that foster a positive attitude toward ourselves, such as our accomplishments or our family. Yet pride is considered one of the seven capital sins. What is the "pride of heart" that Obadiah condemns in this verse? How is it different from a merely positive self-image? How does a wrongful pride impede a relationship with God?

2. **4:** How does God often deal with prideful people, who "soar aloft like the eagle"? What is the difference between humility and humiliation, and from where does each originate? In your experience, has humiliation ever served as a remedy for your pride?

3. **7:** Have you ever felt betrayed by a friend, coworker, or ally? What were the consequences? How did you deal with them? In light of how Jesus forgave those who betrayed him, what do you owe your betrayer?

4. **11–13:** When you learn that this same betrayer has suffered a major disaster through his own fault, such as loss of his livelihood or reputation, how might you be tempted to react? What are some ways you as a Christian might respond?

INTRODUCTION TO JONAH

Author and Date Little is known with certainty about the origins of the Book of Jonah. Neither the author who penned the biblical account nor the date of its composition is mentioned in the book. Its main character, "Jonah the son of Amittai" (1:1), was a prophet from Galilee who lived during the reign of Jeroboam II from 793 to 753 B.C. This information, derived from 2 Kings 14:25 rather than from the Book of Jonah itself, seems to set the story in the first half of the eighth century B.C., although the book makes no claim that Jonah himself was responsible for writing it. It is conceivable, if one grants the possibility of the story having a basis in history, that Jonah could have kept memoirs of such an adventure, which he or someone else relied upon to produce the canonical book, but evidence is lacking to confirm this. The authorship of the book thus remains unknown.

A few contemporary scholars trace the Book of Jonah back to the time of the prophet himself in the eighth century B.C., while most place it in the postexilic period between the fifth and the third century B.C. Unfortunately, a lack of unambiguous evidence makes it difficult to narrow the range of possible dates. Some argue that Aramaisms in the text favor a time of composition in the postexilic period; others contend that several alleged Aramaisms are better viewed as Phoenicianisms, and this suggests an earlier date of composition in the preexilic period. The only certainty is that the Book of Jonah was revered as a book of Sacred Scripture by the third century B.C., since the collection of the "twelve" Minor Prophets was complete when the Book of Sirach was written ca. 180 B.C. (Sir 49:10). Beyond that, evidence bearing on the date of the book is inconclusive.

Title The book is named after its main character, Jonah the son of Amittai, whose Hebrew name *Yônāh* means "dove". The prophet's name appears in the Greek Septuagint in the title *Iōnas*, while this heading is expanded in the Latin Vulgate to *Iona Propheta*, "Jonah the Prophet". English titles for the book follow these ancient traditions.

Place in the Canon Jonah has long been revered as a canonical book of Scripture. In the Jewish Bible, or Tanakh, it stands among the Latter Prophets in a sub-collection of writings known as "the Book of the Twelve". In Christian Bibles, these twelve books are called the Minor Prophets, not because they are less important than Isaiah, Jeremiah, Ezekiel, and Daniel, but because they are comparatively shorter. In ancient Hebrew and Latin manuscripts, Jonah stands fifth among the Minor Prophets between Obadiah and Micah. In ancient Greek manuscripts, it stands sixth in the collection between Obadiah and Nahum.

Structure The Book of Jonah is neatly symmetrical. It divides into two parts that mirror one another, so that each successive theme in the first half has a counterpart in the second half. **(1)** In chapters 1–2, the story unfolds in five steps: the Lord calls Jonah to prophesy (1:1–2); Jonah flees from the Lord's call (1:3); Gentile sailors come to fear the Lord in the midst of a storm (1:4–10); the Lord appoints a fish to return Jonah to land (1:17); and Jonah prays a psalm of thanksgiving for his rescue from death (2:1–10). **(2)** In chapters 3–4, another five steps are visible: the Lord calls Jonah to prophesy (3:1–2); Jonah follows the Lord's call (3:3–4); the Gentile population of Nineveh repents and comes to fear the Lord in view of his sentence of judgment (3:5–10); the Lord appoints a plant to grow and shield Jonah from the sun (4:1–7); and Jonah complains to the Lord about his circumstances and wishes for death (4:8–11).

Literary Genre The vast majority of Jewish and Christian interpreters through the centuries have read the Book of Jonah as a work of prophetic history. It was believed to be a story that rested on actual events of the past, even as its message was believed to teach lessons about faith and life for the People of God. Modern times, however, have seen the rise of a different perspective on Jonah. For some, the book is a work of didactic fiction that is built around a historical person. For others, the book is a work of fiction through and through. No one denies that Jonah was written to instruct readers about God's mercy and concern for peoples beyond Israel. But did the author intend to record events of history? Or was his aim to teach religious truths by means of a partly or entirely fictional narrative? Since Jonah appears in 2 Kings 14:25 as a historical figure who lived in northern Israel in the eighth century B.C., the question of literary genre requires some attention.

It is popular in modern times to read the Book of Jonah as an extended parable, allegory, or folktale. Among the reasons given for this position are the following. (a) The Book of Jonah provides few details about the historical setting of the story. Readers aware of 2 Kings 14:25 will remember that Jonah was a prophet in northern Israel during the reign of Jeroboam II (793–753 B.C.), but the book itself does not supply this information. Nor does it give sufficient information to narrow down when in the first half of the eighth century B.C. the story is situated. Vagueness on the book's historical setting is consistent with didactic fiction but would be unusual for a work that intends to relate history. (b) The Book of Jonah makes extensive use of caricature, irony, and satire. Jonah, who is the only human character in the story given a name, seems like a caricature of a troubled prophet whose unlikely adventure is filled with ironic twists and satirical depictions that poke fun at him. These techniques, which imply a measure of artistic license on the part of the author, seem to many interpreters to be incompatible with writing a straightforward account of history. (c) The story is filled with fantastical elements, e.g., Jonah is cast in the sea by pagan sailors who, contrary to expectations, make vows and offer a sacrifice to the God of Israel; a giant fish swallows Jonah to save him from drowning; the prophet survives in the fish's stomach for three days before he is returned to dry land; the entire population of Nineveh, infamous for its wickedness, turns from sin after a single day of Jonah's preaching; the animals of Nineveh participate in public acts of penitence by wearing sackcloth; and the Lord makes a shade plant grow up over Jonah's shelter in a single night. Without denying that miracles can and do happen, one might hold that the marvels described in Jonah seem *ad hoc*, a point reinforced by the observation that they are unattested in contemporary records outside the Bible. Furthermore, they seem intended to deepen the irony and satire of the story and thus seem less likely to describe historical events. (d) Scholars have noted parallels between the story of Jonah and Near Eastern mythological tales in which journeys to the underworld lasted three days, just as Jonah describes his three days in the fish (1:17) as a descent to the realm of the dead (2:1–6). In view of these observations, it remains possible that the Book of Jonah has a historical core; but if so, the author seems to have greatly embellished it with fictional and satirical elements to drive home the theological theme of the book.

Although a minority position today, some continue to read the Book of Jonah as history. Among the reasons given for this position are the following. (a) The book's main character, Jonah son of Amittai, is not a fictional character. He is a prophet who foretold the expansion of Israel's northern territory in the reign of Jeroboam II (2 Kings 14:25). (b) Locations mentioned in the book such as Joppa, Tarshish, and Nineveh are real places in the biblical world, not creations of the storyteller. (c) Ancient readers treated the Jonah story as historical. For example, the Jewish historian Josephus recounts Jonah's misadventure alongside other events that transpired in the eight century B.C. (*Antiquities* 9, 208–14). Likewise, Church Fathers such as St. Cyril of Jerusalem, St. Gregory Nazianzen, St. Cyril of Alexandria, St. Jerome, and St. Augustine of Hippo considered the book historical, even though they delighted in pointing out the ways that Jonah prefigured Christ and his saving mission. (d) There is no doubt that teachers in ancient Israel sometimes used parables as a tool to communicate their message effectively and memorably, but there are no clear instances outside of the Book of Jonah in which parables relate spectacular miracles. (e) Jesus almost certainly read the book as historical. He compares Jonah's emergence after three days in the belly of the fish to his own burial and rising on the third day (Mt 12:40). While citing a classic story to prepare listeners for a coming event does not require that story to be historical, Jesus also claims: "The men of Nineveh will arise at the judgment with this generation and condemn it; for they repented at the preaching of Jonah" (Mt 12:41; Lk 11:32). At this point, Jesus moves beyond illustrative comparison into the realm of eschatological prophecy. He foresees the Ninevites faring better than some of his own generation at the Last Judgment. Unless he is talking about real people who repented in real history, the criticism of his own generation by comparison rings hollow. One can argue that Jesus' remarks do not settle the historical genre of the book beyond all doubt; but this interpretation remains the most natural understanding of his perspective on the story.

What to make of the fictional and historical readings of the book? On the one hand, there is nothing objectionable about an author using fiction as a genre to convey a spiritual lesson. The prophets of Israel made use of parables in the Old Testament, just as Jesus did in the New Testament. Parables are one form of fiction; there is no reason to suppose other forms—including fiction that features a historical figure—are inappropriate. What is more, many scholars regard other Old Testament works as containing fictional elements. On the other hand, the grand sweep of Jewish and Christian tradition weighs against it. It is difficult to believe that the author's intention was mistaken by practically all ancient readers and only rightly discerned by modern readers who stand at a greater distance from the time it was written.

The Catholic Church, for her part, has taken no official stance on the genre or historicity of the Book of Jonah, and so interpreters are free to investigate these questions and to draw conclusions on the basis of ongoing research. That said, advocates of different positions do well to acknowledge that both historical and fictional genres can be used to impart lessons about faith and life and the plan of God. Both can serve this didactic and religious aim. In the case of the Book of Jonah, its message comes through clearly regardless of its literary genre or relationship to history.

The Message of the Prophet The Book of Jonah is unique among the Bible's prophetic books. Most of the writings in this category feature oracles of the Lord delivered by the prophets to the people of their times. Jonah, however, does not recount the *sayings* of a prophet but rather a *story* about a prophet. Apart from the message, "Yet forty days, and Nineveh shall be overthrown" (3:4), the book is focused entirely on Jonah's actions and dialogues with the Lord. Moreover, even among the Bible's stories about the prophets, the Book of Jonah stands out as unique. Figures such as Elijah complained to the Lord about the hardships of their mission, and figures such as Jeremiah wrestled mightily with their call to deliver an unpopular message. But only in the case of Jonah do we see a prophet whose preaching is astoundingly successful even though he stubbornly refuses to see things God's way.

The message of the Book of Jonah is a message of universalism. It teaches that God wants all people and nations to repent of sin and to receive his mercy, not just Israel. He wants to reveal his grace, already treasured in Israel, to the world beyond its borders. The object of divine mercy in the Jonah story is the city of Nineveh. Not only was this Assyrian city infamous for its evildoing, but the Assyrian Empire represented a serious threat to Israel's national security and even its existence. Only a few decades after Jonah's time, the Assyrians would subjugate and then obliterate the Northern Kingdom of Israel. Yet, from the Lord's perspective, even Israel's enemies are candidates for his compassion.

For Jonah, a patriotic Israelite who loved his country and hated his enemies, this was too much to stomach. So, when the Lord called him to preach repentance to the Ninevites, he found a ship in Joppa and fled in the opposite direction toward Tarshish (1:1–3). Contrary to our first impression, the reason for his flight was not cowardice. Rather, he knew that the Lord was "a gracious God and merciful" to those who repent (4:2). Jonah was troubled by the thought that God might spare this wicked city, which he felt deserved punishment. He did not want to preach to the Ninevites for fear that they might turn from their evil ways and be saved! Jonah was happy to receive mercy in his own life, as when God sent a fish to save him from drowning (1:17—2:10), but he was reluctant to see mercy extended to his enemies, as when Nineveh was saved from destruction (3:1–10).

This unflattering, even at times comical, picture of Jonah continues to the very end of the book. The Lord's decision to spare Nineveh makes the prophet extremely annoyed and "angry" (4:1). He is so upset that he prays for God to take his life (4:3). This request exposes Jonah's rigid fixation with justice and, in view of his recent past, reveals his callousness: he thanked the Lord for saving him from death

(2:9), but now he would rather perish than see an entire repentant city saved from death (4:3). In a final act of desperation, he seats himself east of Nineveh to see if, perhaps, the city will return to its wickedness and bring God's wrath upon itself at last (4:5). Again, God shows Jonah mercy by causing a plant to grow overnight that will shade him from the sun as he sits watching the city (4:6). But the Lord takes it away the next day (4:7) and sends a sultry wind to increase his discomfort, causing Jonah to pray for death a second time (4:8). Still Jonah failed to realize his inconsistency and double standard: he was "angry" to see his enemies receive mercy instead of justice (4:1), and yet he was "angry" to exchange mercy for justice in his own life (4:9).

This tension between the Lord and Jonah is never resolved in the story. Twice the Lord asks the prophet: "Do you do well to be angry?" (4:4, 9). The implied answer is no, but Jonah never accepts the invitation to reflect on his attitude. He remains hardened in his position and refuses to adopt the Lord's perspective. The final line of the book is a question put to Jonah that he never answers. One presumes the prophet still disagrees with God that Nineveh should have been spared. Readers, however, are implicitly invited to see things as God sees them: the Lord's mercy is not reserved exclusively for Israel but is a gift he desires for all.

Christian Perspective The Book of Jonah plays a conspicuous role in the teaching of Jesus. First and foremost, Jesus foretells his burial and Resurrection on the third day by comparing these events to the three days and three nights that Jonah spent in the belly of the whale before emerging alive (Mt 12:40). This same connection between Easter morning and the Jonah story may underlie Paul's reference to Jesus rising again "on the third day in accordance with the Scriptures" (1 Cor 15:4). Besides this, Jesus also draws attention to the repentance of the Ninevites in response to Jonah's preaching in order to scold his generation for resisting the gospel, even though he comes as one "greater than Jonah" (Mt 12:41; Lk 11:32). The figure of Jonah is thus a "sign" pointing forward to the Messiah's proclamation of repentance and of his rising from the dead (Lk 11:29). More generally, God's desire to bring the Ninevites to repentance reflects his universal salvific will, i.e., his desire to see all people and nations turn from evil and be saved from condemnation on the Day of Judgment (1 Tim 2:4; 2 Pet 3:9).

Introduction to Jonah

OUTLINE OF JONAH

1. Jonah Rejects His Mission (1:1—2:10)
    A. The Lord Commissions Jonah (1:1–2)
    B. Jonah Flees from the Lord's Call (1:3)
    C. Pagan Sailors Fear the Lord (1:4–16)
    D. Jonah and the Great Fish (1:17)
    E. Jonah's Prayer to the Lord (2:1–10)

2. Jonah Accepts His Mission (3:1—4:11)
    A. The Lord Commissions Jonah (3:1–2)
    B. Jonah Follows the Lord's Call (3:3–4)
    C. Pagan Ninevites Fear the Lord (3:5–10)
    D. Jonah and the Shade Plant (4:1–7)
    E. Jonah's Dialogue with the Lord (4:8–11)

THE BOOK OF

JONAH

Jonah Tries to Flee God

1 Now the word of the LORD came to Jonah the son of Amit'tai, saying, [2]"Arise, go to Nin'eveh, that great city, and cry against it; for their wickedness has come up before me." [3]But Jonah rose to flee to Tar'shish from the presence of the LORD. He went down to Joppa and found a ship going to Tarshish; so he paid the fare, and went on board, to go with them to Tarshish, away from the presence of the LORD.

4 But the LORD hurled a great wind upon the sea, and there was a mighty tempest on the sea, so that the ship threatened to break up. [5]Then the mariners were afraid, and each cried to his god, and they threw the wares that were in the ship into the sea, to lighten it for them. But Jonah had gone down into the inner part of the ship and had lain down, and was fast asleep. [6]So the captain came and said to him, "What do you mean, you sleeper? Arise, call upon your god! Perhaps the god will give a thought to us, that we do not perish."

7 And they said to one another, "Come, let us cast lots, that we may know on whose account this evil has come upon us." So they cast lots, and the lot fell upon Jonah. [8]Then they said to him, "Tell us on whose account this evil has come upon us. What is your occupation? And from where do you come? What is your country? And of what people are you?" [9]And he said to them, "I am a Hebrew; and I fear the

---

1:1 the word of the LORD: A word of instruction from God, who sends the prophet to preach a message of repentance outside the land of Israel (1:2). See essay: *The Word of the Lord* at Hos 1. **Jonah:** The name means "dove" in Hebrew. Jonah is mentioned in 2 Kings 14:25, which identifies him as a prophet from the town of Gath-hepher, a few miles northeast of Nazareth in lower Galilee. He lived in the days of Jeroboam II, king of the Northern Kingdom of Israel from 793 to 753 B.C. Jonah is also mentioned in Tob 14:4, 8, in the shorter version of the Book of Tobit translated by the RSV2CE; however, the longer edition of Tobit that is translated by the ESVCE identifies Nahum as the prophet of Nineveh's doom, and this edition of the text is more likely original. **Amittai:** Not otherwise known.

📖 **1:2 Arise, go:** The introduction recalls 1 Kings 17:8-9, where "the word of the LORD" came to the prophet Elijah, who was told: "Arise, go to Zarephath." Unlike Elijah, who obeyed the Lord and went to Zarephath, Jonah disobeys and flees in the opposite direction from Nineveh. **Nineveh:** An Assyrian city on the east bank of the Tigris River, over 500 miles away from the land of Israel. The site lies near modern Mosul in Iraq. **great city:** Nineveh was a large metropolis that was infamous for its evildoing in biblical times (Nahum 3:1-4).

1:3 went down: The beginning of Jonah's steady descent toward death. After going down to the seaport, he **went on board** a ship, literally, "he went down in it", then he went down below deck into the hold of the ship (1:5), and soon he would be cast into the sea and would sink down to the realm of the dead (2:3). **Jonah rose to flee:** An act of disobedience (CCC 29). The prophet's motive for running away from his divine calling, unclear at first, is revealed in 4:2: he feared that God, in his abundant mercy, might spare the wicked Ninevites, whom Jonah felt were deserving of destruction. **Tarshish:**

Usually identified as Tartessos in southern Spain, a destination as far in the opposite direction from Nineveh as one could go on a ship sailing in the Mediterranean Sea. Others think the city of Tarsus in Asia Minor is meant. **Joppa:** A port on the Mediterranean coast northwest of Jerusalem (modern Jaffa, near Tel-Aviv). It was about 50 miles from Jonah's hometown of Gath-hepher (2 Kings 14:25). **away from the presence of the LORD:** Jonah foolishly (even humorously) tries to escape from God by going to Tarshish, even though one cannot hope to escape "the God of heaven, who made the sea and the dry land" (1:9).

📖 **1:4-16** The Lord brings a storm upon the sea to prevent Jonah's flight. • The story of Jesus calming a storm on the Sea of Galilee parallels the story of Jonah in several details. In both, the prophet sets sail on a boat, a storm hits and threatens to sink the boat, the sailors begin to panic, the prophet is found sleeping and must be awakened, and the prophet takes steps to make the sea calm again (Mt 8:23-27; Mk 4:35-41). Differences between the two stories are also evident, e.g., Jonah requests to be thrown overboard in order to quiet the tempest and appease the Lord for his disobedience (1:12), whereas Jesus, innocent of disobedience, remains in the boat and calms the storm with a miraculous word.

1:4 hurled: The same Hebrew term describes how the sailors "threw" cargo off the ship (1:5) and how they "threw" Jonah into the sea (1:15) at his request (1:12).

1:5 each cried to his god: The sailors were not Israelites who believed in one God but polytheists who believed in many gods.

1:7 cast lots: A procedure similar to rolling dice that was performed to discern the Lord's will in a particular situation (Josh 18:6; Prov 16:33). Here lots are cast to identify the person responsible for the divine anger that threatens the life of the entire crew.

1:9 a Hebrew: A descendant of Eber, ancestor of Abraham (Gen 11:14). Israelites sometimes used this term to distinguish themselves ethnically from non-Semitic peoples (Gen 40:15; Ex 1:19; 1 Sam 4:6). **I fear the LORD:** A statement of religious affiliation. Ironically, the claim is contradicted by Jonah's flight from the Lord (1:3). Adding to the irony, the pagan sailors show themselves true fearers of God (1:16) and more spiritually alert to the need to seek God's favor than Israel's prophet (1:10, 14). **God ... who made the sea:** Yet another instance of irony: God, the Maker of the sea, uses the sea to foil Jonah's escape.

The Book of Jonah (Jonas) is set in the reign of Jeroboam II (eighth century B.C.), but the book was probably written long after the Exile. This suggests that it is not meant to be taken historically, although the central figure, Jonah, is mentioned in 2 Kings 14:25 and appears to have been a well-known prophet of the time. In this story the writer, making use of many improbable details, teaches that God is merciful even in his punishments, if only his people will repent; and so far from being the God of Israel alone, he is prepared to extend his mercy to others, provided they possess or acquire the necessary dispositions of heart. Our Lord himself quotes the conversion of the Ninevites and the three days Jonah spent inside the great fish (Mt 12:38-41), but this is not a testimony to its historical character. He is concerned rather with its teaching.

Lord, the God of heaven, who made the sea and the dry land." ¹⁰Then the men were exceedingly afraid, and said to him, "What is this that you have done!" For the men knew that he was fleeing from the presence of the Lord, because he had told them.

Jonah Is Thrown into the Sea and Swallowed

11 Then they said to him, "What shall we do to you, that the sea may quiet down for us?" For the sea grew more and more tempestuous. ¹²He said to them, "Take me up and throw me into the sea; then the sea will quiet down for you; for I know it is because of me that this great tempest has come upon you." ¹³Nevertheless the men rowed hard to bring the ship back to land, but they could not, for the sea grew more and more tempestuous against them. ¹⁴Therefore they cried to the Lord, "We beg you, O Lord, let us not perish for this man's life, and lay not on us innocent blood; for you, O Lord, have done as it pleased you." ¹⁵So they took up Jonah and threw him into the sea; and the sea ceased from its raging. ¹⁶Then the men feared the Lord exceedingly, and they offered a sacrifice to the Lord and made vows.

17 ᵃ And the Lord appointed a great fish to swallow up Jonah; and Jonah was in the belly of the fish three days and three nights.

Jonah's Prayer and Deliverance

2 Then Jonah prayed to the Lord his God from the belly of the fish, ²saying,

"I called to the Lord, out of my distress,
and he answered me;
out of the belly of Sheol I cried,
and you heard my voice.
³For you cast me into the deep,
into the heart of the seas,
and the flood was round about me;
all your waves and your billows
passed over me.
⁴Then I said, 'I am cast out
from your presence;

1:17: Mt 12:40.

1:12 throw me into the sea: Jonah prefers death to accepting God's call (4:3). But not even this attempt to evade his mission will be successful, for God will save him from death by sending a fish to swallow him (1:17) and vomit him up on the shore (2:10), giving him a second chance to embrace his calling (3:1-2). **I know it is because of me:** Jonah's conscience is well aware of his wrongdoing.

1:13 the men rowed hard: An act of desperation to avoid hurling Jonah overboard to drown in the sea. This action is ironic and contrary to what readers would expect, given that the men were pagan idolaters and would presumably have no qualms about throwing an Israelite overboard to save their own lives.

1:14 We beg you, O Lord: Even the pagan sailors pray to Yhwh, the God of Israel. Jonah is conspicuous for not praying to the Lord in the midst of the storm. **let us not perish:** The mariners do not wish to be punished as murderers if they comply with Jonah's request. Their words echo the language of Deut 21:8. **for this man's life:** Ironically, the pagan sailors show concern for the life of a single Israelite, while Jonah the Israelite appears to care nothing for the lives of more than 120,000 pagan Ninevites (4:11). **you, O Lord, have done as it pleased you:** A recognition of God's absolute sovereignty over all things, as in Ps 115:3 and 135:6.

1:16 a sacrifice: Either a thank offering in gratitude to God for their survival (Ps 50:23) or a sacrifice of atonement for their part in hurling Jonah to his death (Job 1:1-5). The possibility of Gentiles serving the God of Israel is indicated by the sailors praying and sacrificing to the Lord.

1:17—2:10 Different editions of the Bible number these verses differently. Jewish and some Christian Bibles, such as the NABRE, have sixteen verses in the first chapter of Jonah (1:1-16) and eleven verses in the second chapter (2:1-11). Other translations, such as the RSV2CE and the ESVCE, have seventeen verses in the first chapter (1:1-17) and ten in the second (2:1-10). These differences reflect alternative ways of dividing the Book of Jonah into chapters and verses, not differences in the original text.

1:17 the Lord appointed: God exercises his sovereignty over the natural world to perform a miracle. The same expression is used for the three miracles in 4:6-8. **a great fish:** Not an instrument of death, but the means by which God saves Jonah from drowning and gives him a second chance to fulfill his prophetic mission. The Hebrew is non-specific about the species of marine animal in question; it specifies only its large size. The Greek LXX translates with *kētos*, meaning "sea monster" or possibly "whale". **three days and three nights:** Journeys to the underworld sometimes lasted three days in ancient Near Eastern literature. • Jesus views Jonah's three days in the fish as a prophetic "sign" of his entombment and third-day Resurrection (Mt 12:39-40; CCC 627). • Let us consider which is more difficult: for a man to rise again after being buried or for a man to escape corruption in the heat of a whale's stomach. If one is not believable, neither is the other. Jonah was preserved, since all things are possible with God, and Christ was likewise raised from the dead (St. Cyril of Jerusalem, *Catechesis* 14, 18).

2:1-9 A psalm of thanksgiving. Praying from within the great fish, Jonah remembers calling to God (2:2) as he was sinking in the sea (2:3-7). This may have been **(1)** a near-death experience from which he was saved in the nick of time or **(2)** an actual experience of death by drowning from which he was revived. Either way, the Lord saved him from a watery grave by sending a fish to swallow him (1:17) and return him to dry land (2:10). Jonah vows to offer sacrifice in gratitude for his deliverance (2:9). Notice that Jonah recites a prayer of *thanksgiving* for his rescue from the belly of Sheol; he is not reciting a prayer of *supplication* to be rescued from the belly of the fish. Several expressions and images in his prayer are found also in the Book of Psalms, e.g., Ps 18:4-6; 30:3; 31:6; 42:7; 50:14; 69:2; 71:20; 118:5; 143:4. See note on 2:9.

2:2 Sheol: Hebrew name for the netherworld of the dead (CCC 633). See word study: *Sheol* at Num 16:30.

2:3 you cast me into the deep: Jonah realizes that God accomplished his plan through the hands of the sailors, who actually "threw him into the sea" (1:15).

2:4 your holy temple: The Jerusalem Temple.

ᵃ Ch 2:1 in Heb.

how shall I again look
 upon your holy temple?'
⁵The waters closed in over me,
 the deep was round about me;
weeds were wrapped about my head
⁶ at the roots of the mountains.
I went down to the land
 whose bars closed upon me for ever;
yet you brought up my life from the Pit,
 O LORD my God.
⁷When my soul fainted within me,
 I remembered the LORD;
and my prayer came to you,
 into your holy temple.
⁸Those who pay regard to vain idols
 forsake their true loyalty.
⁹But I with the voice of thanksgiving
 will sacrifice to you;
what I have vowed I will pay.
 Deliverance belongs to the LORD!"

¹⁰And the LORD spoke to the fish, and it vomited out Jonah upon the dry land.

Nineveh Repents

3 Then the word of the LORD came to Jonah the second time, saying, ²"Arise, go to Nin'eveh, that great city, and proclaim to it the message that I tell you." ³So Jonah arose and went to Nin'eveh, according to the word of the LORD. Now Nineveh was an exceedingly great city, three days' journey in breadth. ⁴Jonah began to go into the city, going a day's journey. And he cried, "Yet forty days, and Nin'eveh shall be overthrown!" ⁵And the people of Nin'eveh believed God; they proclaimed a fast, and put on sackcloth, from the greatest of them to the least of them.

6 Then tidings reached the king of Nin'eveh, and he arose from his throne, removed his robe, and covered himself with sackcloth, and sat in ashes. ⁷And he made proclamation and published through

---

2:6 bars: The netherworld of Sheol is pictured as having gates that open and shut to admit the souls of the deceased into its realm (Job 17:16; 38:17). **yet:** The turning point when God intervened to save Jonah. **the Pit:** Another name for the place of the dead (Job 33:22; Ps 30:9).

2:7 my prayer came to you: The Lord in heaven hears prayers directed to his Temple on earth, even by those far away from it (1 Kings 8:30, 35–51; Dan 6:10).

2:8 Those who . . . regard . . . idols: The pagan sailors, who cried each to his own god in the midst of the storm (1:5). Jonah has a strong disdain for idolaters, even though the sailors who cast him into the sea acted more admirably than he, who claimed to "fear the LORD" (1:9) even while fleeing from him (1:3).

2:9 I . . . will sacrifice to you: Jonah vows to make a thank offering in the Temple, at which time he will relate the story of his deliverance to fellow worshipers. For background, see note on Lev 7:12 and essay: *Thanksgiving Psalms* at Ps 30.

2:10 it vomited out Jonah: A miracle that affords the prophet another opportunity to accept his mission from the Lord (3:2).

3:1 the word of the LORD: See note on 1:1.

3:2 Arise, go to Nineveh: Restates the original commission of 1:2. **the message:** The proclamation in 3:4 that Nineveh will be destroyed in forty days. Notice that Jonah's message of judgment does not specify that repentance will successfully avert the coming disaster. Nevertheless, the king and citizens express hope that their penitential actions will move God to spare the city (3:5–9).

3:3 was: Sometimes cited as an indication that the Book of Jonah was written after the fall of Nineveh in 612 B.C. If the book was written later, then use of the verb "was" may be the author's way of looking back on the former glory of the city. But since the story is told in the past tense, "was" may only point to the vastness of the city in Jonah's day. **great city:** A statement about Nineveh's size and importance. For other "great" cities in the Bible, see Josh 10:2; 1 Kings 4:13; Jer 22:8; Rev 11:8. **three days' journey in breadth:** Literally, "a walk of three days". The precise meaning of the expression is disputed. **(1)** The author may mean it would take Jonah three days to walk from one end of the city to the other (as understood by the RSV2CE, which adds the words "in breadth"). If

so, then he is exaggerating Nineveh's size for dramatic effect, since no known city, ancient or modern, has a diameter of 60 miles or more. **(2)** The author may mean that Jonah will need three days to preach the Lord's message in all the districts and neighborhoods of the city and perhaps even in the suburbs. Archaeologists estimate that the city of Nineveh (not including suburbs) was approximately one-square mile in the eighth century B.C.

3:4 Nineveh shall be overthrown!: A conditional prophecy in which the outcome depends on the response of the hearers. This is implicit rather than explicit, since Jonah never promises that God will spare the city if its inhabitants repent in time (in contrast to Jeremiah, who announces that God will show mercy to a sinful nation that repents, Jer 18:7–8). If Nineveh ignores the warning or fails to act within the forty days, it will become like Sodom and Gomorrah, wicked cities that the Lord "overthrew" with fire and brimstone (Gen 19:25). For references to Jonah's preaching in the Book of Tobit, see notes on 1:1 and Tob 14:4.

3:5 Nineveh believed: A stunning response to divine grace. The Ninevites, despite being pagan idolaters, took the message of the foreign prophet to heart and decided to seek the Lord, to turn from their wickedness, and to cry out for divine mercy (3:8). • Jesus cites the repentance of the Ninevites to rebuke his own generation for failing to respond to his preaching, even though he is one "greater than Jonah" (Mt 12:41; Lk 11:32). **a fast:** A public act of penitence, as in Jer 36:9 and Joel 2:15. Here the people abstain from food and water for an unspecified period of time (3:7). For the purposes behind fasting, see note on Joel 1:14. **sackcloth:** A coarse fabric spun from goat hair and worn next to the skin (2 Kings 6:30). Fasting and wearing sackcloth often go together as ritual expressions of mourning (Esther 4:3; Dan 9:3).

3:6 the king of Nineveh: Possibly the king of Assyria, which in the time of Jonah's career was probably Shalmaneser IV (782–773 B.C.) or Ashur-dan III (772–755 B.C.). However, since the Hebrew term for "king" can also designate a lesser "ruler", the expression may refer to a provincial governor who is headquartered in Nineveh. **sat in ashes:** An expression of mourning (Job 2:8; Is 58:5).

3:7 made proclamation: A city-wide ordinance is put into effect.

Nin'eveh, "By the decree of the king and his nobles: Let neither man nor beast, herd nor flock, taste anything; let them not feed, or drink water, [8]but let man and beast be covered with sackcloth, and let them cry mightily to God; yes, let every one turn from his evil way and from the violence which is in his hands. [9]Who knows, God may yet repent and turn from his fierce anger, so that we perish not?"

10 When God saw what they did, how they turned from their evil way, God repented of the evil which he had said he would do to them; and he did not do it.

Jonah's Anger

4 But it displeased Jonah exceedingly, and he was angry. [2]And he prayed to the LORD and said, "I pray you, LORD, is not this what I said when I was yet in my country? That is why I made haste to flee to Tar'shish; for I knew that you are a gracious God and merciful, slow to anger, and abounding in mercy, and that you repent of evil. [3]Therefore now,

O LORD, take my life from me, I beg you, for it is better for me to die than to live." [4]And the LORD said, "Do you do well to be angry?" [5]Then Jonah went out of the city and sat to the east of the city, and made a booth for himself there. He sat under it in the shade, till he should see what would become of the city.

God Reproves Jonah

6 And the LORD God appointed a plant,[b] and made it come up over Jonah, that it might be a shade over his head, to save him from his discomfort. So Jonah was exceedingly glad because of the plant.[b] [7]But when dawn came up the next day, God appointed a worm which attacked the plant,[b] so that it withered. [8]When the sun rose, God appointed a sultry east wind, and the sun beat upon the head of Jonah so that he was faint; and he asked that he might die, and said, "It is better for me to die than to live." [9]But God said to Jonah, "Do you do well to be angry for the plant?"[b] And he said, "I do well to be angry, angry enough to die." [10]And the LORD

3:9: Joel 2:14. **4:2:** Ex 34:6.

3:8 man and beast: For animals participating in community rituals of mourning, see also Jud 4:10 and Herodotus, *Histories* 9, 24. **cry mightily:** Earnest prayers for God to turn away his wrath from the city.

3:9 Who knows ...?: Implies that Nineveh's future is uncertain and that sincere repentance could still lead to a positive outcome (2 Sam 12:22; Joel 2:14; Amos 5:15).

3:10 God repented: A figurative description, not a literal one, since God is unchangeable (Mal 3:6). The point is that God holds back his judgment in response to the city's repentance, which was outward (fasting and sackcloth, 3:5) as well as inward (turning from evil and violence, 3:8). The example illustrates that God is patient with sinners, giving them time to mend their ways (2 Pet 3:9), and that he spares the sinner who seeks his mercy, regardless of nationality (Acts 10:34–35) (CCC 1037). • The saying of Jonah that Nineveh would be destroyed in forty days means "Its merits demand that it should be destroyed." The saying that God repented is metaphorical, insofar as he acts after the manner of one who repents by changing his sentence of judgment (St. Thomas Aquinas, *Summa Theologiae* II-II, 171, 6).

4:1–11 The Lord shows himself generous and merciful, while Jonah comes across as callous, selfish, and foolish—as someone out of touch with God's desire to save the nations beyond Israel. This unflattering picture of the prophet centers on a key contrast: Jonah's personal discomfort (4:7–9) concerns him more than 120,000 people being rescued from destruction (4:1).

4:1 it displeased Jonah exceedingly: Literally, "it was a very great evil to Jonah." The term for evil (Heb., *ra'ah*) is the subject of a wordplay in connection with 3:10: the Ninevites repented of "evil" (= their wicked ways), and so God withdrew his threat of "evil" (= calamity upon the city), and yet Jonah regards this outcome as "evil" (= a failure to punish sin). It is also ironic that Jonah finds it exceedingly evil that God spares Nineveh from destruction (4:1), and yet he is "exceedingly glad" when God saves him from the hot sun (4:6). **he was angry:** Jonah is patriotic to a fault. He is resentful because

he hoped that God would lay waste the Assyrians, who were idolatrous pagans and a looming threat to Israel. His desire to see Nineveh perish explains why he refused to preach to the wicked city in the first place (4:2). Jonah forgets that God has shown him mercy by saving his life (2:6) despite his disobedience (1:3).

4:2 Tarshish: See note on 1:3. **Gracious ... merciful ... slow to anger:** The Lord's most celebrated attributes in the Bible. They were revealed to Moses on Mt. Sinai (Ex 34:6–7) and represent a form of God's "power" over sin (Num 14:17–18).

4:3 take my life: Recalls the despondent words of Elijah in 1 Kings 19:4. Jonah's wish is tragically ironic: he is thankful to have been rescued from death (2:9), yet he would rather die than see Nineveh saved from death (4:9).

4:5 a booth: A makeshift shelter, probably built from tree branches. As soon as its leaves withered, Jonah would again be exposed to the sun. Hence the need for shade again in 4:6. **till he should see:** Jonah wanted to see if the Ninevites would resume their evil ways, prompting the Lord to reconsider his clemency and bring wrath upon the city (3:4).

4:6 appointed: An indication of God's sovereignty over creation, as also in 1:17; 4:7; 4:8. **a plant:** The precise meaning of the Hebrew *qîqāyôn* is uncertain. It is evidently a climbing plant with large leaves that grew up over Jonah's shelter. Possibilities include a gourd plant, a castor oil plant, or a type of ivy. **to save him:** An act of God's kindness.

4:7 worm ... withered: An act of God's discipline.

4:8 east wind: A hot and dry wind, increasing Jonah's discomfort. An "east wind" sometimes represents God's judgment (Is 27:8; Jer 18:17).

4:9 I do well: A stubborn and disrespectful response to God. Jonah still refuses to change his attitude or to see things from God's perspective.

4:10–11 The Lord tries to reason with Jonah: If the prophet finds it acceptable to pity a withering plant, which he neither made nor caused to grow, should not God pity 120,000 people whom he has made in his image and likeness? This final question is not answered by Jonah, leaving it to readers to make the correct response: God's mercy is something to celebrate; it should not provoke criticism or cause consternation.

---

[b] Heb *qiqayon*, probably *the castor oil plant.*

God is relenting (different version)

outcome changed because Ninevites changed their behavior

said, "You pity the plant,**b** for which you did not labor, nor did you make it grow, which came into being in a night, and perished in a night. ¹¹And should not I pity Nin'eveh, that great city, in which there are more than a hundred and twenty thousand persons who do not know their right hand from their left, and also much cattle?"

4:11 their right hand from their left: The Ninevites have a confused sense of what is right and wrong. Still, their culpability for sin is mitigated by not having the divine revelation that Israel possessed in the Scriptures. God has mercy on them in their plight. **much cattle:** Shows the Lord's providential care for animals (CCC 2416). The remark also adds a humorous point, as if to say, "Why should I not spare the city from destruction? There are over 120,000 repentant people there! Besides, look at all the cattle! If you cannot appreciate my mercy to the people, Jonah, perhaps you will at least see that wiping out the city would be a waste of cattle!" Jonah's hypocrisy is once again exposed: he cares about a dying plant, yet he has no qualms about a city teeming with life undergoing destruction.

---

b Heb *qiqayon*, probably *the castor oil plant*.

STUDY QUESTIONS
Jonah

Chapter 1

For understanding

1. **1:3.** What are the stages of Jonah's steady descent toward death? Where is Jonah's motive for running away from his divine calling revealed, and what was his motive? How is Tarshish usually identified, and why is that destination significant? Where is Joppa in relation to Jonah's hometown of Gath-hepher?
2. **1:9.** Who is a Hebrew? Why did Israelites sometimes use this term of themselves? How does Jonah indicate his religious affiliation? Ironically, how is his claim contradicted? What adds to the irony? How is saying that God is the one who made the sea still another irony?
3. **1:14.** To whom do even the pagan sailors pray? What is Jonah conspicuous for not doing? For what do the mariners not wish to be punished? What is the irony between the pagan sailors' concern for the life of a single Israelite and Jonah's apparent attitude?
4. **1:17.** What does the expression "the Lord appointed" show? Where else is the same expression used in this book? Of what does the great fish serve as an instrument? What in terms of the fish is the Hebrew nonspecific about? How does the Greek LXX translate the Hebrew? How long did journeys to the underworld often last in ancient Near Eastern literature? As what does Jesus view Jonah's three days in the fish? What does St. Cyril of Jerusalem say about the believability of Jesus' Resurrection from the tomb and Jonah's escape from the fish?

For application

1. **1:3.** Almost everyone tries at some point to evade a calling that the Lord has given him. Have you ever tried to avoid such a calling? If so, how aware were you that you did not do what the Lord asked of you? What form did your avoidance take?
2. **1:4.** If the Lord has given you a vocation that you have resisted, what winds of circumstance have opposed the decisions you have made? In other words, what plans, life directions, relationships, and so on have either not materialized or have failed? How have circumstances influenced your understanding of the Lord's will for you?
3. **1:5b–6.** To what extent do your responsibilities at home or in your career affect the welfare of others? How diligent are you in carrying out those duties? How have you sought the Lord regarding the performance of your work?
4. **1:9–10.** Among your friends and acquaintances, who knows that you describe yourself as a Catholic? What difference does your Catholicism make to them? What would they say about your practice of the faith?

Chapter 2

For understanding

1. **2:1–9.** With what are these verses concerned? When Jonah remembers praying to God as he was sinking in the sea, what type of experience might he actually have experienced? At any rate, how did the Lord save him? What does Jonah vow to do? What are we to notice about Jonah's prayer? Where else are several expressions and images of Jonah's prayer found?
2. **2:6.** How is the netherworld of Sheol pictured? What is another biblical name for the place of the dead?
3. **2:8.** When Jonah mentions "those who pay regard to vain idols", to whom is he referring? Although Jonah had a strong disdain for idolaters, who acted more admirably than he did, despite his claim to fear the Lord?

For application

1. **2:4.** Have you ever felt cast out of God's presence? How would you identify the cause of this feeling, such as a sense of your sinfulness or because of God's apparent silence? What spiritual steps have you taken to return to God's presence?
2. **2:6.** What has been the lowest time in your spiritual life? What was it like, and how long did it last? How did you maintain hope that the desolation would end? How did the Lord bring you out of it? What did you learn from the experience?
3. **2:9.** Jonah offers his prayer of thanksgiving while still in the belly of the fish. How can praying prayers of thanks while in the midst of suffering help with the suffering itself? How does thanksgiving strengthen faith? At such a time, for what would you give thanks?

Chapter 3

For understanding

1. **3:3.** Of what is the word "was" in this verse sometimes cited as proof? Why is the argument inconclusive? Of what is "a three days' journey" not a measure? Rather, what might the author be intending to stress, or else what is the point of the statement? At the time of the story, how large was the walled city of Nineveh?
2. **3:4.** What is a conditional prophecy? What will happen if Nineveh repents or if it ignores the warning?
3. **3:5.** In their stunning response to divine grace, what do the people do? Why does Jesus cite the repentance of the Ninevites in reference to his own generation? In their public act of penitence, what do the people do, and for how long? How is sackcloth made and worn? Why do fasting and wearing sackcloth go together?
4. **3:10.** How do we understand the description of God repenting here? What is the point? What does the example illustrate? How does St. Thomas Aquinas explain the saying of Jonah that Nineveh would be destroyed in forty days?

For application

1. **3:4.** The wording of this verse suggests that Jonah never completed the three days' journey into Nineveh, that he only went a day's journey into it. What does that suggest about his eagerness to spread God's warning? Have you ever begun an unpleasant spiritual task, such as a fast or a discipline, and failed to complete it?

2. **3:5.** Some religious movements spread like wildfire. What Christian movements can you think of that have spread quickly across this country? Whom did they affect? What long-term impact did they have on Christian life and practice? If you were involved in such a movement, how did it change your faith?

3. **3:6–9.** Religious leaders are often the last to get involved in the spread of a movement. Judging from the response of the king of Nineveh, who published supporting regulations, what is the role of the leader in addressing people's fervid excitement?

Chapter 4

For understanding

1. **4:1.** How is the "evil" of the repentance of Nineveh the subject of a wordplay in connection with the previous verse? What is the irony in Jonah's "exceedingly" strong reactions to God's behavior? Why is Jonah resentful? What does his desire to see Nineveh perish explain? What does Jonah forget?

2. **4:5.** What kind of booth does Jonah build? As soon as its leaves wither, what will happen? What does Jonah want to see?

3. **4:10–11.** How does God try to reason with Jonah? Because this final question is not answered by Jonah, what is left to the reader to do?

4. **4:11.** What do the Ninevites lack? Nevertheless, what mitigates their culpability for sin? What does the detail about the Lord's providential care for animals expose regarding Jonah's hypocrisy?

For application

1. **4:2.** Have you ever tried to convince God that your disobedience was not wrong or that his will for your life is mistaken? How do you recognize the point at which explaining your motives becomes mere rationalizing? When you understand what God's will is, how does resistance to it harm you?

2. **4:4.** St. Paul, quoting Ps 4, says, "Be angry, but sin not" (Eph 4:26; Ps 4:4). When does the emotion of anger become sinful? If you get angry at God, how do you avoid sinning against him?

3. **4:6–8.** The word "appointed" appears three times in these verses. According to the note for v. 6, what does this repetition stress about God's sovereignty? How does Jonah react to the changes in his circumstances? How does your behavior compare with his when your circumstances change in one direction or another?

4. **4:9.** In this verse, Jonah persists in his anger. If you met with such persistence in a child, how would you deal with it? If you met with it in an adult, what would you do? How have you learned or been taught to let your anger go?

INTRODUCTION TO MICAH

Author and Date The superscription traces the oracles of the book to "Micah of Moresheth" (1:1), who spoke the word of the Lord in the latter half of the eighth century B.C. during the reigns of three kings of Judah: Jotham (750–731 B.C.), Ahaz (735–715 B.C.), and Hezekiah (729–686 B.C.). This tells us that Micah ministered at the same time as the prophet Isaiah and was a younger contemporary of the prophet Hosea. Unfortunately, almost nothing more is known about him. No information is given about his genealogy or background, although indications within the book suggest that he, like the prophet Amos, was a man of humble and rural origins. Nevertheless, Micah's prophecies were sufficiently well-known to be quoted more than a century after his lifetime during the trial of Jeremiah in Jerusalem (Jer 26:18). It is unknown whether Micah himself was responsible for preserving his oracles in writing and compiling them into a book or whether this was done by a disciple or scribal associate.

Modern scholarship is divided on the date of the Book of Micah. There is broad agreement that chapters 1–3 come from the time of the prophet in the eighth century B.C., but some have challenged the originality of chapters 4–7, particularly passages that describe events and circumstances of the sixth century B.C. For example, the oracle in 4:10 is explicit that Zion's inhabitants will be exiled to Babylon, even though this city was neither the center of a conquering empire nor a threat to Jerusalem until long after Micah's day, and 7:7–13 is said to reflect the mind-set of the exilic period before Judah's release from Babylon in 538 B.C. Aside from skepticism over theological claims that God revealed the future to his prophets, there is no incontestable evidence that requires dating these and similar passages more than a century after the rest of the book. If Micah was active as a prophet between 735 and 700 B.C., then the book can be reasonably dated around 690 B.C.

Title The book is named after Micah, mentioned in the opening verse. Its Hebrew form, *Mîkhāh*, is an abbreviation for *Mîkhāyāh*, meaning "Who is like Yah(weh)?" or "Who is like the LORD?" (see Jer 26:18 MT). The name appears in the Greek Septuagint in the title *Michaias*, while this heading is expanded in the Latin Vulgate to *Micha Propheta*, "Micah the Prophet". English titles for the book follow these ancient traditions.

Place in the Canon Micah has long been revered as a canonical book of Scripture. In the Jewish Bible, or Tanakh, it stands among the Latter Prophets in a sub-collection of writings known as "the Book of the Twelve". In Christian Bibles, these twelve books are called the Minor Prophets, not because they are less important than Isaiah, Jeremiah, Ezekiel, and Daniel, but because they are comparatively shorter. In the Hebrew Bible and Latin Vulgate, Micah stands sixth among the Minor Prophets, just as it does in English Bibles. In the Greek Septuagint, it is the third book in the collection, standing between Amos and Joel.

Structure The Book of Micah gives the impression of being random and unstructured. It is clearly an anthology of the prophet's messages, but the logic of its arrangement is not obvious to modern readers. That said, a case can be made that its contents have been grouped into three prophetic addresses: chapters 1–2, chapters 3–5, and chapters 6–7. Each of these units begins with an appeal to "Hear" the words of the prophet (1:2; 3:1; 6:1), and each follows a similar progression from oracles of condemnation to oracles of salvation. **(1)** The first address takes aim at the Northern Kingdom of Israel and then at the Southern Kingdom of Judah. Both will suffer the dreadful judgments of God, the north when the city of Samaria is destroyed (1:6), and the south when captives from various cities of the land are taken into exile (1:16). The section ends with a promise that the Lord will regather the scattered sheep of his people (2:12–13). **(2)** The second address denounces Israel's wicked leaders for exploiting God's people and warns of his judgments to come. Following these announcements, Micah foresees a glorious future in which the nations stream to Zion to learn from the God of Israel (4:1–4), while a new Davidic ruler arises from Bethlehem, bringing a new era of peace and spiritual renewal (5:2–15). **(3)** The third address begins with a covenant lawsuit in which Lord brings charges against his sinful people and sentences them to suffer his punishments. Following a lament over the chaos of his times, Micah ends by announcing the restoration of Zion (7:11–12), describing the fear of the nations (7:16–17) and celebrating the mercy and fidelity of God (7:18–20). See also *Outline*.

Historical Background Micah prophesied during a period of Assyrian domination and expansion in the Near East. In the early years of his ministry, the Assyrians dismantled the Northern Kingdom of Israel and destroyed the city of Samaria (722 B.C.); and near the end of his ministry, the Assyrians ravaged multiple cities in the Southern Kingdom of Judah and laid siege to Jerusalem (701 B.C.). These lamentable events are the experiences that Micah shared with his contemporaries, but they are not the only ones envisioned in the book. The prophet also looked beyond the horizon of his own generation to foresee the Babylonian conquest and exile of Jerusalem (586 B.C.) as well as the return of exiles from Babylon soon after the start of the Persian period (539 B.C.). The book is thus anchored in events of the eighth century B.C. as well as events of the sixth century B.C.

Message of the Prophet Like many of the biblical prophets, Micah is a messenger of judgment and restoration. He does not hesitate to denounce wickedness in Israel and to warn that the Lord is coming to discipline his sinful people. At the same time, he is careful not to destroy all hope for the future by implying that God's judgment is the last word. The same Lord who comes to chastise the evildoing of his people also has plans to bless them by gathering a remnant of Israelites from exile and by sending them a ruler-shepherd from Bethlehem to establish peace. History, according to Micah, follows a divine plan that reveals not only God's intolerance for wanton iniquity but also his mercy and faithfulness.

Divine acts of judgment are made necessary by widespread rebellion against the covenant. The prophet directs most of his preaching against sins of worship, greed, and deception. Among their *sins of worship*, the people of Israel are guilty of serving idols and embracing the pagan religious practices of the Canaanites (1:7; 5:13–14). Even when worship is given to the Lord, the prophet faults his fellow Israelites for treating sacrifices as substitutes for what God truly requires—justice, kindness, and humility (6:6–8). In confronting *sins of greed*, Micah goes after powerful oppressors who unjustly seize lands that belong to others (2:1–2, 9). He also rails against prophets and priests who sell their services out of a covetous desire for gain (3:5–7, 11). Judges and princes who deny justice to the common people by accepting bribes are likewise exposed for their corruption (3:11; 7:3). As for *sins of deception*, Micah singles out fraud in the marketplace (6:11) and laments the mass erosion of honesty and truth in all levels of society (7:5–6). On top of all this, religious authorities embrace the false hope that the covenant people have nothing to fear because the Lord, who dwells among them, will never allow their homeland to suffer calamity (3:11). Because of these evils, the Lord intends to devise "evil" against them (2:3). This will take different forms at different times, from the Assyrian conquest of Samaria (1:6–7) and the Assyrian Exile of several cities in Judah in the prophet's lifetime (1:10–16) to the Babylonian desolation and exile of Jerusalem more than a century later (4:10; cf. 3:12; 6:9–16).

Divine acts of mercy and restoration are also envisioned that will begin to reverse the tragedies of Israel's history. Micah insists that God will not forget about the exiles of Israel and Judah that conquering nations will send as captives to foreign lands. On the contrary, he plans to gather the remnant of Israel as a scattered flock is brought back safely into a sheepfold (2:12–13). Later one learns that he will shepherd his restored people through Israel's future ruler, the Messiah, who will come from David's tiny hometown of Bethlehem and yet his greatness will be known to the ends of the earth (5:2–4). Likewise, even though Jerusalem will be reduced to ruins (3:12) and its inhabitants will go to Babylon (4:10), the prophet promises that its walls will be rebuilt and its children regathered (7:11–12), while its enemies will be put to shame (7:10) and come to fear the Lord (7:16–17). In these days of fulfillment, the mountain of the house of the Lord will be exalted as a place of international pilgrimage where the nations of the world go to seek instruction and justice from the God of Israel (4:1–4).

The closing prayer of the book puts Micah's message into a theological framework. It praises God as One who has no equal or rival in "pardoning iniquity" and in showing extraordinary "compassion" to his wayward people (7:18–19). This demonstrates the Lord's "faithfulness" to the covenant that he has sworn to Abraham and the Patriarchs (7:20) that someday blessings will come to all nations of the earth (4:1–3; cf. Gen 22:16–18). The book also shows God's faithfulness to the covenant he made with David to raise up one of his descendants to rule over his kingdom forever and to possess the ends of the earth (5:2–4; cf. 2 Sam 7:12–18; Ps 2:8; 72:8).

Christian Perspective The New Testament both quotes and alludes to the Book of Micah. In the story of the Nativity, Herod inquires about the birthplace of the Messiah, and the chief priests and scribes direct him to Micah's prophecy that Israel's future ruler will come from Bethlehem (5:2; Mt 2:6). Years later, while instructing his disciples, Jesus draws from the words of Micah to warn that commitment to his gospel can create tensions even within families, pitting sons against fathers and daughters against mothers (7:6; Mt 10:35–36; Lk 12:53). Two of Micah's oracles also stand in the background of Jesus' teaching without being cited explicitly. In one, the prophet foresees the Lord gathering the remnant of Israel as a shepherd gathers his sheep into a fold and then leads them out behind him (2:12–13). Parallels suggest that Jesus draws in part from this vision when he declares himself the Good Shepherd who gathers, protects, and leads his sheep (Jn 10:1–18). Similarly, when Jesus announces before his Ascension that "repentance and forgiveness of sins should be preached in his name to all nations, beginning from Jerusalem" (Lk 24:47), he is tapping into the prophetic expectation that, in days to come, "many nations" will seek instruction from the God of Israel and "the word of the LORD" will go forth "from Jerusalem" (4:2; cf. Is 2:2–4).

OUTLINE OF MICAH

1. Judgment of Samaria and Jerusalem (chaps. 1–2)
   A. Superscription (1:1)
   B. The Demise of Samaria (1:2–7)
   C. The Conquest of Cities in Judah (1:8–16)
   D. Evil in Store for the Evil (2:1–11)
   E. The Remnant of Israel Will Be Gathered (2:12–13)

2. Judgment of Israel's Leaders (chaps. 3–5)
   A. Charges against Rulers, Prophets, and Priests (3:1–11)
   B. Forewarning of Jerusalem's Destruction (3:12)
   C. The Exaltation of Zion (4:1–8)
   D. Travail of the Daughter of Zion (4:9—5:1)
   E. Israel's Royal Shepherd from Bethlehem (5:2–15)

3. Judgment of Israel and the Sinful City (chaps. 6–7)
   A. Covenant Lawsuit against Israel (6:1–8)
   B. Desolation of the Sinful City (6:9–16)
   C. Lament over Evil Times (7:1–7)
   D. Jerusalem Vindicated and Restored (7:8–13)
   E. Prayer to the God Feared by the Nations and Faithful to His Covenants (7:14–20)

THE BOOK OF
MICAH

Prophecy concerning Samaria and Judah

1 The word of the Lord that came to Mi′cah of Mo′resheth in the days of Jo′tham, A′haz, and Hezeki′ah, kings of Judah, which he saw concerning Samar′ia and Jerusalem.

²Hear, you peoples, all of you;
    listen, O earth, and all that is in it;
  and let the Lord God be a witness against you,
    the Lord from his holy temple.
³For behold, the Lord is coming forth out of his place,
    and will come down and tread upon the high places of the earth.
⁴And the mountains will melt under him
    and the valleys will be cleft,
  like wax before the fire,
    like waters poured down a steep place.
⁵All this is for the transgression of Jacob
    and for the sins of the house of Israel.

What is the transgression of Jacob?
    Is it not Samar′ia?
And what is the sin of the houseᵃ of Judah?
    Is it not Jerusalem?
⁶Therefore I will make Samar′ia a heap in the open country,
    a place for planting vineyards;
  and I will pour down her stones into the valley,
    and uncover her foundations.
⁷All her images shall be beaten to pieces,
    all her hires shall be burned with fire,
  and all her idols I will lay waste;
  for from the hire of a harlot she gathered them,
    and to the hire of a harlot they shall return.

⁸For this I will lament and wail;
    I will go stripped and naked;
  I will make lamentation like the jackals,
    and mourning like the ostriches.

1:2: 1 Kings 22:28.

1:1 The word of the Lord: Prophetic revelation from God entrusted to a human messenger. See essay: *The Word of the Lord* at Hos 1. **Micah:** A shortened form of the name Micaiah, meaning "Who is like the Lord?". A pun on his name appears in 7:18. Micah was conscious of being inspired and empowered by the Spirit of God to deliver his message (3:8). **Moresheth:** A village in the low hills of western Judah that lay near the Philistine city of Gath. Micah was thus a citizen of the Southern Kingdom of Judah. **Jotham, Ahaz, and Hezekiah:** Three successive kings of Judah whose reigns covered more than half a century, from 750 to 686 B.C. Micah's ministry can probably be dated in the window 735–700 B.C., which was also the time of Isaiah's ministry (Is 1:1). **which he saw:** Divine messages given to the prophets were sometimes visual as well as verbal (Is 1:1; Ezek 7:26; Amos 9:1–10). **Samaria:** Capital of the Northern Kingdom of Israel since the days of King Ahab (1 Kings 16:29). It lay nearly 40 miles north of Jerusalem in the central hill country of Israel. **Jerusalem:** Capital of the Southern Kingdom of Judah. Micah probably did most of his preaching in Jerusalem.

1:2–16 Oracles against Samaria and Jerusalem. Both cities have become strongholds of iniquity, and so the Lord plans to punish their sins by destroying Samaria and its idols (1:6–7) and by chastening Judah with mourning and exile (1:8–16). Historically, these judgments were carried out by the Assyrians, who conquered Samaria in 722 B.C. under King Shalmaneser V (2 Kings 18:9–10) and who devastated numerous towns in Judah in 701 B.C. under King Sennecharib (2 Kings 18:13). Jerusalem was not taken in 701, but the surviving *Annals of*

Sennecharib state that more than 200,000 captives were exiled from Judah at this time (1:16).

1:2 Hear, you peoples: The world is summoned to listen as the Lord brings charges against his rebellious people: Israel and Judah (Is 1:2). It introduces the first division of the book (chaps. 1–2). **his holy temple:** The Lord's Temple in heaven, as indicated by his coming "down" upon the mountaintops in the next verse (1:3). This celestial sanctuary is the unseen counterpart to the Lord's Temple in Jerusalem (Ps 11:4; Wis 9:8; Heb 8:5; Rev 11:19). See essay: *Theology of the Temple* at 2 Chron 5.

1:3 the Lord is coming: I.e., to enforce the terms of his covenant by bringing its curses for disobedience (Deut 28:15–68). Micah describes the event with the poetical language of a theophany, in which creation withers in fear when the Creator's wrath is aroused and his power is revealed.

1:5 the house of Israel: The Northern Kingdom of Israel. **the sins:** The Hebrew term *bāmôt* means "high places". The prophet insinuates by this term that Jerusalem has become a place of corrupt worship. See word study: *High Places* at 2 Kings 23:5. **the house of Judah:** The Southern Kingdom of Judah.

1:6 Samaria: See note on 1:1. **a heap:** A pile of rubble. For the Assyrian conquest of Samaria in 722 B.C., see 2 Kings 17:5–6; 18:10. **a place for planting:** The city will be emptied of its people and revert to farmland (cf. 3:12).

1:7 idols: The Northern Kingdom of Israel was idolatrous from its beginning (1 Kings 12:25–30; 16:32). Its deviant worship became the primary reason for its downfall (2 Kings 17:5–23). **the hire of a harlot:** Prostitution is a common way that Scripture speaks about idolatry. To serve gods other than the Lord is to "play the harlot" (Ex 34:15–16; Lev 20:5; Judg 2:17).

1:8–16 A funeral lament over Judah and Jerusalem. The list of towns probably marks the route taken by the Assyrian army when Sennecharib marched toward Jerusalem from the southwest in 701 B.C. The text displays several wordplays and puns in the Hebrew, many of which are hard to capture in translation.

1:8 I will lament: Micah appears to be the speaker. **stripped and naked:** A symbolic act that dramatizes the prophecy of conquest and exile (cf. Is 20:2–4).

Micah lived and prophesied at about the same time as Isaiah, in the kingdom of Judah. Like his contemporaries, he denounces the evils of his age, which he contrasts dramatically with the requirements of God: "to do justice, and to love kindness, and to walk humbly" with God (6:8). He foretells God's punishments, even the fall of Jerusalem (3:12). At the same time he prophesies, like Isaiah, that a remnant shall be saved (chapters 4–5) and speaks of the Messiah to come (5:2).

ᵃ Gk Tg Compare Syr: Heb *what are the high places.*

⁹For her wound ᵇ is incurable;
   and it has come to Judah,
it has reached to the gate of my people,
   to Jerusalem.

¹⁰Tell it not in Gath,
   weep not at all;
in Beth'-le-aph'rah
   roll yourselves in the dust.
¹¹Pass on your way,
   inhabitants of Sha'phir,
   in nakedness and shame;
the inhabitants of Za'anan
   do not come forth;
the wailing of Beth-e'zel
   shall take away from you its standing
      place.
¹²For the inhabitants of Ma'roth
   wait anxiously for good,
because evil has come down from the LORD
   to the gate of Jerusalem.
¹³Harness the steeds to the chariots,
   inhabitants of La'chish;
you were ᶜ the beginning of sin
   to the daughter of Zion,
for in you were found
   the transgressions of Israel.
¹⁴Therefore you shall give parting gifts
   to Mo'resheth-gath;

the houses of Ach'zib shall be a deceitful thing
   to the kings of Israel.
¹⁵I will again bring a conqueror upon you,
   inhabitants of Mare'shah;
the glory of Israel
   shall come to Adul'lam.
¹⁶Make yourselves bald and cut off your hair,
   for the children of your delight;
make yourselves as bald as the eagle,
   for they shall go from you into exile.

Evils of the People Denounced but a Remnant Will Be Gathered

2 Woe to those who devise wickedness
   and work evil upon their beds!
When the morning dawns, they perform it,
   because it is in the power of their hand.
²They covet fields, and seize them;
   and houses, and take them away;
they oppress a man and his house,
   a man and his inheritance.
³Therefore thus says the LORD:
Behold, against this family I am devising evil,
   from which you cannot remove your necks;
and you shall not walk haughtily,
   for it will be an evil time.
⁴In that day they shall take up a taunt song
   against you,
   and wail with bitter lamentation,

1:9 reached to the gate: The Assyrian siege of Jerusalem in 701 B.C. According to 2 Kings 19:32–35, the Lord intervened in a miraculous way to lift the siege and spare the city (2 Kings 19:32–35).

1:10 Tell it not in Gath: A saying attributed to David when he learned of the death of Saul and his sons (2 Sam 1:20). News of Assyria's capture of Judahite towns should not be publicized in the Philistine city of Gath, lest Judah's enemies rejoice over its distress. **Beth-le-aphrah:** Translates "house of dust".

1:11 Shaphir: Similar in sound to a Hebrew term for "beautiful". **Zaanan:** The name is related to a verb meaning "go out, go forth". **Beth-ezel:** Translates "house standing next to".

1:12 Maroth: A plural adjective meaning "bitter".

1:13 the steeds: The Hebrew term sounds similar to the name Lachish. **Lachish:** A fortified city guarding the approach to Jerusalem from the southwest (Tell el-Duweir). It was assaulted and taken by the Assyrians in 701 B.C. (2 Kings 19:8). **the daughter of Zion:** A poetical personification of Jerusalem. See word study: *The Daughter of Zion* at Lam 1:6.

1:14 parting gifts: Gifts given to a young bride when she left the care of her family. Here a town once belonging to Judah will be claimed by Assyria and forced to pay tribute to its conquerors. **Moresheth-gath:** Micah's hometown (Jer 26:18). See note on 1:1. **Achzib:** Related to a term meaning "deceitful".

1:15 a conqueror: The Hebrew term sounds similar to Mareshah. **the glory of Israel:** Refers to the prominent men of the town, who will be forced to flee before the Assyrians (2 Sam 1:19). **Adullam:** Over 15 miles southwest of Jerusalem. David once made a cave in Adullam one of his hideouts (1 Sam 22:1–2).

1:16 Make yourselves bald: Shaving the head was an ancient mourning ritual (Is 22:12; Jer 16:6; Amos 8:10). **into exile:** Sennacherib's deportation of captive Judahites. See note on 1:2–16.

2:1–5 The sins of Judah that merit "grievous destruction" at the hands of the Lord (2:10). The prophet targets members of the rich and ruling class who have the "power" (2:1) to seize estates from defenseless commoners by deceptive land dealings (2:2). As fitting punishment for this injustice, the robbers of land will become victims of robbery, with their own lands and fields taken by others (2:4). Micah sympathizes with the oppressed, in part because he himself is a man of humble origins (1:1).

2:1 Woe: A cry of lamentation and distress heard at funerals. See word study: *Woe* at Is 28:1. **those who devise wickedness:** Planners and perpetrators of moral iniquity (Heb., 'āven). The Lord is well aware of their evildoing; indeed, he is "devising evil" against them in return (2:3; Jer 18:11). **upon their beds:** Sinister schemes are concocted in the darkness of night.

2:2 They covet fields ... houses: In violation of the tenth commandment of the Decalogue, which forbids coveting a neighbor's property, including his "house" and "field" (Deut 5:21) (CCC 2534). **inheritance:** Family estates unjustly seized by greedy oppressors (2:9).

2:3 this family: The tribal people of Israel. **evil:** The Hebrew ra'ah here means "disaster" or "calamity", not moral evil, as in 2:1. **your necks:** Suggests the yoke of foreign rule is in view (Deut 28:48). **an evil time:** A time of bitter suffering and woe (Amos 5:13).

2:4 a taunt: A proverbial song or saying that mocks the humiliation of the arrogant (Is 14:4; Hab 2:6). **the portion of my people:** The lands apportioned to Israel's tribes and families (Josh 13–21).

ᵇ Gk Syr Vg: Heb *wounds*.
ᶜ Cn: Heb *it was*.

and say, "We are utterly ruined;
    he changes the portion of my people;
how he removes it from me!
      Among our captors[d] he divides our
        fields."
⁵Therefore you will have none to cast the line
    by lot
    in the assembly of the Lord.

⁶"Do not preach"—thus they preach—
    "one should not preach of such things;
    disgrace will not overtake us."
⁷Should this be said, O house of Jacob?
    Is the Spirit of the Lord impatient?
    Are these his doings?
Do not my words do good
    to him who walks uprightly?
⁸But you rise against my people[e] as an enemy;
    you strip the robe from the peaceful,[f]
from those who pass by trustingly
    with no thought of war.
⁹The women of my people you drive out
    from their pleasant houses;
from their young children you take away
    my glory for ever.

¹⁰Arise and go,
    for this is no place to rest;
because of uncleanness that destroys
    with a grievous destruction.
¹¹If a man should go about and utter wind and lies,
    saying, "I will preach to you of wine and
      strong drink,"
he would be the preacher for this people!

¹²I will surely gather all of you, O Jacob,
    I will gather the remnant of Israel;
I will set them together
    like sheep in a fold,
like a flock in its pasture,
    a noisy multitude of men.
¹³He who opens the breach will go up before them;
    they will break through and pass the gate,
    going out by it.
Their king will pass on before them,
    the Lord at their head.

Evil Rulers and Prophets

3 And I said:
Hear, you heads of Jacob
    and rulers of the house of Israel!
Is it not for you to know justice?—

read

2:5 you will have none: The guilty will have no share in the Promised Land after the return from exile, implying their families will have died out, with none left to claim an inheritance. **the assembly:** The restored community of the future, called "the remnant of Israel" in 2:12 (cf. 4:6–7).

2:6–11 Micah's contends with civic leaders and false prophets who oppose his message and want him to keep silent. It is not the prophet but these adversaries who are the real "enemy" of God's people because they scoff at his warning that evil days are coming (2:6) and prefer calls for drinking and celebration instead of repentance (2:11).

2:7 O house of Jacob: The people of Israel. **the Spirit of the Lord:** The divine power behind Micah's preaching (3:8). **impatient?:** Implied answer: No, the Lord denounces sin and warns of future judgment in order to give people an opportunity to turn from their evil ways before time runs out (Rom 2:4; 2 Pet 3:9). **my words do good:** I.e., they encourage victims with assurance that God will bring their oppressors to justice.

2:8 my people: The prophet identifies with the people who have been wronged. **no thought of war:** The victims of fraud and property seizure pose no threat at all to those who exploit them.

2:10 Arise and go: Into exile (1:16). **no place to rest:** Judah cannot expect to live in peace after having committed crimes against innocent "women" and "children" (2:9). **uncleanness:** Implies that injustice is defiling the land.

2:11 wind and lies: Vain and false messages that tell people what they want to hear, not what they need to hear (2 Tim 4:3). **strong drink:** Not distilled liquor, but beer or ale. **He would be the preacher:** Spoken sarcastically.

 2:12–13 A prophecy of restoration after judgment. The Lord will regather the exiles of Israel from foreign lands like a shepherd corrals a flock of scattered sheep into the protection of an enclosure and then leads them out to pasture through the gate (Is 40:11; Ezek 34:11–16). The con-

text suggests Micah envisions a reversal of the Assyrian exiles of the eighth century b.c. (7:12), since Assyria exiled thousands of Israelites from Samaria in 722 b.c. and then deported thousands more from Judah in 701 b.c. The prophet's vision may also include Jerusalem's return from Babylonian Exile in the sixth century b.c., an event that is prophesied later in the book (4:10). See note on 1:2–16. • Jesus seems to allude to this passage in Jn 10:1–18, describing himself as a Good Shepherd who gathers his flock into a sheepfold and then leads them out to pasture by passing through the gate ahead of them (CCC 754). • Christ's Ascension into heaven lifts up our hope. For by placing the human nature that he assumed in heaven, Christ gives us the hope of going there as well. Hence, it is written in Micah: "He shall go up opening the way before them" (St. Thomas Aquinas, *Summa Theologiae* III, 57, 1).

2:12 I will gather: A promise of restoration from exile (Deut 30:3–5). **the remnant:** Refers to a small part of a greater whole. See word study: *Remnant* at Zeph 2:7. **a fold:** A pen or enclosure made of stacked stones with a single entryway. It was used to keep flocks safe from predators and thieves at night.

2:13 Their king: Here identified as the Lord God, but Micah later describes a Davidic ruler from Bethlehem who will "feed his flock in the strength of the Lord" (5:4). In a similar way, Ezekiel promises that both the divine Lord and the Davidic Messiah will shepherd the restored People of God (Ezek 34:15, 23). • Christian faith sees a conjunction of these divine and human roles in the Incarnation, in which Christ the Good Shepherd is both the eternal Son of God and the messianic heir of David (Lk 1:32–34; Rom 1:3–4) (CCC 436–45).

3:1–12 Micah condemns the corruption of Judah's leaders. Political authorities deny justice to the people and hate what is good (3:1–2, 9, 11), while religious authorities are tainted by greed for material gain (3:5, 11). As a consequence of these sins, crooked rulers will not have their prayers answered (3:4), prophets in love with money will not receive divine revelation (3:6), and the city and Temple of Jerusalem will face a threat of destruction (3:12).

3:1 Hear: A summons to listen as the Lord brings charges against evildoers. Following 1:2, it introduces the second

---

[d] Cn: Heb *the rebellious*.
[e] Cn: Heb *yesterday my people rose*.
[f] Cn: Heb *from before a garment*.

2   you who hate the good and love the evil,
who tear the skin from off my people,
and their flesh from off their bones;
³who eat the flesh of my people,
and flay their skin from off them,
and break their bones in pieces,
and chop them up like meat⁹ in a kettle,
like flesh in a caldron.

⁴Then they will cry to the LORD,
but he will not answer them;
he will hide his face from them at that time,
because they have made their deeds evil.

⁵Thus says the LORD concerning the prophets
who lead my people astray,
who cry "Peace"
when they have something to eat,
but declare war against him
who puts nothing into their mouths.
⁶Therefore it shall be night to you, without
vision,
and darkness to you, without divination.
The sun shall go down upon the prophets,
and the day shall be black over
them;

⁷the seers shall be disgraced,
and the diviners put to shame;
they shall all cover their lips,
for there is no answer from God.
⁸But as for me, I am filled with power,
with the Spirit of the LORD,
and with justice and might,
to declare to Jacob his transgression
and to Israel his sin.

⁹Hear this, you heads of the house of Jacob
and rulers of the house of Israel,
who abhor justice
and pervert all equity,
¹⁰who build Zion with blood
and Jerusalem with wrong.
¹¹Its heads give judgment for a bribe,
its priests teach for hire,
its prophets divine for money;
yet they lean upon the LORD and say,
"Is not the LORD in the midst of us?
No evil shall come upon us."
¹²Therefore because of you
Zion shall be plowed as a field;
Jerusalem shall become a heap of ruins,
and the mountain of the house a wooded height.

division of the book (chaps. 3–5). **the house of Israel:** Here refers to the people of Jerusalem (3:9–10), whose population swelled after 722 B.C. with refugees from the northern tribes of Israel (cf. 2 Chron 30:25). **justice:** The Hebrew *mishpaṭ* means an equal application of the Mosaic Law to all members of the covenant community, regardless of a person's wealth or social standing.

3:2–3 Abuse of power is tantamount to cannibalism against the common folk, with rulers acting like butchers processing meat and making stew.

3:4 he will not answer: Sin is a hindrance to effective prayer (Ps 66:18; Is 1:15; 1 Pet 3:7). **he will hide his face:** I.e., God will withhold his favor.

3:5 the prophets: Spokesmen for the Lord who have become corrupted and unreliable. Micah accuses them of changing their message depending on the amount food or money offered to them by inquirers. The Lord will judge them by keeping them in the dark about his plans (3:6) and by bringing shame on them (3:7). **Peace:** The signature message of a false prophet who supports the status quo despite living in evil times (Jer 6:14; 8:11; Ezek 13:10). True prophets do not shy away from decrying sin and warning of its consequences (3:8; Is 58:1).

3:6 darkness: An ironic punishment for those who claim to enlighten others with words from God.

3:7 seers: An archaic name for prophets (1 Sam 9:9). **diviners:** Predicters of the future. Divination is the pagan art of fortune-telling, which is condemned in the Mosaic Law (Deut 18:9–14) (CCC 2116–17). **cover their lips:** Holding a hand over one's mouth indicates there is nothing to say (7:16; Job 21:5). **no answer:** The silence of God is a sign of his displeasure, as in 3:4.

3:8 I am filled with ... the Spirit: Micah is supernaturally empowered to proclaim justice and denounce evil

among the covenant people. The divine Spirit thus enabled his words to "do good" (2:7) and to predict events of the future (e.g., 4:10). Ezekiel was similarly conscious of prophesying by the Spirit (Ezek 2:2; 3:12), as was the apostle John (Rev 1:10). That the Spirit makes possible what is humanly impossible, see note on Judg 3:10. For NT teaching on prophetic inspiration, see 1 Pet 1:10–12; 2 Pet 1:20–21. • In the Nicene Creed, the Spirit is identified as the Divine Person "who has spoken through the prophets" (CCC 687, 702).

3:9 Hear this: See note on 3:1.

3:10 Zion: Jerusalem. See note on 4:2. **with blood:** May have inspired the wording of Hab 2:12.

3:11 for a bribe: Bribery in the courts is a perversion of justice (Deut 16:19) that was also criticized by Isaiah at this time (Is 1:23). **priests:** Commissioned to teach the Torah to the people (Lev 10:11), although not for profit beyond the people's tithes (Num 18:25–32). **prophets:** See note on 3:5. **Is not the LORD in the midst of us?:** A sin of presumption and self-deception. Jerusalem's protection lies not in having the Lord's Temple within its walls but in its people obeying the Lord's covenant (Jer 7:4). The belief that Zion was inviolable may have arisen from an isolated reading of select Scripture passages (e.g., Ps 46:4–5; 48:1–3; Is 31:5).

3:12 Zion shall be plowed: A picture of Jerusalem in the aftermath of divine judgment, with the mighty city destroyed and transformed into a farmed and forested hilltop. Judging from the citation and interpretation of his passage in Jer 26:18–19, this was a conditional prophecy that never came to pass in Micah's day because the city spared the prophet's life and King Hezekiah prayed earnestly for the Lord to protect Zion from Assyrian conquest (2 Kings 19:1–37). Still, the Lord's judgment against the city was not cancelled but postponed: more than a century later, the city would become wicked again and, refusing to repent, would be destroyed by the Babylonians (2 Kings 25:8–10). For another conditional prophecy about a city that was spared for a time, see Jon 3:1–10. **the house:** The Solomonic Temple.

⁹Gk: Heb *as.*

104

Prophecy of Restoration of Zion

4 It shall come to pass in the latter days
    that the mountain of the house of the Lord
shall be established as the highest of the
        mountains,
    and shall be raised up above the hills;
and peoples shall flow to it,
2   and many nations shall come, and say:
"Come, let us go up to the mountain of the Lord,
    to the house of the God of Jacob;
that he may teach us his ways
    and we may walk in his paths."
For out of Zion shall go forth the law,
    and the word of the Lord from Jerusalem.
³He shall judge between many peoples,
    and shall decide for strong nations afar off;
and they shall beat their swords into plowshares,
    and their spears into pruning hooks;
nation shall not lift up sword against nation,
    neither shall they learn war any more;
⁴but they shall sit every man under his vine and
        under his fig tree,
    and none shall make them afraid;
for the mouth of the Lord of hosts has
        spoken.

⁵For all the peoples walk
    each in the name of its god,
but we will walk in the name of the Lord our God
    for ever and ever.

⁶In that day, says the Lord,
    I will assemble the lame
and gather those who have been driven away,
    and those whom I have afflicted;
⁷and the lame I will make the remnant;
    and those who were cast off, a strong nation;
and the Lord will reign over them in Mount Zion
    from this time forth and for evermore.

⁸And you, O tower of the flock,
    hill of the daughter of Zion,
to you shall it come,
    the former dominion shall come,
    the kingdom of the daughter of Jerusalem.

⁹Now why do you cry aloud?
    Is there no king in you?
Has your counselor perished,
    that pangs have seized you like a woman in
        labor?

4:1–3: Is 2:2–4.   **4:4:** Zech 3:10.

4:1–3 A vision of Jerusalem's future glory. Its focal point is the Temple Mount, which will tower above all other heights and become a pilgrimage destination for the world. This will coincide with an era of peace, when disputes are resolved by the Lord, making war a thing of the past. The same vision appears almost verbatim in Is 2:2–4 among the prophecies of Isaiah, a contemporary of Micah. It is unknown whether **(1)** Micah drew from the vision of Isaiah, **(2)** Isaiah drew from the vision of Micah, **(3)** both prophets were inspired with the same vision, or **(4)** both prophets drew upon a common tradition.

4:1 the latter days: A future era of scriptural fulfillment (= messianic times). See word study: *The Latter Days* at Is 2:2. **mountain of the house:** The Temple was built on Mt. Moriah (2 Chron 3:1). In the biblical world, mountains were viewed as places of contact between heaven and earth, the divine and human realms, making them ideal locations for sanctuaries of worship. **highest:** The exaltation of the Temple Mount, which sits lower than its neighboring elevations, Mt. Scopus and the Mount of Olives. The language of the prophet is figurative, not a literal prediction of future changes in the landscape around Jerusalem.

4:2 many nations: Peoples throughout the world will converge on the Temple when they forsake their own gods (4:5) and come as pilgrims to worship the true God of Israel (Is 60:1–7; 66:18–20; Zech 2:11). **Zion:** Jerusalem, which encompasses the Temple Mount. The name Zion originally referred to the southeastern ridge of the city where King David built his royal residence (2 Sam 5:6–12). • According to the NT, the elevation of Zion, crowned with the city of Jerusalem, is a historical sign of a heavenly reality. It points upward to the celestial Mt. Zion, the Jerusalem above, where angels and saints worship the Lord without ceasing (Gal 4:26; Heb 12:22–24; Rev 21:2, 10). **the law:** The Hebrew word is *tôrāh*, which translates "instruction" as well as "law". The going forth of God's instruction from Jerusalem is fulfilled in the proclamation of the gospel to all nations (Lk 24:46–47). • The Spirit prophesied these things to come, and we can show that they actually happened. For a group of twelve men

went out from Jerusalem, and though they were illiterate and without training in speaking, they testified by the power of God to every race that they were sent by Christ to teach the word of God. Now we who were once killed one another not only cease from war but willingly die for confessing our belief in Christ (St. Justin Martyr, *First Apology* 39).

4:3 He shall judge: The Lord will administer perfect justice, leading to a time of peace. **swords into plowshares:** The weapons of the warrior will be refashioned into the tools of the farmer. For a reversal of this imagery, see Joel 3:10.

4:4 under his fig tree: Signifies a time of peace and security when life is untroubled by war (1 Kings 4:25; Zech 3:10).

4:5 we will walk: Micah speaks on behalf of his people.

4:6 In that day: Synchronizes the prophecy of 4:6–8 with "the latter days" of 4:1. **I will assemble:** A promise of restoration from exile (Deut 30:3–5). **the lame:** The captives of Israel and Judah who were "cast off" into exile (4:7; Zeph 3:19) by the Assyrians (1:16) and later by the Babylonians (4:10).

4:7 the remnant: Refers to a small part of a greater whole. See word study: *Remnant* at Zeph 2:7. **the Lord will reign:** The future kingdom of God (Is 52:7–8), when "the Lord will become king over all the earth" (Zech 14:9).

4:8 tower of the flock: The mountain of Jerusalem, imagined as a watchtower from which the Lord looks after his people and keeps them safe. One can also translate "tower of Eder" (as in Gen 35:21). **daughter of Zion:** A personification of Jerusalem, pictured in this chapter as a woman in labor (4:10) as well as a female ox that threshes enemies like grain (4:13). See word study: *The Daughter of Zion* at Lam 1:6.

4:9–5:1 Prophecies about the near future as well as the distant future. The oracles marked by "Now" forecast the siege and deliverance of Jerusalem in 701 B.C. (4:9, 11; 5:1), while the vision of Daughter Zion's labor looks ahead to the Babylonian Exile of Judah and the subsequent return from exile that took place in the sixth century B.C. (4:10).

4:9 no king in you? : A rhetorical question reminding Jerusalem that the Lord dwells in its midst and is more powerful than its enemies (cf. Jer 8:19).

¹⁰Writhe and groan,ʰ O daughter of Zion,
  like a woman with labor pains;
for now you shall go forth from the city
  and dwell in the open country;
  you shall go to Babylon.
There you shall be rescued,
  there the LORD will redeem you
  from the hand of your enemies.

¹¹Now many nations
  are assembled against you,
  saying, "Let her be profaned,
  and let our eyes gaze upon Zion."
¹²But they do not know
  the thoughts of the LORD,
they do not understand his plan,
  that he has gathered them as sheaves to the
    threshing floor.
¹³Arise and thresh,
  O daughter of Zion,
for I will make your horn iron
  and your hoofs bronze;

you shall beat in pieces many peoples,
  and shallⁱ devote their gain to the LORD,
  their wealth to the Lord of the whole earth.

A Ruler from Bethlehem

5 ʲNow you are walled about with a wall;ᵏ
  siege is laid against us;
with a rod they strike upon the cheek
  the ruler of Israel.

²ˡBut you, O Bethlehem Eph′rathah,
  who are little to be among the clans of
    Judah,
from you shall come forth for me
  one who is to be ruler in Israel,
whose origin is from of old,
  from ancient days.
³Therefore he shall give them up until the time
  when she who has labor pains has brought
    forth;
then the rest of his brethren shall return
  to the sons of Israel.

5:2: Mt 2:6; Jn 7:42.

4:10 daughter of Zion: See note on 4:8. **labor pains:** The pangs that Jerusalem will suffer when the Babylonians destroy the city and take its captives into exile. However, just as the agony of childbirth gives way to the joy of new life, so Zion's exiles will later be rescued by the Lord to begin their lives again (Is 54:1–8). **you shall go:** Isaiah, a contemporary of Micah, also foretold this exile (Is 39:6–7). **Babylon:** Did not become the center of a conquering empire until the late seventh century B.C., roughly a century after Micah's lifetime. **redeem:** Means to "buy back" a person from slavery. Judah's return from captivity in Babylon is meant (cf. Is 48:20; 52:11–12). See word study: *Redeem* at Lev 25:25.

4:11 many nations: Refers to the Assyrian siege of Jerusalem in 701 B.C. (5:1). Sennacherib's imperial army included foreign mercenaries among its ranks. **Let her be profaned:** For threats made against the holy city at this time, see 2 Kings 18:17–35.

4:12 his plan: To protect Jerusalem from conquest by a miracle of divine intervention (2 Kings 19:32–36).

4:13 Arise and thresh: Threshing was a process of separating grains from their stalks and husks. It typically involved an ox trampling the sheaves and dragging a sled with a studded underside across them (Deut 25:4). For threshing as an image of judgment, see also Is 21:10; 41:15; Jer 51:33. **daughter of Zion:** See note on 4:8. **devote:** The Hebrew means "place under a *ḥerem* ban". The wealth of the nations, being consecrated to the Lord, is banned from being spoils of wars. See word study: *Devoted* at Josh 6:17.

5:1 the ruler of Israel: Hezekiah was king when Jerusalem was besieged (2 Kings 18:13–17).

5:2–6 A prophecy of the Davidic Messiah. He will be born in Bethlehem (5:2), feed the family of Israel as a faithful

shepherd (5:4), magnify his greatness to the ends of the earth (5:4), and protect God's people with the support of allied shepherds and princes (5:5–6).

5:2 Bethlehem: A small town five miles south of Jerusalem. It was the hometown of King David but was not otherwise significant (1 Sam 17:12). Micah foresees another **ruler** from Bethlehem, i.e., a king from the dynastic line of David who fulfills the Davidic covenant of kingship (2 Sam 7:12–19) and the messianic hopes of Israel's prophets (Is 9:6–7; 11:1–5; Jer 23:5; Ezek 34:23; Hos 3:5) (CCC 436–40). **Ephrathah:** The area around Bethlehem (Gen 35:19; Ruth 4:11). • In the Gospel of Matthew, the chief priests and scribes cite this passage in answer to Herod the Great's inquiry about the birthplace of the Messiah (Mt 2:3–6). Herod, once informed, tried to prevent its fulfillment by slaughtering the infant boys of Bethlehem (Mt 2:16). Other Jews of the NT period shared the expectation that the Messiah would come from David's lineage and birthplace (Jn 7:42). **whose origin is from of old:** Israel's future ruler comes from the distant past. This may mean that God's plan for a future Messiah was formed in ages past, e.g., in the time of David. The text, however, seems to assert the antiquity of the ruler himself. • Christian faith finds the solution to this mystery in the Incarnation: Jesus was the preexistent Son of God before all ages (Jn 8:58), even though he was born the son of David in the course of human history (Mt 1:1) (CCC 461–64).

5:3 he shall give them up: The Lord gave David's kingdom over to destruction in 586 B.C. (Ps 89:38–45). Its restoration awaited the coming of Jesus as the heir to David's throne (Lk 1:32–33). **she who has labor pains:** The mother of the Davidic ruler (5:2). Micah's depiction of her links back to 4:9–10, hinting that she shares in the anguish of Daughter Zion yearning for redemption (CCC 489, 722). • The Book of Revelation uses the language of birth pangs to depict the Mother of Jesus suffering the loss of her Son to Crucifixion before his rebirth in the Resurrection (Rev 12:1–6). This is based in part on the teaching of Jesus, who compared his dying and rising to the agony of childbirth followed by the joy of new life (Jn 16:21–22). **his brethren shall return:** From a state of exile (2:12–13).

ʰ Heb uncertain.
ⁱ Gk Syr Tg: Heb *I will.*
ʲ Ch 4:14 in Heb.
ᵏ Cn Compare Gk: Heb obscure.
ˡ Ch 5:1 in Heb.

⁴And he shall stand and feed his flock in the
　　strength of the Lord,
　　in the majesty of the name of the Lord his God.
　And they shall dwell secure, for now he shall be
　　great
　　to the ends of the earth.

⁵And this shall be peace,
　　when the Assyrian comes into our land
　　and treads upon our soil,ᵐ
　that we will raise against him seven shepherds
　　and eight princes of men;
⁶they shall rule the land of Assyria with the
　　sword,
　　and the land of Nimrod with the drawn sword;ⁿ
　and theyᵒ shall deliver us from the Assyrian
　　when he comes into our land
　　and treads within our border.

⁷Then the remnant of Jacob shall be
　　in the midst of many peoples
　like dew from the Lord,
　　like showers upon the grass,
　which do not depend upon men
　　nor wait for the sons of men.
⁸And the remnant of Jacob shall be among the
　　nations,
　　in the midst of many peoples,
　like a lion among the beasts of the forest,
　　like a young lion among the flocks of sheep,

which, when it goes through, treads down
　　and tears in pieces, and there is none to deliver.
⁹Your hand shall be lifted up over your
　　adversaries,
　　and all your enemies shall be cut off.

¹⁰And in that day, says the Lord,
　　I will cut off your horses from among you
　　and will destroy your chariots;
¹¹and I will cut off the cities of your land
　　and throw down all your strongholds;
¹²and I will cut off sorceries from your hand,
　　and you shall have no more soothsayers;
¹³and I will cut off your images
　　and your pillars from among you,
　and you shall bow down no more
　　to the work of your hands;
¹⁴and I will root out your Ashe′rim from among you
　　and destroy your cities.
¹⁵And in anger and wrath I will execute vengeance
　　upon the nations that did not obey.

What the Lord Requires

6 Hear what the Lord says:
　Arise, plead your case before the mountains,
　　and let the hills hear your voice.
²Hear, you mountains, the controversy of the Lord,
　　and you enduring foundations of the earth;
　for the Lord has a controversy with his people,
　　and he will contend with Israel.

5:4 feed his flock: The Messiah assumes a leading role in the restoration of Israel from exile that Micah prophesied in 2:12-13. **the name:** The divine name YHWH, probably pronounced "Yahweh" and typically translated "Lord" in English Bibles. See note on Ex 3:15. **to the ends of the earth:** Envisions a messianic kingdom of salvation that is global, not merely regional (Is 49:6; Dan 2:31-35, 44).

5:5 the Assyrian: Assyria, which ceased to exist within a century of Micah's lifetime, is projected into the future. It represents all evil empires that threaten God's people through the ages. **comes into our land:** Assaults against the messianic community are imagined after the pattern of Assyria's invasions of Israel and Judah in the seventh century B.C. **shepherds ... princes:** Royal ministers who participate in the reign of the shepherd king from Bethlehem (5:2-4). • The NT portrays the apostles of Jesus in these terms as fellow shepherds and royal officials in God's kingdom (Mt 16:18-19; 19:28; Jn 21:15-17; 1 Pet 5:1-4).

5:6 Nimrod: Identified in Genesis as Noah's great-grandson who founded a kingdom in Mesopotamia (Gen 10:8-10).

5:7 the remnant of Jacob: The exiles of Israel scattered to distant lands by the Assyrians (1:16) and later by the Babylonians (4:10). Micah insists they will be regathered by the Lord (2:12-13; 4:6). **like dew:** God's rescue of the remnant is compared to droplets of water evaporating in the morning sun, despite being spread far and wide over the world.

5:8 like a lion: Israel's exiles, once humiliated victims, will become mighty victors.

5:10-15 In the day of restoration, the Lord will remove all the vanities in which his erring people trusted, from military resources (5:10-11) to superstitious practices (5:12) to idol images (5:13-14).

5:12 sorceries: Forms of witchcraft, which was strictly forbidden in Israel (Deut 18:10). **soothsayers:** Fortune-tellers, also forbidden in Israel (Deut 18:10).

5:13 pillars: Large oblong stones propped upright as cultic monuments dedicated to Baal, the storm and fertility god of Canaanite religion. The Torah commanded these pillars, along with Asherim (5:14), to be destroyed and banished from the land of Israel (Ex 34:14; Deut 7:5; 12:3).

5:14 Asherim: Trees or wooden poles erected at sanctuaries and dedicated to Asherah, the chief fertility goddess of Canaanite religion. These cult objects were outlawed in Israel (Deut 16:21).

6:1-16 The Lord brings Israel to trial for violations of the covenant. He calls witnesses (6:1-2), questions the accused (6:3), defends his innocence and goodness in relation to the accused (6:4-5), specifies what is needed to repair the relationship (6:8), cites specific sins against the covenant (6:10-12, 16), and declares a sentence of punishment on the guilty (6:13-16).

6:1 Hear: A summons to attention. Following 1:2 and 3:1, it introduces the third division of the book (chaps. 6-7). **the mountains ... the hills:** Ancient witnesses to the covenant between God and Israel, which Moses declared in the presence of "heaven and earth" (Deut 4:26; 30:19).

6:2 controversy: The Hebrew term is *rîv*, on which see essay: *Covenant Lawsuit.*

ᵐGk: Heb *in our palaces.*
ⁿCn: Heb *in its entrances.*
ᵒHeb *he.*

³"O my people, what have I done to you?
  In what have I wearied you? Answer me!
⁴For I brought you up from the land of Egypt,
  and redeemed you from the house of bondage;
  and I sent before you Moses,
    Aaron, and Miriam.
⁵O my people, remember what Balak king of Moab
    devised,
  and what Balaam the son of Beor answered
    him,
  and what happened from Shittim to Gilgal,
    that you may know the saving acts of the
    LORD."

⁶"With what shall I come before the LORD,
  and bow myself before God on high?
  Shall I come before him with burnt offerings,
    with calves a year old?
⁷Will the LORD be pleased with thousands of
    rams,
  with ten thousands of rivers of oil?
  Shall I give my first-born for my transgression,
    the fruit of my body for the sin of my soul?"
⁸He has showed you, O man, what is good;
  and what does the LORD require of you
  but to do justice, and to love kindness,ᴾ
    and to walk humbly with your God?

6:4 Moses: Israel's deliverer, lawgiver, and mediator of the covenant (Ex 3:10; 34:27; Deut 29:1). **Aaron:** Moses' older brother and the first high priest of Israel (Ex 6:20; 40:12-13). **Miriam:** Moses' sister, who was a prophetess (Ex 15:20-21; Num 26:59).

6:5 Balak: The Moabite king who feared the Israelites and hired the Mesopotamian soothsayer **Balaam** to curse them in the wilderness (Num 22:1-6). The Lord protected Israel at this time by turning his curses into blessings (Num 23-24). **Shittim to Gilgal:** The final stage of the Exodus journey that saw Israel cross over the Jordan River from the land of Moab (Num 25:1) into Canaan (Josh 4:19).

6:6-8 Micah instructs Israel on God's priorities for his people. A relationship with the Lord demands more than a multitude of Temple sacrifices; it requires a personal commitment to live by the standards of justice, covenant loyalty, and spiritual humility. The rhetorical questions in 6:6-7 escalate from the less costly sacrifice (**calves**) to the more costly (**thousands of**

rams and **ten thousands of rivers of oil**) to the most costly (a **first-born** son). That liturgy cannot be a substitute for morality, see 1 Sam 15:22, Is 1:10-17, Hos 6:6, and note on Amos 5:21-24.

6:6 burnt offerings: See note on Lev 1:3-17.

6:7 the fruit of my body: Not an endorsement of child sacrifice, which is strongly condemned in the Mosaic Law (Lev 20:1-5), but a hypothetical proposal signifying the loss of what is most valuable to a person (cf. Judg 11:29-40).

6:8 justice: In a legal context, justice means an equal application of the Mosaic Law to all members of the covenant community, regardless of a person's wealth or social standing. In a personal context, it means acting rightly, honestly, and equitably toward others in accord with the commandment "You shall love your neighbor as yourself" (Lev 19:18). **kindness:** The Hebrew term *ḥesed* is the devoted love and loyalty expected in a covenant relationship. See word study: *Merciful Love* at Ex 34:7. **walk humbly:** Humility is the acceptance of one's lowliness before God and of one's total dependance upon him. It is the opposite of a prideful attitude of independence from God. As such, humility is the foundation of prayer (CCC 2559).

ᴾ Or *steadfast love.*

Covenant Lawsuit

The relationship between the Lord and Israel is governed by the covenant that binds them together. The covenant spells out the sacred obligations incumbent upon the parties as well as the consequences that follow compliance or noncompliance with its stipulations. The consequences of the Mosaic covenant are set forth in its blessings and curses. If Israel obeys the Lord's commandments, the nation will be blessed and live prosperously in the land of Canaan (Deut 28:1-14). But if Israel turns away from the Lord and disobeys his commandments, the nation will suffer dreadful curses, culminating in military conquest and expulsion from the land (Deut 28:15-68).

The prophets repeatedly confront the people of Israel for sins against the covenant—sins that activate its curses if the invitation to repent and seek reconciliation with the Lord is declined. One way that God brings charges against violators of the covenant is a form of judgment speech called a *rîv*, a legal term that can be translated "controversy" (Mic 6:2), "indictment" (Hos 12:2), or "case" (Is 41:21). Scholars refer to this literary form as a covenant lawsuit. Examples can be found in Is 1, Jer 2, Hos 4, and Mic 6.

In these and similar texts, the Lord initiates legal action through his prophet and presses the case against his disobedient people. Readers listen to a courtroom dialogue in which the plaintiff (= the Lord) presents his case against the defendant (= Israel) for breaking the covenant and failing to fulfill its terms. Biblical examples of the prophetic lawsuit include some or all of the following features:

(1) Summons of the defendant to stand trial (Hos 4:1; Mic 6:2, 9).
(2) Charges brought against the defendant (Is 1:21-23; Jer 2:13; Hos 4:2, 12-13; Mic 6:10-12).
(3) Questions put to the defendant (Is 1:12; Jer 2:5, 11, 18; Mic 6:3).
(4) Invocation of witnesses (Is 1:2; Jer 2:12).
(5) Sentencing of the guilty (Is 1:28-31; Jer 2:35-37; Hos 4:6; Mic 6:13-16).

[9]The voice of the LORD cries to the city—
and it is sound wisdom to fear your name:
"Hear, O tribe and assembly of the city![q]
[10] Can I forget[r] the treasures of wickedness in
the house of the wicked,
and the scant measure that is accursed?
[11]Shall I acquit the man with wicked scales
and with a bag of deceitful weights?
[12]Your[s] rich men are full of violence;
your[s] inhabitants speak lies,
and their tongue is deceitful in their mouth.
[13]Therefore I have begun[t] to strike you,
making you desolate because of your sins.
[14]You shall eat, but not be satisfied,
and there shall be hunger in your inward
parts;
you shall put away, but not save,
and what you save I will give to the sword.
[15]You shall sow, but not reap;
you shall tread olives, but not anoint
yourselves with oil;
you shall tread grapes, but not drink wine.
[16]For you have kept the statutes of Omri,[u]
and all the works of the house of A'hab;
and you have walked in their counsels;
that I may make you a desolation, and your[v]
inhabitants a hissing;
so you shall bear the scorn of the peoples."[w]

Corruption, Repentance, and God's Compassion and Love

7 Woe is me! For I have become
as when the summer fruit has been gathered,
as when the vintage has been gleaned:
there is no cluster to eat,
no first-ripe fig which my soul desires.
[2]The godly man has perished from the earth,
and there is none upright among men;
they all lie in wait for blood,
and each hunts his brother with a net.
[3]Their hands are upon what is evil, to do it
diligently;
the prince and the judge ask for a bribe,
and the great man utters the evil desire of his
soul;
thus they weave it together.
[4]The best of them is like a brier,
the most upright of them a thorn hedge.
The day of their[x] watchmen, of their[x]
punishment, has come;
now their confusion is at hand.
[5]Put no trust in a neighbor,
have no confidence in a friend;
guard the doors of your mouth
from her who lies in your bosom;
[6]for the son treats the father with contempt,
the daughter rises up against her mother,

7:6: Mt 10:21, 35, 36; Mk 13:12; Lk 12:53.

6:9–16 The sentencing of a **city** (6:9) to the punishment of **desolation** (6:16). The prophet targets either the northern capital of Samaria, which fell to the Assyrians in 722 B.C. (1:6), or the southern capital of Jerusalem, which fell to the Babylonians in 586 B.C. (3:12; 4:10). Both cities fit the prophecy: the reference in 6:16 to Omri and Ahab, kings of northern Israel, favor an address to Samaria, but Jerusalem could be faulted for imitating the wickedness of Samaria. See note on 1:2–16.

6:9 wisdom: On fear of the Lord as the beginning of wisdom, see note on Prov 1:7.

6:11 wicked scales: A condemnation of dishonest business practices (Prov 11:1; Hos 12:7; Amos 8:5).

6:13 I have begun to strike: If Samaria is in view, this may refer to Assyrian conquests in Galilee (2 Kings 15:29) that took place a full decade before the city fell in 722 B.C. (2 Kings 17:5–6). If Jerusalem, then the Assyrian invasion of Judah in 701 B.C. is likely intended. See note on 6:9–16.

6:14–15 Various curses of the Mosaic covenant (Lev 26:16, 25–26; Deut 28:39–40).

6:16 Omri: King of Israel from 885 to 874 B.C. He is remembered in Scripture as an extremely wicked king who founded Samaria as the capital of northern Israel (1 Kings 16:24–26). **Ahab:** Son of Omri and King of Israel from 874 to 853 B.C. He was infamous for making Samaria a center of Canaanite idolatry (= Baal worship, 1 Kings 16:31–32). **hissing:** An expression of derision (Jer 19:8).

7:1–7 Micah laments the evil that flourishes in his day. Everywhere he sees treachery and dishonesty, while godly men and women seem to have disappeared (7:2). Enmity abounds even among neighbors, friends, and family members (7:5–6). Despite this crisis, the prophet refuses to lose hope in the saving power of God (7:7).

7:1 no cluster to eat: Creates a feeling of deep disappointment.

7:2 there is none upright: A way of saying that sin and corruption have overrun the majority of the covenant people (Ps 14:3; Is 59:3–8). Paul cites similar passages of Scripture when he charges that all peoples, Jews and Gentiles alike, are under the power of sin (Rom 3:9–18).

7:3 bribe: Swaying rulers and authorities with money and gifts is forbidden because "a bribe blinds the eyes of the wise and subverts the cause of the righteous" (Deut 16:19). **the great man:** One who wields power over others.

7:4 a brier ... a thorn: Jagged, fruitless, and a danger to others. **watchmen:** A sentry posted on a tower or wall who looks out for messengers or armies approaching a city (2 Sam 18:24; Is 21:6–9; Ezek 3:17). **their punishment:** The Assyrian invasion of Judah in 701 B.C. (1:8–16) or perhaps the Babylonian conquest of Judah in 586 B.C. (4:10).

7:5 guard the doors: It is wise to be careful what you say in evil times, lest even people you trust turn against you. **her who lies in your bosom:** A man's wife.

7:6 son ... father ... daughter ... mother: Strife within families, which are typically bound together with the strongest ties of loyalty, shows the full extent of the moral and spiritual chaos erupting in the prophet's day. • Jesus draws from Micah's words when he spells out the consequences of

[q] Cn Compare Gk: Heb *and who has appointed it yet.*
[r] Cn: Heb uncertain.
[s] Heb *whose.*
[t] Gk Syr Vg: Heb *have made sick.*
[u] Gk Syr Vg Tg: Heb *the statutes of Omri are kept.*
[v] Heb *its.*
[w] Gk: Heb *my people.*
[x] Heb *your.*

the daughter-in-law against her mother-in-law;
    a man's enemies are the men of his own house.
⁷But as for me, I will look to the L ORD,
    I will wait for the God of my salvation;
    my God will hear me.

⁸Rejoice not over me, O my enemy;
    when I fall, I shall rise;
when I sit in darkness,
    the L ORD will be a light to me.
⁹I will bear the indignation of the L ORD
    because I have sinned against him,
until he pleads my cause
    and executes judgment for me.
He will bring me forth to the light;
    I shall behold his deliverance.
¹⁰Then my enemy will see,
    and shame will cover her who said to me,
    "Where is the L ORD your God?"
My eyes will gloat over her;
    now she will be trodden down
    like the mire of the streets.

¹¹A day for the building of your walls!
    In that day the boundary shall be far extended.
¹²In that day they will come to you,
    from Assyria toʸ Egypt,
and from Egypt to the River,
    from sea to sea and from mountain to mountain.

¹³But the earth will be desolate
    because of its inhabitants,
    for the fruit of their doings.

¹⁴Shepherd your people with your staff,
    the flock of your inheritance,
who dwell alone in a forest
    in the midst of a garden land;
let them feed in Bashan and Gilead
    as in the days of old.

¹⁵As in the days when you came out of the land of
    Egypt
    I will show themᶻ marvelous things.

¹⁶The nations shall see and be ashamed
    of all their might;
they shall lay their hands on their mouths;
    their ears shall be deaf;
¹⁷they shall lick the dust like a serpent,
    like the crawling things of the earth;
they shall come trembling out of their
      strongholds,
    they shall turn in dread to the L ORD our God,
    and they shall fear because of you.

¹⁸Who is a God like you, pardoning iniquity
    and passing over transgression
    for the remnant of his inheritance?

---

discipleship. Because he demands a personal commitment that takes precedence over kinship ties, adherence to the gospel can turn even the closest family members against one another (Mt 10:35–36; Lk 12:53).

7:7 I will look to the L ORD: Micah refuses to despair of God's goodness and help, even when most of his generation has gone astray. He clings to the Lord in the hope of future deliverance (Ps 130:5), confident that the promises of restoration and peace revealed to him will come to pass (2:12–13; 4:1–3; 5:2–6) (CCC 2090–91).

7:8–10 An individual speaking in the first person (I, me, my) addresses an enemy in the third person (her, 7:10). It announces a reversal of fortunes, so that she who mocked the speaker and rejoiced in her demise will be shamed and trampled down in turn. The speaker appears to be Jerusalem and the enemy Babylon (cf. Is 51:21–23).

7:9 I have sinned: Jerusalem was destroyed and exiled in 586 B.C. for its great wickedness (Jer 9:11–16).

7:10 her who said: Babylon. Cities are often portrayed in the Bible in feminine terms (e.g., Babylon is a "daughter" in Ps 137:8). **Where is . . . your God?:** The scoffing words of foreign conquerors (Ps 79:10; Joel 2:17). **like the mire of the streets:** Indicates total defeat (Is 10:6).

7:11–13 Envisions a restoration of Jerusalem, when its walls are rebuilt (7:11) and its scattered children return to it (7:12). Judean exiles began to repopulate the city in ca. 538 B.C. (Ezra 2:1–70), and its walls were reconstructed ca. 445 B.C. (Neh 3:1–32).

7:12 Assyria to Egypt: Lands north(east) and south of Israel. **the River:** The Euphrates (Gen 15:18).

7:14 Shepherd your people: Micah's prayer for Israel, pictured as a flock of sheep that the Lord gathers, protects, and feeds (2:12–13; Ps 23:1–4; 95:6–7). See note on 2:13. **Bashan and Gilead:** Fertile grazing lands east of the Sea of Galilee and the Jordan River (Deut 32:14; Num 32:1; Jer 50:19).

7:15 I will show them: The Lord's answer to the prophet's prayer in 7:14. **marvelous things:** Akin to the wonders of the Exodus, from plagues and judgments to saving miracles (Ex 3:20; Deut 6:22; Neh 9:9–12). See essay: *The New Exodus in Isaiah* at Is 44.

7:16 The nations: The peoples of the world besides Israel. Even the mightiest of them will tremble with fear when the Lord does "marvelous things" again (7:15). Their conversion may be hinted at as well since Micah foresaw that "many nations" would come to worship the Lord at his Temple (4:2).

7:17 lick the dust: The complete humiliation of an enemy (Ps 72:9; Is 49:23). **like a serpent:** Perhaps thought to eat dust, among other things (Is 65:25). According to the curse of Gen 3:14, the serpent who instigated the first human sin was consigned to eat "dust" for the rest of its days.

7:18 Who is a God like you . . . ?: The Lord, the God of Israel, surpasses all and has no rival or equal who compares to him in treating sinners mercifully (7:18–19) and keeping covenants faithfully (7:20). The question involves a wordplay on the name Micah, a shortened form of Micaiah, meaning "Who is like Yah(weh)?" or "Who is like the L ORD?". **pardoning iniquity:** An expression taken from Ex 34:7, translated "forgiving iniquity", where the Lord reveals to Moses that mercy and faithfulness are among his greatest attributes, along with his graciousness, patience, and justice. • God shows mercy, not by acting contrary to justice, but by doing more than justice requires. A man who pays someone two hundred coins when he only owes one hundred coins

---

ʸ Cn: Heb *and cities of*.
ᶻ Heb *him*.

He does not retain his anger for ever
   because he delights in mercy.
[19]He will again have compassion upon us,
   he will tread our iniquities under foot.
You will cast all our[a] sins
   into the depths of the sea.

[20]You will show faithfulness to Jacob
   and mercy to Abraham,
   as you have sworn to our fathers
   from the days of old.

7:20: Lk 1:55.

---

acts generously and mercifully. It is the same with pardoning an offense, since in pardoning he bestows a gift (St. Thomas Aquinas, *Summa Theologiae* I, 21, 3). **the remnant:** Refers to a small part of a greater whole, in this case those of Israel and Judah who receive the Lord's pardon (Jer 50:20). See word study: *Remnant* at Zeph 2:7. **mercy:** The Hebrew term *ḥesed* is the devoted love and loyalty expected in a covenant relationship. See word study: *Merciful Love* at Ex 34:7.

7:19 cast ... into the depths: One of several ways that Scripture speaks about the expiation of sins. They are also said to be blotted out (Is 43:25), swept away (Is 44:22), put away (2 Sam 12:13), taken away (Zech 3:4), and removed as far away as the east is from the west (Ps 103:12).

7:20 sworn to our fathers: Refers to the covenant God made by oath to the Patriarchs (Gen 15:18–21; 22:16–18; 26:3–5; Lk 1:72–73).

---

[a] Gk Syr Vg Tg: Heb *their*.

STUDY QUESTIONS
Micah

Chapter 1

For understanding
1. **1:2–16.** In these oracles, since Samaria and Jerusalem have become strongholds of iniquity, how does the Lord plan to punish their sins? Historically, who carried out these judgments? Though Jerusalem was not taken in 701, what do the surviving *Annals of Sennecharib* state did happen?
2. **1:2.** To what is the world summoned to listen? How is the Lord's holy Temple in heaven indicated? To what is this celestial sanctuary the unseen counterpart?
3. **1:8–16.** In this funeral lament over Judah and Jerusalem, what route does the list of towns probably mark? What technique does the text display?
4. **1:10.** To whom is the saying "tell it not in Gath" attributed? Why should news of Assyria's capture of Judahite towns not be publicized in the Philistine city of Gath? What is the translation for the name Beth-le-aphrah?

For application
1. **1:2.** Why do human beings tend to ignore prophets who warn that God is not pleased with their conduct? Which modern prophets have been warning about the moral condition of society? Who is paying attention?
2. **1:5.** If Micah were prophesying today, which cities do you think he would indict as representing the sins of the country? The note for this verse singles out corrupt worship. What might he say corrupts our worship?
3. **1:7.** According to St. Paul in 1 Cor 3:10–15, what workmanship must those who preach the gospel employ to build upon the foundation of the faith? How will it be tested? How do his words apply to the preaching of the gospel today?
4. **1:10.** When the sins of Church ministers are publicly revealed, who rejoices? What benefits do such revelations provide for the Church as a whole?

Chapter 2

For understanding
1. **2:2.** Why is woe invoked on those who covet fields and houses? What is the inheritance to which the verse refers?
2. **2:6–11.** With whom is Micah contending? Who are the real "enemy" of God's people, and why?
3. **2:12–13.** With what is this prophecy concerned? How will the Lord regather the exiles of Israel from foreign lands? What does the context suggest that Micah envisions? How does Jesus seem to allude to this passage in Jn 10:1–18? How does St. Thomas Aquinas apply this passage to our hope of heaven?
4. **2:13.** Though "their king" is here identified as the Lord God, which ruler does Micah later describe? In a similar way, what does Ezekiel promise? What conjunction of the ruler's divine and human roles in the Incarnation does Christian faith see?

For application
1. **2:2.** If the desires for possessions is good in itself (CCC 2535), what makes coveting a neighbor's property a grave (i.e., mortal) sin? To what virtue does it stand in opposition?
2. **2:6.** When is the last time you heard a homily or sermon in which the preacher corrected his congregation for an abuse? If you have heard such a correction, how did the congregation receive it? In a Catholic parish, what would happen if the congregation rebelled against its pastor on account of such preaching?
3. **2:11.** For what qualities should a parish hope in a good preacher? What may be the spiritual fate of a parish whose pastor preaches only what his congregation wants to hear?
4. **2:12.** Read the note for this verse. In John 10:7–9, Jesus identifies himself as the gate of the fold. Why should there be only one gate? Why is Jesus the gate rather than someone else?

Chapter 3

For understanding
1. **3:5.** To which prophets is Micah referring? Of what does he accuse them? How will the Lord judge them? Why is "Peace" the signature message of these prophets? From what do true prophets not shy away?
2. **3:8.** What is Micah supernaturally empowered to proclaim? What did the divine Spirit thus enable his words to accomplish? Which other prophets were similarly conscious of prophesying by the Spirit? In the Nicene Creed, how is the Spirit identified?
3. **3:11.** Why is bribery in the courts condemned? What remuneration were priests commissioned to teach the Torah to the people supposed to receive? Where does Jerusalem's protection lie? How might the belief that Zion was inviolable have arisen?
4. **3:12.** What picture does Micah present of Jerusalem in the aftermath of divine judgment? Judging from the citation and interpretation of this passage in Jer 26:18–19, what kind of prophecy was this, and why? If the Lord's judgment against the city was not cancelled, what came of it? To what house is the reference?

For application
1. **3:1–3.** Why does the prophet use such graphic hyperbole in his message? Can you think of some examples when Jesus used hyperbole in his preaching? What message is the audience supposed to get from this technique?

2. **3:4.** How often have you prayed and received no answer from the Lord? According to the note for this verse, what is an obstacle to effective prayer? What are some other obstacles? If you do not detect an answer from the Lord, does that mean he is keeping silent?

3. **3:8.** According to 1 Cor 14:23-33, what is the context in which prophecy is normally exercised? For whom is prophecy intended? How would a prophet know that he is being inspired to prophesy? How would others present know that the prophecy is from the Lord (cf. v. 29)?

4. **3:11.** Although Jesus is always present in his Church, what danger does she face from a smug complacency that no evil will happen to her? What protection does she have from the kinds of punishment threatened against Jerusalem here?

Chapter 4

For understanding
1. **4:1.** To what does the expression "the latter days" refer? Where was the Temple built? In the biblical world, how were mountains viewed? How is the mountain of the Lord's house to be considered the highest despite being lower in elevation than Mt. Scopus and the Mount of Olives?

2. **4:2.** When will peoples throughout the world converge on the Temple? To what did the name Zion originally refer? According to the NT, of what is the elevation of Zion, crowned with the city of Jerusalem, a historical sign? How can the Hebrew word *tôrāh* be translated? How is the going forth of God's instruction from Jerusalem fulfilled? According to St. Justin Martyr, who prophesied these things to come, and with what result?

3. **4:9—5:1.** With what are these prophecies concerned? What do the oracles marked by "Now" forecast, and to what does the vision of Daughter Zion's labor look ahead?

4. **4:13.** What does the process of threshing accomplish, and how is it done? What does the Hebrew for "devote" mean, and how does it apply to the wealth of nations?

For application
1. **4:1-2.** What is the purpose of a religious pilgrimage? If you have ever made such a pilgrimage, what was its effect on your spiritual life? If you have never gone on a pilgrimage, even to a site near you, what is to prevent you from making one?

2. **4:5.** How determined are you and your household to serve the Lord (cf. Josh 24:15)? How explicit is that determination? What does that service involve?

3. **4:12.** In Eph 1:3-14, St. Paul summarizes God's plan of salvation. To whom does it apply? As you look back on your life, what pattern can you trace of the Lord's plan for you? How does it seem to be unfolding for you? Where is it leading?

4. **4:13.** Threshing is sometimes used as an image of purification through suffering. How might it apply to the purification of the Church? How might it apply to one's personal life?

Chapter 5

For understanding
1. **5:2.** Where is Bethlehem, and what was its significance? What ruler does Micah see coming from Bethlehem? Where is Ephrathah? In the Gospel of Matthew, when did the chief priests cite this passage, and what happened as a result? What expectation did other Jews of the NT period share? What could it mean that Israel's future ruler comes from the distant past? However, what does the text seem to assert? How does Christian faith find the solution to this mystery in the Incarnation?

2. **5:3.** Since the Lord gave David's kingdom over to destruction in 586 B.C., whose coming did its restoration await? Who is "she who has labor pains"? At what does Micah's depiction of her hint? What does the Book of Revelation use the language of birth pangs to depict? On what is this based in part?

3. **5:7.** Who are the remnant of Jacob? What does Micah insist about them? To what is God's rescue of the remnant compared?

4. **5:13.** To what pillars is Micah referring? What did the Torah command about these pillars?

For application
1. **5:2.** How does Mary's Magnificat reflect the Lord's tendency to use small and insignificant things, people, and places to accomplish great things, while ignoring more "important" ones? What unimportant person or event has exercised the most influence on your life?

2. **5:4.** In Jn 10:1ff., Jesus calls himself the Good Shepherd and also the gate of the sheepfold. What does he say about the security of his flock? How far is he willing to go to ensure their security? For whose security are you responsible? How would you imitate the Good Shepherd?

3. **5:10-15.** Why does Jesus expect his followers to renounce all their possessions to follow him (cf. Mk 10:23-31)? What benefit is there in the spiritual life for the Lord to cut off from us the resources we have or on which we rely?

4. **5:13.** Against what kind of images is Micah prophesying here? Why is the Christian veneration of images not forbidden? What does the *Catechism* have to say about veneration of images of Jesus, Mary, and the saints (CCC 2129-32)?

Chapter 6

For understanding
1. **Essay: Covenant Lawsuit.** What does the covenant regarding the relationship between the Lord and Israel spell out? What is one way that God brings charges against violators of the covenant? In these and similar texts, how does the Lord initiate legal action through his prophet and press the case against his disobedient people? In biblical examples, what are some of the features of the prophetic lawsuit?

2. **6:6–8.** As Micah instructs Israel on God's priorities for his people, what does he say a relationship with the Lord demands? How do the rhetorical questions in 6:6–7 escalate? For what is the liturgy no substitute?
3. **6:8.** In a legal context, what does justice mean? In a personal context, what does it mean? What is expected in a covenant relationship? What is humility, and what is its opposite? As such, of what is humility the foundation?
4. **6:9–16.** To what is the city sentenced? Which city does the prophet target? How do both cities fit the prophecy?

For application
1. **6:3.** This verse is the basis of the list of reproaches sung during the Good Friday liturgy. What reproach would the Lord level against his people today? What return to the Lord have you made for all the good he has done for you?
2. **6:6–8.** Would your spiritual life improve if you multiplied devotional practices and penances? What problem in your relationship with the Lord would piling on more commitments solve? What instead would be a better solution? How would you implement Micah's recommendation in v. 8?
3. **6:14–15.** Which of your devotional practices seem to amount to fruitless effort? As you examine your conscience, what might the Lord be telling you through this lack of fruit? For example, whom have you refused to forgive? What other faults lie hidden that you have not addressed?

Chapter 7

For understanding
1. **7:2.** What is "there is none upright" a way of saying? When does Paul cite similar passages of Scripture?
2. **7:6.** What does strife within families, which are typically bound together with the strongest ties of loyalty, show? How does Jesus draw from Micah's words? Because he demands a personal commitment that takes precedence over kinship ties, what can adherence to the gospel do?
3. **7:7.** What does Micah refuse to do? Why does he cling to the Lord?
4. **7:8–10.** Whom does an individual speaking in the first person (I, me, my) address here? What does his speech announce? Who do the speaker and the enemy appear to be?
5. **7:18.** How does the Lord, the God of Israel, surpass all and show that he has no rival or equal? What wordplay does Micah's question involve? With the expression taken from Ex 34:7, translated "forgiving iniquity", what does the Lord reveal about himself to Moses? According to St. Thomas Aquinas, how does God show mercy? To what does the concept of a remnant refer? To what does the Hebrew term *ḥesed*, here translated mercy, refer?

For application
1. **7:2.** What evils in society most concern you? How often do they prompt you to utter cynical remarks in front of your family or neighbors? If you voice cynicism frequently, what hope do you bring others? If it is true that the mouth speaks what is in the heart (Lk 6:45), what is in yours?
2. **7:6.** Read the note for this verse. How have varying commitments to the faith caused strife within your family? How have you taken sides in the midst of such division? If speaking about religion at home seems counterproductive, what does refusing to speak of it solve? How do you resolve this dilemma?
3. **7:8.** How upset do you become with yourself when you sin? When you do fall, how quickly do you arise? What steps do you take to recover, especially if your fault is public?
4. **7:18.** How has God shown mercy toward you, especially in the face of all your sins? If he has been so merciful in the past, how will he regard you in the future? How has God shown delight in loving you?

INTRODUCTION TO NAHUM

Author and Date The Book of Nahum, according to its superscription, consists of "the vision of Nahum of Elkosh" (1:1). Nothing further is known about Nahum, nor is he mentioned by name elsewhere in the Bible (except in the long Greek LXX text of Tobit 14:4 preserved in *Codex Sinaiticus*). It is clear from the contents of the book that he was skilled at writing picturesque and sometimes graphic poetry, but little else about his personality or background can be said with confidence. Not even the prophet's hometown of Elkosh has been securely identified.

The book can be dated between the conquest of Thebes in 663 B.C. and the conquest of Nineveh in 612 B.C. The former is mentioned as a past event in 3:8, and the latter is foreseen as a future event in 3:1–7. Pinpointing a specific date within this historical window is difficult. Some estimate that the book was written around 650 B.C., while others prefer a date around 620 B.C. Judgments of this sort are sometimes based on the silence of the book. For instance, the superscription in 1:1 does not synchronize the time of Nahum's ministry with the reign of any contemporary king of Judah, as do most of the other prophetic books of Scripture. This suggests to some that Nahum was written during the days of Manasseh, Judah's most wicked king, on the premise that a prophet would be unlikely to mention such a godless figure (696–642 B.C.). On the other hand, the book makes no attempt to denounce the sins of God's people, a feature that is also characteristic of most of the prophetic books. This suggests to others that Nahum was written during the days of Josiah, Judah's great reformer king, who made every effort to lead the covenant people back to the Lord (640–609 B.C.). In the end, neither argument for a specific date is conclusive. So long as one situates the message of Nahum within the parameters noted above, the interpretation of the book is not greatly affected by the exact date one assigns to its composition.

Title The book is named after Nahum, mentioned in the opening verse. Its Hebrew form, *Naḥûm*, means "consolation" or "comfort". His name appears in the Greek Septuagint in the title *Naoum*, a heading that is expanded in the Latin Vulgate to *Naum Propheta*, "Nahum the Prophet". English titles for the book follow these ancient traditions.

Place in the Canon Nahum has long been revered as a canonical book of Scripture. In the Jewish Bible, or Tanakh, it stands among the Latter Prophets in a sub-collection of writings known as "the Book of the Twelve". In Christian Bibles, these twelve books are called the Minor Prophets, not because they are less important than Isaiah, Jeremiah, Ezekiel, and Daniel, but because they are comparatively shorter. In the Hebrew Bible as well as in the Latin Vulgate, Nahum stands seventh among the Minor Prophets between Micah and Habakkuk. This is also its position in most English Bibles. In the Greek Septuagint, it stands between Jonah and Habakkuk.

Structure Nahum divides into three parts that align with its three chapters. **(1)** Chapter 1 announces that God is a Divine Warrior who brings judgment upon those who defy him and salvation to those who trust in him. This timeless truth has a direct application to the prophet's own day: the Lord is about to destroy the wicked city of Nineveh and to free the people of Judah from the yoke of its tyranny. **(2)** Chapter 2 presents readers with scenes of the coming attack on Nineveh. From bloodied warriors and flashing chariots racing through the streets to the desolation and ruin left behind, the prophet paints a graphic picture of the city's violent conquest. **(3)** Chapter 3 explains why Nineveh is doomed to this fate. Among its many crimes, the city is guilty of wanton violence, shameless lies, boundless greed, and smug arrogance. In a word, it is to be judged for its history of "unceasing evil" (3:19). See also *Outline*.

Historical Background The Assyrian Empire reached the summit of its power in the middle of the seventh century B.C. under Ashurbanipal, its last mighty king (r. 669–627 B.C.). Ashurbanipal both retained and extended Assyria's dominion over the Near East with the weapons of savage cruelty and terrorizing propaganda. Small nations such as the Southern Kingdom of Judah lived in constant fear of this godless empire, which had already destroyed the Northern Kingdom of Israel in the eighth century B.C. and was only prevented by a miracle of God from overthrowing Jerusalem in 701 B.C. Nineveh, its capital, was the seat of Assyrian rule and a sign of its power. Few suspected this fortified metropolis was conquerable. Following the death of Ashurbanipal, however, Assyria's overextended empire began to show signs of weakness. Assyrian cities began to fall one by one to besieging armies starting in 616 B.C., and in 612 B.C. a coalition of Medes, Babylonians, and Scythians destroyed the city of Nineveh. A few members of the Assyrian court escaped this disaster and clung to power for a brief time, but subsequent defeats at Haran in 610 B.C. and at Carchemish in 605 B.C. brought death to Assyria once and for all.

Message of the Prophet The Book of Nahum is focused entirely on the fall of Nineveh. This event is prophesied, not as an event that seemed inevitable in light of the political realities of the day, but as God's stern punishment on an evil and arrogant empire. The book thus affirms the Bible's theology of history, which claims that the Lord is sovereign over all creation, that he controls the rise and fall of nations, and that he exercises moral governance over all peoples on earth, holding them accountable for their ways. To the human eye, there was no greater power in the world of the seventh century B.C. than the kingdom of Assyria. But to the eye of the prophet, enlightened by the vision of divine revelation, even the mightiest of nations was no match for the God of Israel. Assyria had long terrorized the Near East, and the Lord's patient endurance of its evil had finally run out. Its thuggish abuse of power would not be allowed to continue indefinitely. Nahum was called to announce that Nineveh's time was up: the Lord was coming in judgment, and the wicked city would fall. The book presents readers with poetical accounts of Nineveh's demise, from the initial stages of the attack (2:3–9) to the corpses and ruins left behind in the aftermath (2:10; 3:3, 10).

If the subject of the book is the fall of Nineveh, the audience of the book is the Southern Kingdom of Judah (1:15). This is significant because, for the people of Israel, the Assyrians were long feared and despised as enemy oppressors (see *Historical Background* above). News of Nineveh's demise, then, could only come as welcome news to small countries under the heel of its authority. It meant that Assyria was getting the divine justice it deserved. It meant that Israel's faith in a God who does not overlook evil and who blesses those who trust in him was reinforced (1:7–8). The prophecies of Nahum, whose name means "consolation", thus function as messages of consolation to the covenant people after more than a century of tyranny. Once the prophecy was fulfilled with the overthrow of Nineveh in 612 B.C., nations like Judah had reason to "clap their hands" in celebration (3:19).

Christian Perspective The NT never quotes from the Book of Nahum directly, although indirect links to the prophet's oracles are discernable. The closest one gets to a citation is Rom 10:15, where Paul quotes the words of Is 52:7 to support the need for Christian evangelists to proclaim the good news of the gospel to others. Nearly identical language appears in 1:15, where Nahum also envisions messengers traveling from afar with the "good tidings" that God has overthrown the evil that held them in bondage. Also, the harlot city that is denounced and destroyed in the Book of Revelation (Rev 17–18) is prefigured in part by the wicked city of Nineveh, which is condemned to extinction for being a "harlot" who seduces "nations" with her wiles (3:4). In general, Nahum's message that no one is beyond the reach of divine justice and that the Lord will judge not only individuals but entire nations is reaffirmed in the teaching of Jesus and the apostles (Mt 25:31–46; Acts 17:30–31; 2 Cor 5:10; Rev 20:11–13). In later Christian tradition, the fall of Nineveh was considered a preview of the end of the world.

OUTLINE OF NAHUM

1. The Fall of Nineveh Is Announced (1:1–15)
   A. Superscription (1:1)
   B. Hymn of the Divine Warrior, Avenger, and Savior (1:2–8)
   C. Enemies Will Be Cut Off, Judah Will Have Peace (1:9–15)

2. The Fall of Nineveh Is Described (2:1–13)
   A. Attack on Nineveh (2:1–10)
   B. Taunt against Nineveh (2:11–13)

3. The Fall of Nineveh Is Explained (3:1–19)
   A. Woe to Nineveh (3:1–3)
   B. Taunt against Nineveh (3:4–7)
   C. Example of Thebes (3:8–13)
   D. Nineveh's Doom (3:14–17)
   E. Ninevites Dead and Dispersed (3:18–19)

THE BOOK OF
NAHUM

God's Wrath toward Nineveh and Peace for Judah

1 An oracle concerning Nin'eveh. The book of the vision of Na'hum of El'kosh.
²The Lord is a jealous God and avenging,
  the Lord is avenging and wrathful;
the Lord takes vengeance on his adversaries
  and keeps wrath for his enemies.
³The Lord is slow to anger and of great might,
  and the Lord will by no means clear the guilty.

His way is in whirlwind and storm,
  and the clouds are the dust of his feet.

⁴He rebukes the sea and makes it dry,
  he dries up all the rivers;
Bashan and Carmel wither,
  the bloom of Lebanon fades.
⁵The mountains quake before him,
  the hills melt;
the earth is laid waste before him,
  the world and all that dwell therein.

⁶Who can stand before his indignation?
  Who can endure the heat of his anger?
His wrath is poured out like fire,
  and the rocks are broken asunder by him.

1–3: Is 10:5–34; Zeph 2:12–15.

1:1 oracle: The Hebrew term *massaʾ* is a pronouncement of judgment on those who oppose the Lord, whether the people of Israel (Mal 1:1) or a foreign nation (Is 13:1; 17:1; 19:1; 21:13; Hab 1:1; Zech 9:1). **Nineveh:** Capital of the mighty Assyrian Empire for most of the seventh century B.C. It stood on the east bank of the Tigris River near modern Mosul, Iraq. Its long history of wickedness made it a target of God's judgment more than once in ancient times (Jon 3:1–10). See introduction: *Historical Background.* • The prophecy refers anagogically to the consummation of the world. It is designed to comfort the saints, that they might despise the visible things of this passing and perishing world and ready themselves for the Day of Judgment, when the Lord will come in vengeance against the true Assyrians (St. Jerome, *Commentary on Nahum*, preface). **book of the vision:** Suggests to some scholars that the Book of Nahum is a literary prophecy, meaning the Lord's revelation was written down from the start without first being delivered orally (cf. Rev 1:11). **Nahum:** The name in Hebrew translates "consolation" or "comfort". **Elkosh:** The prophet's hometown. Scholars have reached no agreement on its location. It has been argued that Elkosh is **(1)** the town of El-Kauzeh in Galilee, **(2)** the lakeside town of Capernaum in Galilee, **(3)** the village of al-Kush on the banks of the Tigris River, or **(4)** a town in southwest Judah near modern Beit Jibrin.

1:2–8 A victory hymn to the Lord, the Divine Warrior, who is hailed a wrathful Avenger (1:2) and a mighty Savior (1:7). Although the Assyrians were "strong and many" (1:12) at the time of writing, the prophet was so certain that God would destroy Nineveh that he celebrates its demise years before its fall in 612 B.C. Nahum depicts the coming judgment as a theophany—an overwhelming manifestation of the Lord's glory and power using the imagery of a violent thunderstorm (1:3–5; cf. Ps 18:7–15; Is 29:6). This way of speaking recalls the display of God's presence on Mt. Sinai (Ex 19:16–19). Literarily, the hymn may be a partial acrostic poem that follows the sequence of the first half of the Hebrew alphabet, although the text as it stands presents conflicting evidence that casts doubt on the author's intention to employ this technique.

1:2 a jealous God: Divine jealousy is expressed as a divine commitment to judge offenders who impugn his honor and the honor of Israel, his bride by covenant (Is 54:5; Jer 2:2; Hos 1–3). The jealousy of God is affirmed many times in Scripture, often to stress that he demands exclusive loyalty and tolerates no rivals for Israel's love and worship (Ex 20:5; 34:14; Deut 4:24; Josh 24:19, etc.). **his adversaries:** The Assyrians, who were guilty of "unceasing evil" against God, Israel, and other nations (3:19).

1:3 slow to anger: God's patience with sinners as revealed to Moses on Mt. Sinai (Ex 34:6). The Lord is slow to execute judgment in order to give transgressors time to repent (Wis 11:23; Rom 2:4). **and of great might:** A striking departure from an OT pattern, in which the Lord's slowness to anger is normally coupled with his merciful love (Ex 34:6; Num 14:18; Ps 86:15; 103:8; Joel 2:13, etc.). In this case, the expected reference to divine mercy is replaced with a reference to divine might, hinting that Nineveh has exhausted the Lord's patience and must now face his dreadful power and wrath. For the repentance of Nineveh more than a century before Nahum's day, see Jon 3:1–10. • The mercy of God is limitless in itself, but the free choice of men and women can put limits on its reception. People can close their hearts to divine mercy by refusing to admit their faults and by denying forgiveness to others (CCC 1847, 2840). **by no means clear the guilty:** Also part of the Sinai revelation (Ex 34:7). The Lord not only made known his patience and mercy to Moses but equally affirmed his justice in holding sinners accountable for evil.

1:4 rebukes the sea: The Lord's sovereign command over the waters is affirmed many times in Scripture (Gen 1:9; Ex 14:21; Josh 3:14–17; Ps 106:9; Is 42:15; Jer 51:36). Here his voice is compared to a warrior's battle cry. **Bashan ... Carmel:** Locations in northern Israel, east and west of the Sea of Galilee and noted for their lush landscapes. **Lebanon:** Directly north of Israel, famous in the biblical world for its majestic cedar trees (Ps 92:12; Ezek 31:3).

1:5 mountains: Symbolize pride and immovable strength. The message is that nothing in this world, no matter how mighty or seemingly indestructible (= Assyrian Empire), can stand before the Lord when he comes with retribution for sin (1:6). **melt:** A reaction of fear (Ex 15:15; Josh 2:9).

The opening words of the Book of Nahum announce the central theme—the coming destruction of Nineveh, the great oppressor of God's people. The passion with which this lyric poetry is imbued is explained by the tyranny endured for so long by Israel. But the deliverance announced will not, unfortunately, be of long duration. The fall of Nineveh (612 B.C.) will be followed by the fall of Jerusalem, but that is not part of the prophet's message.

⁷The LORD is good,
　　a stronghold in the day of trouble;
　　he knows those who take refuge in him.
⁸But with an overflowing flood
　　he will make a full end of his adversaries, ᵃ
　　and will pursue his enemies into darkness.
⁹What do you plot against the LORD?
　　He will make a full end;
　　he will not take vengeanceᵇ twice on his foes. ᶜ
¹⁰Like entangled thorns they are consumed, ᵈ
　　like dry stubble.
¹¹Did one notᵉ come out from you,
　　who plotted evil against the LORD,
　　and counseled villainy?

¹²Thus says the LORD,
　"Though they be strong and many, ᶠ
　　they will be cut off and pass away.

Though I have afflicted you,
　　I will afflict you no more.
¹³And now I will break his yoke from off you
　　and will burst your bonds asunder."

¹⁴The LORD has given commandment about you:
　"No more shall your name be perpetuated;
　from the house of your gods I will cut off
　　the graven image and the molten image.
　I will make your grave, for you are vile."

¹⁵ᵍBehold, on the mountains the feet of him
　　who brings good tidings,
　　who proclaims peace!
　Keep your feasts, O Judah,
　　fulfil your vows,
　for never again shall the wicked come against you,
　　he is utterly cut off.

1:15: Is 40:9; 52:7; Acts 10:36; Rom 10:15.

1:7 The LORD is good: Reassurance for all who trust in God and his lordship over the world. Nahum's message is that the Lord's punishment of the wicked is simultaneously an act of his kindness toward the righteous, who delight, not in God's fury, but in the relief he brings to them when the powers of evil and oppression are overthrown. This general truth sets the stage for Nineveh's destruction, which will bring "peace" to Judah (1:15) and move peoples formerly conquered by Assyria to "clap their hands" (3:19).

1:8 overflowing flood: An image of overwhelming judgment (Gen 6–7; Is 8:7–8; Jer 47:2; Dan 9:26). **into darkness:** Into the realm of the dead, called Sheol or the Pit, where darkness prevails (Job 17:13; 18:18).

1:9 will not take vengeance twice: Nineveh will not need to be punished twice, since the Lord's wrath will be fully unleashed, leaving the city unable to rise again.

1:11 one: Sennacherib, king of Assyria from 705 to 681 B.C. He invaded the land of Judah in 701 B.C., captured multiple cities and towns, and arrogantly threatened to conquer Jerusalem before the Lord intervened to protect the city (2 Kings 18:13—19:37). Sennacherib also enlarged the city of Nineveh and made it Assyria's capital in the early eighth century B.C. **from you:** The pronoun is feminine, referring to Nineveh.

1:12 strong and many: The mighty Assyrians, whose "yoke" of imperial rule was pressed upon the neck of small states like Judah (1:13). **you:** Judah (1:15).

1:14 you: The king of Assyria, who is denied a dynasty of successors and assured that the idols in his temple will be unable to defend him.

1:15 Behold: The RSV2CE follows the Latin Vulgate by making this the final verse of chapter 1. In the Hebrew MT and Greek LXX, this passage appears as 2:1, an alternative verse numbering that is followed by some modern translations (e.g., NABRE, NJB). **brings good tidings:** Nahum envisions a messenger traveling on foot to deliver news of victory from the battlefront (cf. 2 Sam 18:24–27). Here the herald comes over

the mountains of Judah with the report that Nineveh is fallen. A similar image is found in Is 52:7. **Keep your feasts:** The weekly and yearly religious festivals of Lev 23:1–44. **O Judah:** An address to the Southern Kingdom of Judah. **your vows:** Perhaps vows to offer sacrifices of thanksgiving to the Lord (Lev 7:16). **never again:** Not a promise of everlasting peace in this world but a promise that Assyria will no longer be a threat to the covenant people.

WORD STUDY

Peace (1:15)

Shālôm (Heb.): a noun that appears over 200 times in the Old Testament. It has a rich depth of meaning and a broad range of usage. It is spoken in greetings that offer wishes of well-being (1 Sam 25:6) as well as words of encouragement (Dan 10:19) or reassurance (Gen 43:23, where "Rest assured" is literally "Peace to you"). In other contexts, it is closely connected with prosperity (Ps 37:11), physical rest and security (Ps 4:8), health or wellness (Gen 37:14), serenity in death (Jer 34:5), and relational concord between persons who could potentially be at odds (Ex 4:18). To have *shālôm* is to have freedom from fear and to enjoy God's blessing of protection from hostile threats (Lev 26:6). This applies not only to individuals but to cities and societies (Jer 29:7). Peace is the benefit that comes when justice is upheld for all (Zech 8:16). The Lord has plans for the welfare or peace of the entire People of God (Jer 29:11). Prophecies of the messianic age thus foresee a new covenant between God and his people as a "covenant of peace" that reconciles sinners with the Lord (Is 54:10; Ezek 34:25; cf. Jer 31:31–34). The bringer of this eschatological peace is none other than the Davidic Messiah, who is called "Prince of Peace" (Is 9:6).

ᵃ Gk: Heb *her place.*
ᵇ Gk: Heb *rise up.*
ᶜ Cn: Heb *distress.*
ᵈ Heb *are consumed, drunken as with their drink.*
ᵉ Cn: Heb *fully.*
ᶠ Heb uncertain.
ᵍ Ch 2:1 in Heb.

The Overthrow of Nineveh

2 The shatterer has come up against you.
Man the ramparts;
watch the road;
gird your loins;
collect all your strength.

[2](For the Lord is restoring the majesty of Jacob
as the majesty of Israel,
for plunderers have stripped them
and ruined their branches.)

[3]The shield of his mighty men is red,
his soldiers are clothed in scarlet.
The chariots flash like flame[h]
when mustered in array;
the chargers[i] prance.
[4]The chariots rage in the streets,
they rush back and forth through the squares;
they gleam like torches,
they dart like lightning.
[5]The officers are summoned,
they stumble as they go,
they hasten to the wall,
the mantelet is set up.
[6]The river gates are opened,
the palace is in dismay;
[7]its mistress[j] is stripped, she is carried off,
her maidens lamenting,

moaning like doves,
and beating their breasts.
[8]Nin'eveh is like a pool
whose waters[k] run away.
"Halt! Halt!" they cry;
but none turns back.
[9]Plunder the silver,
plunder the gold!
There is no end of treasure,
or wealth of every precious thing.
[10]Desolate! Desolation and ruin!
Hearts faint and knees tremble,
anguish is on all loins,
all faces grow pale!
[11]Where is the lions' den,
the cave[l] of the young lions,
where the lion brought his prey,
where his cubs were, with none to disturb?
[12]The lion tore enough for his whelps
and strangled prey for his lionesses;
he filled his caves with prey
and his dens with torn flesh.

Utter Ruin of the Evil City

13 Behold, I am against you, says the Lord of hosts, and I will burn your[m] chariots in smoke, and the sword shall devour your young lions; I will cut off your prey from the earth, and the voice of your messengers shall no more be heard.

2:1-10 A poetic description of Nineveh under attack. The city is overrun by warriors spattered with blood (2:3), thundering through the streets on chariots (2:4) and looting the city of its valuables (2:9). Nahum's message: Nineveh will be like a captive noblewoman (2:7), and nothing but anguish and ruin will be left behind (2:10). • Satan, too, was plundered by Christ and then by the holy apostles. Those who are precious to Satan come to faith when Christ, the Savior of all, leads them to fear God, and the apostles persuade them to do the same (St. Cyril of Alexandria, *Commentary on Nahum* 2).

2:1 The shatterer: Nineveh's conquerors, who will send its inhabitants fleeing in all directions (2:8; 3:18). Historical sources indicate that the city was taken in 612 B.C. by an alliance of Medes, Babylonians, and Scythians. **Man the ramparts:** A sarcastic use of battle commands. The prophet orders Assyrian soldiers to defend their capital, knowing full well that its demise is assured.

2:2 For the Lord ... branches: The parentheses around this verse in the RSV2CE indicate that its location in the book is uncertain. It appears here in ancient manuscripts, yet it seems to disrupt the flow of the prophet's thought. Perhaps it originally stood after 1:15. **restoring:** God is restoring the honor of his people after years of foreign domination and humiliation. **plunderers:** The Assyrians, whose tyranny left Judah like a ravaged vine (Is 5:5-6).

2:3 chariots flash: Chariots were made of wood but typically had metal fittings and coverings that could reflect the sunlight. The Canaanites, for example, had "chariots of iron" (Josh 17:16; Judg 1:19).

2:5 mantelet: A portable covering that shielded attacking soldiers from projectiles hurled down from the top of city walls (spears, arrows, rocks, etc.).

2:6 river gates: Canals channeled water from the nearby Tigris and Khoser rivers into the walled city of Nineveh. Attackers may have used them as weapons: by damming the rivers, they would not only cut off a vital water supply from the besieged population, but quickly unblocking the rivers would send powerful waves crashing against the city wall, thus weakening Nineveh's defenses.

2:7 its mistress: Possibly a statue of the goddess Ishtar, worshiped by the Assyrians, that is confiscated by enemy invaders as a trophy of war (cf. Jer 43:12).

2:11-13 Nineveh, the **den** of Assyria, is about to be empty with its **young lions** slain. Its conquerors will triumph because the Lord, who steers the direction of world history and holds nations accountable for their ways, is set against the wicked city. Four different words are used in this passage for lions, a technique seen in Job 4:10-11 (in reference to lions) and in Joel 1:4 (in reference to locusts).

2:13 I am against you: Ominous words of doom spoken when nations are about to face divine judgment (Jer 50:31; 51:25; Ezek 21:3; 35:3; 38:3). **the Lord of hosts:** A title for the Lord as commander of the heavenly army of angels (Josh 5:14) as well as the military forces of Israel (1 Sam 17:45). In this context, it hints that the Lord commands even pagan armies—Median, Babylonian, and Scythian forces—whom he will use to punish Nineveh, just as Assyria itself was a "rod" of divine anger that God wielded against others (Is 10:5-6).

---

[h]Cn: The meaning of the Hebrew word is uncertain.
[i]Cn Compare Gk Syr: Heb *cypresses.*
[j]The meaning of the Hebrew is uncertain.
[k]Cn Compare Gk: Heb *from the days that she has become, and they.*
[l]Cn: Heb *pasture.*
[m]Heb *her.*

3 Woe to the bloody city,
 all full of lies and booty—
  no end to the plunder!
[2]The crack of whip, and rumble of wheel,
  galloping horse and bounding chariot!
[3]Horsemen charging,
  flashing sword and glittering spear,
 hosts of slain,
  heaps of corpses,
 dead bodies without end—
  they stumble over the bodies!
[4]And all for the countless harlotries of the harlot,
  graceful and of deadly charms,
 who betrays nations with her harlotries,
  and peoples with her charms.

[5]Behold, I am against you,
  says the LORD of hosts,
  and will lift up your skirts over your face;
 and I will let nations look on your nakedness
  and kingdoms on your shame.
[6]I will throw filth at you
  and treat you with contempt,
  and make you an object of scorn.
[7]And all who look on you will shrink from you
   and say,
 Wasted is Nin eveh; who will moan over her?
  from where shall I seek comforters for her?[n]

[8]Are you better than Thebes[o]
  that sat by the Nile,

with water around her,
  her rampart a sea,
  and water her wall?
[9]Ethiopia was her strength,
  Egypt too, and that without limit;
  Put and the Libyans were her[p] helpers.

[10]Yet she was carried away,
  she went into captivity;
 her little ones were dashed in pieces
  at the head of every street;
 for her honored men lots were cast,
  and all her great men were bound in chains.
[11]You also will be drunken,
  you will be dazed;
 you will seek
  a refuge from the enemy.
[12]All your fortresses are like fig trees
  with first-ripe figs—
 if shaken they fall
  into the mouth of the eater.
[13]Behold, your troops
  are women in your midst.
 The gates of your land
  are wide open to your foes;
  fire has devoured your bars.
[14]Draw water for the siege,
  strengthen your forts;
 go into the clay,
  tread the mortar,
  take hold of the brick mold!

3:1 Woe: A cry of anguish heard at funerals. Here it announces Nineveh's imminent death. See word study: *Woe* at Is 28:1. **bloody city:** Or "city of bloodshed", implying that it is punished in kind for its murderous violence against others. **the plunder:** The wealth that Assyria gained from spoils of war and from tribute imposed upon subjugated nations.

3:2-3 Sights and sounds of the military assault on Nineveh. The prophet invites readers to watch and listen as the city descends into chaos and becomes a mass grave.

3:4 the harlot: Nineveh, pictured as a prostitute. Defiled by a myriad of sins and indiscretions, it is about to be stripped naked and publicly shamed like a convicted adulteress (3:5-7; Ezek 16:35-39; Hos 2:3). Since harlotry is a common metaphor in Scripture for idolatry, Nineveh's service to a pantheon of false gods may be in view as well (Ex 34:14-16; Hos 2:2; Jer 3:1-9). **her charms:** Her techniques of enticement and seduction.

3:5 Behold, I am against you: Repeated from 2:13. Emphasis on the Lord's opposition to Nineveh reinforces the certainty of the city's destruction.

3:7 comforters: The word in Hebrew shares the same root as the name Nahum, meaning "comfort". This points to a contrast: Nineveh's demise will bring comfort to the victims of its oppression, but no comfort will be found for the city itself.

3:8 Thebes: Greek name for the city of No, longtime capital of southern (= Upper) Egypt. It stood beside the Nile, roughly 400 miles upriver from the Mediterranean, and was dedicated to the god Amon. Being a fortified city deep in Egyptian territory, it was thought to be unconquerable; nevertheless, the Assyrians destroyed Thebes in 663 B.C. Nahum puts this incident forward as an object lesson: Nineveh may appear to be impregnable as well, but history shows that no city is safe from conquest. **water around her:** Water canals fed by the Nile were part of the strategic defenses of Thebes.

3:9 Ethiopia ... Put ... Libyans: North African peoples who supplied Egypt with military aid (Jer 46:8-9).

3:10 little ones were dashed: The massacre of infants and children was a horrific practice of ancient warfare, intended in part to destroy an enemy's future warriors (2 Kings 8:12; Ps 137:9; Is 13:16; Hos 10:14).

3:11 You: The pronoun is feminine, referring to Nineveh. **drunken:** The terror and confusion of war induces a state of disorientation similar to intoxication. **you will seek a refuge:** Assyrian survivors who escaped the fall of Nineveh regrouped in Haran, but these too were overthrown by the Babylonians and their allies in 610 B.C.

3:13 your troops are women: Fear of the enemy will turn Nineveh's brave soldiers into the equivalent of frightened female civilians (cf. Is 19:16; Jer 51:30). **your bars:** Wooden crossbeams that reinforced city gates from the inside.

3:14 Draw water: In anticipation of the enemy cutting off the city's water supply. **take hold of the brick mold:** Last-minute efforts to strengthen the city's defensive wall are in view. The prophet's commands are spoken sarcastically. See note on 2:1.

---

[n] Gk: Heb *you.*
[o] Heb *No-amon.*
[p] Gk: Heb *your.*

[15]There will the fire devour you,
the sword will cut you off.
It will devour you like the locust.

Multiply yourselves like the locust,
multiply like the grasshopper!
[16]You increased your merchants
more than the stars of the heavens.
The locust spreads its wings and flies away.
[17]Your princes are like grasshoppers,
your scribes[q] like clouds of locusts
settling on the fences
in a day of cold—
when the sun rises, they fly away;
no one knows where they are.

[18]Your shepherds are asleep,
O king of Assyria;
your nobles slumber.
Your people are scattered on the mountains
with none to gather them.
[19]There is no assuaging your hurt,
your wound is grievous.
All who hear the news of you
clap their hands over you.
For upon whom has not come
your unceasing evil?

3:15–17 The prophet employs two analogies based on locust infestations. The overthrow of Nineveh is compared to the mass *destruction* that locusts bring upon fields and crops (3:15), and the panicked flight of the Ninevites is compared to the swift *departure* of locust swarms that fly away when no vegetation is left (3:16–17). Four distinct words for "locust" are used in this passage, just as four different words for "lion" were used in 2:11–12.

[q]Or *marshals.*

3:16 merchants: Those who increased Nineveh's enormous wealth are among the first to flee.

3:18 O king of Assyria: Assyria's humiliated ruler. Nahum contends that the monarchy in Nineveh suffered a lethal blow from which it will not recover. **Your people are scattered:** The Assyrians are like sheep, dispersed and preyed upon by enemies while their national leaders are sleeping.

3:19 clap their hands: The destruction of Nineveh is a cause for celebration among the victims of Assyrian cruelty. In biblical times, clapping was an expression not only of approval but of joy (Ps 47:1).

STUDY QUESTIONS
Nahum

Chapter 1

For understanding

1. **1:2–8.** As a victory hymn to the Lord, the Divine Warrior, in what role is he hailed? Although the Assyrians were "strong and many" at the time of writing, of what was the prophet so certain that he did years in advance? How does Nahum depict the coming judgment? What does this way of speaking recall? Although literarily, the hymn may be a partial acrostic poem, what conflicting evidence does the text as it stands present?

2. **1:3.** What does God's slowness to anger mean? How is the phrase "and of great might" a striking departure from an OT pattern? In this case, with what is the expected reference to divine mercy replaced? While the mercy of God is limitless in itself, what can put limits on its reception? As part of the Sinai revelation where the Lord made known his patience and mercy to Moses, what was equally affirmed there?

3. **1:7.** As reassurance for all who trust in God and his lordship over the world, what is Nahum's message? For what does this general truth set the stage and what will it bring?

4. **Word Study: Peace (1:15).** How many times does the Hebrew word *shālôm* appear in the Old Testament? With its rich depth of meaning and a broad range of usage, how is it spoken? In other contexts, with what is it closely connected? What is it to have *shālôm*, and for whom does it apply? When does the benefit of peace come? What do prophecies of the messianic age thus foresee? Who is the bringer of this eschatological peace?

For application

1. **1:3.** What happens within you when you become angry? Does your anger rise quickly and subside slowly, or does it ignite slowly and subside quickly? When you do get angry, what sorts of damage are you capable of causing? Why is the slowness of God's "anger" measured in years or centuries? How does his might manifest itself then?

2. **1:7.** According to the note for this verse, how is the goodness of God compatible with his punishments? Why does God impose discipline on his children (Prov 3:11–12, Heb 12:5)? How might his discipline of yourself even be considered a way of leading you to take refuge within him?

3. **1:15.** According to the word study on the word *shālôm*, "The Lord has plans for the welfare or peace of the entire People of God", citing Jer 29:11. According to subsequent verses in that chapter of Jeremiah (i.e., vv. 11–14), how do you discover what those plans are? How have you experienced his plans for your welfare?

Chapter 2

For understanding

1. **2:1–10.** Of what are these verses a poetical description? What is Nahum's message here? According to St. Cyril of Alexandria, how is Satan, too, plundered by Christ and then by the holy apostles?

2. **2:1.** Who is "the shatterer"? What do historical sources indicate about how the city was taken? As a sarcastic use of battle commands, what does the prophet order Assyrian soldiers to do?

3. **2:6.** What were the river gates? How may attackers have used them?

4. **2:11–13.** As the den of Assyria, what will happen to Nineveh? Why will its conquerors triumph? How many different words are used in this passage for lions?

For application

1. **2:3.** Read the note for this verse. Modern armies try to develop weapons that disorient, confuse, or frighten their enemies. What are some examples of such weapons? What are some of the ways Satan can disorient or frighten you? How do you resist his tactics?

2. **2:9.** Jesus said that where your treasure is, there will your heart be (Lk 12:34). What is your treasure? What treasure have you stored up for heaven? How vulnerable is it to attack from either the devil or the world?

3. **2:10.** Imagine yourself in a game, such as soccer, where your team is playing all-out for a title and you realize that crushing defeat is looming. How would you resist the dread of defeat? How would you try to keep the team in the game? In the spiritual life, when failure looms, how do you stir up hope in yourself and encourage it in others?

Chapter 3

For understanding

1. **3:7.** With what does the word in Hebrew for "comforters" share the same root? To what contrast does this point?

2. **3:8.** For what city is Thebes the Greek name? Where was it located, and to whom was it dedicated? Why was it thought to be unconquerable, and nonetheless what happened to it? Why does Nahum put this incident forward? Of what were the water canals around Thebes a part?

3. **3:15–17.** What two analogies based on locust infestations does the prophet employ? How many words for "locust" are used in this passage?

4. **3:19.** Why do people clap their hands at the destruction of Nineveh? In biblical times, of what was clapping an expression?

For application

1. **3:4–7.** After the fall of the Nazi empire in 1945, the atrocities of that regime were revealed to the world. How would the nations who were victimized by Germany most likely have regarded it as a nation? How was the effort to create a plan for

Study Questions

Germany's relief and restoration in the best interests of the victorious Allies? Why should a former victim choose to come to the aid of a defeated tormentor?

2. **3:10.** In describing the future destruction of Jerusalem at the hands of the Romans, why did Jesus express sorrow for pregnant women and nursing mothers (Mt 24:19)? What is often the fate of women and children at the hands of an invading army? What has the Church in your area done for refugees and other victims of war and violence?

3. **3:12–15.** Since modern cities cannot rely on defensive walls, what defenses do they have against attack? How reliable are they? What defenses do most citizens have in the event of a natural disaster, such as a flood or forest fire? How reliable are they?

4. **3:19.** The words of this verse can apply to the defeat of the devil and of Death and Hades in Rev 20:10–14. What form does gloating over their defeat take among the saints (cf. Rev 19:1–8))? When you experience victory over the devil and his temptations, what form does your celebration take?

INTRODUCTION TO HABAKKUK

Author and Date Little is known about the prophet whose name is attached to this book (1:1). It says nothing about his genealogy, his occupation, or his place of residence. Fragments of information appear in the Greek Septuagint translation of Daniel, which includes two deuterocanonical chapters that are not part of the Hebrew/Aramaic text of Daniel (chaps. 13–14). Here we learn that Habakkuk's father's name was "Joshua" and that he was descended from "the tribe of Levi" (Dan 14:1 LXX = *Bel and the Dragon* 1). Daniel 14 also includes the miraculous story of Habakkuk being transported by an angel to Babylon in order to provide food for the prophet Daniel in the lions' den (Dan 14:31–39). From evidence within the Book of Habakkuk itself, we can sketch a profile of the author as both a prophet and a Psalmist. He was given an "oracle" (1:1) about God's intention to bring judgment on Judah (1:5–11) and eventually on the Babylonians (2:2–20). At the same time, he is credited with the lyrics of the closing hymn or "prayer" (3:1), which was meant to be sung to the accompaniment of "stringed instruments" (3:19). This suggests that Habakkuk, besides being a prophet, may have been a Levite who performed sacred music in the Jerusalem Temple (1 Chron 23:1–5; Neh 12:27). Some of these Levitical musicians also prophesied, according to 1 Chron 25:1–6.

Efforts to date the book are hampered by limited information. A few have dated the book in the early seventh century B.C., and a few have even placed it as late as the fourth century B.C. The majority of scholars, however, place the Book of Habakkuk near the end of the seventh century B.C., a time when the Babylonians freed themselves from Assyrian rule, asserted themselves as an independent kingdom, and began the process of building an empire. Evidence for this historical backdrop is found in 1:6, which describes the Chaldeans (= Babylonians) as victorious conquerors, and in 1:12–17, which indicates the growing reputation of their army as merciless and unstoppable. It is thus reasonable to assign a date for the book between 626 B.C., when the Babylonians gained their independence, and 605 B.C., the year that King Nebuchadnezzar of Babylon besieged Jerusalem for the first time and claimed the kingdom of Judah as a vassal state (Dan 1:1–4). Within this twenty-year window, a date closer to 605 in the early years of King Jehoiakim's reign (609–598 B.C.) seems preferable, as it allows sufficient time for the Babylonians to have acquired the reputation for ruthless conquest evidenced in 1:6–11, 14–17. This would make Habakkuk a contemporary of the prophets Jeremiah, Nahum, and Zephaniah.

Title The book is named after Habakkuk, mentioned in the opening verse. Its Hebrew form, *Ḥabaqqûq*, either means "embraced" or is related to an Akkadian name for a type of garden plant. His name appears in the Greek Septuagint in the title *Ambakoum* and in the expanded heading of the Latin Vulgate, *Abacuc Propheta*, "Habakkuk the Prophet". English titles for the book follow these ancient traditions.

Place in the Canon Habakkuk has long been revered as a canonical book of Scripture. In the Jewish Bible, or Tanakh, it stands among the Latter Prophets in a sub-collection of writings known as "the Book of the Twelve". In Christian Bibles, these twelve books are called the Minor Prophets, not because they are less important than Isaiah, Jeremiah, Ezekiel, or Daniel, but because they are comparatively shorter. In the Hebrew Bible, the Greek Septuagint, and the Latin Vulgate, Habakkuk stands eighth among the Minor Prophets between Nahum and Zephaniah. This is also its position in most English Bibles.

Structure The Book of Habakkuk divides cleanly into three parts, two that are cast as a dialogue and one that takes the form of a psalm. **(1)** The book opens with Habakkuk setting a problem before the Lord (1:1–4), to which the Lord answers with his solution (1:5–11). **(2)** The book continues with Habakkuk setting a second problem before the Lord (1:12–17), and this is followed by the Lord's second answer, revealing again his solution (2:2–20). **(3)** The book closes with a hymn of praise to the Lord as the Divine Warrior who comes with wrath for his enemies and salvation for his people (3:1–19). See *Outline*.

Historical Background Habakkuk lived in the declining years of the Southern Kingdom of Judah. Internally, this was a time of serious societal breakdown among the covenant people when violence and lawlessness was the norm (1:2–4). Externally, the Babylonians were rising rapidly under the general-king Nebuchadnezzar to succeed the Assyrians as the next Mesopotamian empire with ambitions to dominate the Near East. Nevertheless, the prophet's fellow Judahites seemed at this point to think that a Babylonian conquest of Judah was unthinkable (1:5). They breathed a sigh of relief at the fall of Nineveh, capital of Assyria, in 612 B.C., but they overestimated the strength of the Egyptians to hold the Babylonians at bay. This would prove to be a serious tactical mistake. The Babylonian victory at the Battle of Carchemish in 605 not only crushed the last remnants of Assyria but caused their Egyptian allies to retreat and withdraw from Syria-Palestine. If a Babylonian subjugation of Judah seemed unlikely before this, it was no longer so afterward. Habakkuk's prophecy that God was rousing the Babylonians ("the Chaldeans", 1:6) to chastise the sinful people of Judah would soon become a reality: Nebuchadnezzar besieged Jerusalem and took a modest number of persons into exile in 605 (Dan 1:1–4); he invaded again and took many more captives to Babylon in 597 (2 Kings 24:10–17); and he returned yet again to dismantle the Judahite monarchy, to destroy the Jerusalem Temple, and to deport even more Judeans into exile in 586 B.C. (2 Kings 25:1–12).

Message of the Prophet The Book of Habakkuk is unique among the prophetic books of Scripture. It is usually the case that prophets rebuke the erring People of God and call them back to the Lord and his covenant. In Habakkuk, however, the prophet delivers no message of repentance. Instead, readers listen to a dialogue between God and the prophet in which Habakkuk voices his complaints to the Lord and the Lord responds by revealing his plans to take action (1:1—2:20). The final segment of the book is also unique: it is a hymn in which Habakkuk sings of the Lord's almighty power to judge and to save (3:1–15). The closest parallels to Habakkuk's psalm are found, not in the prophetic books of Scripture, but in the lyrical compositions featured in the Book of Psalms. Together these features make the Book of Habakkuk one of the most distinctive of the Minor Prophets.

Habakkuk's dialogue with the Lord is focused on theodicy: the justification of God's mysterious ways. The conversation falls into two parts. **(1)** In the first exchange, the prophet complains that God is silent and inactive in the face of sin (1:2–4). Habakkuk looks around and sees violence, conflict, and lawlessness flourishing in Judah. Justice is perverted and even the righteous are made to suffer at the hands of the wicked. This is a problem for faith since the Lord, who forged a covenant with Israel, is responsible for enforcing the covenant when it is broken. Habakkuk is concerned that God is neglecting his duties. God is supposed to judge violations of the covenant by administering its curses (Lev 26:3–45; Deut 28:1–68), but the prophet can see no sign of its enforcement. The Lord then answers with strong assurance that Judah's sins will not go unpunished (1:5–11). Unbeknownst to the prophet, he has already begun "rousing the Chaldeans" (1:6 = Babylonians), who will march against Judah and bring chastisement upon its rebellious people. **(2)** In the second exchange, Habakkuk complains that God's solution to the first problem is itself problematic (1:12–17). How can the Lord, who is supremely "Holy" (1:12), make use of the wicked and treacherous Babylonians to punish the "more

righteous" people of Judah (1:13)? This seems to the prophet incompatible with the justice and righteousness of God. If the people of Judah deserve judgment, then the Babylonians deserve it far more, and yet the Lord seems to be standing by, allowing them to conquer one nation after another (1:17). The Lord's second answer also comes with strong words of assurance: the Babylonians, whom he will wield as the rod of his anger against Judah, will themselves come to judgment (2:2–20). The punisher will himself be punished in due time. This is indicated by five "woes" or funeral laments that announce Babylonia's coming demise (2:6, 9, 12, 15, 19). God allowed the Babylonians to grow strong, and he would use their strength to discipline his sinful people, but this was merely a prelude to their own day of reckoning. The Babylonians, too, will be held accountable for their evildoing when they are forced to drink "the cup" of Lord's wrath (2:16).

In both cases, then, it is a question of the Lord's timing. His people may be asked to "wait" for him to act, but the day of his justice "will surely come" (2:3). This is precisely the lesson that Habakkuk comes to learn by the end of the book: after calling to mind a report of divine interventions in the past (3:3–15), the prophet declares that he will "quietly wait" for God to fulfill his plans for both Judah and Babylonia (3:16). He is confident that, no matter what calamities lie ahead, he can trust in God's promise that "the righteous shall live by his faith" (2:4). The Lord may appear at times to be silent and inactive, to be unconcerned with justice, but these are times of waiting that call for patient endurance and faithful reliance on God.

Christian Perspective The Book of Habakkuk has made a clear impact on the New Testament. Its general theme of God's moral government of the world, by which he judges not only individuals but entire nations, is clearly affirmed in the teaching of Jesus (Mt 25:31–46). In terms of specific passages, Habakkuk is cited to shed light on distinctively Christian beliefs and circumstances. In the Book of Acts, Paul quotes the Greek LXX translation of 1:5 to warn that God is doing something that disbelievers reject to their own peril. Habakkuk was talking about scoffers who dismissed a Babylonian invasion of Judah, whereas Paul applies the warning to those who reject the forgiveness of sins offered in Christ (Acts 13:40). Likewise, Paul cites a Greek version of 2:4 as a key to the doctrine of justification. The passage shows that justification (= becoming righteous before God and destined for eternal life) takes place by faith and not by observing the works of the Mosaic Law (Rom 1:17; Gal 3:11). This same passage is quoted more fully in the Book of Hebrews, which draws from it the lesson that believers must persevere in faith as they endure persecution and await the Lord's coming (Heb 10:37–38).

OUTLINE OF HABAKKUK

1. The First Problem and God's Solution (1:1–11)
    A. Superscription (1:1)
    B. Habakkuk Questions God about Evil in Judah (1:2–4)
    C. God Answers Habakkuk about Punishing Judah (1:5–11)

2. The Second Problem and God's Solution (1:12—2:20)
    A. Habakkuk Questions God about Using the Babylonians (1:12—2:1)
    B. God Answers Habakkuk about Punishing the Babylonians (2:2–20)

3. The Psalm of Habakkuk (3:1–19)
    A. Superscription (3:1)
    B. Prayer for Mercy amidst Wrath (3:2)
    C. Theophany of the Divine Warrior (3:3–15)
    D. Waiting for the Day of Trouble (3:16–19)

THE BOOK OF

HABAKKUK

The Prophet's Complaint

1 The oracle of God which Habak'kuk the prophet saw.

²O Lord, how long shall I cry for help,
  and you will not hear?
  Or cry to you "Violence!"
  and you will not save?
³Why do you make me see wrongs
  and look upon trouble?
  Destruction and violence are before me;
  strife and contention arise.
⁴So the law is slacked
  and justice never goes forth.
  For the wicked surround the righteous,
  so justice goes forth perverted.

⁵Look among the nations, and see;
  wonder and be astounded.
  For I am doing a work in your days
  that you would not believe if told.
⁶For behold, I am rousing the Chalde'ans,
  that bitter and hasty nation,
  who march through the breadth of the
   earth,
  to seize habitations not their own.
⁷Dread and fearsome are they;
  their justice and dignity proceed from
   themselves.
⁸Their horses are swifter than leopards,
  more fierce than the evening wolves;
  their horsemen press proudly on.

1:2: Is 13:1–14:23; 47; Jer 50–51. **1:5:** Acts 13:41. **1:6:** Rev 20:9.

1:1–4 Habakkuk laments the violence, destruction, and lawlessness that prevails in Judah. The prophet is troubled by God's inaction, and so he questions why the Lord allows wickedness to flourish unpunished. After all, it is God's responsibility to enforce the terms of his covenant with Israel by putting its curses for disobedience into effect (Deut 28:15–68). His concern will be addressed by the divine response in 1:5–11. The first part of the book, from 1:2—2:20, is thus presented as a "dialogue" between God and the prophet.

1:1 oracle: The Hebrew term *massā'* is a pronouncement of judgment on those who oppose the Lord, either the people of Israel (Mal 1:1) or more often a foreign nation (Is 13:1; 17:1; 19:1; 21:13; Nahum 1:1; Zech 9:1). **Habakkuk:** Meaning uncertain. The name may be derived from a Hebrew verb that can mean "embrace" or is related to an Akkadian name for a type of garden plant. **the prophet:** A title also given to Habakkuk in 3:1 and Dan 14:33. **saw:** God imparts revelation to the prophets in visual as well as verbal ways (Is 1:1; 2:1; 6:1; Ezek 7:26).

1:2 O Lord, how long: Words of anguish and growing impatience. The prophet yearns to see an end to the evil that surrounds him. The same cry is heard frequently in the Psalter (e.g., Pss 6:3; 13:1; 62:3; 79:5; 82:2). **Violence!:** The unjust use of force to inflict damage, injury, and suffering is decried several times in the book (1:3, 9; 2:8, 17). For the many injustices in Judah during the early years of Jehoiakim's reign, see Jer 22:13–19.

1:4 the law: The Torah or Law of Moses, which codified the Lord's instruction for Israel's faith, life, and worship. Transgressing the Law is tantamount to breaking the Lord's covenant with Israel (Hos 4:6; 8:1). **slacked:** Could also be translated "numb" or "incapacitated". **justice:** The Hebrew *mishpaṭ* means a fair and unprejudiced application of the Torah to the entire covenant community. Lawless corruption

in Judah is evidence that justice has been compromised. **the righteous:** The few devout persons left in Judah.

1:5–11 The Lord responds to Habakkuk's complaints in 1:2–4. He assures the prophet that Judah's sin has not escaped his notice, nor will it escape his justice. On the contrary, a plan is already in motion to chastise Judah by means of the Babylonians ("the Chaldeans" of 1:6).

📖 **1:5 Look:** Just as Habakkuk could "see" and "look upon" the problem of evil in Judah (1:3), so he and his fellow Judahites are invited to "look" and "see" God's solution in the rise of the Babylonians. **in your days:** Most likely the early years of King Jehoiakim (r. 609–598 B.C.). It was unclear before 605 B.C. that the Babylonians were destined to become an imperial superpower who could pose an existential threat to Judah. Few, in other words, were likely to **believe** what the Lord was about to do. • Paul cites the Greek LXX version of this passage in Acts 13:41 to warn against those who reject God's wondrous work in their days. In the apostle's time, the wondrous work of God was the dying and rising of Jesus for the forgiveness of sins.

1:6 the Chaldeans: Semitic tribal groups in southern Mesopotamia near the Persian Gulf. They seized the throne of Babylon soon after the death of the Assyrian king Ashurbanipal in 627 B.C. and established the Chaldean dynasty of the Neo-Babylonian empire. Key figures in the reemergence of Babylonian power at this time include Nabopolassar (626–605 B.C.) and Nebuchadnezzar (605–562 B.C.). The prophet learns that God intends to use Babylonia as a rod of correction to punish his wayward people, just as he had used the Assyrians to administer the curses of the covenant against Israel in the eighth century (Is 10:5–6). The Chaldeans are better known as the Babylonians. **march ... seize habitations:** Babylonian military conquests are in view. Nebuchadnezzar in particular will play the role of God's "servant" (Jer 25:9) by invading the land of Judah several times (2 Kings 24:1; 25:1; Dan 1:1).

1:7 justice ... from themselves: The arrogance of a people that "makes its own rules".

📖 **1:8 like an eagle:** Or "like a vulture". • The image, drawn from Deut 28:49, represents a foreign nation that God will use to administer covenant curses on disobedient Israel. Hosea earlier applied this image to the Assyrians (Hos 8:1), and Jesus will similarly describe the Romans (Mt 24:28).

There is not much evidence for the date of the Book of Habakkuk (Habacuc), but it is likely that the prophet is speaking against the Chaldeans under Nebuchadnezzar, who destroyed Jerusalem in 586 B.C. The book starts with a dialogue between the prophet and God—the prophet complaining, and the Lord explaining and foretelling the coming destruction of the oppressor. All this took place probably before the fall of Jerusalem. Habakkuk has some originality; he asks God to explain his thought: for example, why does he punish his erring people by a nation more wicked than itself? And hence, why does wickedness seem to triumph? This is the problem found all through the Old Testament.

Yes, their horsemen come from afar;
    they fly like an eagle swift to devour.
[9]They all come for violence;
    terror[a] of them goes before them.
They gather captives like sand.
[10]At kings they scoff,
    and of rulers they make sport.
They laugh at every fortress,
    for they heap up earth and take it.
[11]Then they sweep by like the wind and go on,
    guilty men, whose own might is their god!

[12]Are you not from everlasting,
    O Lord my God, my Holy One?
We shall not die.
O Lord, you have ordained them as a judgment;
    and you, O Rock, have established them for
    chastisement.
[13]You who are of purer eyes than to behold evil
    and cannot look on wrong,
why do you look on faithless men,
    and are silent when the wicked swallows up
    the man more righteous than he?
[14]For you make men like the fish of the sea,
    like crawling things that have no ruler.
[15]He brings all of them up with a hook,
    he drags them out with his net,

he gathers them in his seine;
    so he rejoices and exults.
[16]Therefore he sacrifices to his net
    and burns incense to his seine;
for by them he lives in luxury,[b]
    and his food is rich.
[17]Is he then to keep on emptying his net,
    and mercilessly slaying nations for
    ever?

God's Reply

2 I will take my stand to watch,
    and station myself on the tower,
and look forth to see what he will say to me,
    and what I will answer concerning my
    complaint.
[2]And the Lord answered me:
"Write the vision;
    make it plain upon tablets,
    so he may run who reads it.
[3]For still the vision awaits its time;
    it hastens to the end—it will not lie.
If it seem slow, wait for it;
    it will surely come, it will not delay.
[4]Behold, he whose soul is not upright in him
    shall fail,[c]
    but the righteous shall live by his faith.[d]

2:1: Is 21:8. **2:3:** Heb 10:37. **2:4:** Rom 1:17; Gal 3:11; Heb 10:38–39.

1:9 captives: Removing mass numbers of conquered people from their homeland was a feature of Babylonian warfare (2 Kings 24:10–14; 25:11; Jer 52:28–30).

1:10 heap up earth: Refers to the building of siege ramps to overthrow walled cities (2 Sam 20:15).

1:12–17 Habakkuk questions the justice of God's plan to punish sinful Judah by means of the more sinful Babylonians (1:5–11). The Lord's "solution" seems to compound the problem of injustice rather than offer a satisfying answer. To the mind of the prophet, evildoers should not be *instruments* of divine punishment but *objects* of divine punishment.

1:12 Are you not: The question is rhetorical. **from everlasting:** God is as old as history itself, since he lives outside of history in the limitless realm of eternity (Deut 33:27; Is 57:15). **Holy One:** The Lord is supremely holy, untainted by any impurity of sin (Is 6:3). **We shall not die:** The prophet, speaking on behalf of his people, expresses confidence that God will not allow Israel to perish entirely. **O Rock:** The Lord is the strength and defense of his people (Gen 49:24; Deut 32:4; Ps 18:2; Is 26:4). **ordained them:** The Babylonians. **as a judgment:** I.e., as a rod of correction to discipline Judah.

1:13 why: Habakkuk is again puzzled by God's lack of intervention in the face of evil (1:3). Why does the Lord tolerate the extreme wickedness of the Babylonians? Why does he not bring them to justice? Why does he allow this godless and arrogant empire to conquer nation after nation with ruthless force? This is the theological conundrum that prompts the divine response in 2:2–20. **the man more righteous:** Judah, who is comparatively less evil than Babylonia.

1:15 He: The king of Babylon, who gathers up helpless nations like a great fisherman (1:17; 2:5). **seine:** A dragnet.

1:16 sacrifices ... burns incense: The Babylonians make idols of their military might and of the wealth that comes from their conquests (CCC 2113).

2:1 I will take my stand: Habakkuk resolves to wait for the Lord's answer. He imagines himself as a sentry on a city wall or tower, scanning the horizon for a runner or horseman bringing news from afar (cf. 2 Sam 18:24; Is 21:8–9).

2:2–20 The Lord responds to Habakkuk's complaint in 1:12–17. He assures the prophet that the Babylonians will not escape justice for their wickedness. Again, as in 1:5–11, it is simply a question of timing (2:3). God is sending the Babylonians to punish sinful Judah; but once this is accomplished, they too will be punished. Historically, Babylon fell in 539 B.C. to the Medo-Persians under Cyrus II the Great. For other prophecies of the fall of Babylon, see Is 13:1–22; 21:1–10; Jer 50–51.

2:2 the vision: Divine revelation about the future that must be preserved in writing. **make it plain:** The prophecy must be written legibly and displayed publicly, so that even a runner hurrying by can read its words clearly. After the prophecy is fulfilled, this monument will serve as a witness that God is true to his word (Is 30:8). **tablets:** The Hebrew term can indicate boards or planks (Ezek 27:5) as well as stone tables (Ex 31:18). Isaiah was similarly told to write prophetic words on a display placard (Is 8:1).

2:3 it will not lie: Assurance that the prophecy will be fulfilled, even if it seems long in coming (cf. 2 Pet 3:8–9).

2:4 whose soul is not upright: One who is puffed up with pride and out of alignment with the covenant. The wicked in Judah appear to be meant (1:4). **the righteous:** The person who trusts in the Lord, waits for his promises, and keeps his covenant (Deut 6:25; Lk 1:6). **shall live:** The righteous one will survive the judgment that is coming upon Judah. Even in the midst of national judgment, the Lord will mercifully protect the righteous remnant from perishing. • Paul cites this passage in Rom 1:17 and Gal 3:11, where faith in the gospel is the means by which one is justified

---

[a] Cn: Heb uncertain.

[b] Heb *his portion is fat.*

[c] Cn: Heb *is puffed up.*

[d] Or *faithfulness.*

⁵Moreover, wine is treacherous;
  the arrogant man shall not abide.ᵉ
His greed is as wide as Sheol;
  like death he has never enough.
He gathers for himself all nations,
  and collects as his own all peoples."

⁶Shall not all these take up their taunt against him, in scoffing derision of him, and say,
  "Woe to him who heaps up what is not his
    own—
  for how long?—
  and loads himself with pledges!"
⁷Will not your debtors suddenly arise,
  and those awake who will make you tremble?
  Then you will be booty for them.
⁸Because you have plundered many nations,
  all the remnant of the peoples shall plunder
    you,
  for the blood of men and violence to the earth,
  to cities and all who dwell therein.

⁹Woe to him who gets evil gain for his house,
  to set his nest on high,
  to be safe from the reach of harm!
¹⁰You have devised shame to your house
  by cutting off many peoples;
  you have forfeited your life.
¹¹For the stone will cry out from the wall,
  and the beam from the woodwork respond.

¹²Woe to him who builds a town with blood,
  and founds a city on iniquity!
¹³Behold, is it not from the LORD of hosts
  that peoples labor only for fire,
  and nations weary themselves for nothing?
¹⁴For the earth will be filled
  with the knowledge of the glory of the LORD,
  as the waters cover the sea.

¹⁵Woe to him who makes his neighbors drink
  of the cup of his wrath,ᶠ and makes them drunk,
  to gaze on their shame!

2:14: Is 11:9.

---

in Christ, saved from judgment, and made an heir of eternal life. A fuller citation of the passage appears in Heb 10:37–38, which urges believers to persevere in faith without shrinking back in fear or doubt before Christ comes again to judge the world. • Baptism initiates a new life of righteousness; it is also an enlightenment of faith by which one receives spiritual life. This accords with the words of Habakkuk: "but the righteous one lives by faith." Baptism, which is a declaration of faith, is thus a sacrament of faith (St. Thomas Aquinas, *Summa Theologiae* III, 66, 1).

2:5 wine: Recklessly craved by those who are drunk. Babylon, like an intoxicated man, was never satisfied by its conquests; it always wanted more. **greed:** Lust for the spoils of war (2:6). **Sheol:** The realm of the dead with its insatiable "appetite" for the living (Is 5:14). See word study: *Sheol* at Num 16:30.

2:6–19 The Babylonian empire, when it finally falls in 539 B.C., will be taunted by its victims and made to pay for its crimes. Their ridicule is expressed in five "woes" or funeral laments (2:6, 9, 12, 15, 19). Use of this literary form is sarcastic: Babylon's demise is an occasion for mockery rather than mourning by those who suffered under its tyranny.

2:6 Woe: A cry of anguish heard at funerals. See word study: *Woe* at Is 28:1. **heaps up:** Babylonia is guilty of enriching itself at the expense of other nations. **pledges:** Items of value kept by a lender until the borrower pays off his debt (Deut 24:10–13).

2:8 plunder you: A punishment that fits the crime.

2:9 evil gain: Wealth acquired unjustly by extortion, theft, conquest, etc.

2:10 forfeited your life: The Babylonian empire is doomed to perish.

2:11 the stone will cry out: Babylon's "house" (2:9) is personified and heard protesting the injustice of its builders. Jesus used this language during his triumphal entry into Jerusalem, except on that occasion "the very stones would cry out" that he was coming to the city as its blessed King (Lk 19:40).

2:13 is it not from the LORD: Babylonia's imperial conquests are permitted by God, even enabled by him in some respects. This is not a sign of his favor but a prelude to divine judgment. The Lord allows some nations to become extremely powerful in order to show that he is more powerful still when he brings divine judgment upon them.

2:14 the earth will be filled: The fall of Babylon, foretold by the prophet, will teach the onlooking world that Israel's God is the sovereign judge of all nations.

2:15 their shame: Literally, "their private parts". Humiliation by exposing nakedness is meant (Is 47:3; Lam 1:8; Nahum 3:5). Prisoners of war were sometimes treated in this way (Is 20:4; cf. 2 Chron 28:14–15).

ᵉ The Hebrew of these two lines is obscure.
ᶠ Cn: Heb *joining to your wrath.*

WORD STUDY

Faith (2:4)

'Emûnāh (Heb.): a noun that typically denotes "faithfulness" or "fidelity" to a relationship or commitment. The Lord is preeminently a "God of faithfulness" insofar as he is always right and just in his dealings with the covenant people (Deut 32:4; Ps 33:4). As their divine Husband, he always acts with the "faithfulness" of a loyal and loving spouse (Hos 2:20). Israel, his bride, is also called to this steadfast fidelity. The people show faithfulness by their obedience to his Law (Ps 119:30); and when they prove loyal, they are rewarded by the Lord (1 Sam 26:23) with abundant blessings (Prov 28:20). Other times the term refers specifically to "truthfulness" in speech or action (Prov 12:22; Is 59:4; Jer 7:28). The English word "faith" that appears in Hab 2:4 only captures its meaning imperfectly, since trusting the Lord and believing his promises is only part of what it means show 'emûnāh. It also means staying true to his covenant over the long haul. It is a firm personal loyalty that remains steady throughout a long-term relationship. Isaiah expected the Davidic Messiah to exemplify this enduring faithfulness to the Lord (Is 11:5).

¹⁶You will be sated with contempt instead of glory.
 Drink, yourself, and stagger!ᵍ
The cup in the LORD right hand
 will come around to you,
 and shame will come upon your glory!
¹⁷The violence done to Lebanon will overwhelm you;
 the destruction of the beasts will terrify you,ʰ
for the blood of men and violence to the earth,
 to cities and all who dwell therein.

¹⁸What profit is an idol
 when its maker has shaped it,
 a metal image, a teacher of lies?
For the workman trusts in his own creation
 when he makes dumb idols!
¹⁹Woe to him who says to a wooden thing, Awake;
 to a mute stone, Arise!
Can this give revelation?
Behold, it is overlaid with gold and silver,
 and there is no breath at all in it.

²⁰But the LORD is in his holy temple;
 let all the earth keep silence before him.

Habakkuk's Prayer

3 A prayer of Habak'kuk the prophet, according to Shigion'oth.

²O LORD, I have heard the report of you,
 and your work, O LORD, I fear.
In the midst of the years renew it;
 in the midst of the years make it known;
 in wrath remember mercy.
³God came from Te man,
 and the Holy One from Mount Par an.
His glory covered the heavens,
 and the earth was full of his praise.   *Selah*
⁴His brightness was like the light,
 rays flashed from his hand;
 and there he veiled his power.
⁵Before him went pestilence,
 and plague followed close behind.
⁶He stood and measured the earth;
 he looked and shook the nations;
Then the eternal mountains were scattered,
 the everlasting hills sank low.
His ways were as of old.
⁷I saw the tents of Cush'an in affliction;
 the curtains of the land of Mid'ian trembled.
⁸Was your wrath against the rivers, O LORD?
 Was your anger against the rivers,
 or your indignation against the sea,
when you rode upon your horses,
 upon your chariot of victory?

2:20: Zeph 1:7; Zech 2:13.

2:16 The cup: An image of judgment in which evildoers are made to drink the wine of God's wrath, causing them to stumble in a drunken stupor toward destruction (Ps 75:8; Ezek 23:31-34; Obad 16; Rev 18:6). Many nations of the biblical world were made to consume this wine, including Babylon (Jer 25:18-26). See note on Is 51:17.

2:17 Violence done to Lebanon: The majestic cedars of Lebanon, flourishing north of Israel, were coveted as premium lumber for large building projects (1 Kings 5:6; Is 37:24). The Babylonians, in their greed, were guilty of plundering its cedar forests (Is 14:8).

2:18-20: A prophetic critique of idolatry that ridicules idol images, their makers, and their worshipers. The final verse underscores the contrast between lifeless pagan idols and the living God of Israel before whom all the earth stands in speechless awe (2:20). For similar idol polemics in Scripture, see Ps 115:3-8; Is 44:9-20; Jer 10:1-10; Bar 6:1-73.

2:20 his holy temple: The Temple in Jerusalem, which was an architectural representation of the Lord's eternal Temple in heaven (Ps 11:4; Mic 1:2; Rev 11:19). See essay: *Theology of the Temple* at 2 Chron 5. **silence:** In anticipation of divine judgment (Zeph 1:7; Zech 2:13).

3:1-19 The book closes with a psalm originally set to music. It resembles a psalm of lament that begins with anxious petition (3:2) and ends with the Psalmist resolving to wait upon the Lord (3:16) as the source of his strength (3:19). Between these endpoints, Habakkuk describes a divine theophany in which the Lord, the Divine Warrior, manifests his power and majesty (3:3-7) and then marches against enemy nations to save his people (3:8-15). His awesome fury strikes fear into the hearts of onlookers (3:7). For similar passages, see Deut 33:2-5; Jud 4:4-5; Ps 68:7-18.

3:1 prayer: The petition of an individual in distress. This is suggested by the appearance of the same term in the superscriptions of Pss 17, 86, 90, 102, and 142. **Habakkuk the prophet:** The author or composer of the psalm. See note on 1:1. **Shigionoth:** The plural form of "Shiggaion", a word of uncertain meaning that appears in the superscription of Ps 7. It may be the name of the melody to be played by musicians when the psalm was sung (3:19).

3:2 the report: The awe-inspiring description of God in 3:3-15. **renew it:** A petition that God will act again to bring his enemies low, as in the past, when he "trampled the nations in anger" (3:12). **remember mercy:** The prophet knows that Judah deserves chastisement (1:2-4), but he appeals to God's compassion for a measure of restraint (Ex 34:6-7). In effect, Habakkuk desires both justice and mercy.

3:3 Teman: In Edomite territory south of the Dead Sea. **Mount Paran:** The mountainous wilderness of the northeast Sinai Peninsula, extending into Edom. Israel was originally commanded to invade the land of Canaan from its camp at Kadesh in the wilderness of Paran (Num 12:16; 13:3, 26). **His glory:** Manifest on Mt. Sinai as fire and lightning wrapped in a thick cloud (Ex 19:16-18). **Selah:** A musical notation of uncertain meaning. It occurs three times in this chapter (3:3, 9, 13) and 71 times in the Book of Psalms. Scholars surmise that it called for an instrumental interlude or liturgical response from the congregation.

3:4 rays: The Hebrew reads "two horns", perhaps referring to bolts of lightning in both of God's hands (Job 36:32).

3:5 pestilence ... plague: Personified as warriors in God's advancing retinue.

3:6 mountains ... hills: The epitome of things ancient and permanent (Gen 49:26). Even these give way and disperse before the fury of the Lord of hosts (Ps 97:5; Nahum 1:5).

3:7 Cushan ... Midian: Tent-dwelling peoples who lived south of Edom. **in affliction:** Or "in terror".

3:8 the sea: Represents the world of nations hostile to Israel (3:15; Dan 7:2-3), including Babylonia (Jer 51:36-37). The Lord's victory over these earthly powers is described in 3:12, 15. **your chariot:** The clouds of the sky (Ps 104:3; Is 19:1).

ᵍCn Compare Gk Syr: Heb *be uncircumcised.*
ʰGk Syr: Heb *them.*

⁹You stripped the sheath from your bow,
 and put the arrows to the string.ⁱ *Selah*
 You split the earth with rivers.
¹⁰The mountains saw you, and writhed;
 the raging waters swept on;
the deep gave forth its voice,
 it lifted its hands on high.
¹¹The sun and moon stood still in their habitationʲ
 at the light of your arrows as they sped,
 at the flash of your glittering spear.
¹²You bestrode the earth in fury,
 you trampled the nations in anger.
¹³You went forth for the salvation of your people,
 for the salvation of your anointed.
 You crushed the head of the wicked,ᵏ
 laying him bare from thigh to neck.ˡ *Selah*
¹⁴You pierced with yourᵐ shafts the head of his
 warriors,ⁿ
 who came like a whirlwind to scatter me,
 rejoicing as if to devour the poor in secret.
¹⁵You trampled the sea with your horses,
 the surging of mighty waters.

¹⁶I hear, and my body trembles,
 my lips quiver at the sound;
rottenness enters into my bones,
 my steps totterᵒ beneath me.
I will quietly wait for the day of trouble
 to come upon people who invade us.

¹⁷Though the fig tree does not blossom,
 nor fruit be on the vines,
 the produce of the olive fail
 and the fields yield no food,
 the flock be cut off from the fold
 and there be no herd in the stalls,
¹⁸yet I will rejoice in the Lord,
 I will joy in the God of my salvation.
¹⁹God, the Lord, is my strength;
 he makes my feet like deer's feet,
 he makes me tread upon my high places.

To the choirmaster: with stringedᵖ instruments.

3:10 lifted its hands: Poetically, the sea churned up by the storm is lifting its hands in the swelling of its waves, praying for a calming of God's anger (Ps 28:2).

3:11 sun and moon stood still: Reminiscent of the divine help given to Joshua in his victory over the Canaanite kings at Gibeon in Josh 10:12–14. Here, too, the Psalmist pictures God warring against his adversaries with the weapons of nature. Upheaval in the heavens is a traditional feature in apocalyptic scenes of judgment in Scripture (Is 13:10; Ezek 32:7–8; Amos 8:9; Joel 2:10; Mt 24:29; Rev 6:12).

3:13 salvation: Divine deliverance. **your anointed:** The poetic parallelism of the verse suggests this refers to Israel.

However, since use of the term "anointed" is not clearly applied elsewhere to the whole covenant community, some think it refers to the Davidic king of Judah, who represents his people and who achieves success on the battlefield with the Lord's help (2 Sam 22:51). See note on 1 Sam 2:10.

3:16–19 Habakkuk trembles before the Lord's power and anger described in the "report" (3:2, referring to 3:3–7), and yet he trusts that God will be true to his word and bring judgment on the Babylonian invaders of Judah ("the Chaldeans", 1:6). He is also prepared to face the hardships that lie ahead, even a severe food shortage (3:17), knowing that God gives "salvation" (3:18) to the righteous man who lives by faith (2:4).

3:16 the day of trouble: The time of Babylon's doom. History places this in 539 B.C.

3:19 like deer's feet: Able to escape dangers and surmount obstacles with ease (2 Sam 22:34; Ps 18:33). **choirmaster:** Probably a Levite in charge of music in the Jerusalem Temple. This type of musical notation is typical of psalms used in a liturgical setting. See, e.g., the superscriptions attached to Pss 4, 6, 54, 55, 61, 67, 76. **stringed instruments:** Such as harps and lyres.

ⁱ Cn: Heb obscure.
ʲ Heb uncertain.
ᵏ Cn: Heb *head from the house of the wicked.*
ˡ Heb obscure.
ᵐ Heb *his.*
ⁿ Vg Compare Gk Syr: Heb uncertain.
ᵒ Cn Compare Gk: Heb *I tremble because.*
ᵖ Heb *my stringed.*

STUDY QUESTIONS
Habakkuk

Chapter 1

For understanding

1. **1:1–4:** What does Habakkuk lament? Troubled by God's inaction, what does he question? When will his concern be addressed? Thus, how is the first part of the book presented?
2. **1:1:** To what does the Hebrew term *massāʾ* refer? What is the meaning of Habakkuk's name? How does God impart revelation to prophets?
3. **1:4:** What did the Torah or Law of Moses codify? What was transgressing the Law tantamount to doing? What does the Hebrew word *mishpaṭ* mean? Of what is lawless corruption in Judah the evidence? Who are the righteous?
4. **1:5:** Just as Habakkuk could "see" and "look upon" the problem of evil in Judah, what are he and his fellow Judahites invited to do? When did this most likely occur? Because it was unclear before 605 B.C. that the Babylonians were destined to become an imperial superpower who could pose an existential threat to Judah, what were few people likely to believe would happen? Why does Paul cite the Greek LXX version of this passage in Acts 13:41?
5. **1:6:** Who were the Chaldeans, and when did they seize the throne of Babylon? Who were key figures in the reemergence of Babylonian power? For what does the prophet learn that God intends to use Babylonia? What role would Nebuchadnezzar in particular play?

For application

1. **1:4:** What makes enforcement of a law credible to those it addresses? When should a strict law be relaxed? On the other hand, what problems arise from relaxing a law that is strict but fair?
2. **1:5:** The note for this verse refers to Acts 13:41. In Paul's sermon to the Jews in Pisidian Antioch (Acts 13:16–41), how does he use OT history to show that the message of salvation has actually been sent to them (v. 38)? What Scriptures does he cite to prove his point? Why does he end with the warning from Habakkuk?
3. **1:13:** How would you answer Habakkuk's complaint that the Lord uses bad people to chastise others more righteous than they? Why do bad things happen to good people?

Chapter 2

For understanding

1. **2:2:** What vision does the Lord want Habakkuk to write down? Why must the prophecy be written legibly and displayed publicly? What can the Hebrew term for tables indicate? Who else was similarly told to write on a display placard?
2. **2:4:** Who is the person whose soul is not upright? Who is the righteous person, and what will happen to him in the judgment coming upon Judah? What points does Paul make by citing this passage in Rom 1:17 and Gal 3:11? What does the fuller citation of the passage appearing in Heb 10:37–38 urge believers to do? According to St. Thomas Aquinas, how does Baptism, which initiates a new life of righteousness and enlightenment of faith, accord with the words of Habakkuk?
3. **Word Study: Faith (2:4):** What does the Hebrew noun *ʾemûnāh* typically denote? How does the Lord show himself preeminently a "God of faithfulness" to the covenant people? How do the people show their faithfulness? At other times, to what does the term specifically refer? Why does the English word "faith" that appears in Hab 2:4 only capture its meaning imperfectly? What does it mean doing over the long haul? What did Isaiah expect of the Davidic Messiah?
4. **2:17:** For what were the majestic cedars of Lebanon, flourishing north of Israel, coveted? What were the Babylonians, in their greed, guilty of doing?

For application

1. **2:1:** Describe a time when you and the Lord had a dialogue going during prayer, where one initiated the dialogue and the other responded. Have you ever argued with the Lord over an issue? If so, how did he respond and how did you receive his answer?
2. **2:4:** Heb 10:38 quotes this verse in the context of the need for endurance. How challenging has living the life of faith been for you? In times of difficulty or personal loss, what have you done to retain and build up your faith in God's good will toward you?
3. **2:7:** How do you feel about the pricing policies of drug manufacturers? How able are you to pay for medications you need? If your medications are too expensive, what recourse do you have to obtain lower prices? What group efforts are being made to challenge the manufacturers?
4. **2:14:** Compare this verse in its context with that of Is 11:9 in its context. What are the main similarities and differences? To what fulfillment is each prophet looking forward?

Chapter 3

For understanding

1. **3:1–19:** How does the book close? What kind of psalm does it resemble? Between these endpoints, what does Habakkuk describe?
2. **3:3:** Where are "Teman" and "Mt. Paran"? From where was Israel originally commanded to invade the land of Canaan? How was God's glory manifested on Mt. Sinai? What does "selah" mean, and where does it occur? What do scholars speculate it calls for from the congregation?
3. **3:11:** Of what is "the sun and moon stood still" reminiscent? How does the Psalmist picture God warring against adversaries? Of what is upheaval in the heavens a traditional feature?

4. **3:16–19:** Before what power is Habakkuk trembling, and yet what does he trust that God will do? What is he also prepared to face?

For application
1. **3:2:** At the beginning of the Second Vatican Council, Pope St. John XXIII prayed for a new outpouring of the Holy Spirit. How has that prayer been answered? What problems in the Church remain? What work of the Lord would you most like him to renew in our day?
2. **3:16:** What prospect for the future most terrifies you? For example, how concerned are you that death and judgment are both imminent? How quiet is your waiting for that day to arrive?
3. **3:17–18:** Since times will not always be good, have you tested the limits of your trust in the Lord's provision for you? How willing are you to rejoice in him if the economy should fail and the stores run out of supplies?

INTRODUCTION TO ZEPHANIAH

Author and Date The opening verse credits the prophecies of the book to "Zephaniah the son of Cushi", whose ancestry is traced back four generations to "Hezekiah" (1:1). If this is a reference to the famous King Hezekiah, who ruled the Southern Kingdom of Judah from 729 to 686 B.C., then the prophet was a relative of the Davidic royal family. The reference to Jerusalem as "this place" in 1:4 further implies that Zephaniah ministered in the holy city. Beyond that, nothing certain is known about his background.

A general date for the book is also indicated in the superscription which states that Zephaniah prophesied during "the days of Josiah ... king of Judah" (1:1). This means that he delivered the oracles of the book sometime between 640 and 609 B.C. These parameters can be narrowed by noting that the fall of Nineveh, which took place in 612 B.C., is an event that lies in the future, according to 2:13. Also, it is often felt that because Judah and Jerusalem are still engaged in flagrant idolatry in 1:3–6, the prophet is most likely addressing the situation prior to 622 B.C., the year that King Josiah renewed his efforts to purge the land of Judah and its worship of pagan contamination (2 Kings 23:1–25). The decade between 635 and 625 B.C. is thus a reasonable estimate for the time that Zephaniah was actively preaching in Jerusalem. This would make him a contemporary of the prophets Jeremiah, Nahum, and Habakkuk.

That said, some scholars hold that certain sayings, e.g., 2:8–11 and 3:14–20, are later additions made to the book by exilic or postexilic editors. Hypotheses such as these are not impossible, since later editors could have been divinely inspired to make contributions to an existing collection of prophecies, but identifying later additions is often a speculative enterprise, and no hypothesis has won a consensus among scholars or has been demonstrated beyond a reasonable doubt. In fact, there are no indisputable signs that a long period of time elapsed between Zephaniah's ministry and the time when his prophecies were written down. Nor is it apparent that parts of the book come from an author different from the one who composed the bulk of the work.

Title The book is named after Zephaniah, mentioned in the opening verse. Its Hebrew form, *Ṣephanyāh*, means "the LORD has hidden". His name appears in the Greek Septuagint in the title *Sophonias*, while this heading is expanded in the Latin Vulgate to *Sofonias Propheta*, "Zephaniah the Prophet". English titles for the book follow these ancient traditions.

Place in the Canon Zephaniah has long been revered as a canonical book of Scripture. In the Jewish Bible, or Tanakh, it stands among the Latter Prophets in a sub-collection of writings known as "the Book of the Twelve". In Christian Bibles, these twelve books are called the Minor Prophets, not because they are less important than Isaiah, Jeremiah, Ezekiel, and Daniel, but because they are comparatively shorter. In the Hebrew Bible, Greek Septuagint, and Latin Vulgate, Zephaniah stands ninth among the Minor Prophets between Habakkuk and Haggai, just as it does in English Bibles.

Structure Zephaniah divides neatly into three major parts. **(1)** Following a superscription (1:1), the book opens with oracles of judgment directed against the earth in general (1:2–3) and then against Judah and Jerusalem in particular (1:4–13). All are warned that the approaching day of the Lord will be a day of distress and darkness (1:14–18), and so an appeal for repentance follows (2:1–3). **(2)** The middle of the book consists of oracles against regional nations such as Philistia (2:4–7), Moab and Ammon (2:8–11), Ethiopia (2:12), and Assyria (2:13–15), culminating with a "woe" or funeral lament for Jerusalem (3:1–7). **(3)** The book ends with oracles of restoration, foreseeing a time when Gentile peoples will come to serve the Lord (3:8–10), followed by two prophecies of salvation for the faithful remnant in Jerusalem along with the exiles who return (3:11–13, 14–20). See also *Outline*.

Historical Background Zephaniah lived during a time of spiritual crisis, when the Southern Kingdom of Judah was struggling to recover from decades of state-sponsored idolatry under the regimes of Manasseh (696–642 B.C.) and Amon (642–640 B.C.), who both "did what was evil in the sight of the LORD" (2 Kings 21:2, 20). These long decades of corrupt leadership and paganized worship had taken a heavy toll on the people and their relationship with God. Judah was in desperate need of reform. King Josiah, whose reign from 640 to 609 B.C. was the backdrop to Zephaniah's ministry (1:1), began to address these problems in 628 B.C. (2 Chron 34:3), but it was not until "the book of the law" was discovered in the Temple in 622 B.C. (2 Kings 22:8) that his most aggressive efforts were made to rid the land of Judah of idolatrous practices (2 Kings 23:4–14). Zephaniah, who denounces the same corruption at the same time in history, may have helped to inspire Josiah in his efforts by his warnings of imminent judgment. According to the prophet, Judah and Jerusalem were approaching a day of apocalyptic disaster, a day of "trumpet blast and battle cry" (1:16). He envisions, not an Assyrian conquest of the land and capital, as the Assyrian Empire was declining rapidly at this point in history, but a Babylonian conquest that ended with the destruction of Jerusalem in 586 B.C.

Message of the Prophet The main focus of the Book of Zephaniah is the coming judgment of God, which he calls the "day of the LORD" (1:7, 14). This is a day of divine intervention in history when the Lord brings the wicked of the world to justice. The prophet describes it as a time of distress and devastation on an epic scale. Its essential features can be broken down into four categories.

(1) *Scope of the Judgment.* Zephaniah's opening words in 1:2–3 warn of a universal judgment that sweeps over all the earth, leaving no realm of living creatures untouched by the Lord's decree of death. Mankind, beasts, birds, and fish will all be impacted by this calamity. The words of 1:18 and 3:8 likewise depict the whole world consumed in the fire of the Lord's indignation. Other passages, however, seem to describe a regional rather than a global event. In 1:4 and 3:1–7, the prophet narrows the focus of coming judgment to Judah and Jerusalem. Then, in 2:4–15, he widens the target area to prophesy judgment on nations that live west (Philistines), east (Moab, Ammon), south (Ethiopia), and north (Assyria) of Judah. This could suggest the prophet uses the language of cosmic destruction and woe to indicate how "world-shaking" the coming judgment will be. Or it may be that he views the smaller-scale judgments against Judah and its neighbors as a foretaste of the universal judgment that God will bring at the end of history.

(2) *Timing of the Judgment.* Zephaniah's oracles are marked by a sense of urgency. The judgment of God, he insists, is "at hand" (1:7) and "hastening fast" (1:14). It is clear from this that he is talking about calamitous events of the not-too-distant future, e.g., the fall of Nineveh, capital of Assyria, in 612 B.C., and the overthrow of Judah by the Babylonians, culminating with the destruction of Jerusalem in 586 B.C. The nearness of this latter event explains why he makes a strong appeal to his fellow Judahites to repent and seek the Lord before the day of his wrath arrives (2:1–3).

(3) *Reason for the Judgment.* Nations are singled out for chastisement "because they have sinned against the LORD" (1:17). Judah and Jerusalem are guilty of forsaking the Lord to worship idols (1:4–6), of perpetrating violence and fraud (1:9), and of losing faith in God's sovereignty over the fortunes of his people (1:12). Jerusalem's leaders in particular are charged with oppression and corruption (3:1–4, 7). Other nations, too, are set for humiliation because they have grown proud and boastful (2:8, 10, 15).

(4) *Purpose of the Judgment.* Several passages make clear that purgation rather than annihilation is the goal of the coming judgment. Initially it sounds as if God intends to snuff out all life from the face of the earth (1:2–3, 18). But later it becomes clear that his mercy will restrain his justice from destroying all. For instance, no sooner is "all the earth" consumed in his anger than "the peoples" beyond Israel come to serve the Lord by calling upon his name with the pure speech of praise (3:8–9). In other words, judgment poured out on the nations has brought about conversions to the God of Israel. Likewise, the prophet can urge the devout remnant in Judah to seek the Lord in the hope of being "hidden" (= protected) on the day when judgment comes (2:3). The chastisement envisioned will remove the "proudly exultant ones" (3:11) from Judah and Jerusalem and leave behind a people who are "humble and lowly" (3:12) and who tell "no lies" (3:13). So even though Zephaniah's message is dreadful and severe, it is not relentlessly negative. On the other side of judgment, he sees restoration and a new beginning. The Jerusalem that emerges from the judgment will sing with joy that the Lord dwells in its midst and has restored its honor, its exiles, and its fortunes (3:14–20). Even God will raise his voice with "loud singing" over the faithful remnant of his people in this glorious time (3:17).

Christian Perspective The New Testament makes limited reference to the Book of Zephaniah, although a few clear allusions are detectable. In Luke's story of the Annunciation, the angel Gabriel appears to echo the words of 3:14–17, suggesting that Mary, the humble maiden from Nazareth, exemplifies the faithful daughter of Zion who is called to rejoice in the Lord's presence within her (Lk 1:26–38). Likewise, when the Book of Revelation describes a vision of the Lamb standing on Mt. Zion, he stands with the redeemed of Israel, who have no lie in their mouths (Rev 14:5), recalling the vision of the prophet that no deceitful tongue would be found in the mouths of the remnant of Israel (3:13). Finally, Zephaniah's emphasis on "the day of the LORD" as a day of apocalyptic judgment and wrath (1:7–18) takes a new form in apostolic teaching about the Last Judgment, which is designated "the day of the Lord Jesus" (1 Cor 5:5; 2 Cor 1:14; cf. Acts 17:31) as well as "the day of wrath" (Rom 2:5; cf. 1 Thess 1:10).

OUTLINE OF ZEPHANIAH

1. Oracles of Coming Judgment (1:1—2:3)
A. Superscription (1:1)
B. Judgment of the Earth (1:2–3)
C. Judgment of Judah and Jerusalem (1:4–13)
D. The Day of the Lord (1:14–18)
E. Call to Repentance (2:1–3)

2. Oracles against Nations and Cities (2:4—3:7)
A. Oracle against Philistines (2:4–7)
B. Oracle against Moabites and Ammonites (2:8–11)
C. Oracle against Ethiopians (2:12)
D. Oracle against Assyrians (2:13–15)
E. Oracle against Jerusalem (3:1–7)

3. Oracles of Future Restoration (3:8–20)
A. Nations Will Serve the Lord (3:8–10)
B. Jerusalem Purified (3:11–13)
C. Rejoicing and Restoration of Zion (3:14–20)

THE BOOK OF
ZEPHANIAH

Last prophet to warn Judah (handwritten note)

The Day of the Lord

1 The word of the LORD which came to Zephani′ah the son of Cu′shi, son of Gedali′ah, son of Amari′ah, son of Hezeki′ah, in the days of Josi′ah the son of A′mon, king of Judah.

2"I will utterly sweep away everything
   from the face of the earth," says the LORD.
3"I will sweep away man and beast;
   I will sweep away the birds of the air
   and the fish of the sea.
 I will overthrow[a] the wicked;
   I will cut off mankind
   from the face of the earth," says the LORD.
4"I will stretch out my hand against Judah,
   and against all the inhabitants of Jerusalem;

and I will cut off from this place the remnant
   of Ba′al
   and the name of the idolatrous priests;[b]
5those who bow down on the roofs
   to the host of the heavens;
 those who bow down and swear to the LORD
   and yet swear by Milcom;
6those who have turned back from following
   the LORD,
 who do not seek the LORD or inquire of
   him."

7Be silent before the Lord GOD!
   For the day of the LORD is at hand;
 the LORD has prepared a sacrifice
   and consecrated his guests.

1:7: Hab 2:20; Zech 2:13.

1:1 The word of the LORD: Prophetic revelation from God communicated to the prophet. See essay: *The Word of the LORD* at Hos 1. **Zephaniah:** The name in Hebrew means "the LORD has hidden". He appears to have ministered in Jerusalem, but little else is known about him. **son ... son ... son ... son:** It is unusual for a prophet to trace his genealogy beyond his father (Is 1:1; Jer 1:1; Ezek 1:3; Hos 1:1, etc.). Zephaniah traces his ancestry three generations farther, most likely because his great-great-grandfather **Hezekiah** is the famous king of Judah who reigned from 729 to 686 B.C. If so, the prophet was related by blood to the ruling house of David. **Josiah:** Reigned over Judah from 640 to 609 B.C. For more on the time frame of the book, see introduction: *Author and Date*.

1:2-6 The judgment and devastation to come when God acts against the wicked. The scale of the disaster, which leaves no realm of creation untouched, calls to mind the extent of the flood (Gen 6:5-7). **Judah** and **Jerusalem**, who had forsaken the Lord to serve idols, stand at the center of this terrifying event (1:4-6). They are to be judged in the midst of the nations because they have become like the nations—immoral and idolatrous.

1:2 earth: The Hebrew term can also be translated "land", and so the judgment prophesied may be global (worldwide) or regional (affecting specifically the nations named in 2:1-15). The language of universal destruction may be understood literally in reference to the Last Judgment but may be read as

hyperbole for the judgment aimed at Judah and the peoples that surround it (1:4, 14).

1:4 stretch out my hand: An act of divine chastisement (2:13; Is 5:25; Jer 51:25). **this place:** Jerusalem, whose sins are known to the prophet (3:1-4). **Baal:** The storm and fertility god of the Canaanite religion. Worship of Baal had been firmly established in Judah by this time, due to its promotion by the wicked King Manasseh, whose reign lasted from 696 to 642 B.C. (2 Kings 21:1-3) and whose policies were kept in place by his son Amon, who reigned from 642 to 640 B.C. (2 Kings 21:19-22). The **remnant** of Baal is a group of followers who remain attached to this false god. This may suggest that Zephaniah ministered between 628 B.C., when Josiah began to purge Judah's worship of idolatry (2 Chron 34:3-4), and 622 B.C., when he expanded the reform (2 Kings 23:1-14). See word study: *Baal* at Hos 2:8. **idolatrous priests:** Made offerings to foreign gods (2 Kings 23:5; Hos 10:5).

1:5 on the roofs: Where incense was burned to astral deities (Jer 19:13). **the host of the heavens:** The sun, moon, stars, and visible planets. Israel was forbidden to worship these luminaries of the day and night sky (Deut 4:19), but disobedience to God's Law is attested (2 Kings 17:16; 23:4-5; Ezek 8:16; Amos 5:26). Astral cults were popular among the Assyrians and others (CCC 57). **Swear ... yet swear:** Evidence of a syncretism that mixed pagan cult practices with the religious observances of Israel. **Milcom:** Chief god of the Ammonites, who dwelt east of the Jordan River (1 Kings 11:5, 33; 2 Kings 23:13). The Hebrew reads "their king", but a reference to the deity Milcom is probably intended.

1:7 Be silent: There can be no protest when the Lord acts as Judge, only speechless awe and dread (Zech 2:13). **the day of the LORD:** A day of cataclysmic judgment that is fast approaching (1:14). The prophet foresees the conquest of Judah and Jerusalem, which eventually will occur in 586 B.C. When this day of reckoning arrives, Babylonian warriors will destroy the city, set fire to the Lord's Temple, and take thousands of captives into exile. See word study: *The Day of the Lord* at Joel 1:15. **a sacrifice:** A sacrificial banquet in which the invited guests become the victims of slaughter. For the image of a feast of judgment, see also Is 34:6; Jer 46:10; Ezek 39:17-20.

Zephaniah (Sophonias) prophesied shortly before the religious reform of Josiah, i.e., about the year 630 B.C., and he proclaims in clarion tones the "day of the LORD," when his people will be crushed by their enemies because of their sins; cf. Amos. The words of Zephaniah (1:15) remind one of the *Dies irae*, which seems to have drawn its imagery from here. The prophet foretells punishment not only for Judah but also for the nations round about (2:4-15). Then, after more threats against Jerusalem (3:1-8), he utters consolations (3:9-20): the people will be restored, but chastened and humble. The reform of Josiah was too short-lived to affect the results of these prophecies—the Exile and the return followed within the century.

[a] Cn: Heb *the stumbling blocks.*
[b] Compare Gk: Heb *idolatrous priests with the priests.*

141

⁸And on the day of the LORD's sacrifice—
"I will punish the officials and the king's sons
and all who clothe themselves in foreign attire.
⁹On that day I will punish
every one who leaps over the threshold,
and those who fill their master's house
with violence and fraud."

¹⁰"On that day," says the LORD,
"a cry will be heard from the Fish Gate,
a wail from the Second Quarter,
a loud crash from the hills.
¹¹Wail, O inhabitants of the Mortar!
For all the traders are no more;
all who weigh out silver are cut off.
¹²At that time I will search Jerusalem with lamps,
and I will punish the men
who are thickening on their dregs,
those who say in their hearts,
'The LORD will not do good,
nor will he do ill.'
¹³Their goods shall be plundered,
and their houses laid waste.
Though they build houses,
they shall not inhabit them;
though they plant vineyards,
they shall not drink wine from them."

¹⁴The great day of the LORD is near,
near and hastening fast;
the sound of the day of the LORD is bitter,
the mighty man cries aloud there.

¹⁵A day of wrath is that day,
a day of distress and anguish,
a day of ruin and devastation,
a day of darkness and gloom,
a day of clouds and thick darkness,
¹⁶ a day of trumpet blast and battle cry
against the fortified cities
and against the lofty battlements.

¹⁷I will bring distress on men,
so that they shall walk like the blind,
because they have sinned against the LORD;
their blood shall be poured out like dust,
and their flesh like dung.
¹⁸Neither their silver nor their gold
shall be able to deliver them
on the day of the wrath of the LORD.
In the fire of his jealous wrath,
all the earth shall be consumed;
for a full, yes, sudden end
he will make of all the inhabitants of the
earth.

Judgment on Israel's Enemies

2 Come together and hold assembly,
O shameless nation,
²before you are driven away
like the drifting chaff, ᶜ
before there comes upon you
the fierce anger of the LORD,
before there comes upon you
the day of the wrath of the LORD.

1:8–13 An oracle against Jerusalem and its rebellious citizens.
1:8 officials: Members of the royal government. **the king's sons:** Members of the royal family. **foreign attire:** Another sign of alien, possibly idolatrous, influence in Israel (2 Kings 10:22).
1:9 leaps over the threshold: Meaning obscure. A pagan religious superstition may be in view (1 Sam 5:5).
1:10 the Fish Gate: In the north wall of Jerusalem (Neh 3:3). **the Second Quarter:** A newer district of the city, either on the western hill or north of the Temple (2 Kings 22:14).
1:11 the Mortar: Apparently a hollow place, resembling a stone mortar, that served as a marketplace in Jerusalem. **traders are no more:** Suggests a judgment for corrupt business practices (Amos 8:5–6; Mic 6:10–11).
1:12 thickening on their dregs: The men of Jerusalem are like wine that is going bad because it sat too long without being strained of solid particles that settled at the bottom of the storage bottle or cask. **will not do good, nor ... ill:** Zephaniah's generation no longer believes that the Lord acts in the life of the nation to bring either prosperity or punishment. Denial of God's lordship over his people and their history is not only a form of practical atheism but is tantamount to apostasy.
1:13 not inhabit ... not drink wine: Loss of houses recently built and vineyards recently planted are listed as curses of the covenant triggered by Israel's disobedience in Deut 28:30.
1:14 the day of the LORD: Lest any mistake what is coming for good news, the prophet stresses that Judah (and the whole

region) is about to face the justice of God against wickedness. See note on 1:7. **near and hastening fast:** Adds a sense of alarm and imminent doom to the prophet's message (Rev 1:1; 22:6–7).
1:15–16 The day soon to come will bring divine punishment (**wrath**), psychological pain (**distress, anguish**), physical destruction (**ruin, devastation**), terror and dread (**darkness, gloom**), and the sounds of war (**trumpet blast, battle cry**).
1:17 they have sinned: E.g., by committing idolatry (1:4–5), perpetrating violence, fraud, and oppression (1:9; 3:1), turning away from the Lord (1:6), losing faith in the Lord (1:12), rebelling against the Lord (3:1), refusing correction from the Lord (3:2), and embracing corruption (3:7). **like dust ... dung:** I.e., like things of no value.
1:18 their silver ... gold: Idol images, cast or overlaid with precious metals, will afford no protection from the Lord's day of reckoning (Is 2:20; Jer 10:4–5). **all the earth:** Or "all the land". See note on 1:2.
2:1–3 An urgent call to repentance **before** time runs out and Judah faces the Lord's stern punishment. Zephaniah does not say that Judah and Jerusalem can still *avoid* this catastrophe, which is already fixed in the plan of God (2 Kings 23:27–29), but he offers hope that some can *survive* the catastrophe if they seek the Lord and return to righteousness and humility (cf. Hab 2:4).
2:1 hold assembly: A national gathering for prayer and fasting may be meant (Joel 1:14; Jon 3:6–9). **shameless nation:** Judah (1:4).
2:2 chaff: The useless husks that are separated from grains on threshing floors and carried away by the wind (Job 21:18; Ps 1:4; Is 17:13).

ᶜCn Compare Gk Syr: Heb *before a decree is born; like chaff a day has passed away.*

[3]Seek the LORD, all you humble of the land,
who do his commands;
seek righteousness, seek humility;
perhaps you may be hidden
on the day of the wrath of the LORD.
[4]For Gaza shall be deserted,
and Ash'kelon shall become a desolation;
Ash'dod's people shall be driven out at noon,
and Ek'ron shall be uprooted.
[5]Woe to you inhabitants of the seacoast,
you nation of the Cher'ethites!
The word of the LORD is against you,
O Canaan, land of the Philis'tines;
and I will destroy you till no inhabitant is left.
[6]And you, O seacoast, shall be pastures,
meadows for shepherds
and folds for flocks.

[7]The seacoast shall become the possession
of the remnant of the house of Judah,
on which they shall pasture,
and in the houses of Ash'kelon
they shall lie down at evening.
For the LORD their God will be mindful of
them
and restore their fortunes.

[8]"I have heard the taunts of Moab
and the revilings of the Am'monites,
how they have taunted my people
and made boasts against their territory.
[9]Therefore, as I live," says the LORD of hosts,
the God of Israel,
"Moab shall become like Sodom,
and the Am'monites like Gomor'rah,

2:4 f. Is 11.00–01, Jer 17; Ezek 25:15–17; Joel 2:4–8; Amos 1:6–8; Zech 9:5–7
2:8–11: Is 15–16; 25:10–12; Jer 48; Ezek 25:8–11; Amos 2:1–3.

2:3 Seek the LORD: Instead of other gods (1:4-6). **you humble:** The prophet addresses the ʿanawim or devout poor in Judah who remained faithful to the Lord in the midst of widespread apostasy (CCC 716). See word study: *The Afflicted* at Ps 22:26. **his commands:** Literally, "his justice". **seek righteousness:** By careful observance of the covenant commandments (Deut 6:25; Lk 1:6). **seek humility:** By relying upon the Lord, taking refuge in him, and renouncing pride (Prov 15:33; CCC 2559, 2631). **perhaps:** Zephaniah speaks with cautious optimism, knowing that God is merciful, but not with prophetic certainty (cf. Ex 32:30). Divine mercy is something to seek and to hope for; it is not something to presume upon (Amos 5:15; Joel 2:12-14; Rom 2:2-5). **hidden:** In the sense of being "protected" or "sheltered" from the approaching storm of God's wrath.
2:4—3:7 Oracles against foreign nations and cities culminating with a denunciation of Jerusalem. Judah stands at the center of this regional map, surrounded by the Philistines to the west (2:4-7), the Moabites and Ammonites to the east (2:8-11), the Ethiopians to the south (2:12), and the Assyrians to the north (2:13-15). For a similar sequence of oracles that target foreign nations and climax with Judah and Israel, see Amos 1:3—2:16. See essay: *Oracles against the Nations in the Minor Prophets* at Amos 1.
2:4 Gaza ... Ashkelon ... Ashdod ... Ekron: Philistine coastal cities in southwest Canaan, all traditional enemies of Judah. For oracles against Philistia, see also Is 14:28-32; Jer 47:1-7; Ezek 25:15-17; Amos 1:6-8.
2:5 Woe: A cry of anguish heard at funerals. Here it anticipates Philistia suffering mass casualties. See word study: *Woe* at Is 28:1. **Cherethites:** People from the island of Crete (1 Sam 30:14). The Philistines, known in ancient Egyptian texts as the "sea peoples", migrated to the Near East from various islands of the Mediterranean. **the LORD is against you:** Ominous words of doom addressed to nations that are about to incur divine judgment (Jer 50:31; Ezek 21:3; Nahum 2:13).
2:7 restore their fortunes: Anticipates the restoration of Judah and Jerusalem foreseen in 3:14-20.
2:8 Moab ... Ammonites: Distant relatives of the people of Israel who lived east of the Dead Sea (= Moab) and the Jordan River (= Ammon). They are faulted mainly for their boastful "pride" (2:10). According to Genesis, both peoples were born of incest after the Lord overthrew Sodom and Gomorrah (Gen 19:30-38). Ironically, they escaped the fate of these cities at the time of their conception, but they will share their fate at the time of their death (2:9). For oracles against Moab and Ammon, see also Is 15-16; Jer 48:1—49:6; Ezek 25:1-11; Amos 1:13—2:3.

2:9 as I live: A divine oath formula (Deut 32:40). **Sodom ... Gomorrah:** Cities infamous for their wickedness and destroyed by fire from heaven (Gen 19:24-29). In the aftermath, only a scorched and salty wasteland remained, serving as a witness to the Lord's judgment for future generations (Deut 29:23). **my nation:** Judah.

WORD STUDY

Remnant (2:7)

She'erît (Heb.): a noun meaning "what is left". It refers to a small portion that remains of a larger group or thing, such as the "rest" of a group that has not yet been counted (Neh 7:17), the "rest" of a tree that is left after part of it has been burned (Is 44:17), or a "remnant" of descendants whose survival keeps a family from perishing (Gen 45:7; 2 Sam 14:7). The notion of a remnant also bears theological significance in the Bible. Sometimes the Lord brings judgment against a wicked people so that none remain alive, not even a remnant (Is 14:30; Jer 11:23; Amos 1:8). Some even feared that God, in his wrath, would punish Israel to such an extent that none would be left (Ezra 9:14; Ezek 9:8). The prophets, however, teach that the Lord sometimes judges his people harshly, but he never destroys them completely. He may reduce them to a small number, but his mercy places a limit on his severity, lest none be left alive to bear his blessings into the future. Even though the Assyrians and Babylonians carried thousands of Israelites into exile, God left a "remnant" of his people in the land (2 Chron 34:9) and promised to save and regather a "remnant" from among the exiles (Jer 23:3; 31:7; Mic 2:12). In several places in the Minor Prophets, the remnant blessed by God is the small community of survivors and returnees from Babylonian exile that occupy Judah and Jerusalem (Zeph 2:7, 9; 3:13; Hag 1:12; Zech 8:12).

a land possessed by nettles and salt pits,
  and a waste for ever.
The remnant of my people shall plunder them,
  and the survivors of my nation shall possess
    them."
¹⁰This shall be their lot in return for their
    pride,
  because they scoffed and boasted
  against the people of the LORD of hosts.
¹¹The LORD will be terrifying against them;
  yes, he will famish all the gods of the
    earth,
  and to him shall bow down,
    each in its place,
  all the lands of the nations.

¹²You also, O Ethiopians,
  shall be slain by my sword.
¹³And he will stretch out his hand against the
    north,
  and destroy Assyria;
  and he will make Nin'eveh a desolation,
    a dry waste like the desert.
¹⁴Herds shall lie down in the midst of her,
  all the beasts of the field;ᵈ
  the vultureᵉ and the hedgehog
    shall lodge in her capitals;
  the owlᶠ shall hoot in the window,
    the ravenᵍ croak on the threshold;
  for her cedar work will be laid bare.

¹⁵This is the exultant city
  that dwelt secure,
  that said to herself,
    "I am and there is none else."
What a desolation she has become,
  a lair for wild beasts!
Every one who passes by her
  hisses and shakes his fist.

Wickedness of the Nations

3 Woe to her that is rebellious and defiled,
  the oppressing city!
²She listens to no voice,
  she accepts no correction.
She does not trust in the LORD,
  she does not draw near to her God.

³Her officials within her
  are roaring lions;
  her judges are evening wolves
    that leave nothing till the morning.
⁴Her prophets are wanton,
  faithless men;
  her priests profane what is sacred,
    they do violence to the law.
⁵The LORD within her is righteous,
  he does no wrong;
  every morning he shows forth his justice,
    each dawn he does not fail;
  but the unjust knows no shame. /

2:12: Is 18. **2:13–15:** Is 10:5–34; Nahum.

2:11 all the gods: The idols of the world will be exposed as false and weak, at which time their pagan devotees will have a change of heart and bow to the God of Israel instead (cf. 3:9-10).

2:12 Ethiopians: Or "Cushites". An Ethiopian dynasty ruled Egypt just prior to Zephaniah's time, i.e., before the Assyrian conquest of the city of Thebes in 663 B.C. Some think the prophet foresees the victory of Cambyses II of Persia over Egypt in 525 B.C. For another oracle against Ethiopia, see Is 18:1-6.

2:13 stretch out his hand: An act of divine chastisement (1:4; Is 5:25; Jer 51:25). **Assyria:** The most powerful empire in the Near East for much of the seventh century B.C. It was centered around the Tigris River in upper Mesopotamia. Zephaniah foresees its imminent demise. Historically, Assyria declined rapidly after Babylon achieved its independence in 626 B.C. For oracles against Assyria, see also Is 10:5-34; 14:24-27. **Nineveh:** Capital of Assyria until its conquest by an alliance of Babylonians, Medes, and Scythians in 612 B.C. The entire Book of Nahum is devoted to prophesying this event.

2:14 vulture ... raven: Beasts and birds that dwell in abandoned cities (Is 34:11).

2:15 the exultant city: Nineveh (2:13). **I am and there is none else:** Nineveh's arrogant self-perception (cf. Is 47:8, 10). It sees itself as the greatest of all cities, invulnerable and secure. Its pride will be cast down when God reduces the

mighty metropolis to uninhabited ruins. **hisses and shakes his fist:** The fallen city will be taunted and treated with contempt.

3:1-7 Zephaniah's final oracle of judgment is aimed at Jerusalem. The Lord who dwells in the city is **righteous**, yet nearly everyone else is **rebellious**. God is no longer trusted or approached in faith (3:2). Jerusalem's civil leaders prey upon the defenseless underclasses (3:3), and its religious leaders are scandalously corrupt (3:4). Instead of repenting, the city refuses to learn from the mistakes of nations who have been severely judged by God in the past (3:6-7). Jeremiah likewise denounced the wickedness of Jerusalem in the decades before its destruction in 586 B.C.

3:1 Woe: A cry of anguish heard at funerals. Here it anticipates Jerusalem's death by foreign conquest. See word study: *Woe* at Is 28:1. **rebellious:** Against the Lord (Jer 4:16-17). **defiled:** By such things as violent crimes (Is 59:3) and defective sacrifices (Mal 1:7). **the oppressing city:** Jerusalem, not to be confused with "the exultant city" of Nineveh in 2:15.

3:2 listens to no voice: Refers to willful disobedience (Jer 22:21). **accepts no correction:** The city spurns the Lord's discipline, which comes in measured ways and amounts to encouraging repentance (Lev 26:14-45). **does not draw near:** Sincere and heartfelt worship of the Lord is lacking (Is 29:13).

3:3-4 The sins of Jerusalem's leadership, decried in similar words by Ezekiel (Ezek 22:25-27).

3:4 prophets: False prophets who dismissed predictions of woe and foolishly assured the city of "peace" (Jer 6:14; 8:11; Ezek 13:10). **priests:** Responsible for distinguishing the holy from the common and for instructing the people in the Mosaic Law (Lev 10:10-11).

3:5 righteous: Faithful to the covenant and fair in administering justice. See word study: *Righteous* at Neh 9:8.

ᵈ Tg Compare Gk: Heb *nation*.
ᵉ The meaning of the Hebrew word is uncertain.
ᶠ Cn: Heb *a voice*.
ᵍ Gk Vg: Heb *desolation*.

⁶"I have cut off nations;
  their battlements are in ruins;
I have laid waste their streets
  so that none walks in them;
their cities have been made desolate,
  without a man, without an inhabitant.
⁷I said, 'Surely she will fear me,
  she will accept correction;
she will not lose sight[h]
  of all that I have enjoined upon her.'
But all the more they were eager
  to make all their deeds corrupt."

⁸"Therefore wait for me," says the Lord,
  "for the day when I arise as a witness.
For my decision is to gather nations,
  to assemble kingdoms,
to pour out upon them my indignation,
  all the heat of my anger;
for in the fire of my jealous wrath
  all the earth shall be consumed.

Restoration of Israel

⁹"Yes, at that time I will change the speech of the
    peoples
  to a pure speech,
that all of them may call on the name of the Lord
  and serve him with one accord.

¹⁰From beyond the rivers of Ethiopia
  my suppliants, the daughter of my dispersed
    ones,
  shall bring my offering.

¹¹"On that day you shall not be put to shame
  because of the deeds by which you have
    rebelled against me;
for then I will remove from your midst
  your proudly exultant ones,
and you shall no longer be haughty
  in my holy mountain.
¹²For I will leave in the midst of you
  a people humble and lowly.
They shall seek refuge in the name of the
    Lord,
¹³ those who are left in Israel;
they shall do no wrong
  and utter no lies,
nor shall there be found in their mouth
  a deceitful tongue.
For they shall pasture and lie down,
  and none shall make them afraid."

¹⁴Sing aloud, O daughter of Zion;
  shout, O Israel!
Rejoice and exult with all your heart,
  O daughter of Jerusalem!

3:13: Rev 14:5.

3:6 their cities ... desolate: Like Sodom and Gomorrah (2:9).
3:8 wait for me: A call for patient endurance addressed to the "humble of the land" (2:3). Waiting for the Lord includes confident trust that he will fulfill his promises in due time (Is 8:17; Hab 2:3). **the day:** Described in 1:14–16. **gather nations ... kingdoms:** The focus widens from Judah to the peoples singled out for judgment in 2:4–15. **all the earth:** Or "all the land". See note on 1:2.
3:9–10 The conversion of the nations following their chastisement (3:8). If the negative side of judgment is bitterness, grief, and destruction (1:14–16), the positive side is a spiritual awakening to the folly of idols and the majesty of the one true God (2:11). Zephaniah foresees survivors among the Gentiles calling upon the Lord with a **pure speech**, i.e., with lips that are cleansed of lies and deceit (3:13) and that no longer utter the names of false gods (1:5). For prophecies that envision a future when all peoples join themselves to the God of Israel, see Is 2:2–3; 18:7; 19:23–25; Jer 3:17; Zech 2:11; 14:16. • According to Vatican II, the Church still awaits the day, which is known to God alone, when all peoples of the world will call upon the Lord with a single voice and serve him side by side (*Nostra aetate* 4).
3:9 call on the name: An act of prayer and praise (Gen 4:26; 12:8; Ps 116:17).
3:10 From beyond: From lands as far away as Africa (Is 18:1). **the rivers:** The Blue Nile and the White Nile. **suppliants:** People who pray. **my dispersed ones:** Zephaniah foresees a great ingathering of Israel's exiles that coincides with all nations turning from idols to serve the Lord (as in Is 49:22; 66:18–20). **my offering:** The Hebrew *minḥāh* designates a cereal or grain sacrifice. See note on Lev 2:1–16.

3:11–13 Jerusalem will see better days after the purifying judgment of God. It will be rid of pompous leaders (3:11) and purged of sins of speech (3:13), and the remnant that remains in the city will be a devout community that seeks refuge in the Lord (3:12).
3:11 that day: A day of restoration that will follow the day of reckoning (1:4; 2:1–3). **exultant ones:** The same language used in 2:15, implying that Jerusalem will be purged of corrupt leaders who have become as haughty as the arrogant city of Nineveh. **my holy mountain:** Mt. Zion, crowned with the city of Jerusalem and sanctified by the Lord's presence in his Temple (Ps 2:6; Joel 2:1).
3:12 humble and lowly: The faithful who recognize their need for God and trust him to bless them (Is 57:13; Nahum 1:7). Their lowliness is thus a spiritual stance of reliance upon the Lord, regardless of their socioeconomic status. • The Greek equivalents of these terms, *praüs* and *tapeinos*, are used when Jesus describes himself as "gentle and lowly" in heart in Mt 11:29.
3:13 those who are left: The remnant of God's people who are kept "hidden" from the Lord's judgment (2:3). **nor ... in their mouth a deceitful tongue:** This passage is referenced in the Book of Revelation, where the remnant of Israel, the 144,000 redeemed by God, is seen standing with the Lamb on Mt. Zion and "in their mouth no lie was found" (Rev 14:5). **they shall pasture:** An image of God's people as a flock of sheep that he leads and cares for (Pss 79:13; 95:7; Is 40:11; Jn 10:11–16).
3:14–17 An oracle that celebrates God's restoration of Jerusalem. The city, after enduring the fires of divine judgment, will be purged of evil and delivered from fear and shame. In the midst of "those who are left" (3:13) the Lord will reign as the **King of Israel** (3:15) and as a **warrior** who triumphs over all enemies (3:17). The humble community

---

[h] Gk Syr: Heb *and her dwelling will not be cut off.*

¹⁵The Lᴏʀᴅ has taken away the judgments against
  you,
   he has cast out your enemies.
  The King of Israel, the Lᴏʀᴅ, is in your midst;
   you shall fear evil no more.
¹⁶On that day it shall be said to Jerusalem:
  "Do not fear, O Zion;
   let not your hands grow weak.
¹⁷The Lᴏʀᴅ, your God, is in your midst,
   a warrior who gives victory;
  he will rejoice over you with gladness,
   he will renew youⁱ in his love;
  he will exult over you with loud singing
¹⁸   as on a day of festival.^j
  "I will remove disaster^k from you,
   so that you will not bear reproach for it.

¹⁹Behold, at that time I will deal
   with all your oppressors.
  And I will save the lame
   and gather the outcast,
  and I will change their shame into praise
   and renown in all the earth.
²⁰At that time I will bring you home,
   at the time when I gather you together;
  yes, I will make you renowned and praised
   among all the peoples of the earth,
  when I restore your fortunes
   before your eyes," says the Lᴏʀᴅ.

---

on Zion will then be renewed in his **love** (3:17). Additional blessings are revealed in 3:18–20, with the Lord speaking directly in the first person ("I, me, my"). • At the Annunciation, Gabriel greets Mary with words that echo Zephaniah's prophecy. His introductory "Hail!" (Lk 1:28) can also be translated "Rejoice!" (3:14); the angel's assurance that "the Lord is with you" (Lk 1:28) resembles the words "the Lᴏʀᴅ ... is in your midst" (3:15); the appeal "Do not be afraid" (Lk 1:30) recalls the words "Do no fear" (3:16); and the announcement that Mary will conceive "the Son of God" in her womb (Lk 1:35) resonates with the message that "God ... is in your midst" (3:17). These echoes imply that Mary, the Mother of Jesus, exemplifies the devout remnant of Israel. • Owing in part to this prophecy, Catholic tradition has thus come to view Mary as the beloved "Daughter of Sion" (Vatican II, *Lumen Gentium* 55; St. John Paul II, *Redemptoris Mater* 3; CCC 489). • The passage commands Jerusalem to rejoice and be glad that its transgressions are wiped away by Christ. The Church, who

is the spiritual and holy Zion, is justified in Christ alone, and through his mediation we have been rescued from the powers of evil (St. Cyril of Alexandria, *Commentary on Zephaniah* 43).

3:14 Sing ... shout ... Rejoice: Invitations to praise the Lord for his grace and salvation. **daughter of Zion:** Jerusalem and its people are personified as a young woman. See word study: *The Daughter of Zion* at Lam 1:6. For background on Zion, see note on 2 Sam 5:7.

3:15 King of Israel: Israel designates the whole tribal family descended from Jacob, suggesting the homecoming envisioned in 3:20 goes beyond retrieving the captives of Judah taken to Babylon in the sixth century ʙ.c. In concert with other prophets, Zephaniah anticipates a reunion of all twelve tribes of Israel, including the northern tribes exiled by the Assyrians in the eighth century ʙ.c. (Is 11:11–12; 27:12–13; Jer 3:17–18; Ezek 37:15–28; Hos 1:11).

3:17 a warrior: God showed himself "a man of war" when he freed the Israelites from Egypt (Ex 15:3) and fought alongside them for the Promised Land (Josh 10:14). **loud singing:** An image of God taking delight in his people (Is 65:19). This is the only passage in Scripture that depicts the Lord singing (cf. Lk 15:11–32).

3:20 I will bring you home: From the distant lands of exile (2 Kings 15:29; 17:6; 24:15; 25:11; Jer 52:28–30).

ⁱ Gk Syr: Heb *he will be silent.*
^j Gk Syr: Heb obscure.
^k Cn: Heb *they were.*

STUDY QUESTIONS
Zephaniah

Chapter 1

For understanding
1. **1:4.** What does it mean that God stretches out his hand? To which place does the prophet refer? Who promoted the worship of Baal, the storm and fertility god of Canaanite religion, that had been firmly established in Judah? Who is the remnant of Baal, and what may its mention suggest about when Zephaniah ministered? Who are the idolatrous priests?
2. **1:7.** If one cannot protest when the Lord acts as judge, what is the only possible response? What is "the day of the Lord"? What does the prophet foresee? What will happen when this day of reckoning arrives? What sacrifice has the Lord prepared?
3. **1:12.** How are the men of Jerusalem like wine? What does Zephaniah's generation no longer believe? To what does denial of God's lordship over his people and their history amount?
4. **1:14.** Lest any mistake what is coming for good news, what does the prophet stress that Judah (including Jerusalem) is about to face? What sense does the expression "near and hastening fast" add to the prophet's message?

For application
1. **1:5.** What is a "divided heart" when it comes to things of God? How do you think God responds to the prayers of those whose hearts are divided?
2. **1:7.** What does the command to be silent in a courtroom call upon those present to do besides stop talking? What attitudes of attention and respect are indicated? Why is silence before the Lord appropriate?
3. **1:12.** What is your view of the Lord's role in everyday life? How do you answer someone who maintains that "the Lord will not do good, nor will he do ill"—that God is absent or is unconcerned with how people behave?
4. **1:15.** The hymn "Dies Irae" was once sung at funeral liturgies. What do the words mean? To what do they refer? Why do you think this sequence is no longer sung at funerals? What view of death has taken its place?

Chapter 2

For understanding
1. **2:3.** In urging his audience to seek the Lord instead of other gods, whom does the prophet address? How do they seek righteousness? How do they seek humility? Why does Zephaniah speak with cautious optimism? If divine mercy is not something upon which to presume, how does one attain it?
2. **2:4—3:7.** Against whom are these oracles addressed? Standing at the center of this regional map, by whom is Judah surrounded?
3. **Word study: Remnant (2:7).** To what does the Hebrew noun *she'ērît* meaning "what is left" refer? What theological significance does the notion of a remnant bear in the Bible? Even though the Assyrians and Babylonians carried thousands of Israelites into exile, what did God do with the remnants? In several places in the Minor Prophets, which was the remnant blessed by God?
4. **2:8.** Who were the Moabites and the Ammonites? For what are they mainly faulted? According to Genesis, how were both peoples born? While, ironically, they escaped the fate of these cities at the time of their conception, what will happen to them now?

For application
1. **2:3.** In an unsettled time such as this, for what might observant Catholics pray by seeking the Lord through prayer and fasting? From what wrath would they hope to be hidden?
2. **2:7.** Given that large numbers of people have been abandoning the faith as the world and even the Church become secularized, what hope do Christians have if only a small remnant is left? What will this remnant be like?
3. **2:9.** Zephaniah predicts that the remnant of Judah will possess the lands of Moab and Ammon. How does the possibility of a declining Christian population accord with Jesus' command to make disciples of all nations? How might this remnant renew the Church?

Chapter 3

For understanding
1. **3:1–7.** At whom is Zephaniah's final oracle of judgment aimed? Although the Lord who dwells in the city is righteous, what is nearly everyone else like? Because God is no longer trusted or approached in faith, what do Jerusalem's civil and religious leaders do? Instead of repenting, what does the city do?
2. **3:9–10.** With what are these verses concerned? If the negative side of judgment is bitterness, grief, and destruction, what is the positive side? What does Zephaniah foresee that survivors among the Gentiles will be doing? According to Vatican II, what day known to God alone does the Church still await?
3. **3:13.** Who are "those who are left"? How is this passage referenced in the Book of Revelation?
4. **3:14–17.** What does this oracle that celebrates God's restoration of Jerusalem predict about the city? In the midst of "those who are left", who will reign? What will happen to the humble community on Zion? At the Annunciation, how does Gabriel's greeting to Mary resemble Zephaniah's language? Owing in part to this prophecy, how has Catholic tradition thus come to view Mary?

Study Questions

1. **3:4-5.** How valid are the sacraments if they are administered by priests who do not believe the gospel they preach? For example, how valid is a Mass if a priest does not believe that the Consecration of the elements confects anything (CCC 1128, 1550, 1584)?
2. **3:8.** According to the note for this verse, what does it mean to wait for the Lord? How do you wait for the Lord to act in your own life? In the lives of those whom you love or for whom you pray?
3. **3:9.** What do you think Zephaniah means by a "pure speech"? What kind of purity is involved here?
4. **3:17.** The note for this verse says that this is the only passage in Scripture that depicts the Lord singing. When Jesus rejoiced, how did he act (Lk 10:21)? About what did he rejoice? For what does Jesus encourage his disciples to rejoice (e.g., Mt 5:12; Lk 10:20; Jn 14:28, 16:22)?

INTRODUCTION TO HAGGAI

Author and Date Minimal controversy surrounds the origin of the Book of Haggai. It consists mainly of oracles spoken by "Haggai the prophet" (1:1; 2:1, 10, 20) that are framed by short notices indicating the dates when the prophet received his messages from the Lord. Because these notices refer to Haggai in the third person (he, him, his) instead of the first person (I, me, my), it is possible that a disciple or associate of the prophet preserved Haggai's sayings in writing and compiled them into the book we have today. It is likewise plausible, however, that Haggai himself was responsible for its composition. Unfortunately, very little is known about the prophet whose name is attached to the book except that he ministered in Judah and Jerusalem at the same time as the prophet Zechariah (Ezra 5:1; 6:14). Jewish tradition further holds that he was one of the Jewish exiles who returned to Judah from Babylon. The Greek Septuagint version of the Book of Psalms credits Haggai with co-authoring Psalms 145–48, although his name does not appear in the superscriptions of the Hebrew Psalter, and so the historical value of this tradition is uncertain.

The date of the book can be determined fairly precisely. Haggai's prophecies are all dated in 520 B.C., the second year of Darius I Hystaspes, ruler of Persia from 522 to 486 B.C. Moreover, nothing in the book suggests that long years elapsed between the proclamation of Haggai's messages and the time when his sayings were written down. On the contrary, the book's silence on the completion and rededication of the Jerusalem Temple in 515 B.C. favors a date prior this landmark event. The Book of Haggai can thus be dated within a five-year window between 520 and 515 B.C.

Title The book is named after Haggai, mentioned in the opening verse. Its Hebrew form, *Ḥaggay*, is related to the noun *ḥag*, meaning "feast, festival". He may have received this name because he was born during one of Israel's liturgical feasts. His name appears in the Greek Septuagint in the title *Aggaios*, while this heading is expanded in the Latin Vulgate to *Aggeus Propheta*, "Haggai the Prophet". English titles for the book follow these ancient traditions.

Place in the Canon Haggai has long been revered as a canonical book of Scripture. In the Jewish Bible, or Tanakh, it stands among the Latter Prophets in a sub-collection of writings known as "the Book of the Twelve". In Christian Bibles, these twelve books are called the Minor Prophets, not because they are less important than Isaiah, Jeremiah, Ezekiel, and Daniel, but because they are comparatively shorter. In the Hebrew Bible, Greek Septuagint, and Latin Vulgate, Haggai stands tenth among the Minor Prophets between Zephaniah and Zechariah, just as it does in English Bibles.

Structure The book consists of four prophetic addresses arranged in chronological order. **(1)** Haggai's first address, dated August 29, 520 B.C., is an appeal to the small community in Judah to finish the task of rebuilding the Jerusalem Temple (1:1–15). **(2)** The second address, dated October 17, encourages the builders with the Lord's promise to make the glory of the latter Temple outshine even Solomon's Temple (2:1–9). **(3)** The third address, dated December 18, contrasts the frustrations of the past with the blessings that will come now that God's people have responded to the prophet's appeal with obedience (2:10–19). **(4)** The fourth address, also dated December 18, informs Zerubbabel, governor of Judah, that God is about to overthrow the mighty powers of the world, although the governor is favored by the Lord and chosen as his signet ring (2:20–23). See also *Outline*.

Historical Background The book unfolds in the early Persian period after an initial wave of Jewish exiles returned to Judah from Babylon. Cyrus II of Persia took control of the Babylonian empire when he captured the city of Babylon in 539 B.C. and released all foreign exiles in 538 B.C., allowing them to return to their native lands (Ezra 1:2–4). Not long afterward, thousands of Judeans who had been living for decades in Babylon made the journey home to reestablish the covenant community in Judah. The obstacles faced by these returnees were formidable. Many of the villages, farms, and homes in Judah lay in ruins since the Babylonian conquest of 586 B.C., as did the city and Temple of Jerusalem. But thanks to the strong leadership of Zerubbabel, the governor, and Jeshua, the high priest, an initial effort was made to rebuild the Jerusalem Temple, with the altar of sacrifice being restored in the fall of 537 B.C. (Ezra 3:1–7) and the foundation stones being laid in the spring of 536 B.C. (Ezra 3:8–11). However, opposition from the local population soon brought the project to a standstill, and work on the sanctuary was halted for the next sixteen years (Ezra 4:1–24). Haggai was commissioned to speak for the Lord at the end of this long interruption. His task was to encourage the community in Judah to complete the work of rebuilding the Temple, an undertaking that was resumed in 520 and finished in 515 B.C. (Ezra 6:15).

The Message of the Prophet Despite being small in size and succinct in expression, the Book of Haggai is rich in theological content. The prophet mainly delivers words of correction and encouragement. Correction is needed for the people of Judah because they have neglected their duty to rebuild the Temple in Jerusalem, which had been destroyed and left in ruins for more than six decades. But instead of making the reconstruction of the Lord's house a national priority, the community of returnees focused their efforts on building comfortable houses for themselves (1:4) on the excuse that it was "not yet" time to resume work on the Temple (1:2). This proved to be a costly misjudgment. The prophet, speaking for the Lord, invites the people to think back on how they have fared in recent years (1:5; 2:16). Far from prospering under the Lord's blessing, the people of Judah have barely produced enough food to survive (1:6, 9). They have been struggling against crop failure and meager harvests caused by drought, blight, mildew, and hail (1:11; 2:17). None of this, according to the prophet, was by accident. These agricultural calamities were chastisements sent by the Lord to discipline his people and to bring them to repentance (1:11; 2:17). It is not that the people repudiated the Lord or wantonly rejected his Torah; rather, the Lord had ceased to be the center of their lives. Selfish priorities and pursuits had been pushed ahead of spiritual priorities. The Lord's presence among his people was not sufficiently treasured to make a difference in their daily lives, and so they withheld the labor and resources that were needed to build a sanctuary for God's glory. In this way the remnant in Judah made itself and its worship "unclean" in God's eyes (2:14). However, thanks to a movement of grace in the spirits of the people (1:14), the Judeans and their leaders responded to Haggai's message. They "obeyed the voice of the LORD" (1:12) and "worked on the house of the LORD" (1:14). The Lord promised in turn to "bless" his people and their work in the days ahead (2:19).

Besides correction for inaction, encouragement for the task of restoring the Temple was also needed in the midst of the effort. Zerubbabel, the governor of Judah, Joshua, the high priest, and the people of the land are all addressed with the words: "take courage" (2:4). Twice the Lord assures the builders of his divine presence and help by saying, "I am with you" (1:13; 2:4), and once he declares, "My Spirit abides among you" (2:5). To these promises of present assistance, he adds two promises of future glory. In the first, the Lord announces his plan to shake heaven and earth, with the result that all nations of the world will bring their treasures to the Temple in Jerusalem, causing its future glory to outshine even the legendary glory of the Temple built by Solomon (2:6–9). This is heartening news for the community in Judah, for whom the Second Temple was a glaring disappointment, given its smaller size and humbler construction in comparison to the former sanctuary (2:3). In the second promise, the Lord announces again that he will shake heaven and earth, this time shattering the strength of the world's kingdoms and defeating their armies (2:21–22). The bright side is that God has chosen Zerubbabel, a royal descendant of David, to be his "signet ring" (2:23). The implication is that God remains committed to his everlasting covenant of kingship with David (2 Sam 7:12–19). Zerubbabel himself will not reign as a king, but he will extend the line of David's heirs into the future until the Davidic Messiah comes to rule on David's throne (cf. Lk 1:32; Acts 2:30–33). The remnant community in Judah is thus invited to see its work as a small part of a much larger plan of salvation history that the Lord intends to accomplish.

Christian Perspective Only once does the New Testament quote the Book of Haggai. This occurs when the author of Hebrews contrasts the earthquake that shook Mt. Sinai with the promise in Haggai that God will shake the heavens as well (2:6, referenced in Heb 12:26–27). Interpreted, this means that what is shaken passes away (= Old Covenant), leaving behind what cannot be shaken as lasting (= New Covenant). Beyond this sole citation, one can also discern thematic links with the book. For example, Haggai's call to prioritize work on the Temple so that Lord will meet the material needs of his people resonates with Jesus' teaching in the Sermon on the Mount: "But seek first [God's] kingdom and his righteousness, and all these things shall be yours as well" (Mt 6:33). Likewise, Haggai's vision of the "latter splendor" of the Temple surpassing its "former" glory (2:9) fits the Christian belief that God's greatest Temple is the risen and glorified Body of Christ (Mt 12:6; Jn 2:21). All nations contribute to its glory by accepting the gospel and becoming members of the Church, which is a Temple built of living stones and indwelt by the Holy Spirit (1 Cor 3:16; Eph 2:11–21; 1 Pet 2:4–5). Lastly, the closing oracle of the book, which announces a special role in God's plan for Zerubbabel, the son of Shealtiel, points ultimately to Matthew's genealogy of Jesus (Mt 1:1–16), which traces his lineage back to King David through his royal heirs "Shealtiel" and "Zerubbabel" (Mt 1:12).

OUTLINE OF HAGGAI

1. Haggai's First Address (1:1–15)
- A. Chronological Note (1:1)
- B. Appeal to Rebuild the Temple (1:2–11)
- C. Response of the People (1:12–15)

2. Haggai's Second Address (2:1–9)
- A. Chronological Note (2:1)
- B. Splendor of the Future Temple (2:2–9)

3. Haggai's Third Address (2:10–19)
- A. Chronological Note (2:10)
- B. Uncleanness of the Past (2:11–17)
- C. Blessing for the Future (2:18–19)

4. Haggai's Fourth Address (2:20–23)
- A. Chronological Note (2:20)
- B. Zerubbabel, the Lord's Signet Ring (2:21–23)

THE BOOK OF

HAGGAI

The Command to Rebuild the Temple

1 In the second year of Dari'us the king, in the sixth month, on the first day of the month, the word of the LORD came by Hag'-gai the prophet to Zerub'babel the son of She-al'ti-el, governor of Judah, and to Joshua the son of Jehoz'adak, the high priest, 2"Thus says the LORD of hosts: This people say the time has not yet come to rebuild the house of the LORD." 3Then the word of the LORD came by Hag'gai the prophet, 4"Is it a time for you yourselves to dwell in your paneled houses, while this house lies in ruins? 5Now therefore thus says the LORD of hosts: Consider how you have fared. 6You have sown much, and harvested little; you eat, but you never have enough; you drink, but you never have your fill; you clothe yourselves, but no one is warm; and he who earns wages earns wages to put them into a bag with holes.

7 "Thus says the LORD of hosts: Consider how you have fared. 8Go up to the hills and bring wood and build the house, that I may take pleasure in it and that I may appear in my glory, says the LORD. 9You have looked for much, and behold, it came to little; and when you brought it home, I blew it away. Why? says the LORD of hosts. Because of my house that lies in ruins, while you busy yourselves each with his own house. 10Therefore the heavens above you have withheld the dew, and the earth has withheld its produce. 11And I have called for a drought upon the land and the hills, upon the grain, the new wine, the oil, upon what the ground brings forth, upon men and cattle, and upon all their labors."

1:1-15 Haggai's first prophetic address, dated August 29, 520 B.C.

1:1 In the second year: The first of five chronological notes in the book (1:15; 2:1, 10, 20). **Darius:** Darius I Hystaspes, ruler of Persia from 522 to 486 B.C. **sixth month:** Known in postexilic times as Elul. **the word of the LORD:** Prophetic revelation from God entrusted to a human messenger. See essay: *The Word of the Lord* at Hos 1. **Haggai:** Nothing certain is known about his family or background. His name is related to the Hebrew term *hag*, meaning "feast, festival", and has been found on seals dating back to the postexilic period. Haggai is also mentioned in Ezra 5:1; 6:14. **Zerubbabel:** Grandson of Jehoiachin, king of Judah, who was exiled to Babylon in 597 B.C. (2 Kings 24:15). Zerubbabel thus stood in the royal line of David, although the institution of the Davidic monarchy did not survive the Babylonian conquest of Judah in 586 B.C. He is the subject of the final oracle of the book (2:20-23). **son of She-alti-el:** Also stated in Ezra 3:2, 8; Neh 12:1; Mt 1:12. For Zerubbabel's genealogy, see note on 1 Chron 3:19. **governor:** Not a king or ruler of an independent state but an appointed administrator of the Persian province of Judah, called Yehud. Zerubbabel appears to have been the second governor of Judah in the postexilic period, following Sheshbazzar (Ezra 1:8; 5:14). **Joshua the son of Jehozadak:** The same person as "Jeshua the son of Jozadak" in the Book of Ezra (Ezra 3:2, 8; 5:2; 10:18). Jehozadak, Joshua's father and predecessor as high priest, was taken into exile by the Babylonians in the early sixth century B.C. (1 Chron 6:15). **the high priest:** Shows that the hereditary line of Israel's high priests remained unbroken and intact despite the Babylonian Exile. Ultimately, Joshua is a descendant of Aaron and his grandson Phinehas (1 Chron 6:1-15), with whom the Lord made a covenant of perpetual priesthood (Num 25:10-13). The joint leadership of Zerubbabel (civil) and Joshua (religious) in rebuilding the Temple is celebrated in Sir 49:11-12.

1:2 the LORD of hosts: A title for the Lord as the commander of the heavenly armies of angels (Josh 5:13-14) as well as the military forces of Israel (1 Sam 17:45). Haggai uses it 14 times in this short book. **not yet:** An excuse for postponing the reconstruction of the Jerusalem Temple. This is the central problem addressed by Haggai: no work has been done since the foundations of the sanctuary were laid in 536 B.C., some 16 years earlier (Ezra 3:8-11), thanks to local opposition from Samaritans and others (Ezra 4:1-24). Now the time has come to finish the work (1:8). See introduction: *Historical Background*.

1:4 your paneled houses: The Judeans have invested time, energy, and resources into building comfortable homes for themselves while the Lord's house sits "in ruins" (1:9). Haggai rebukes them for allowing selfish and material concerns to take priority over spiritual concerns. Also, he may allude to Solomon's Temple, which had wood paneling on its interior floor and walls (1 Kings 6:15).

1:5 how you have fared: An invitation to reflect on the causes of current struggles. The people fail to realize that meager harvests, limited food and clothing, and economic strain are the result of neglecting the Temple's reconstruction. In this case, the adversity suffered by the community stems from their spiritual indifference. They fail to see that the Lord's Temple is a source of blessing for his people (cf. 1 Kings 8:27-53).

1:8 bring wood: For timber beams to be laid in the walls (Ezra 5:8). **that I may take pleasure:** The Lord tells his people what they must do to turn his displeasure into delight. **may appear in my glory:** Or "may be glorified". The Lord is glorified when his will is accomplished. This will be shown concretely when the divine glory (= the luminous cloud of God's presence) returns to inhabit the Second Temple (Ezek 43:1-5) after departing from the Solomonic Temple (Ezek 11:23).

1:11 drought: A form of divine discipline for unfaithfulness (Deut 28:22). Like all chastisements from above, this one is an expression of the Lord's fatherly love that aims at correction of misbehavior and a recommitment to following the covenant (Prov 3:11-12; Heb 12:5-11).

Haggai (Aggeus) is the first of the postexilic prophets and differs considerably from the earlier. No longer do we read threats of punishment for sin or words of consolation. The people need to be helped in their work of restoration and encouraged to persevere. Haggai first insists that the temple must be built before they think of anything else. This is to be the focal point of their life, as it was in the past, and they cannot hope for any prosperity without it. In spite of its humble appearance, the Spirit of God will rest upon it and the "latter splendor of this house shall be greater than the former, says the LORD of hosts" (2:9).

The People Obey

12 Then Zerub′babel the son of She-al′ti-el, and Joshua the son of Jehoz′adak, the high priest, with all the remnant of the people, obeyed the voice of the LORD their God, and the words of Hag′gai the prophet, as the LORD their God had sent him; and the people feared before the LORD. [13]Then Hag′gai, the messenger of the LORD, spoke to the people with the LORD's message, "I am with you, says the LORD." [14]And the LORD stirred up the spirit of Zerub′babel the son of She-al′ti-el, governor of Judah, and the spirit of Joshua the son of Jehoz′adak, the high priest, and the spirit of all the remnant of the people; and they came and worked on the house of the LORD of hosts, their God, [15]on the twenty-fourth day of the month, in the sixth month.

The Splendor of the Temple

2 In the second year of Dari′us the king, [1]in the seventh month, on the twenty-first day of the month, the word of the LORD came by Hag′gai the prophet, [2]"Speak now to Zerub′babel the son of She-al′ti-el, governor of Judah, and to Joshua the son of Jehoz′adak, the high priest, and to all the remnant of the people, and say, [3]'Who is left among you that saw this house in its former glory? How do you see it now? Is it not in your sight as nothing? [4]Yet now take courage, O Zerub′babel, says the LORD; take courage, O Joshua, son of Jehoz′adak, the high priest; take courage, all you people of the land, says the LORD; work, for I am with you, says the LORD of hosts, [5]according to the promise that I made you when you came out of Egypt. My Spirit abides among you; fear not. [6]For thus says the LORD of hosts: Once again, in a little while, I will shake the heavens and the earth and the sea and the dry land; [7]and I will shake all nations, so that the treasures of all nations shall come in, and I will fill this house with splendor, says the LORD of hosts. [8]The silver is mine, and the gold is mine, says the LORD of hosts. [9]The latter splendor of this house shall be greater than the former, says the LORD of hosts; and in this place I will give prosperity, says the LORD of hosts.'"

2:6: Heb 12:26.

1:12 remnant of the people: Either the small community in Judah that returned from exile in Babylon or possibly the faithful Jews among them. See word study: *Remnant* at Zeph 2:7. **obeyed:** By restarting the building project, which is evidence of repentance. **feared:** Fear of the Lord is a holy reverence that seeks to honor God by obedience and to avoid offending him by sin (Ex 20:20; Deut 13:4; Job 1:1).

1:13 I am with you: A promise of divine help (2:4). These words of reassurance are often spoken when God's people are faced with a difficult mission and need his sustaining grace (Gen 28:15; Jer 1:8, 19; Mt 28:19–20; Acts 18:9–10).

1:14 the LORD stirred up: A divine action that moves people to accomplish God's purposes (2 Chron 21:16; Ezra 1:1; Is 41:25; Jer 51:11).

1:15 twenty-fourth day: The people's response is dated September 21, 520 B.C., twenty-three days after Haggai delivered his first message (1:1). Presumably, this time was spent collecting materials, recruiting laborers, and gathering in the fall harvest.

2:1–9 Haggai's second prophetic address, dated October 17, 520 B.C.

2:1 Darius: See note on 1:1. **seventh month:** Known in postexilic times as Tishri. **twenty-first day:** The seventh day of the annual Feast of Booths/Tabernacles (Lev 23:33–43).

2:2 remnant: See note on 1:12.

2:3 Who is left: The Solomonic Temple was destroyed 66 years earlier in 586 B.C. Only the elderly would have memories of its grandeur. For those who did, the Second Temple was a painful disappointment in comparison (Ezra 3:12–13). Haggai thus offers words of encouragement in 2:4–5.

2:4 take courage: Or "be strong". David used these words to encourage Solomon to build the first Temple (1 Chron 22:13; 28:20). **Zerubbabel ... Joshua:** See note on 1:1. **people of the land:** An expression used in different ways at different times. In the preexilic period, it designates a class of influential citizens in Judah who supported the ruling house of David (2 Kings 11:14; 21:24; 23:30). In the postexilic period, it sometimes refers to foreign populations, distinct from the Jewish community, who occupied the land of Israel during the Babylonian Exile (Ezra 4:4; 9:1; 10:2). Here it seems to mean the people of Judah.

2:5–9 Haggai prophesies a world-shaking event that will draw all nations to the Lord's Temple with gifts of silver and gold. When this day comes, the Second Temple, small and unimpressive, will give way to one that is far more glorious and worthy of the divine presence. • These future events are patterned on the events of the Exodus, e.g., the Israelites who escaped bondage assembled at Mt. Sinai, which the Lord shook with a mighty earthquake (Ex 19:18; Ps 68:8); they built a Tabernacle for the Lord (Ex 25–30) with the silver and gold they had gotten from the Egyptians (Ex 12:35–36); its architects were endowed with skills of craftsmanship by the same Spirit (Ex 31:1–11) who abides in postexilic Judah (2:5).

2:5 the promise: The Lord's pledge to Moses that his "presence" would go with the Israelites into the Promised Land (Ex 33:14).

2:6 Once again ... I will shake: This passage is quoted in Heb 12:26–27 to draw a contrast between the shaking of earth, which removes things that are temporary, and the shaking of heaven, which leaves only the eternal kingdom of Christ standing. • Haggai offers a clear prophecy of Christ and the Church, one that is partly fulfilled now but will come to completion at the end of time. The Lord shook the heavens when the angels and the star bore witness to Christ's birth; he shook the earth by the miracle of the virgin birth; and he shook the sea and land when Christ was proclaimed throughout the world. We observe all nations being shaken when they come to faith in Christ (St. Augustine, *City of God* 18, 35).

2:7 the treasures: For a similar vision of Gentiles coming to Zion with their wealth, see Is 60:3–14.

2:9 The latter splendor: On a material level, the Second Temple was funded in part by tribute money from the Persian royal treasury (Ezra 6:8–10) and then enlarged and adorned by Herod the Great beginning ca. 19 B.C. • From the perspective of the NT, the Temple that exceeds in glory every previous sanctuary is the Temple of Christ's risen body (Jn 2:21), into which believers from all the nations are incorporated as living stones indwelt by the Spirit (Eph 2:11–21; 1 Pet 2:4–5). See essay: *Theology of the Temple* at 2 Chron 5. **prosperity:** The Hebrew is *shālôm*. See word study: *Peace* at Nahum 1:15.

A Rebuke and a Promise

10 On the twenty-fourth day of the ninth month, in the second year of Dari′us, the word of the LORD came by Hag′gai the prophet, [11]"Thus says the LORD of hosts: Ask the priests to decide this question, [12]'If one carries holy flesh in the skirt of his garment, and touches with his skirt bread, or pottage, or wine, or oil, or any kind of food, does it become holy?'" The priests answered, "No." [13]Then said Hag′gai, "If one who is unclean by contact with a dead body touches any of these, does it become unclean?" The priests answered, "It does become unclean." [14]Then Hag′gai said, "So is it with this people, and with this nation before me, says the LORD; and so with every work of their hands; and what they offer there is unclean. [15]Please now, consider what will come to pass from this day onward. Before a stone was placed upon a stone in the temple of the LORD, [16]how did you fare?[a] When one came to a heap of twenty measures, there were but ten; when one came to the winevat to draw fifty measures, there were but twenty. [17]I struck you and all the products of your toil with blight and mildew and hail; yet you did not return to me, says the LORD. [18]Consider from this day onward, from the twenty-fourth day of the ninth month. Since the day that the foundation of the LORD temple was laid, consider: [19]Is the seed yet in the barn? Do the vine, the fig tree, the pomegranate, and the olive tree still yield nothing? From this day on I will bless you."

God's Promise to Zerubbabel

20 The word of the LORD came a second time to Hag′gai on the twenty-fourth day of the month, [21]"Speak to Zerub′babel, governor of Judah, saying, I am about to shake the heavens and the earth, [22]and to overthrow the throne of kingdoms; I am about to destroy the strength of the kingdoms of the nations, and overthrow the chariots and their riders; and the horses and their riders shall go down, every one by the sword of his fellow. [23]On that day, says the LORD of hosts, I will take you, O Zerub′babel my servant, the son of She-al′ti-el, says the LORD, and make you like a signet ring; for I have chosen you, says the LORD of hosts."

2:10–19 Haggai's third prophetic address, dated December 18, 520 B.C.

2:10 the ninth month: Known in postexilic times as Kislev. **Darius:** See note on 1:1.

2:11 the priests: In charge of making legal distinctions between what is holy, clean, and unclean (Lev 10:10). They teach, according to the following examples, that ordinary food is not made holy by contact with a garment that touched consecrated meat; however, food is made unclean by contact with a person who is defiled for touching a corpse. Unfortunately, the priests failed to realize that worship in Jerusalem was unacceptable to God so long as rebuilding his Temple was neglected and the problem of spiritual apathy was not addressed. Because the people of Judah were defiled, their works and offerings became "unclean" as well (2:14).

2:12 holy flesh: Whatever touches the meat of a sin offering is made holy (Lev 6:27).

2:13 contact with a dead body: Contact with a human corpse, bone, or grave causes seven days of uncleanness (Num 19:11–22).

2:15 from this day onward: Resuming construction on the Temple in 1:14 was an act of obedience that secured the Lord's blessing of abundant harvests (2:19).

2:16 how did you fare: Repeats the invitation to self-reflection given several months earlier (1:5).

2:17 blight and mildew: Haggai may be echoing the words of Amos 4:9. **yet you did not return:** Divine chastisement promotes repentance. See note on 1:11.

2:18 the foundation: The Temple foundation was laid 16 years earlier in 536 B.C. (Ezra 3:10–13).

2:20–23 Haggai's fourth prophetic address, dated December 18, 520 B.C. Unlike the first three, this one is a private message for Zerubbabel. It promises an apocalyptic upheaval in which the Lord shakes heaven and earth, shatters world powers and their armies, and establishes his own reign as supreme (as in Dan 2:31–45). Zerubbabel, from the royal line of David, is chosen for a special role in this divine plan. Although he never becomes king himself, God's favor toward him signifies his commitment to preserve the Davidic line of kings after the Exile. • Zerubbabel thus appears in the Matthean genealogy of Jesus, which verifies his messianic identity by linking him to the royal line of David that passes through "Shealtiel" and "Zerubbabel" (Mt 1:12).

2:20 twenty-fourth day: The same day Haggai's message in 2:10–19 was received.

2:21 Zerubbabel, governor: See note on 1:1.

2:22 chariots ... horses ... riders: Recalls the Lord's triumph over the armies of Pharaoh at the time of the Exodus (Ex 14:23–28; 15:1–5).

2:23 a signet ring: A ring bearing royal insignia that was pressed into a clay or wax seal. The impression was equivalent to the king's signature, even when used by a lesser official authorized to act on the king's behalf. Here it signifies the right to rule on David's throne. **chosen:** The language of divine election. See word study: *Chose* at Ps 78:68. • Haggai's message to Zerubbabel echoes the words of Jeremiah's curse against Zerubbabel's grandfather King Jehoiachim/Coniah (Jer 22:24–30). Jehoiachim was likened to a "signet ring" that the Lord would tear off his hand—a sign of judgment that the king would be exiled to Babylon and none of his sons in exile would sit on David's throne after him. Here the sign of the ring is reversed, with Zerubbabel, grandson of Jehoiachim, being not rejected but chosen as the Lord's "signet ring" to keep the Davidic line alive and to restore hope that one of David's heirs (= the Messiah) will rule again.

---

[a] Gk: Heb *since they were.*

STUDY QUESTIONS
Haggai

Chapter 1

For understanding
1. **1:2.** What does the title "LORD of hosts" mean as a title for the Lord? How often does Haggai use it in this short book? What excuse do people make that the right time has not yet come? What is the central problem addressed by Haggai? What time has now come?
2. **1:4.** What were Judeans investing time, energy, and resources in doing? For what does Haggai rebuke them? To what may he also be alluding?
3. **1:12.** Who are the remnant of the people? How will this remnant give evidence of their repentance? What does fear of the Lord mean?
4. **1:15.** When is the people's response dated? How was this time presumably spent?

For application
1. **1:2.** Have you delayed building in your heart—or even your family home—a house for the Lord? If you have delayed, when will a more opportune time come? What does building that house entail for you?
2. **1:5–6.** What efforts have you made to improve your spiritual life, even if you seem to have few positive results to show for it? What have you considered to be potential obstacles? In what ways have you avoided surrendering yourself to Jesus?
3. **1:9.** If the Lord were to charge you with paying more attention to your own needs than to him, to what in your conduct could he point? What excuses would you make for yourself? If you accepted the correction, what changes do you think you would have to make?
4. **1:13.** Look up passages in Scripture where an emissary of the Lord announces that the Lord is with a person or group (e.g., Judg 6:12; Lk 1:28). Why is this reassurance being given? When the celebrant at the liturgy says "the Lord be with you", what does that statement usually preface? Why is the Lord's presence in a task so important?

Chapter 2

For understanding
1. **2:4.** How did David encourage Solomon to build the first Temple? How is the expression "people of the land" used in preexilic times? In the postexilic period? What does it seem to mean here?
2. **2:5–9.** About what does Haggai prophesy? When this day comes, to what will the Second Temple, small and unimpressive, give way? On what events are these future events patterned?
3. **2:20–23.** How is Haggai's fourth prophetic address, dated December 18, 520 B.C., unlike the first three? What does it promise? For what is Zerubbabel, from the royal line of David, chosen? Although he never becomes king himself, what does God's favor toward him signify? What does Zerubbabel's appearance in the Matthean genealogy of Jesus verify about Jesus' identity?
4. **2:23.** For what is a signet ring used? To what was its impression equivalent? What does it signify here? What words of Jeremiah does Haggai's message to Zerubbabel echo? How was Jehoiachim likened to a "signet ring"? How is the sign of the ring reversed here?

For application
1. **2:3.** What is your opinion of the state of the Church today? How do you think it compares with previous ages? How do the problems you perceive in the Church affect your faith?
2. **2:5–9.** What activity of the Holy Spirit do you see going on in the Church now? Where does the Church seem to be thriving? What renewal movements are making a significant impact? How are you called to participate in Church renewal?
3. **2:11–14.** The note for v. 11 refers to spiritual apathy, or lack of concern for spiritual things. According to the *Catechism*, how do acedia, or spiritual sloth, and related problems impede growth in charity (CCC 2094)? How does acedia interfere with prayer (CCC 2733)? Has this problem affected your spiritual development? If so, in what ways?
4. **2:15–19.** How would you describe your vocation in life? Was there ever a time when you resisted it? If so, how happy were you? How has obedience to your vocation resulted in a blessing?

INTRODUCTION TO ZECHARIAH

Author and Date The superscription traces the oracles of the book to "Zechariah the son of Berechiah, son of Iddo, the prophet" (1:1). It is generally thought that the prophet's grandfather Iddo was one of the leading priests who returned to Judah from Babylon with Zerubbabel the governor and Joshua the high priest (Neh 12:4, 16). This would make Zechariah a descendant of Aaron and a member of the tribe of Levi. Little else is known about him, except that he was a younger contemporary of the prophet Haggai (Ezra 5:1; 6:14).

Modern scholarship broadly accepts that chapters 1–8 come from Zechariah and can be dated to the years 520–518 B.C., as indicated by the historical notations in 1:1, 1:7, and 7:1. It is also the majority view, however, that chapters 9–14 are the oracles of one or more unnamed prophets who lived after the time of Zechariah. This judgment is based on striking dissimilarities between the book's two main parts. Chapters 1–8, for instance, attach calendar dates to the prophet's messages; they are written entirely in prose; they address the concerns of Zechariah's day; they name the leaders of the community in Judah; and they consist of visions, sermons, and short narratives. Chapters 9–14, by contrast, form a collection of undated revelations; they combine poetry with prose; they are said to reflect circumstances that postdate the lifetime of Zechariah; they identify no individuals by name; and they consist of symbolic apocalyptic messages. In view of these differences in style, genre, and presumed audience, many scholars attribute chapters 9–14 to an anonymous prophet conventionally called Second Zechariah. Others make a further distinction between Second Zechariah, whose work is identified with chapters 9–11, and Third Zechariah, another unnamed prophet who is said to have written chapters 12–14.

The distinctiveness of chapters 9–14 in comparison with chapters 1–8 is undeniable. It does not follow, however, that the Book of Zechariah is necessarily a composite work that stems from more than one author. The hypothesis of multiple authors is consistent with the differences noted above but is not demanded by them. Hence there continue to be scholars who argue that Zechariah is the work of a single author, alleging that differences between earlier and later chapters are capable of other explanations. For example, sorting prophetic messages into dated and undated collections, into distinct literary genres, and into material that addresses different historical situations—these could just as well be the signs of a work that follows a single author's logical plan of composition. Likewise, some surmise that the division of the book into two main parts reflects a chronological progression in Zechariah's career, so that chapters 1–8 record his earliest visions and oracles, while chapters 9–14 preserve apocalyptic revelations that he received later in life. Finally, crediting the book to a single author has the advantage of explaining why common themes are spread across the various parts of the book (e.g., Jerusalem as the spiritual center of the world, the cleansing in the covenant community, Gentile nations seeking the God of Israel, etc.).

Different views on the literary unity of the book inevitably lead to different views on when its final form appeared. Some scholars who regard Zechariah as the author of the entire book date its final form around 518 B.C., soon after the last date mentioned in the book (7:1); others, interpreting chapters 9–14 as prophetic messages that Zechariah received at a later time, date its final form near the end of the sixth century B.C. or even in the early decades of the fifth century B.C., sometimes as a late as 480 B.C. As for scholars who posit a Second and Third Zechariah, suggested dates vary widely. Some maintain that a handful of passages in chapters 9–14 may come from the preexilic period, but generally the final form of the book is dated either in the Persian period following the reconstruction of the Temple (after 515 B.C.) or during the Hellenistic period (after 332 B.C.). A few have dated the finished book as late as the Maccabean period (after 164 B.C.).

Title The book is named after Zechariah, mentioned in the opening verse. Its Hebrew form, *Zekharyāh*, means "the LORD has remembered" and was a popular name in biblical times, appearing more than two dozen times in the Bible. It appears in the Greek Septuagint in the title *Zacharias*, while this heading is expanded in the Latin Vulgate to *Zaccharias Propheta*, "Zechariah the Prophet". English titles for the book follow these ancient traditions.

Place in the Canon Zechariah has long been revered as a canonical book of Scripture. In the Jewish Bible, or Tanakh, it stands among the Latter Prophets in a sub-collection of writings known as "the Book of the Twelve". In Christian Bibles, these twelve books are called the Minor Prophets, not because they are less important than Isaiah, Jeremiah, Ezekiel, and Daniel, but because they are comparatively shorter. In the Hebrew Bible, Greek Septuagint, and Latin Vulgate, Zechariah stands before Malachi as the eleventh of the Minor Prophets, just as it does in English Bibles.

Structure Zechariah divides into two main parts, chapters 1–8 and 9–14, each of which has two primary subdivisions. **(1)** Following a short prologue (1:1–6), the prophet describes a series of night visions he received from the Lord (1:7—6:15). This is followed by an account of inquiry regarding the custom of fasting for Jerusalem and an announcement of the Lord's plan to restore Jerusalem (7:1—8:23). **(2)** The second half of the book consists of two prophetic collections, each marked by the heading "An Oracle" (9:1; 12:1). Chapters 9–11 are devoted to matters of leadership in the covenant community, exposing the problem of wicked shepherds and announcing the coming of a humble and righteous king. Chapters 12–14 look toward a future day when the nations will mount an assault on Jerusalem, who sinned by turning against one of its own, only to find that God will open a fountain of mercy for his people and come as the city's defender and King. See also *Outline*.

Historical Background The Book of Zechariah shares the same historical background as the Book of Haggai. Both are set in the early Persian period after an initial wave of Jewish exiles returned to Judah from Babylon. This was the result of Cyrus II of Persia seizing control of the Babylonian empire in 539 B.C. and giving permission in 538 B.C. for all foreign captives to return to their native lands (Ezra 1:2–4). Soon thousands of Judeans who had been living for decades in Babylon made the journey home to reestablish the covenant community in Judah. Many of the villages, farms, and homes in Judah had sat in ruins since the Babylonian conquest of 586 B.C., as did the city and Temple of Jerusalem. But under the strong leadership of Zerubbabel, the governor, and Joshua, the high priest, an initial effort was made to rebuild the Jerusalem Temple. The altar of sacrifice was restored in the fall of 537 B.C. (Ezra 3:1–7), and the foundation was laid in the spring of 536 B.C. (Ezra 3:8–11). Despite this promising start, local opposition and political turmoil brought the project to a standstill, and work on the Temple was halted for the next sixteen years (Ezra 4:1–24). Zechariah was called to speak for the Lord at the end of this long interruption. His task was to encourage the community in Judah to complete the work of rebuilding the sanctuary. Thanks in part to the ministry of Zechariah, construction was resumed in 520 and finished in 515 B.C. (Ezra 5:1–2; 6:15).

Message of the Prophet The Book of Zechariah is the longest of the Minor Prophets and arguably the most difficult to interpret. Much of its message is encrypted in dream-like visions, symbolic enactments, and apocalyptic scenes of judgment and renewal. It has been said that Zechariah is to the Old Testament what the Book of Revelation is to the New—a dramatic unveiling of God's plans for the future that seems to conceal as much as it reveals. This is no argument for avoiding the book, however, since the New Testament shows that Jesus and his disciples found much in the pages of Zechariah that points to the messianic kingdom of God.

The main themes and concerns of the book can be grouped under three headings:

(1) *The Lord's Covenant People.* The initial focus of the book is on the small community in Judah in the late sixth century B.C. This was the remnant that returned from exile in Babylon almost two decades before Zechariah received the word of the Lord. The prophet encouraged them to continue the work of rebuilding the Lord's Temple in Jerusalem (8:9), but he also urged them to repent of their sins and to rebuild their relationship with God (1:3–6). He assured them of the Lord's desire to show "compassion" (1:16) and to do "good" to them (8:15), yet he was equally emphatic that thieves and perjurers must be removed from Judah (5:1–4), along with every trace of idolatry and false prophecy (5:5–11; 13:2–3). More important than fasting in memory of Jerusalem's destruction in 586 B.C. was the need for God's people to show kindness and mercy to one another (7:4–14). If the struggling people of Judah would enjoy the Lord's blessings once again, they must earnestly commit themselves to speaking the truth and seeking justice for everyone (8:16–17).

Looking beyond the community in Judah, the prophet also reveals God's plan to restore the people of Israel who remained in exile at this time. This includes not only the Jews still living in Babylon (2:6–7) but also the dispersed tribes of northern Israel who never returned from the Assyrian Exile in the eighth century B.C. The Lord's interest in these "lost" tribes appears in several oracles that distinguish the people of Judah from the northern Israelites, variously called "Israel" (1:19), the "house of Israel" (8:13), the "house of Joseph" (10:6), and "Ephraim" (9:13; 10:7). God's plan of restoration embraces the whole People of God, for "all the tribes of Israel" belong to him (9:1). But even this expectation fails to capture the full extent of God's saving purposes. Beyond Judah and Israel lies the world of Gentile nations, and these too are the beneficiaries of his future blessings. Following Zechariah's third vision, the Lord informs the prophet that "many nations shall join themselves to the LORD … and shall be my people" (2:11). This means that Gentiles who turn from idols to serve the Lord will become members of his covenant people. Along the same lines, the prophet declares that "strong nations shall come to seek the LORD of hosts in Jerusalem" (8:22) because they have heard that God is with the people of Judah (8:23). The final vision of the book likewise foresees "all the nations" worshiping the Lord and celebrating his feasts (14:16). The book thus traces the expansion of the Lord's covenant community from a small remnant in postexilic Judah to a worldwide assembly of all Israel and all nations.

(2) *The Lord's City and Temple.* If the book foresees a restoration of Judah, Israel, and the Gentiles, it ties all these events to Jerusalem and its sanctuary. Zion is the center of gravity for every expectation in the book. Initially the prophet's concern is with the beleaguered capital in sixth-century Judah. But this is only a starting point because much of what he says about Jerusalem is projected into the future. The Lord is zealous to restore Zion (1:14–17) and to transform it into a "faithful city" (8:3), a city with a fountain that cleanses his people from sin (13:1). He is calling Zion's captives in exile to return to it (2:6–7) so that it can grow and flourish (2:4–7; 8:7–8) and its mourning can be turned into joy once again (8:19). The Lord promises to be its wall of defense against enemies (2:5; 9:8). But, for reasons not explained in the book, the prophet also foresees Jerusalem falling to besieging armies once again (14:2). It is only after this eschatological defeat of the city, when the Lord comes to bring its attackers to judgment (14:3–5), that the kingdom of God is firmly established and his promise to create a new and glorious Jerusalem is fully realized (14:6–21).

A similar narrative develops around the Lord's Temple. God's desire is to "dwell" again in the holy city (2:10) and to be its "glory" (2:5). For this reason, he urges the postexilic community to finish the task of rebuilding the Temple (8:9), assuring the people that Zerubbabel the provincial governor will complete the reconstruction by the power of the Spirit (4:6–10; cf. 1:16). The international "rest" that characterizes the Persian Empire at this time makes it the ideal time for sanctuary construction to progress toward this end (1:11). But, again for reasons not explained in the book, Zechariah also looks beyond the horizons of his own day to the building of a future Temple. This will be the work of a royal and eschatological figure, named the Branch, "who shall build the temple of the Lord" in the coming days of his kingship (6:12–13). The prophet does not clarify how this house of worship to be raised by the Davidic Messiah relates to the Second Temple in postexilic Judah. He only hints that this will be the place where "all the nations" come as pilgrims to worship the divine King and to celebrate his religious feasts (14:16).

(3) *The Lord's King and Kingdom.* Although Zechariah was written after the disappearance of the monarchy in Judah, the book is marked by royal expectations for the future. A day will come, says the prophet, when kingship will be reborn among God's people. This is made evident first in the words and actions surrounding Joshua, the high priest, who is told that the Lord will send his servant "the Branch" (3:8), which is a title for the Davidic Messiah drawn from the prophet Jeremiah (Jer 23:5; 33:15). Zechariah learns that this figure, like King Solomon of old, will "build the temple of the Lord" (6:12) and will wear a royal crown when

he rules "upon his throne" (6:13). Anticipation of a future king in the likeness of Solomon is even more explicit in a later oracle, where the prophet sees the arrival of Israel's "king" in Jerusalem—a humble and peaceful figure who will ride into the city on a donkey (9:9), even though he is a mighty world ruler whose dominion stretches to "the ends of the earth" (9:10). No timetable is given for his arrival, but it likely corresponds to the day when the Lord brings cleansing and a new beginning to "the house of David" (13:1).

In addition to Davidic kingship, Zechariah is also concerned with divine kingship. At various places in the book, the Lord appears as the Creator (12:1), Defender (2:5), and Savior of his people (8:7). He brings natural blessings such as prosperity (1:17) and rain (10:1) as well as spiritual blessings such as the words spoken through the prophets (7:12) and the removal of sin (3:9; 13:1). But the capstone is set in the final chapter of the book, which paints a picture of the kingdom of God. This is the vision of a "day of the Lord" (14:1), when the Almighty becomes "king over all the earth" (14:9) in an exalted Jerusalem (14:10). At this highpoint in salvation history, not only Israel but "all the nations" will pay him homage as the divine "King" enthroned in his Temple (14:16).

Christian Perspective Zechariah's prophecies deeply impacted Christian thinking about messianic times. This is clear already in the Passion narratives of the Gospels, where Jesus' triumphal entry into Jerusalem on a donkey fulfills the expectation of Israel's Davidic Messiah coming to the city as a peaceful king (9:9; Mt 21:4–5; Jn 12:14–15). Likewise, Judas' betrayal of Jesus for thirty pieces of silver replicates how the prophet himself was called to be a good shepherd to God's people, only to be rejected and valued at thirty shekels of silver, a paltry sum that was cast into the Temple (11:4–14; Mt 26:15; 27:3–5). Jesus himself notes that God's plan to "[s]trike the shepherd, that the sheep may be scattered" is realized in his own life when his arrest in Gethsemane causes his disciples to flee in fear (13:7; Mt 26:31; Mk 14:27). An additional link with Zechariah's oracles is discerned in the events of the Crucifixion, where Jesus' body is pierced with nails and a Roman spear, signaling that Jerusalem will one day mourn over "him whom they have pierced" (12:10; Jn 19:34; Rev 1:7). All of this culminates in the Book of Revelation and its vision of the kingdom and city of God. This concluding book of the NT draws heavily on imagery from Zechariah when it describes God's judgments on the earth (e.g., compare 1:7–17 and 6:1–8 with Rev 6:1–8) and especially when it describes the new Jerusalem as a heavenly city where the Lord dwells with his people in perpetual light and perfect holiness (compare 14:1–11 and Rev 21–22).

OUTLINE OF ZECHARIAH

1. Visions and Messages of Restoration (chaps. 1–8)
    A. Symbolic Visions of the Night (1:1—6:15)
        1. Prologue (1:1–6)
        2. The Four Horsemen (1:7–17)
        3. The Four Horns (1:18–21)
        4. The Measuring Line (2:1–13)
        5. Joshua the High Priest (3:1–10)
        6. The Golden Lampstand and Olive Trees (4:1–14)
        7. The Flying Scroll of Judgment (5:1–4)
        8. The Woman in the Basket (5:5–11)
        9. The Four Chariots (6:1–8)
      10. Epilogue (6:9–15)
    B. Response to an Inquiry about Fasting (7:1—8:23)
        1. Hypocrisy and True Covenant Commitment (7:1–14)
        2. Israel and Judah's Restoration from Exile (8:1–17)
        3. The Fasts Will Become Feasts (8:18–19)
        4. Gentiles Will Seek the Lord in Jerusalem (8:20–23)

2. Visions and Messages of Judgment and the Kingdom to Come (chaps. 9–14)
    A. The First Oracle: Shepherds Good and Bad (9:1—11:17)
        1. The Lord's Victorious March (9:1–8)
        2. The Humble Davidic King and His Kingdom (9:9–10)
        3. Salvation for Israel and Judgment for Enemies (9:11—11:3)
        4. The Good and Worthless Shepherds (11:4–17)
    B. The Second Oracle: Jerusalem Assaulted, Cleansed, and Exalted (12:1—14:21)
        1. The Day of Deliverance and Cleansing (12:1—13:6)
        2. Purification of the Remnant (13:7–9)
        3. Jerusalem and the Kingdom of God (14:1–21)

THE BOOK OF
ZECHARIAH

Israel Urged to Repent

1 In the eighth month, in the second year of Dari'us, the word of the LORD came to Zechari'ah the son of Berechi'ah, son of Iddo, the prophet, saying, ²"The LORD was very angry with your fathers. ³Therefore say to them, Thus says the LORD of hosts: Return to me, says the LORD of hosts, and I will return to you, says the LORD of hosts. ⁴Be not like your fathers, to whom the former prophets cried out, 'Thus says the LORD of hosts, Return from your evil ways and from your evil deeds.' But they did not hear or heed me, says the LORD. ⁵Your fathers, where are they? And the prophets, do they live for ever? ⁶But my words and my statutes, which I commanded my servants the prophets, did they not overtake your fathers? So they repented and said, As the LORD of hosts purposed to deal with us for our ways and deeds, so has he dealt with us."

First Vision: The Horsemen

7 On the twenty-fourth day of the eleventh month which is the month of Shebat', in the second year of Dari'us, the word of the LORD came to Zechari'ah the son of Berechi'ah, son of Iddo, the prophet; and Zechariah said, ⁸"I saw in the night, and behold, a man riding upon a red horse! He was standing

---

1:1-6 Zechariah opens with an appeal for repentance and renewal. For the prophet, this is the spiritual side of the effort needed to finish rebuilding the Jerusalem Temple. The people's relationship with God needs attention no less than God's house.

1:1 eighth month: Marshevan, which falls in October/November. Haggai began his ministry two months earlier (Hag 1:1), making the two prophets contemporaries (Ezra 5:1; 6:14). **second year:** 520 B.C. This is the first of three calendar dates in the book (also 1:7; 7:1). **Darius:** Darius I Hystaspes, king of Persia from 522 to 486 B.C. **the word of the LORD:** Prophetic revelation from God entrusted to a human messenger. See essay: *The Word of the Lord* at Hos 1. **Zechariah:** Translates "Yah(weh) has remembered" or "the LORD has remembered." More than two dozen individuals have this name in the Bible. **Berechiah:** Not otherwise known but also named as the father of Zechariah in Mt 23:35. **Iddo:** A priest who returned to Judah from Babylon around 538 B.C. (Neh 12:16). Zechariah was thus from a priestly family of the tribe of Levi. **the prophet:** Zechariah's title.

1:2 your fathers: Past generations who rebelled against the Mosaic covenant and brought the curses of conquest and exile upon Judah and Jerusalem in 586 B.C.

1:3 them: The people of Judah who returned from exile almost 20 years earlier. They are urged to learn from their ancestors' mistakes. **the LORD of hosts:** A title for the Lord as the commander of the heavenly armies of angels (Josh 5:13-14). **Return:** The language of repentance, which includes a turning away from sin and a restored commitment to the Lord. See word study: *Return* at Jer 3:1. **I will return to you:** I.e., with the blessings of a renewed relationship. • Free will and divine grace are simultaneously affirmed when God says, "Return to me, and I will return to you." The invitation to return to God belongs to our will, while his promise to return to us belongs to his grace. We should not fail to observe,

however, that our turning to God is itself his gift (St. Augustine, *On Grace and Free Will* 10). • The Council of Trent cited this passage to affirm that sinners who have turned away from God remain free to accept or reject the grace that God offers them to move toward repentance. At the same time, the council acknowledged that no one can be justified by free will apart from divine grace (*Decree on Justification*, Session 6, chap. 5).

1:4 the former prophets: The prophets from earlier times who called the people of Israel to repentance and obedience (Moses, Elijah, Amos, Hosea, Isaiah, Micah, Jeremiah, et al.).

1:6 my words and my statutes: The commandments of the Mosaic covenant (Deut 4:1-2; 17:19; 27:8, 10). It was the curses of this broken covenant that "overtook" the rebellious generations of the past (Deut 28:15-68). The word of God stands firm and remains effective even after the prophets who delivered it to Israel have died (Is 40:8). **they repented:** The response of Zechariah's hearers (the same people identified as "them" in 1:3). **so has he dealt with us:** An acknowledgment that the Lord does not make idle threats but justly and faithfully enforces his covenants.

1:7-6:8 Zechariah receives eight visions from the Lord. These come "in the night" (1:8) and have the surreal quality of symbolic dreams. Each vision features an angel who dialogues with the prophet and interprets the meaning of what he sees. Collectively, the visions announce **(1)** that the Lord has authority over the whole earth, **(2)** that he plans to purge Judah and Jerusalem of sin and restore them to prosperity, and **(3)** that his anger against Judah and Jerusalem in the past (1:2) is now turned against their enemies (1:15). For other visions given to God's prophets, see Is 6:1-13; Ezek 1:1-28; Dan 7:1-28; Amos 7-9; Rev 1:10-20.

1:7-17 The first vision: Zechariah sees four horsemen who patrol the earth on colored horses and now report that the world is "at rest" (1:11). The message: the time is ripe for completing the reconstruction of the Temple (1:16), which in turn will bring blessings to Judah (1:17). For parallels between Zechariah's first and last visions, see note on 6:1-8.

1:7 twenty-fourth day: February 15, 519 B.C., more than two months after Zechariah received the initial message in 1:1-6. This appears to be the date when all the visions in chaps. 1-6 were received. **Darius ... Zechariah ... Iddo:** See note on 1:1.

1:8 a man: Identified in 1:11 as "the angel of the LORD". He is the leader among the four horsemen and the one who beseeches divine mercy in 1:12. The other three riders are presumably angels as well. See word study: *Angel of the LORD* at Gen 16:7. **standing:** He was mounted on a horse that was standing still rather than trotting or galloping. **glen:** Or "ravine". **sorrel:** Reddish brown.

Zechariah (Zacharias) prophesied at the same time as Haggai, about 520 B.C. and, like him, exhorted the people to press on with the building of the temple, but he goes on to develop the plans for the national restoration. He speaks in terms of a Messianic era in which the priesthood is supreme but the royal prerogatives are possessed by "the Branch" (6:12), a Messianic term for Zerubbabel. Chapters 1–8 relate a series of visions and are apocalyptic in tone. The second part (chapters 9–14) is quite different, and consists of a collection of prophecies dating from the fourth century and edited later during the Greek period. These are chiefly noteworthy for the Messianic passages in them, especially 9:9, fulfilled on Palm Sunday, and 12:10: "when they look on him whom they have pierced, they shall mourn."

among the myrtle trees in the glen; and behind him were red, sorrel, and white horses. ⁹Then I said, 'What are these, my lord?' The angel who talked with me said to me, 'I will show you what they are.' ¹⁰So the man who was standing among the myrtle trees answered, 'These are they whom the LORD has sent to patrol the earth.' ¹¹And they answered the angel of the LORD who was standing among the myrtle trees, 'We have patrolled the earth, and behold, all the earth remains at rest.' ¹²Then the angel of the LORD said, 'O LORD of hosts, how long will you have no mercy on Jerusalem and the cities of Judah, against which you have had indignation these seventy years?' ¹³And the LORD answered gracious and comforting words to the angel who talked with me. ¹⁴So the angel who talked with me said to me, 'Cry out, Thus says the LORD of hosts: I am exceedingly jealous for Jerusalem and for Zion. ¹⁵And I am very angry with the nations that are at ease; for while I was only a little angry they

furthered the disaster. ¹⁶Therefore, thus says the LORD, I have returned to Jerusalem with compassion; my house shall be built in it, says the LORD of hosts, and the measuring line shall be stretched out over Jerusalem. ¹⁷Cry again, Thus says the LORD of hosts: My cities shall again overflow with prosperity, and the LORD will again comfort Zion and again choose Jerusalem.'"

Second Vision: Four Horns and Four Smiths

18ªAnd I lifted my eyes and saw, and behold, four horns! ¹⁹And I said to the angel who talked with me, "What are these?" And he answered me, "These are the horns which have scattered Judah, Israel, and Jerusalem." ²⁰Then the LORD showed me four smiths. ²¹And I said, "What are these coming to do?" He answered, "These are the horns which scattered Judah, so that no man raised his head; and these have come to terrify them, to cast down

---

1:9 The angel who talked with me: The heavenly messenger who interprets the visions for Zechariah (1:9, 19; 2:3; 4:1, 5; 5:5, 10; 6:4–5).

1:11 at rest: Peacetime is the ideal time for building the Lord's Temple (Deut 12:10–11; 2 Sam 7:1–5).

1:12 seventy years: A round number that approximates the time between the Babylonian conquest of Judah in 586 B.C. and the date of Zechariah's vision in 519 B.C. During this period, the city and Temple of Jerusalem were either lying in ruins or awaiting their full restoration. The seventy years of Zechariah's vision overlap the "seventy years" of Judah's subjugation to Babylon that Jeremiah prophesied, but the two are not identical. See note on Jer 25:11.

1:14 exceedingly jealous: See note on 8:2.

1:15 the nations: The many peoples who made up the vast Persian Empire at this time. **furthered the disaster:** Judah's conquerors made the suffering of the covenant people worse than God had intended (Is 47:5–7; Jer 50:29; 51:24).

1:16 compassion: For the Hebrew term, see word study: *Compassion* at Ps 145:8. **my house:** The Temple in Jerusalem. **shall be built:** Reconstruction was completed in 515 B.C., four years after this vision (Ezra 6:14–15). **measuring line:** A cord or rope used by surveyors for construction projects (2:1).

1:17 comfort: Divine consolation that follows a time of calamity (Is 40:1–2). **again choose:** The Lord will reaffirm his election of Zion as his dwelling place (2 Chron 6:6; Ps 78:68; 132:13).

1:18–21 The second vision: Zechariah sees four horns toppled by four smiths. This signifies the Lord's judgment on the world powers (1:21) who conquered and exiled his people over the centuries (1:19; Hag 2:21–22). The Assyrians and Babylonians are foremost in mind, but smaller states who collaborated in the overthrow of Judah may be meant as well (e.g., Syria, Moab, Ammon, Edom, Philistia, 2 Kings 24:2; Ezek 25:1–17; Obad 10–14). Horns are symbols of strength in the Bible (Deut 33:17; Ps 75:10), and the number four, indicating the four cardinal directions, signifies the wider world beyond Israel (2:6; Is 11:12).

1:19 the angel who talked: See note on 1:9. **scattered:** The language of exile (10:9; Lev 26:33). **Judah:** The Southern Kingdom of Judah, carried into captivity by the Babylonians in the sixth century B.C. (2 Kings 24:10–16; 25:11). **Israel:** The Northern Kingdom of Israel, carried into captivity by the Assyrians in the eighth century B.C. (2 Kings 15:29; 17:5–6; 1 Chron 5:26).

1:20 smiths: Or "craftsmen". They are angels who bring the Lord's judgment on the enemies of his people, perhaps by stirring up other conquering nations against them (cf. 2 Sam 24:16; Ps 78:49; Rev 8:7–9:19).

ªCh 2:1 in Heb.

Zechariah's Night Visions		
Sequence	*Verses*	*Description*
Vision 1	1:7–17	Four horsemen on colored horses patrol the earth and find it at peace.
Vision 2	1:18–21	Four horns that scattered Judah are thrown down by four smiths.
Vision 3	2:1–5	A measuring line to rebuild the wall of Jerusalem will not be necessary.
Vision 4	3:1–10	The high priest is disrobed of iniquity and reclothed in a clean raiment.
Vision 5	4:1–14	A golden lampstand between two olive trees supply its oil.
Vision 6	5:1–4	A giant flying scroll brings judgment on the land of Judah.
Vision 7	5:5–11	A woman in a lidded ephah is flown back to Babylon.
Vision 8	6:1–8	Four chariots with colored horses subdue nations north and south.

the horns of the nations who lifted up their horns against the land of Judah to scatter it."

Third Vision: The Man with a Measuring Line

2 ᵇAnd I lifted my eyes and saw, and behold, a man with a measuring line in his hand! ²Then I said, "Where are you going?" And he said to me, "To measure Jerusalem, to see what is its breadth and what is its length." ³And behold, the angel who talked with me came forward, and another angel came forward to meet him, ⁴and said to him, "Run, say to that young man, 'Jerusalem shall be inhabited as villages without walls, because of the multitude of men and cattle in it. ⁵For I will be to her a wall of fire round about, says the LORD, and I will be the glory within her.'"

6 Ho! ho! Flee from the land of the north, says the LORD; for I have spread you abroad as the four winds of the heavens, says the LORD, ⁷Ho! Escape to Zion, you who dwell with the daughter of Babylon. ⁸For thus said the LORD of hosts, after his glory sent me to the nations who plundered you, for he who touches you touches the apple of his eye: ⁹"Behold, I will shake my hand over them, and they shall become plunder for those who served them. Then you will know that the LORD of hosts has sent me. ¹⁰Sing and rejoice, O daughter of Zion; for behold, I come and I will dwell in the midst of you, says the LORD. ¹¹And many nations shall join themselves to the LORD in that day, and shall be my people; and I will dwell in the midst of you, and you shall know that the LORD of hosts has sent me to you. ¹²And the LORD will inherit Judah as his portion in the holy land, and will again choose Jerusalem."

13 Be silent, all flesh, before the LORD; for he has roused himself from his holy dwelling.

Fourth Vision: Joshua and Satan

3 Then he showed me Joshua the high priest standing before the angel of the LORD, and

---

2:13: Hab 2:20; Zeph 1:7.

2:1–5: The third vision: Zechariah sees a man who sets out to take measurements for the rebuilding of Jerusalem's outer wall. The prophet learns, however, that **(1)** God will make the city's population too numerous to contain within a wall; **(2)** he will defend the city by encircling it with the fire of his presence; and **(3)** his glory will again dwell within the city (2:10). The message: the new Jerusalem protected and indwelt by God will be teeming with life and secure from outside threats (cf. 8:3–6).

2:1 measuring line: A cord or rope used by surveyors for construction projects (1:16).

2:3 the angel who talked: See note on 1:9.

2:4 young man: The Hebrew term covers a range of ages from an adolescent boy to a young man in his twenties. This detail suggests that Zechariah was a younger contemporary of Haggai (Ezra 5:1), and that he may have lived into the early decades of the fifth century B.C. See introduction: *Author and Date*.

2:5 wall of fire: Reminiscent of the pillar of cloud and fire that protected Israel from attack at the time of the Exodus (Ex 13:21; 14:19–20). **the glory:** The luminous cloud of the Lord's presence in the sanctuary (Ex 40:34–35; 1 Kings 8:11).

2:6–13 An address to Judahites still living in Babylon. They are urged to flee the wicked city (2:6) and return home to Jerusalem (2:7), where the Lord will dwell again (2:10). The regathering of exiles to Zion will also be a time of conversion when Gentiles embrace the God of Israel and become full members of the covenant community (2:11).

2:6 Flee: A summons to depart from Babylon (cf. Is 48:20; Jer 50:8; 51:6). In Zechariah's day, a small community of exiles from Babylon had returned to live in Judah, but a larger number of Jews remained in Babylon. Some would choose to stay there permanently; others would return in the fifth century B.C. (e.g., Ezra 7–8). **land of the north:** The land of Babylon, whose armies invaded Israel from the north. See note on Jer 1:14. **the four winds of the heavens:** Indicates the broad extent of the Exile (Deut 30:4; cf. Jer 49:36).

2:7 Zion: The mountain height of Jerusalem. See note on 2 Sam 5:7. **the daughter of Babylon:** A poetic personification of the city (Ps 137:8; Is 47:1; Jer 50:42).

2:8 touches: I.e., with hostile intent. **the apple of his eye:** Refers to the pupil, the most sensitive part of the eye that is carefully protected from harm (Deut 32:10; Ps 17:8). What was promised to Abraham and Jacob's descendants in Gen 12:3 and 27:29 remains true for the covenant people in the prophet's day.

2:9 shake my hand: In order to strike a blow (Is 11:15) or signal an attack (Is 13:2).

2:10 Sing and rejoice, O daughter of Zion: Echoes the words of Zeph 3:14 in which Jerusalem is personified as a woman who is blessed and indwelt by the Lord's presence. See note on Zeph 3:14–17 and word study: *The Daughter of Zion* at Lam 1:6.

2:11 join themselves to the LORD: Implies a conversion from idolatry to the worship of the one true God (Jer 16:19–21; 1 Thess 1:9). **my people:** Gentiles will become members of God's covenant people (8:22–23). Prior to messianic times, only Israel was called the Lord's special people (Ex 19:5; Lev 26:12). The prophets, however, foresaw all nations becoming his people (Is 19:25) after streaming to Zion to seek the Lord (Is 2:2–3; 66:18–20; Jer 3:17; Mic 4:1–3; Zeph 3:8–9). This will fulfill God's oath to Abraham to bless "all the nations of the earth" (Gen 22:18). • Paul pictures the Gentiles entering the Lord's covenant as branches being grafted onto the olive tree of Israel and sharing in its spiritual blessings (Rom 11:17–24; 15:27). **you shall know:** The fulfillment of the prophecy will verify that Zechariah was truly the Lord's messenger (Deut 18:21–22).

2:12 again choose: See note on 1:17.

2:13 Be silent: An act of reverential awe and adoration (CCC 2143). Silence can also indicate a sense of dread at the Lord's coming judgment (Hab 2:20; Zeph 1:7). **his holy dwelling:** The Lord's heavenly Temple, from which he comes forth (Mic 1:2). This celestial sanctuary is the unseen counterpart to his dwelling in Jerusalem (Ps 11:4; Wis 9:8; Rev 11:19). See essay: *Theology of the Temple* at 2 Chron 5.

3:1–10 The fourth vision: Zechariah sees Joshua, the high priest, standing trial in the heavenly court. He is prosecuted by Satan (3:1) and defended by the angel of the Lord (3:3), who orders the removal of his filthy garments (3:4). The prophet then calls for his reclothing with ceremonial attire (3:4–5). The redressing of Joshua, as the high priest who represents his people before the Lord, reveals God's intention to remove guilt

---

ᵇ Ch 2:5 in Heb.

Satan standing at his right hand to accuse him. ²And the Lord said to Satan, "The Lord rebuke you, O Satan! The Lord who has chosen Jerusalem rebuke you! Is not this a brand plucked from the fire?" ³Now Joshua was standing before the angel, clothed with filthy garments. ⁴And the angel said to those who were standing before him, "Remove the filthy garments from him." And to him he said, "Behold, I have taken your iniquity away from you, and I will clothe you with rich apparel." ⁵And I said, "Let them put a clean turban on his head." So they put a clean turban on his head and clothed him with garments; and the angel of the Lord was standing by.

6 And the angel of the Lord enjoined Joshua, ⁷"Thus says the Lord of hosts: If you will walk in my ways and keep my charge, then you shall rule my house and have charge of my courts, and I will give you the right of access among those who are standing here. ⁸Hear now, O Joshua the high priest, you and your friends who sit before you, for they are men of good omen: behold, I will bring my servant the Branch. ⁹For behold, upon the stone which I have set before Joshua, upon a single stone with seven facets, I will engrave its inscription, says the Lord of hosts, and I will remove the guilt of this land in a single day. ¹⁰In that day, says the Lord of hosts, every one of you will invite his neighbor under his vine and under his fig tree."

Fifth Vision: The Lampstand and Olive Trees

4 And the angel who talked with me came again, and waked me, like a man that is wakened out

---

3:2: Jude 9. **3:8:** Is 4:2; Jer 23:5; 33:15; Zech 6:12. **3:10:** Mic 4:4.

---

from the land of Judah (3:9). Purification from the defilements of the past creates new opportunities for blessing in the future.

3:1 Joshua: The son of Jehozadak (Hag 1:1) and one of the leading priests of the first wave of exiles to return to Jerusalem from Babylon in 538 B.C. (Ezra 2:1-2; 3:2). His priestly line is traced through Zadok back to Aaron, Israel's first high priest (1 Chron 6:3-15). Early Christians often viewed Joshua as a type of Jesus, not least because, in the Greek Bible, the two names are identical (Gk., *Iēsous*). **the angel of the Lord:** Speaks on behalf of the Lord as his representative. See word study: *Angel of the Lord* at Gen 16:7. **Satan:** Or "the Adversary", a legal title for a prosecutor in court (Ps 109:6). The heavenly trial scene suggests that he, too, is an angel, only he appears, not as a servant of God's will, but as an antagonist who is rebuked in the name of the Lord for pressing the case against Joshua (3:2). Christian tradition identifies this figure as the devil, leader of the fallen angels (CCC 391-92, 2851). See word study: *Satan* at Job 1:6. **to accuse him:** I.e., of being unfit for priestly ministry due to his "iniquity" (3:4). • The Book of Revelation alludes to this vision when it describes the devil, or Satan, as "the accuser" who is expelled from heaven for bringing charges against the saints "day and night before our God" (Rev 12:10).

3:2 the Lord said: The speaker is the "angel of the Lord" from 3:1. **the Lord rebuke you:** A word of judgment. • The Book of Jude recounts a tradition in which the archangel Michael, during a dispute over the body of Moses, pronounced identical words against the devil: "The Lord rebuke you" (Jude 9). **chosen:** See note on 1:17. **a brand plucked:** Judah has been saved from perishing in exile like a smoldering stick that is pulled from the fire before flames consume it (Amos 4:11; Jude 23).

3:3 filthy: Soiled with excrement, representing defilement (3:4). The Mosaic Law forbids the priests of Israel to minister in a state of "uncleanness" (Lev 22:3).

3:4 rich apparel: The reclothing of Joshua signifies his passage from impurity to purity, making him fit for priestly ministry. His "clean turban" (3:5) is the distinctive headdress of Israel's high priests (Ex 28:4; 29:6). See also note on 6:11. • Zechariah prophesies clearly of Jesus, who was clothed with filthy garments, stripped, and adorned with clean and beautiful attire. This was to teach us in a figurative way that, in Baptism, we put off our sins like a ragged garment and are clothed with the holy and splendid attire of rebirth (St. Gregory of Nyssa, *On the Baptism of Christ*). • This revelation was given to believers in Christ the high priest. At one time, we fornicated and engaged in filthy behavior, but now, by the grace of our Jesus, we have cast off those befouled garments. Even

though the devil stands ready to oppose us, the angel of God, which is the divine power sent through Christ, rebukes him. We have been snatched from the fire that our sins deserved and from the trying torments of the devil and his company (St. Justin Martyr, *Dialogue with Trypho* 116).

3:6 walk in my ways: A basic requirement for living in covenant with God (Deut 10:12; 28:9). **keep my charge:** By observance of the priestly laws (Ezek 44:16).

3:7 rule my house: Authority over the Temple and its precincts is granted. **the right of access:** The privilege of acting as Judah's high priest, who alone could enter the sanctuary's innermost chamber on the Day of Atonement (Lev 16:2-4; Heb 9:7).

3:8 your friends: Perhaps his fellow priests. **my servant:** An honorary epithet for one who accomplishes God's purposes in salvation history (Num 12:7-8; Josh 24:29; Ps 89:3). **the Branch:** A royal figure who will come in the future to "build the temple of the Lord" (6:12). He is often identified with Zerubbabel, the royal descendant of David who will complete the rebuilding of the postexilic Temple (4:9). However, since Zerubbabel never ruled as king, and since he has been a member of the Judean community for nearly two decades at this point, he does not fit the description of a coming one who will rule upon a "throne" (6:13). Zerubbabel is better viewed as one who prefigures the Branch, which Jeremiah identifies with the Davidic Messiah (Jer 23:5; 33:15). Like Solomon, the Branch will be a king who sprouts from David's line, rules on David's throne, and builds the Lord's future house—the Temple of greater splendor that Haggai foretold at roughly the same time (Hag 1:9). See note on 6:12 and word study: *Branch* at Jer 23:5.

3:9 the stone: A foundation stone, or possibly "the top stone" of 4:7. It will bear an inscription identifying the Lord's house as a place of atonement for sin. • Jesus and the apostles read various OT prophecies about a "stone" (Ps 118:22; Is 28:16; Dan 2:44-45) as fulfilled in the Messiah (Lk 20:17-18; Acts 4:11; Rom 9:32-33; 1 Pet 2:4-8). Paul identifies Jesus as the cornerstone of God's new and living Temple, the Church indwelt by the Spirit (Eph 2:19-22). **seven facets:** Literally, "seven eyes", which symbolize the Lord's universal knowledge and watchfulness over "the whole earth" (4:10).

3:10 under his vine ... fig tree: Points to a time of security and prosperity when life will be undisturbed by war, as in the days of Solomon (1 Kings 4:25; Mic 4:4).

4:1-14 The fifth vision: Zechariah sees a golden lampstand fed by a reservoir of oil and flanked by two olive trees. The lampstand represents the Temple, the seat of the Lord's presence; its supply of oil is the Spirit of the Lord (4:6); and its

of his sleep. ²And he said to me, "What do you see?" I said, "I see, and behold, a lampstand all of gold, with a bowl on the top of it, and seven lamps on it, with seven lips on each of the lamps which are on the top of it. ³And there are two olive trees by it, one on the right of the bowl and the other on its left." ⁴And I said to the angel who talked with me, "What are these, my lord?" ⁵Then the angel who talked with me answered me, "Do you not know what these are?" I said, "No, my lord." ⁶Then he said to me, "This is the word of the LORD to Zerub'babel: Not by might, nor by power, but by my Spirit, says the LORD of hosts. ⁷What are you, O great mountain? Before Zerub'babel you shall become a plain; and he shall bring forward the top stone amid shouts of 'Grace, grace to it!'" ⁸Moreover the word of the LORD came to me, saying, ⁹"The hands of Zerub'babel have laid the foundation of this house; his hands shall also complete it. Then you will know that the

LORD of hosts has sent me to you. ¹⁰For whoever has despised the day of small things shall rejoice, and shall see the plummet in the hand of Zerub'babel.

"These seven are the eyes of the LORD, which range through the whole earth." ¹¹Then I said to him, "What are these two olive trees on the right and the left of the lampstand?" ¹²And a second time I said to him, "What are these two branches of the olive trees, which are beside the two golden pipes from which the oil ᶜ is poured out?" ¹³He said to me, "Do you not know what these are?" I said, "No, my lord." ¹⁴Then he said, "These are the two anointed who stand by the Lord of the whole earth."

Sixth Vision: The Flying Scroll

5 Again I lifted my eyes and saw, and behold, a flying scroll! ²And he said to me, "What do you see?" I answered, "I see a flying scroll; its length is twenty cubits, and its breadth ten cubits." ³Then

---

4:3, 11–14: Rev 11:4.   **4:10:** Rev 5:6.

---

seven flames stand for the eyes of the Lord (4:10). Zechariah, puzzled by the vision, needs the help of the angel to interpret its meaning (4:4–5, 11–13). The message: Zerubbabel, governor of Judah, will finish rebuilding the Jerusalem Temple (4:9), but he must draw strength for the task from the Spirit (4:6). Judah will then recognize that its completion is due to God's grace (4:7).

4:1 the angel who talked: See note on 1:9. **waked me:** The prophet, still in a visionary state, is aroused to take notice of something new.

4:2 lampstand: A menorah, the golden candelabra that illuminated the inside of the Mosaic Tabernacle (Ex 37:17–24) and Solomonic Temple (1 Kings 7:48–49). Each lamp consisted of a wick placed in a small cup of oil. In the vision, these seven cups are fed with oil from fourteen tubes or channels running down from an elevated bowl (4:2). See note on Ex 25:31–37. **seven lips:** The Hebrew reads "seven and seven spouts/tubes".

4:3 two olive trees: Represent the two heads of the postexilic community, Zerubbabel, the governor, and Joshua, the high priest (3:1; 4:9). These two oversaw the initial work on the Temple years earlier (Ezra 3:2–13; Hag 1:1–8). Because olive oil was used to anoint Israel's kings and priests, they also represent the continuation of the royal line of David and the priestly line of Aaron after the Babylonian Exile. • The Book of Revelation uses this image of two olive trees to represent two Christian witnesses who prophesy in Jerusalem before the city's demise (Rev 11:4).

4:6 Zerubbabel: The second governor of Judah in the postexilic period, following Sheshbazzar (Ezra 1:8; 5:14). He was the grandson of Jehoiachin, king of Judah, who was exiled to Babylon in 597 B.C. (2 Kings 24:15). See note on Hag 2:20–23. **my Spirit:** The source of divine wisdom and strength that Zerubbabel needs to complete work on the Temple. Abilities required for building the Tabernacle and its furnishings were likewise supplied by "the Spirit of God" in the days of Moses (Ex 31:1–11).

4:7 mountain ... plain: God will enable Zerubbabel to remove every obstacle that stands in the way of fulfilling his

mandate (Is 40:4; Mk 11:23). Perhaps these challenges to rebuilding are pictured as the rubble of the destroyed Temple, which Zerubbabel's workers must have removed to prepare the site for its new foundation back in 536 B.C. (Ezra 3:8–11). **the top stone:** Appears to be a capstone that represents the completion of the project. Some identify it with the inscribed "stone" in the fourth vision (3:9).

4:10 the day of small things: The day of painful disappointment when those who remembered the glory of Solomon's Temple lamented the much smaller and humbler foundations of the Second Temple (Ezra 3:12; Hag 2:3). **the plummet:** Either a builder's tool used to set the final stone of the sanctuary in place or possibly a metallic plate with a dedicatory inscription (cf. 3:9). **These seven:** The seven lamps of the menorah (4:2). **the eyes of the LORD:** Their movement throughout the world signifies God's omniscience or comprehensive knowledge of all things (2 Chron 16:9; Rom 11:33). For the idea that eyes emit light as lamps do, see Tob 10:5; Prov 15:30; Sir 23:19; Mt 6:22.

4:14 anointed: Literally, "sons of oil". See note on 4:3. **who stand by the Lord:** As servants ready to do God's will.

5:1–4 The sixth vision: Zechariah sees a giant flying scroll that brings judgment on sinners in Judah. It measures roughly 30 feet long by 15 feet in diameter (5:2). The scroll is the Torah, a covenant document that bestows blessings on those who follow the statutes and commandments (Deut 28:1–14) and imposes sanctions or curses on those who violate its commandments (Deut 28:15–68). Persons guilty of thievery and perjury—sins against God and neighbor—are cut off from the land (5:3), and their homes are doomed to decay (5:4). The message: God intends to purge the postexilic community of sin and to restore obedience to the Torah.

5:2 cubits: A cubit is roughly 18 inches, the distance between the elbow and fingertips.

5:3 one who steals: Theft is a violation of the seventh commandment (Ex 20:15; Deut 5:19). **cut off:** By death or banishment. Either way, the perpetrator's home is abandoned to disrepair (5:4). **one who swears falsely:** Taking false oaths is a form of taking the Lord's name in vain and thus a violation of the second commandment (Ex 20:7; Deut 5:11). God is said to "hate" a false oath in 8:17. The two transgressions noted in this verse, one against neighbor and one against God, stand for all violations of the covenant.

ᶜ Cn: Heb *gold.*

165

he said to me, "This is the curse that goes out over the face of the whole land; for every one who steals shall be cut off henceforth according to it, and every one who swears falsely shall be cut off henceforth according to it. [4]I will send it forth, says the LORD of hosts, and it shall enter the house of the thief, and the house of him who swears falsely by my name; and it shall abide in his house and consume it, both timber and stones."

Seventh Vision: The Woman in an Ephah

5 Then the angel who talked with me came forward and said to me, "Lift your eyes, and see what this is that goes forth." [6]And I said, "What is it?" He said, "This is the ephah that goes forth." And he said, "This is their iniquity [d] in all the land." [7]And behold, the leaden cover was lifted, and there was a woman sitting in the ephah! [8]And he said, "This is Wickedness." And he thrust her back into the ephah, and thrust down the leaden weight upon its mouth. [9]Then I lifted my eyes and saw, and behold, two women coming forward! The wind was in their wings; they had wings like the wings of a stork, and they lifted up the ephah between earth and heaven. [10]Then I said to the angel who talked with me,

"Where are they taking the ephah?" [11]He said to me, "To the land of Shi'nar, to build a house for it; and when this is prepared, they will set the ephah down there on its base."

Eighth Vision: Four Chariots

6 And again I lifted my eyes and saw, and behold, four chariots came out from between two mountains; and the mountains were mountains of bronze. [2]The first chariot had red horses, the second black horses, [3]the third white horses, and the fourth chariot dappled gray [e] horses. [4]Then I said to the angel who talked with me, "What are these, my lord?" [5]And the angel answered me, "These are going forth to the four winds of heaven, after presenting themselves before the LORD of all the earth. [6]The chariot with the black horses goes toward the north country, the white ones go toward the west country, [f] and the dappled ones go toward the south country." [7]When the steeds came out, they were impatient to get off and patrol the earth. And he said, "Go, patrol the earth." So they patrolled the earth. [8]Then he cried to me, "Behold, those who go toward the north country have set my Spirit at rest in the north country."

6:1-3: Rev 6:2-8.   **6:5:** Rev 7:1.

5:5-11 The seventh vision: Zechariah sees a woman transported to Babylon in a container smaller than a bushel. She represents the wickedness that God's people brought home to Judah from the Exile (5:8). Now she is being sent back, secured under a heavy lid, and flown away by two hybrid creatures that look like women with stork wings (5:9). Since an ephah is too small to contain a living person, the woman may be the figurine of a goddess whose image is banished from the land and installed in an idol temple (5:11). The message: the postexilic community must rid itself of pagan practices that its people adopted while living in Babylon.
5:5 the angel who talked: See note on 1:9.
5:6 ephah: A dry measure. Here it is a small, lidded container or basket with a capacity of five to six gallons.
5:9 The wind: Or "the Spirit". The wording seems to recall how "the Spirit" lifted up the prophet Ezekiel "between earth and heaven" and transported him from Babylon to Jerusalem to witness the idolatry taking place there (Ezek 8:3). **a stork:** An unclean animal (Lev 11:19; Deut 14:18).
5:11 the land of Shinar: Babylonia, a kingdom centered in lower Mesopotamia before the Persians became masters of the Near East (Gen 10:10; 11:2; Dan 1:2). **a house:** A pagan temple. **base:** A pedestal used to display a cult object.
6:1-8 The eighth vision: Zechariah sees four chariots charging out from between two bronze mountains. Each is drawn by a team of colored horses (6:2-3), and three of the chariot teams wheel off to the north and south after an audience with the Lord (6:5-6). No charioteers are described, and the chariot with red horses is given no patrolling assignment. The message: the Lord's anger is assuaged when the nations hostile to Israel are subdued. Zechariah's first and last visions, which form a bracket around the rest, exhibit several

parallels: both feature horses of various colors; both divide the horses into four groups, three of which are sent by the Lord to patrol the earth; both portray the red horse(s) as the leader of the group; and both visions are concerned with the Lord's anger against the nations (compare 1:8-11, 15, and 6:1-8).
6:1 mountains of bronze: Bronze represents unconquerable strength (Jer 1:18). Since the four chariots emerge from the Lord's presence (6:5), the two bronze pillars that stood beside the entrance to Solomon's Temple may be symbolized (1 Kings 7:15-22).
6:2-3 The four colors of the horses distinguish the four chariots, but their symbolism is not explained. • The Book of Revelation draws from this vision (and 1:8) when it describes riders mounted on colored horses—white, red, black, and pale—going forth from the presence of the Lord to execute divine judgments on the earth with bow, sword, famine, and pestilence (Rev 6:2-8).
6:3 dappled gray: Or "spotted".
6:4 the angels who talked: See note on 1:9.
6:5 the four winds: Or "the four spirits". Elsewhere in Scripture, spirits (= angels) are sent forth from the Lord's heavenly court to administer his will on earth (e.g., 1 Kings 22:19-23; Ps 103:20-21; Heb 1:14). **before the LORD:** They go forth from the divine presence with instructions to "patrol the earth" (6:7). Chariots, being weapons of war, are usually thought to bring judgments against the lands they patrol (9:10).
6:6 the north country: Babylonia, conqueror of Judah in the early sixth century B.C. (2:6). See note on Jer 1:14. **the west country:** A scholarly conjecture. The Hebrew MT, Greek LXX, and Latin Vulgate all state that the white horses followed the black horses galloping north. **the south country:** Egypt, another traditional enemy of Israel.
6:8 my Spirit: Possibly the divine Spirit, as in 4:6, but more likely a reference to the Lord's anger, which was pacified or put at ease by Babylon's fall to Persia in 539 B.C. The Hebrew *ruah*, often translated "wind" or "Spirit", sometimes means "anger" (as in Prov 29:11; Eccles 10:4).

---

[d] Gk Compare Syr: Heb *eye*.
[e] Compare Gk: The meaning of the Hebrew word is uncertain.
[f] Cn: Heb *after them*.

The Crown and the Branch

9 And the word of the LORD came to me: [10]"Take from the exiles Hel'dai, Tobi'jah, and Jedai'ah, who have arrived from Babylon; and go the same day to the house of Josi'ah, the son of Zephani'ah. [11]Take from them silver and gold, and make a crown,[g] and set it upon the head of Joshua, the son of Jehoz'adak, the high priest; [12]and say to him, 'Thus says the LORD of hosts, "Behold, the man whose name is the Branch: for he shall grow up in his place, and he shall build the temple of the LORD. [13]It is he who shall build the temple of the LORD, and shall bear royal honor, and shall sit and rule upon his throne. And there shall be a priest by his throne, and peaceful understanding shall be between them both."' [14]And the crown[h] shall be in the temple of the LORD as a reminder to Hel'dai,[i] Tobi'jah, Jedai'ah, and Josi'ah[j] the son of Zephani'ah.

15 "And those who are far off shall come and help to build the temple of the LORD; and you shall know that the LORD of hosts has sent me to you. And this shall come to pass, if you will diligently obey the voice of the LORD your God."

Hypocritical Fasting Condemned

7 In the fourth year of King Dari'us, the word of the LORD came to Zechari'ah in the fourth day of the ninth month, which is Chis'lev. [2]Now the people of Bethel had sent Share'zer and Reg'em-mel'ech and their men, to entreat the favor of the LORD, [3]and to ask the priests of the house of the LORD of hosts and the prophets, "Should I mourn and fast in the fifth month, as I have done for so many years?" [4]Then the word of the LORD of hosts came to me: [5]"Say to all the people of the land and the priests, When you fasted and mourned in the fifth month and in the seventh, for these seventy years, was it for me that you fasted? [6]And when you eat and when you drink, do you not eat for yourselves and drink for yourselves? [7]When Jerusalem was inhabited and

---

6:12: Zech 3:8; Is 4:2; Jer 23:5; 33:15.

6:9–15 The crowning of Joshua, which forms an epilogue to Zechariah's night visions (1:7—6:8). It builds on visions three and four, which feature Joshua, the high priest (3:1–10), and Zerubbabel, the governor, who will finish building the Temple (4:1–14). Many obscurities make these verses difficult to interpret.

6:9 the word of the LORD: A divine instruction given to Zechariah (1:1; 7:1, 8; 8:1, 18).

6:10 the exiles: The community in Judah that returned from exile in Babylon. **Heldai, Tobijah, and Jedaiah:** Otherwise unknown but presumably wealthy since they donate gold and silver (6:11). Jedaiah may be the priest of this name in Ezra 2:36. **Josiah:** Perhaps a metalsmith who will forge the crowns.

6:11 a crown: Follows the Greek LXX; the Hebrew MT and Latin Vulgate have the plural, "crowns". The term in question refers to royal headpieces worn by kings and queens in biblical times (2 Sam 12:30; Ps 21:3; Jer 13:18). One crown is placed on the head of Joshua, the high priest, and the other is placed in the Temple until its designated wearer, "the Branch" (6:12), comes as the Davidic Messiah to rule upon "his throne" (6:13). Joshua, who already wore a priestly crown on his linen turban (the gold "plate" in Ex 28:36–38), is now given a king's crown. Wearing two crowns, he prefigures the royal-priestly Messiah to come. See note on 3:4. • This expectation is fulfilled in Jesus, a royal descendant of David (Mt 1:1–16) who assumes the two offices of king and high priest (Heb 7–9; CCC 436). The link is strengthened by the shared name: Joshua is a longer form of the name Jeshua/Jesus. **Joshua:** See note on 3:1.

6:12 the Branch: Also foreshadowed by Zerubbabel, the provincial governor of Judah descended from David (Mt 1:12). See note on 3:8. **he shall build the temple:** Zerubbabel, who laid the foundations of the Temple years earlier (Ezra 3:8–11), would complete its rebuilding in 515 B.C. (Ezra 6:14–15). • The governorship of Zerubbabel prefigures the messianic kingship of the Branch; his work on building the Temple also prefigures the work of the Branch, who will build the Church

as God's living Temple on the foundation of the apostles (Mt 16:18; Eph 2:19–22).

6:13 his throne: The throne of David, which the Messiah will occupy (Is 9:6–7; Lk 1:32; Acts 2:29–31).

6:14 reminder: Or "memorial" (Heb., *zikkārôn*).

6:15 those who are far off: The people of Israel who remain in exile (Is 57:19) as well as Gentiles who will come to Zion to seek the Lord (8:20–23; Is 2:2–4; Mic 4:1–2).

7:1–8:23 Prophetic messages given to Zechariah in response to an inquiry about fasting.

7:1 King Darius: Darius I Hystaspes, ruler of Persia from 522 to 486 B.C. **the word of the LORD:** A divine instruction given to the prophet (1:1; 7:8; 8:1, 18). **fourth day ... Chislev:** December 7, 518 B.C., roughly 22 months after Zechariah received his night visions (1:7). This is the last date given in the book (1:1, 7).

7:2 Bethel: A town ten miles north of Jerusalem that appears to have been resettled by a small community of Bethelites after the first wave of exiles returned from Babylon (Ezra 2:28). It had been the site of an idolatrous calf cult in the preexilic period (1 Kings 12:28–29). **Sharezer ... Regem-melech:** Otherwise unknown.

7:3 the priests: In Jerusalem. **the house of the LORD:** The Temple, under construction for more than two years at this point, i.e., since September 21, 520 B.C. (Hag 1:14–15). **the fifth month:** Av, which falls in July/August. This was the month in 586 B.C. when Babylonian conquerors burned the city and Temple of Jerusalem (2 Kings 25:8–9). Surviving Jews established an annual tradition of fasting in the fifth month in memory of this calamity. The question of the delegation is whether this tradition should continue now that the Temple is being rebuilt. The Lord's answer is given in 8:19.

7:5 the seventh: Tishri, which falls in September/October. Fasting in the seventh month (besides the Day of Atonement, Lev 16:29) commemorated the assassination of Gedaliah, governor of Judah after the fall of Jerusalem (2 Kings 25:25; Jer 41:1–2). **seventy years:** See note on 1:12. **was it for me ...?:** Fasting in remembrance of Jerusalem's demise is criticized for being self-serving rather than an act of service to God (Is 58:3). The motive rather than the practice as such was the problem.

7:7 inhabited ... prosperity: Recalls the days of Zion's glory before the Babylonian conquest of Judah and its capital. **the former prophets:** See note on 1:4.

---

[g] Gk Mss: Heb *crowns.*
[h] Gk: Heb *crowns.*
[i] With verse 10: Heb *Helem.*
[j] With verse 10: Heb *Hen.*

in prosperity, with her cities round about her, and the South and the lowland were inhabited, were not these the words which the LORD proclaimed by the former prophets?"

Punishment for Rejecting God's Commands

8 And the word of the LORD came to Zechari'ah, saying, ⁹"Thus says the LORD of hosts, Render true judgments, show kindness and mercy each to his brother, ¹⁰do not oppress the widow, the fatherless, the sojourner, or the poor; and let none of you devise evil against his brother in your heart." ¹¹But they refused to listen, and turned a stubborn shoulder, and stopped their ears that they might not hear. ¹²They made their hearts like adamant lest they should hear the law and the words which the LORD of hosts had sent by his Spirit through the former prophets. Therefore great wrath came from the LORD of hosts. ¹³"As I called, and they would not hear, so they called, and I would not hear," says the LORD of hosts, ¹⁴"and I scattered them with a whirlwind among all the nations which they had not known. Thus the land they left was desolate, so that no one went back and forth, and the pleasant land was made desolate."

God's Promise to Zion

8 And the word of the LORD of hosts came to me, saying, ²"Thus says the LORD of hosts:

I am jealous for Zion with great jealousy, and I am jealous for her with great wrath. ³Thus says the LORD: I will return to Zion, and will dwell in the midst of Jerusalem, and Jerusalem shall be called the faithful city, and the mountain of the LORD of hosts, the holy mountain. ⁴Thus says the LORD of hosts: Old men and old women shall again sit in the streets of Jerusalem, each with staff in hand for very age. ⁵And the streets of the city shall be full of boys and girls playing in its streets. ⁶Thus says the LORD of hosts: If it is marvelous in the sight of the remnant of this people in these days, should it also be marvelous in my sight, says the LORD of hosts? ⁷Thus says the LORD of hosts: Behold, I will save my people from the east country and from the west country; ⁸and I will bring them to dwell in the midst of Jerusalem; and they shall be my people and I will be their God, in faithfulness and in righteousness."

9 Thus says the LORD of hosts: "Let your hands be strong, you who in these days have been hearing these words from the mouth of the prophets, since the day that the foundation of the house of the LORD of hosts was laid, that the temple might be built. ¹⁰For before those days there was no wage for man or any wage for beast, neither was there any safety from the foe for him who went out or came in; for I

7:8–14 An oracle about social responsibility and the lessons of history. The Lord wills that his covenant people care for those at greatest risk of social and economic hardship. This was expected of them before the Exile, and it remains so afterward. Fasting to commemorate tragic events, while not wrong in itself, is less important than the higher duty of loving neighbor and securing justice for all. The stubborn refusal to live according to God's priorities is what led to the desolation and dispersion of Judah in the first place. For a similar message about fasting, see Is 58:1–7. • If those addressed by the prophet acquired no benefit from fasting without doing other good works or driving evil intentions against their neighbor out of their hearts, what excuse can we have when more is required of us? We are not only to abstain from such things but also to love our enemies and show kindness to them (St. John Chrysostom, *Homilies on Genesis* 4, 17).

7:9 true judgments: Israel's prophets frequently demanded justice in the covenant community (8:16; Is 1:16–17; Jer 7:5–7; Amos 5:15, 24; Mic 6:8).

7:10 the widow, the fatherless: Of special concern to the Lord (Ex 22:22–24; Ps 68:5; 146:9; CCC 238). **sojourner:** Oppression of a foreigner who lived among the Israelites was strictly forbidden (Ex 22:21).

7:11 turned a stubborn shoulder: An act of defiance, like an ox resisting the yoke of the plowman (Neh 9:29).

7:12 his Spirit: Inspired the prophets with words from the Lord (Neh 9:30; Mic 3:8; 2 Pet 1:20–21).

7:14 I scattered them: Or "I blew them away". Exile from the land of Israel is one of the curses of the Mosaic covenant (Lev 26:33; Deut 28:64).

8:1–23 The question about fasting in 7:3 is answered and explained. Times of fasting and mourning that memorialize the fall of Jerusalem will become "seasons of joy and gladness" (8:19). For the Lord plans to reverse this national disaster by doing "good" to Judah and Jerusalem (8:15) in place of the "evil" he sent in the past (8:14). He will "save" his people from exile (8:7) and turn their name into a "blessing" (8:13).

Zion will be repopulated with people of all ages (8:4–5), and the land will become fruitful once again (8:12). At one level, the restoration of Zion signals the return of God's favor to his disgraced people; at another, it opens a new chapter in salvation history, when all nations will stream to Zion to seek the Lord who dwells with his people (8:23). For prophecies of Jerusalem's future glory, see also Is 62:11–12; 65:19–20; Zeph 3:14–20.

8:2 Thus says the LORD: An expression repeated nine times in this chapter alone (8:2, 4, 6, 7, 9, 14, 19, 20, 23). **I am jealous:** Divine jealousy is an expression of divine love that burns like a fire (Deut 4:24). On the one hand, it implies that God will stop at nothing to do good to his beloved people. On the other, his jealousy is aroused to anger against those who would harm or humiliate his beloved. Zechariah spoke of this zealous affection earlier in 1:14–17 and 2:7–13. **Zion:** The mountain height of Jerusalem. See note on 2 Sam 5:7.

8:3 I ... will dwell in: For the Lord's presence in the new Jerusalem, see also Zeph 3:14–17. **the faithful city:** Or "truthful city". A new commitment to truth is stressed in this oracle (also 8:16, 19).

8:6 the remnant: The postexilic community in Judah. See word study: *Remnant* at Zeph 2:7.

8:7 the east ... the west: The faraway lands of Israel's exile, which stretch from the rising of the sun to its setting (Ps 107:2–3; Is 43:5–6).

8:8 my people ... their God: Reaffirms the covenant bond between the Lord and Israel. Statements of mutual belonging are known as the "covenant formula" (Lev 26:12; Jer 30:22; Ezek 37:27; Hos 2:23).

8:9 Let your hands be strong: Encouragement from the Lord to continue the arduous work of rebuilding the Temple. **the prophets:** Haggai and Zechariah (1:1; Ezra 5:1; Hag 1:1). **the day:** September 21, 520 B.C., the date when Temple construction was resumed: (Hag 1:14–15).

8:10 there was no wage: For Judah's economic woes at this time, see Hag 1:6.

set every man against his fellow. ¹¹But now I will not deal with the remnant of this people as in the former days, says the LORD of hosts. ¹²For there shall be a sowing of peace; the vine shall yield its fruit, and the ground shall give its increase, and the heavens shall give their dew; and I will cause the remnant of this people to possess all these things. ¹³And as you have been a byword of cursing among the nations, O house of Judah and house of Israel, so will I save you and you shall be a blessing. Fear not, but let your hands be strong."

14 For thus says the LORD of hosts: "As I planned to do evil to you, when your fathers provoked me to wrath, and I did not relent, says the LORD of hosts, ¹⁵so again I have planned in these days to do good to Jerusalem and to the house of Judah; fear not. ¹⁶These are the things that you shall do: Speak the truth to one another, render in your gates judgments that are true and make for peace, ¹⁷do not devise evil in your hearts against one another, and love no false oath, for all these things I hate, says the LORD."

Joyful Fasting

¹⁸And the word of the LORD of hosts came to me, saying, ¹⁹"Thus says the LORD of hosts: The fast of the fourth month, and the fast of the fifth, and the fast of the seventh, and the fast of the tenth, shall be to the house of Judah seasons of joy and gladness, and cheerful feasts; therefore love truth and peace.

Many Peoples Will Be Drawn to Jerusalem

²⁰"Thus says the LORD of hosts: Peoples shall yet come, even the inhabitants of many cities; ²¹the inhabitants of one city shall go to another, saying, 'Let us go at once to entreat the favor of the LORD, and to seek the LORD of hosts; I am going.' ²²Many peoples and strong nations shall come to seek the LORD of hosts in Jerusalem, and to entreat the favor of the LORD. ²³Thus says the LORD of hosts: In those days ten men from the nations of every tongue shall take hold of the robe of a Jew, saying, 'Let us go with you, for we have heard that God is with you.'"

Judgment on Israel's Enemies

9

An Oracle

The word of the LORD is against the land of Had'rach
  and will rest upon Damascus.
For to the LORD belong the cities of Ar'am, ᵏ
  even as all the tribes of Israel;

8:16: Eph 4:25.

8:12 the vine ... the ground: Judah's farmlands had been languishing during the years when the Temple sat unfinished and in ruins (Hag 1:9–11). The implication is that God's presence in the sanctuary brings blessing and prosperity to his people (Hag 2:18–19).

8:13 byword of cursing: The name of God's people was uttered in curses pronounced against others (cf. Jer 29:22). **Judah:** The Southern Kingdom of Judah, carried into captivity by the Babylonians in the sixth century B.C. (2 Kings 24:10–16; 25:11). **Israel:** The Northern Kingdom of Israel, carried into captivity by the Assyrians in the eighth century B.C. (2 Kings 15:29; 17:5–6; 1 Chron 5:26).

8:14 do evil to you: Not moral evil, since God cannot sin, but national calamities that God brings to discipline his rebellious people.

8:16 Speak the truth to one another: The Greek LXX translates: "Speak truth, each one to his neighbor." Zephaniah likewise calls for truthful speech among the remnant in Zion (Zeph 3:13). • Paul cites a Greek translation of this passage when he urges Christians to be honest with one another in Eph 4:25. **gates:** Entryways into walled cities were places where legal disputes were resolved (Ruth 4:1–6).

8:19 The fast: The custom of fasting in the fifth and seventh months was noted in 7:3, 5. Here we learn that fasting was also practiced in the **fourth** month, marking the time when the Babylonians breached the wall of Jerusalem (2 Kings 25:3–4), and the **tenth** month, marking the time when the final siege of the city began (2 Kings 25:1; Jer 39:1).

8:20–23 A vision of Gentiles from all over the world streaming to Zion to seek the God of Israel. In an earlier vision, Zechariah saw them joining themselves to the Lord and becoming members of his covenant people (2:11). In a later one, he pictures them as pilgrims who come to Jerusalem to serve the Lord as King (14:16–17). For similar prophecies in the OT, see Is 2:2–4; 60:1–18; Jer 3:17; Mic 4:1–3.

8:23 those days: The future days of messianic fulfillment, sometimes called "the latter days" (Num 24:14; Is 2:2; Dan 2:28; Hos 3:5). **Jew:** Or "Judean". **Let us go with you:** Envisions the conversion of the nations as an event simultaneous with the homecoming of Israel's exiles (as in Is 49:22; 66:18–20). **God is with you:** The nations will come to see that God is known in Judah (Ps 76:1) and is present in a special way in Jerusalem (Ps 78:68–69). This will prompt them to seek the God of Israel as their Savior (Is 45:22). • Jesus likely had this passage in mind when he affirmed that "salvation is from the Jews" (Jn 4:22). See note on 2:11.

9:1–14:21 Chapters 9–14 are markedly different from chapters 1–8 in style and subject matter. They focus, not on circumstances in the prophet's own day, but on God's eschatological plan for the future of Israel, Zion, and the world. Some scholars believe that Zechariah received these revelations many years after the visions and oracles recorded in chaps. 1–8. Others view these final chapters as the work of one or more prophets whose names and dates are unknown. For some of the differences between earlier and later chapters of the book, see introduction: *Author and Date*.

9:1–8 The defeat of Israel's enemies, which is a prelude to the coming of Israel's king (9:9–10). The path of conquest moves from north to south, from the Syrians (9:1) to the Phoenicians (9:2–4) to the Philistines (9:5–7). These cities and nations lay within the full extent of the Promised Land, a territory once governed by King Solomon and now reclaimed (1 Kings 4:21; 8:65; cf. Gen 15:18–21; Deut 1:6–8). Some detect an allusion to Alexander the Great's sweep down the Mediterranean coast in 332 B.C., but this is uncertain.

9:1 An Oracle: The Hebrew term *massā'* is a pronouncement of judgment on those who oppose the Lord (Is 13:3; 17:1; 19:1; 23:13). This heading appears in 9:1 and 12:1, introducing the final two collections of prophecies in the book (chaps. 9–11 and 12–14, respectively). **Hadrach:** A region of northern Syria. **Damascus:** Capital of one of the Aramean kingdoms of Syria, located about 60 miles northeast of the Sea of Galilee.

ᵏCn: Heb *the eye of Adam* (or *man*).

²Hamath also, which borders thereon,
  Tyre and Si′don, though they are very wise.
³Tyre has built herself a rampart,
  and heaped up silver like dust,
  and gold like the dirt of the streets.
⁴But behold, the Lord will strip her of her
    possessions
  and hurl her wealth into the sea,
  and she shall be devoured by fire.

⁵Ash′kelon shall see it, and be afraid;
  Gaza too, and shall writhe in anguish;
  Ek′ron also, because its hopes are confounded.
The king shall perish from Gaza;
  Ashkelon shall be uninhabited;
⁶a mongrel people shall dwell in Ash′dod;
  and I will make an end of the pride of Philis′tia.
⁷I will take away its blood from its mouth,
  and its abominations from between its teeth;
it too shall be a remnant for our God;
  it shall be like a clan in Judah,
  and Ek′ron shall be like the Jeb′usites.

⁸Then I will encamp at my house as a guard,
  so that none shall march back and forth;
no oppressor shall again overrun them,
  for now I see with my own eyes.

The Coming of Israel's King

⁹Rejoice greatly, O daughter of Zion!
  Shout aloud, O daughter of Jerusalem!
Behold, your king comes to you;
  triumphant and victorious is he,
humble and riding on a donkey,
  on a colt the foal of a donkey.
¹⁰I will cut off the chariot from E′phraim
  and the war horse from Jerusalem;
and the battle bow shall be cut off,
  and he shall command peace to the nations;
his dominion shall be from sea to sea,
  and from the River to the ends of the earth.

¹¹As for you also, because of the blood of my
    covenant with you,
  I will set your captives free from the waterless
    pit.

9:9: Mt 21:5; Jn 12:15.

9:2 Hamath: Northeast of Damascus. **Tyre and Sidon:** Two port cities on the Mediterranean coast of Phoenicia (modern Lebanon). Owing to prosperous maritime trade, Tyre in particular was known for its extraordinary "wealth" (9:4; Ps 45:12). For similar prophecies of the downfall of Tyre and Sidon, see Ezek 26–28 and Amos 1:9–10. **very wise:** A reputation also noted in Ezek 28:1–7.

9:3 rampart: The Hebrew *māṣôr* is a play on the name Tyre (*ṣôr*). The city was built on an offshore island and surrounded by a fortified wall, making it eminently defensible. Alexander the Great had to build a causeway out to the city in order to conquer it in 332 B.C.

9:5–7 Divine judgment on Philistine cities in southwest Canaan. Four of its five confederated cities are mentioned (**Ashkelon, Gaza, Ekron, Ashdod**). Despite the defeat of these traditional enemies of Israel, the Lord will claim a remnant of the Philistines for himself and teach them observance of the Law (9:7).

9:6 I will make an end: The Lord speaks in the first person (I, me, my) from 9:5 to 9:13.

9:7 blood ... abominations: Refers to the consumption of blood and unclean animals, both of which are violations of the Torah's dietary laws (Lev 11:1–47; 17:10–12). The correction of Philistine eating habits implies their incorporation into the covenant community (as in 2:11). **Jebusites:** Canaanites who occupied Jerusalem before David seized the city and made it Israel's capital (2 Sam 5:6–9).

9:8 my house: The Temple. **as a guard:** In the third night vision, Zechariah learned that God would form a fiery wall of protection around Jerusalem (2:5).

9:9–10 The coming of the Davidic Messiah, who rides into Jerusalem on a young donkey, just as King Solomon rode into the city on David's mule at his coronation (1 Kings 1:38–40). He brings not war but peace to Israel and the nations, and his dominion extends over the whole earth, fulfilling a hope that was only imperfectly realized by the vastness of Solomon's empire (compare 9:10 with the prayer for an expansion of Solomon's realm in Ps 72:8). This event signals the rebirth of kingship in Jerusalem, which disappeared with the collapse of the Davidic monarchy in 586 B.C., through a restoration of the royal "house of David" (12:7–8).

9:9 Rejoice: Recalls the summons in 2:10. **daughter of Zion:** A poetic personification of Jerusalem. See note on Zeph 3:14–17 and word study: *The Daughter of Zion* at Lam 1:6. **your king:** The royal figure or "Branch" prophesied earlier in the book. See notes on 3:8 and 6:12. **triumphant:** Or "righteous". **donkey:** The mount of the messianic king expected to come from the royal tribe of Judah (Gen 49:10–11). The picture contrasts Jerusalem's peaceful king with the typical conqueror who rides before his subjects in a "chariot" or atop a "war horse" (9:10). • The evangelists Matthew and John both see a fulfillment of this prophecy in Jesus' triumphal entry into Jerusalem on Palm Sunday at the start of Holy Week (Mt 21:4–5; Jn 12:14–15; CCC 559). • The donkey brought to the Lord is the Church, upon which the Son of God will sit when he brings her into the heavenly Jerusalem. This fulfills what the Scriptures say: "Behold, your king comes to you, gentle and riding on a beast"—a donkey, which is the Jews who come to believe, and a young colt, which is the Gentiles who believe in Christ (St. Caesarius of Arles, *Sermon* 113).

9:10 peace: Recalls the peace of Solomon's reign (1 Kings 4:24; 1 Chron 22:9). **his dominion:** Defined by the following expressions, which come from the prayer for Solomon in Ps 72:8. Sirach equates these dimensions with all the nations, whom the Lord promised to bless through Abraham's offspring (Sir 44:21, referring to God's oath in Gen 22:16–18). **from sea to sea:** From the Mediterranean Sea (west of Israel) to the Red Sea, which wraps around the Arabian Peninsula (south and east of Israel). **the River:** The Euphrates (Gen 15:18). **the ends of the earth:** Thought to be the Atlantic coast of Europe. • Peace of soul, the peace beyond all understanding. When the form of this world passes away, everyone will take up the sword that cuts to the soul's marrow to destroy the chariot of Ephraim and the horse of Jerusalem. Then peace will be achieved over the passions of the body and over the minds of unbelievers, so that Christ may be formed in all and offer all subdued to the Father (St. Ambrose, *Letters* 80).

9:11–17 The exiles of Israel are reclaimed by the Lord, just as lands once belonging to Israel are recovered by the Lord in 9:1–7.

9:11 you: The pronoun is feminine singular, meaning the oracle addresses the "daughter of Zion" (9:9). **the blood of**

¹²Return to your stronghold, O prisoners of hope;
  today I declare that I will restore to you double.
¹³For I have bent Judah as my bow;
  I have made E′phraim its arrow.
 I will brandish your sons, O Zion,
  over your sons, O Greece,
  and wield you like a warrior's sword.

¹⁴Then the LORD will appear over them,
  and his arrow go forth like lightning;
 the Lord GOD will sound the trumpet,
  and march forth in the whirlwinds of the south.
¹⁵The LORD of hosts will protect them,
  and they shall devour and tread down the
   slingers;¹
 and they shall drink their blood^m like wine,
  and be full like a bowl,
  drenched like the corners of the altar.

¹⁶On that day the LORD their God will save them
  for they are the flock of his people;
 for like the jewels of a crown
  they shall shine on his land.
¹⁷Yes, how good and how fair it shall be!
  Grain shall make the young men flourish,
  and new wine the maidens.

Restoration of Judah and Israel

10 Ask rain from the LORD
  in the season of the spring rain,
 from the LORD who makes the storm clouds,
  who gives men showers of rain,
  to every one the vegetation in the field.
²For the teraphim utter nonsense,
  and the diviners see lies;
 the dreamers tell false dreams,
  and give empty consolation.
 Therefore the people wander like sheep;
  they are afflicted for want of a shepherd.

³"My anger is hot against the shepherds,
  and I will punish the leaders;^n
 for the LORD of hosts cares for his flock, the house
   of Judah,
  and will make them like his proud steed in
   battle.
⁴Out of them shall come the cornerstone,
  out of them the tent peg,
 out of them the battle bow,
  out of them every ruler.
⁵Together they shall be like mighty men in
   battle,
  trampling the foe in the mud of the streets;

---

my covenant: The blood that sealed the covenant between the Lord and Israel at Mt. Sinai (Ex 24:8; Heb 9:19-20). Some detect a reference to the Lord's election of Zion/Jerusalem as his dwelling place (Ps 132:13-14). **the waterless pit:** The foreign lands where most of "the tribes of Israel" who belong to the Lord remain in captivity (9:1). The land of Israel, by contrast, is well watered by the Lord (10:1). Christian tradition has seen in this verse a promise that Christ would rescue the souls of the righteous held captive in Hades and bring them to heaven (e.g., St. Cyril of Jerusalem, *Catechesis* 13, 34).
9:12 I will restore ... double: Similar to Isaiah's promise that Zion will inherit "a double portion" (Is 61:7).
9:13 Judah ... Ephraim: Envisions a reunion of the southern and northern tribes of Israel, which Ezekiel links to the reign of the Davidic Messiah (Ezek 37:15-28) and Jeremiah links to the "new covenant" that the Lord will make with the houses of Israel and Judah (Jer 31:31-34). **Greece:** Known in the Bible as the sons of "Javan" (Gen 10:4; Is 66:19). Despite contrary claims, mention of the Greeks does not require this passage to have been written as late as the Hellenistic period (332-166 B.C.). Greece was recognized as a world power after defeating the Persians at Marathon in 490 B.C., most likely within Zechariah's lifetime.
9:14 them: The captives of Zion that remain in exile (9:11). These will be identified as the houses of Judah and Joseph (10:6). **Lightning ... whirlwinds:** Visions of the Lord coming as a mighty Warrior often depict the event as a violent thunderstorm (Ps 18:7-15; Nahum 1:3-5; Hab 3:3-15).
9:16 the flock: An image of the people of Israel under the watchful care of the Lord, their divine Shepherd (10:3; Ps 95:7; Is 40:11; Jer 31:10; Mic 7:14). Israel's exiles are just as much a part of the Lord's flock as those already restored to Judah (10:3).

10:1 Ask rain: Prayers for abundant rainfall before the next harvest season were typically made during the autumn Feast of Booths, also called Tabernacles (14:16-17). Here the rains symbolize God's blessings of life and refreshment (Hos 6:3) following the "waterless" days of exile (9:11). **the LORD:** Promises to water the earth and increase its yield when his covenant is faithfully obeyed (Deut 11:13-17). **spring rain:** Showered the lands of Israel in March/April.
10:2 teraphim: Small household idols that were consulted for information from the spirit world (Gen 31:19; Ezek 21:21). Teraphim were abominations worthy of destruction (2 Kings 23:24). **diviners:** Augurers who performed techniques such as inspecting animal organs to foretell the future. Divination was strictly forbidden in Israel (Deut 18:10). **dreamers:** False dreamers who lead the covenant people astray (Deut 13:1-5). **want of a shepherd:** Refers to the lack of a trustworthy king to guide and protect the Lord's flock. The prophet is pointing to Israel's need for the coming Davidic Messiah (Ezek 37:24; Hos 3:4-5; Mic 5:2-4). • The Gospels echo the language of this and similar passages when they describe Jesus having compassion on his people for being "like sheep without a shepherd" (Mt 9:36; Mk 6:34).
10:3 the shepherds: Leaders in postexilic Judah who angered the Lord by oppressing, exploiting, and misleading the covenant people (11:5). Jeremiah and Ezekiel also pronounced God's judgment on the wicked shepherds of Judah in the preexilic period (Jer 10:21; 23:1-2; Ezek 34:1-10). **leaders:** Literally, "male goats", which flock animals tend to follow (Jer 50:8). **his flock:** See note on 9:16.
10:4 cornerstone: An epithet for a chief or leader (Judg 20:2; 1 Sam 14:38; Is 19:13). For the cornerstone as an image of the Messiah, see notes on Ps 118:22 and Eph 2:20. **peg:** An image of firmness and stability (Is 22:23). **battle bow:** An image of triumph over foes. **every ruler:** Powerful leaders who dominate their opponents.
10:5 the LORD is with them: The guarantee of their victory (Deut 7:23-24; Josh 1:5; Ps 44:4-8).

---

¹ Cn: Heb *the slingstones.*
^m Gk: Heb *be turbulent.*
^n Or *he-goats.*

they shall fight because the LORD is with them,
and they shall confound the riders on horses.

[6]"I will strengthen the house of Judah,
and I will save the house of Joseph.
I will bring them back because I have compassion
on them,
and they shall be as though I had not rejected
them;
for I am the LORD their God and I will answer
them.
[7]Then E′phraim shall become like a mighty warrior,
and their hearts shall be glad as with wine.
Their children shall see it and rejoice,
their hearts shall exult in the LORD.

[8]"I will signal for them and gather them in,
for I have redeemed them,
and they shall be as many as of old.
[9]Though I scattered them among the nations,
yet in far countries they shall remember me,
and with their children they shall live and
return.
[10]I will bring them home from the land of Egypt,
and gather them from Assyria;
and I will bring them to the land of Gilead and to
Lebanon,
till there is no room for them.

[11]They shall pass through the sea of Egypt,[o]
and the waves of the sea shall be struck
down,
and all the depths of the Nile dried up.
The pride of Assyria shall be laid low,
and the scepter of Egypt shall depart.
[12]I will make them strong in the LORD
and they shall glory[p] in his name," says the
LORD.

11 Open your doors, O Lebanon,
that the fire may devour your cedars!
[2]Wail, O cypress, for the cedar has fallen,
for the glorious trees are ruined!
Wail, oaks of Ba′shan,
for the thick forest has been felled!
[3]Listen, the wail of the shepherds,
for their glory is despoiled!
Listen, the roar of the lions,
for the jungle of the Jordan is laid waste!

Two Kinds of Shepherd

4 Thus said the LORD my God: "Become shepherd of the flock doomed to slaughter. [5]Those who buy them slay them and go unpunished; and those who sell them say, 'Blessed be the LORD, I have become rich'; and their own shepherds have no pity on them. [6]For I will no longer have pity on the inhabitants of

---

10:6—11:3 The Lord pledges to reunite the tribes of Israel that remain in exile in the postexilic period. Just as he scattered them to foreign lands in the past, the northern tribes by the Assyrians (2 Kings 15:29; 17:6) and the southern tribes by the Babylonians (2 Kings 24:15; 25:11), so he will "bring them home" to himself in the future (10:10). For the fulfillment of this hope in the Messiah, see note on 9:13 and essay: *The Salvation of All Israel* at Rom 11.

10:6 house of Judah: The southern tribes of Israel. **house of Joseph:** The northern tribes of Israel. **bring them back:** Into full covenant communion as God's people (Hos 1:10–11). **compassion:** The basis of Israel's restoration (Deut 30:3).

10:7 Ephraim: Another name for the northern tribes of Israel (9:13). See note on Hos 4:17.

10:8 I will signal: With an audible sound such as the blast of a trumpet (Is 27:13) or the roar of a lion (Hos 11:10). **many as of old:** The multiplication of God's people is also prophesied in Zechariah's third vision (2:4).

10:9 scattered: The language of exile (1:19; Lev 26:33). **they shall live:** Or "they shall come to life". Perhaps Israel's restoration is envisioned as a national resurrection, as in Ezek 37:1–14 and Hos 6:1–2.

10:10 Egypt … Assyria: Mighty nations that enslaved and exiled God's people in ancient times. Here they symbolize all hostile nations where Israel's exiles remain in captivity and from whose lands the Lord will regather them (Is 27:12–13; Hos 11:10–11). **Gilead:** East of the Jordan. **Lebanon:** North of the Sea of Galilee.

10:11 the Nile dried up: Recalls how the Lord made a dry path through the sea for his redeemed to escape Egypt in the days of Moses (Ex 14:21–22). For the return of

Israel's exiles as an event patterned on the Exodus story, see essay: *The New Exodus in Isaiah* at Is 44.

11:1–3 The Lord will bring judgment on the wicked shepherds of Judah (10:3), who will become like **cedars** that are destroyed by forest fires and **lions** that are deprived of their habitat. Other leaders, represented by a **cypress** and **oaks**, wail in distress at the sight of God's severity. For trees as images of mighty rulers, see Is 10:33–34; Ezek 31:1–18; Dan 4:20–26.

11:1 Lebanon: North of the Sea of Galilee. Its towering cedar trees were prized as premium lumber for large-scale construction projects (1 Kings 5:6; 7:1–3).

11:2 Bashan: North and east of the Sea of Galilee. It was famous for its lush grazing lands and sturdy oak trees (Is 2:13).

11:3 lions: Symbolize powerful rulers (Ezek 19:6–7; Nahum 2:12). **jungle of the Jordan:** The thick growth that clusters around the river valley (Gen 13:10).

11:4–17 One of the most difficult sections of Zechariah to interpret. Many details are obscure, but the basic storyline is clear: The prophet calls the prophet to become the **shepherd** of his people in place of the **shepherds** who take advantage of them. For this task, he takes **two staffs** that represent the blessings of God's covenant (**Grace**) and Israel's unity (**Union**). Although he is a good and reforming shepherd, the sheep despise him, and the sheep merchants insult him with a minuscule payment of **thirty shekels**—money the prophet casts into the Temple. To signify that God's blessings have been nullified toward his rebellious people, he breaks both staffs (11:10, 14). Finally, the Lord recruits the prophet a second time to prefigure the **worthless shepherd** he will send against his flock in the future. Many scholars read the episode as an allegory or visionary experience.

11:5 Those who buy … sell: Sheep traffickers who profit from the exploitation of others (11:7, 11).

11:6 I will deliver none: The Lord judges his sinful people by giving them over to the evil they refuse to renounce (Ps 81:11–12).

---

[o] Cn: Heb *distress*.
[p] Gk: Heb *walk*.

this land, says the LORD. Behold, I will cause men to
fall each into the hand of his shepherd, and each into
the hand of his king; and they shall crush the earth,
and I will deliver none from their hand."

7 So I became the shepherd of the flock doomed
to be slain for those who trafficked in the sheep.
And I took two staffs; one I named Grace, the other
I named Union. And I tended the sheep. 8In one
month I destroyed the three shepherds. But I became
impatient with them, and they also detested me. 9So
I said, "I will not be your shepherd. What is to die,
let it die; what is to be destroyed, let it be destroyed;
and let those that are left devour the flesh of one
another." 10And I took my staff Grace, and I broke
it, annulling the covenant which I had made with
all the peoples. 11So it was annulled on that day,
and the traffickers in the sheep, who were watching
me, knew that it was the word of the LORD. 12Then
I said to them, "If it seems right to you, give me my
wages; but if not, keep them." And they weighed
out as my wages thirty shekels of silver. 13Then the
LORD said to me, "Cast it into the treasury"[q]—the
lordly price at which I was paid off by them. So I
took the thirty shekels of silver and cast them into
the treasury[q] in the house of the LORD. 14Then I broke
my second staff Union, annulling the brotherhood
between Judah and Israel.

15 Then the LORD said to me, "Take once more the
implements of a worthless shepherd. 16For behold, I
am raising up in the land a shepherd who does not
care for the perishing, or seek the wandering,[r] or
heal the maimed, or nourish the sound, but devours
the flesh of the fat ones, tearing off even their hoofs.
17Woe to my worthless shepherd,
 who deserts the flock!
May the sword strike his arm
 and his right eye!
Let his arm be wholly withered,
 his right eye utterly blinded!"

Jerusalem's Victory

12

An Oracle

The word of the LORD concerning Israel: Thus
says the LORD, who stretched out the heavens and
founded the earth and formed the spirit of man

11:12–13: Mt 26:15; 27:9.

11:7 Grace ... Union: The names of the two staffs. The first signifies a "covenant" the Lord has made with "all the peoples" (11:10); the second signifies the bond of "brotherhood" that unites Judah and Israel (11:14). The symbolism may be rooted in the founding of the Davidic monarchy in the tenth century B.C. At this time, the Lord made a covenant of kingship with David (2 Sam 7:12–19), giving him dominion over the tribes of Israel and even over neighboring peoples in the region (2 Sam 5:1–5; 8:1–14; Ps 18:43). David's kingdom held together under Solomon, his son and successor (1 Kings 4:20–25), but afterward it broke apart, with northern Israel forming its own rival kingdom in opposition to Judah (1 Kings 12:1–33) and with subject peoples gradually freeing themselves from Israelite rule (2 Kings 1:1; Ps 2:1–6).

11:8 one month: Represents a short period of time. **three shepherds:** Three powerful figures deposed from office. One possibility is that they symbolize Jehoiakim, Jehoiachin, and Zedekiah—the last three kings of Judah who reigned before the Babylonian conquest of Jerusalem and the collapse of the Davidic monarchy in 586 B.C.

11:9 devour the flesh: The horrors of cannibalism, a covenant curse (Lev 26:29; Deut 28:53–57) that accompanied the Babylonian siege of Jerusalem (Lam 2:20; 4:10).

11:12 thirty shekels of silver: The price of a gored slave (Ex 21:32). It was hardly a just wage for the prophet's benevolent services. Casting away the coins signifies his rejection of the payment (11:13). • Matthew sees a messianic fulfillment of this episode when the chief priests pay Judas Iscariot thirty pieces of silver to betray Jesus into their hands (Mt 26:14–16). But after learning of Jesus' condemnation, Judas rejects the silver coins and throws them down in the Temple (Mt 27:3–10). For the evangelist, the prophet prefigures Jesus as the Good Shepherd who is despised and valued at a mere thirty shekels; at the same time, he foreshadows Judas in receiving the payment and casting it into the sanctuary.

11:13 the treasury: Follows an ancient Syriac translation. The Hebrew MT reads "the potter/moulder", and the Greek LXX reads "the furnace" (used for smelting metals, Wis 3:6). Scholars disagree on what exactly the Hebrew text envisions. Insofar as pottery shops had piles of ruined vessels and broken shards, they were known as places where useless items were discarded. It is also possible the coins were given to a foundry where they would be melted down and recast into something new. **lordly price:** The description is meant sarcastically and indignantly.

11:14 Judah and Israel: Traditional names for the Southern and Northern Kingdoms. See note on 8:13.

11:16 a shepherd who does not care: Fitting punishment for ungrateful sheep who "detested" the Lord's good shepherd (11:8). The identity of this figure is unknown. Some view him as the Antichrist of the last days, the man of sin who will exalt himself as a god until he is slain by the Lord Jesus (2 Thess 2:3–12; CCC 675).

11:17 Woe: A cry of anguish heard at funerals. See word study: *Woe* at Is 28:1. **May the sword strike:** A prayer of imprecation that calls down God's judgment on the wicked. See essay: *Imprecatory Psalms* at Ps 109.

12:1—14:21 Prophetic visions of the coming kingdom of God. Its scope will be universal, embracing all nations (14:16), but its epicenter will be Jerusalem, the city that the Lord defends (12:1–5), cleanses (13:1–6), and makes the seat of his kingly reign (14:1–19).

12:1 An Oracle: Usually a pronouncement of judgment on godless foreign nations but here spoken to the restored people of Israel in messianic times (cf. Mal 1:1). The following references to God as Creator stress that he is more than sufficiently powerful to shape the course of history and accomplish the redemption of entire nations. See note on 9:1. **stretched out the heavens:** Like a tent or tabernacle over the earth (Jer 10:12). See note on Is 40:22. **the spirit of man:** The breath of life, infused into the human race at creation (Gen 2:7; Job 32:8).

[q]Syr: Heb *to the potter.*
[r]Syr Compare Gk Vg: Heb *the youth.*

within him. 2"Behold, I am about to make Jerusalem a cup of reeling to all the peoples round about; it will be against Judah also in the siege against Jerusalem. 3On that day I will make Jerusalem a heavy stone for all the peoples; all who lift it shall grievously hurt themselves. And all the nations of the earth will come together against it. 4On that day, says the LORD, I will strike every horse with panic, and its rider with madness. But upon the house of Judah I will open my eyes, when I strike every horse of the peoples with blindness. 5Then the clans of Judah shall say to themselves, 'The inhabitants of Jerusalem have strength through the LORD of hosts, their God.'

6"On that day I will make the clans of Judah like a blazing pot in the midst of wood, like a flaming torch among sheaves; and they shall devour to the right and to the left all the peoples round about, while Jerusalem shall still be inhabited in its place, in Jerusalem.

7"And the LORD will give victory to the tents of Judah first, that the glory of the house of David and the glory of the inhabitants of Jerusalem may not be exalted over that of Judah. 8On that day the LORD will put a shield about the inhabitants of Jerusalem so that the feeblest among them on that day shall be like David, and the house of David shall be like God, like the angel of the LORD, at their head. 9And on that day I will seek to destroy all the nations that come against Jerusalem.

Mourning for the Pierced One

10 "And I will pour out on the house of David and the inhabitants of Jerusalem a spirit of compassion and supplication, so that, when they look on him whom they have pierced, they shall mourn for him, as one mourns for an only child, and weep bitterly over him, as one weeps over a first-born. 11On that day the mourning in Jerusalem will be as great as the mourning for Ha'dad-rim'mon in the plain of Megid'do. 12The land shall mourn, each family by itself; the family of the house of David by itself, and their wives by themselves; the family of the house

---

12:10: Jn 19:37.

12:2 cup of reeling: Filled with wine or alcoholic drink. The drunken stupor that results from drinking it is a form of divine judgment (Ps 75:8; Is 51:21–23; Jer 25:15–29; Ezek 23:31–34). **the siege:** An international assault on Jerusalem is envisioned (12:3). • According to the Book of Revelation, which draws from this and similar oracles (especially Ezek 38–39), history will near its end when the nations of the world besiege "the camp of the saints and the beloved city", which God defends with fire from heaven (Rev 20:9). These appear to be images of the Church undergoing her final trial before the triumphant return of Christ (CCC 675–77).

12:3 that day: A day of divine judgment and salvation, also known as the "day of the LORD" (14:1). Some form of the expression is used nearly 20 times in the final chapters of Zechariah (12:4, 6, 8, 9, 11, etc.). See word study: *The Day of the LORD* at Joel 1:15. **heavy stone:** I.e., no longer a hapless victim of conquest and exile.

12:6 blazing pot: A ceramic pot filled with live coals. The two images in this verse are pictures of God's people empowered to vanquish their enemies.

12:7 the house of David: Features prominently in the final prophecies of the book (12:8, 10, 12; 13:1). It points to a restoration of David's rule, not in a historical rebuilding of the Davidic monarchy, but in the heavenly enthronement of the Davidic Messiah (Lk 1:32–33; Acts 2:29–36).

12:8 a shield: Recalls the Lord's protective "wall of fire" around Jerusalem in Zechariah's third vision (2:5). **like David:** Remembered in the Bible as valiant warrior (1 Sam 17:12–54; 18:1–7). **angel of the LORD:** A messenger from heaven and minister of God's will. See word study: *Angel of the LORD* at Gen 16:7.

12:9 destroy all the nations: The judgment destined for evildoers and unbelievers among the nations. Gentiles who "join themselves to the LORD" (2:11) and "worship ... the LORD of hosts" (14:16) will be the redeemed of the nations who become part of the covenant people.

12:10 I will pour out: The prophets use this language for God bestowing his divine Spirit upon his people (Is 32:15; 44:3; Ezek 39:29; Joel 2:28). **spirit of compassion:** Or "a spirit of grace". It is a divine gift that moves the people to contrition, repentance, and reconciliation with God (CCC 1432). **supplication:** The desire to petition God is also a gift of grace (CCC 2559–61). **they look on him:** The Hebrew reads "they look to me". **whom they have pierced:** Either the Lord, whose rejection by Jerusalem is figuratively described as a violent attack on him, or a prophet of the Lord, who was slain by the city on the charge of being a false prophet (notice that parents are to "pierce" a son with death if he becomes a false prophet, 13:3). Either way, whether piercing the Lord is a metaphor or involves an actual murder, intense mourning will follow when the city realizes its mistake (12:11–14). Some ancient Jews connected this verse to the slaying of an anointed figure who would precede the Davidic Messiah (Babylonian Talmud, *Sukkah* 52a). See word study: *Pierce* at 13:3. • According to the NT, the oracle has a messianic fulfillment when Jesus is crucified and thrust through with a spear (Jn 19:34). Afterward, those who plotted his death will wail when they see the Lord coming in judgment (Rev 1:7). **a first-born:** The first son born to a woman who stood to inherit a double portion of his father's estate (Deut 21:15–17). In the NT, Jesus is the first-born of Mary (Lk 2:7) as well as the first-born of the Father who enters the world by his Incarnation (Heb 1:6), inherits all of creation (Col 1:15), and precedes all others in being resurrected in glory (Col 1:18; Rev 1:5). • Christ's body is now immortal and worthy of a heavenly dwelling. He will also return in human form, so that those on both his right and his left will see him, as it is written: "They shall look on him whom they have pierced." They will behold the same body they impaled with a spear, despite the Word being untouched by it (St. Augustine, *Tractates on John* 21, 3).

12:11 Hadad-rimmon: Evidently a site near Megiddo where the death of King Josiah of Judah was remembered and mourned. He died after being pierced with an arrow in a battle with Egyptian forces in 609 B.C., and his untimely death was lamented long afterward (2 King 23:29; 2 Chron 35:20–25). Others relate the name to an annual ritual of weeping for the Semitic storm god, Baal or Hadad, whose mythical death was lamented every dry season (cf. Ezek 8:14). **Megiddo:** A fortified settlement overlooking a fertile plain on the southern edge of Galilee. It was the scene of several battles in biblical times (Josh 12:21; Judg 5:19; 2 Kings 23:29).

12:12 the house of David: The royal family in Israel (2 Sam 7:11–12). **by themselves:** Repentance is the responsibility of every individual, not just the collective responsibility of a city, nation, or clan. **the house of Nathan:** The descendants of David's third son (2 Sam 5:14; 1 Chron 3:5).

of Nathan by itself, and their wives by themselves; [13]the family of the house of Levi by itself, and their wives by themselves; the family of the Shime′ites by itself, and their wives by themselves; [14]and all the families that are left, each by itself, and their wives by themselves.

13 On that day there shall be a fountain opened for the house of David and the inhabitants of Jerusalem to cleanse them from sin and uncleanness.

The Wounded Prophet

2 "And on that day, says the LORD of hosts, I will cut off the names of the idols from the land, so that they shall be remembered no more; and also I will remove from the land the prophets and the unclean spirit. [3]And if any one again appears as a prophet, his father and mother who bore him will say to him, 'You shall not live, for you speak lies in the name of the LORD'; and his father and mother who bore him shall pierce him through when he prophesies. [4]On that day every prophet will be ashamed of his vision when he prophesies; he will not put on a hairy mantle in order to deceive, [5]but he will say, 'I am no prophet, I am a tiller of the soil; for the land has been my possession[t] since my youth.' [6]And if one asks him, 'What are these wounds on your back?' he will say, 'The wounds I received in the house of my friends.'"

[7]"Awake, O sword, against my shepherd,
  against the man who stands next to me,"
                    says the LORD of hosts.

reminisant of Amos
Passion of Lord

13:7: Mt 26:31; Mk 14:27.

12:13 the house of Levi: The priestly tribe in Israel (Deut 33:8–11). **Shimeites:** Levites of the clan of Gershon (Ex 6:16–17; Num 3:21).

13:1–6 The Lord will open a spring of divine mercy to wash away the sins and impurity (13:1) his people incurred by involvement in idolatry and false prophecy, practices that will also be removed from the covenant community (13:2).

✝ **13:1 that day:** The day of the Lord. See note on 12:3. **fountain opened:** Signifies an abundant and constant supply of divine forgiveness and life. See note on 14:8. • This fountain is the same that gushes from the house of the Lord in Ezekiel, the one that swells into a river and gives life to all. It refers to the Church and to the knowledge of Scripture, from which all can be reborn in Christ and from which we can be cleansed of our sins in the waters of Baptism (St. Jerome, *Commentary on Zechariah* 13, 1).

13:2 the idols: The Lord's plan to banish idolatry from the land was also revealed in Zechariah's seventh vision (5:5–11). **prophets:** False prophets, as specified in the Greek LXX. The problem of false prophecy, while more serious in preexilic times (Jer 23:9–22), lingered on into the postexilic period (Neh 6:12–14). **the unclean spirit:** Perhaps a lying spirit that God allowed to deceive the false prophets, as in 1 Kings 22:19–23.

13:3 You shall not live: The Law of Moses demanded the execution of a false prophet so that evil might be purged from Israel (Deut 13:1–11; 18:20). **you speak lies:** False prophets speak presumptuously, as if they have been sent by the Lord to deliver a specific message when they have not (Deut 18:20–22).

13:4 hairy mantle: The distinctive dress of a prophet. Garments made of animal hair were worn by Elijah (2 Kings 1:8) and John the Baptist (Mt 3:4).

13:5 I am no prophet: Perhaps an intentional echo of Amos 7:14.

13:6 wounds: Lacerations to the body made during idolatrous rites, as when the prophets of Baal cut themselves in a ritual frenzy to gain the deity's favor (1 Kings 18:28). This type of self-mutilation was forbidden in Israel (Lev 19:28; Deut 14:1). **your back:** Or "your chest". **the house of my friends:** False prophets will be so afraid of exposure they will make up stories to conceal the real reason for their scars.

13:7–9 The Lord will cut down his shepherd (13:7) and part of his flock (13:8) and will purify the remnant that remains (13:9). Many read these verses as a continuation of the shepherd allegory in 11:4–17.

📖 **13:7 O sword:** Personified as an instrument of the Lord's will (Deut 32:41; Jer 12:12; Ezek 21:8–17). **my shepherd:** Often identified with the "worthless shepherd" of 11:17, although his position as one who **stands next to** the Lord weighs against this interpretation because it suggests the shepherd is a faithful servant. Insofar as kings are regularly portrayed as shepherds in the Bible, it is better to view this figure as the royal Davidic Branch whom the Lord calls "my servant" (3:8). **Strike the shepherd:** The shepherd-king will be

---

[t] Cn: Heb *for man has caused me to possess.*

WORD STUDY

Pierce (13:3)

Dāqar (Heb.): a verb meaning "pierce" or "stab" or "run through" that appears 11 times in the Hebrew OT. In one case, it is used metaphorically for a person who is stricken with sharp pangs of hunger (Lam 4:9), but, otherwise, it indicates the penetration of the human body with a pointed object, causing a serious or fatal wound (Jer 37:10; 51:4). Most often a person who is pierced is killed by being thrust through with a spear or sword (Num 25:8; Judg 9:54; 1 Sam 31:4; Is 13:15). Impalement by sword or spear is envisioned when the parents of a false prophet put him to death by piercing him through (Zech 13:3). An element of mystery surrounds the use of this verb when the Book of Zechariah foresees the inhabitants of Jerusalem mourning a figure "they have pierced" (Zech 12:10). The Hebrew favors identifying the Lord as the One pierced by the rejection of his people, in which case the language would be metaphorical rather than literal. However, since the remainder of the verse speaks of the victim in the third person ("him"), one senses that a significant person has been killed in a violent way, and the city comes to realize this murder was actually a tragic martyrdom. This second interpretation is followed by the NT, which relates the passage to the Crucifixion of Jesus, whose body was pierced with nails and a spear (Jn 19:34).

"Strike the shepherd, that the sheep may be
scattered;
  I will turn my hand against the little
  ones.
⁸In the whole land, says the LORD,
  two thirds shall be cut off and perish,
  and one third shall be left alive.
⁹And I will put this third into the fire,
  and refine them as one refines silver,
  and test them as gold is tested.
They will call on my name,
  and I will answer them.
I will say, 'They are my people';
  and they will say, 'The LORD is my God.'"

The Day of the Lord Is Coming

14 Behold, a day of the LORD is coming, when the spoil taken from you will be divided in the midst of you. ²For I will gather all the nations against Jerusalem to battle, and the city shall be taken and the houses plundered and the women ravished; half of the city shall go into exile, but the rest of the people shall not be cut off from the city. ³Then the LORD will go forth and fight against those nations as when he fights on a day of battle. ⁴On that day his feet shall stand on the Mount of Olives which lies before Jerusalem on the east; and the Mount of Olives shall be split in two from east to west by a very wide valley; so that one half of the Mount shall withdraw northward, and the other half southward. ⁵And the valley of my mountains shall be stopped up, for the valley of the mountains shall touch the side of it; and you shall flee as you fled from the earthquake in the days of Uzzi'ah king of Judah. Then the LORD your ᵘ God will come, and all the holy ones with him. ᵛ

6 On that day there shall be neither cold nor frost.ʷ ⁷And there shall be continuous day (it is known to the LORD), not day and not night, for at evening time there shall be light.

---

struck down by divine decree, causing his flock to be scattered, judged, and reduced to a remnant (13:8). • Jesus cited this passage before his arrest in Gethsemane to say that his abandonment by the disciples would be a fulfillment of Scripture (Mt 26:31; Mk 14:27). He thus appears to have read this verse as a messianic prophecy; however, some, holding that judgment against the worthless shepherd of 11:17 is meant, maintain that Jesus invoked the passage as a proverb or maxim that applies to any situation where the death or capture of a leader causes his followers to be dispersed (cf. Acts 5:36–37).

13:8 two thirds: The majority of the covenant community will face divine judgment and death for following idols and false prophets (13:2–6). **one third:** The remnant of survivors will undergo a divine cleansing from sin (13:1).

13:9 into the fire: Refining fires of trial and suffering that purge the remnant, just as impurities and alloys are separated from precious metals by smelting them in a furnace (Is 1:25; Prov 17:3; Sir 2:5; 1 Pet 1:6–7). **my people ... my God:** Reaffirms the covenant bond between the Lord and Israel (8:8), which will expand to include the nations in messianic times (2:11). The statement is a variation on the traditional "covenant formula" (Lev 26:12; Jer 30:22; Ezek 37:27; Hos 2:23).

14:1–21 An apocalyptic vision of the coming kingdom of God. It centers on Jerusalem, the city ravaged by hostile nations (14:2) but afterward defended (14:3–5), held aloft (14:10), and made holy by the Lord (14:20–21). The sequence of the prophecy moves from a conquered Jerusalem to a highly exalted Jerusalem that is destined to be the seat of Lord's reign (14:9) and a place of pilgrimage for all the nations (14:16). • This final vision, which foresees another conquest of Jerusalem, stands in the background of Jesus' Olivet Discourse in the Synoptic Gospels (Mt 24; Mk 13; Lk 21). Its picture of the new Jerusalem also influenced John's description of the heavenly Jerusalem in Rev 21–22. This celestial city, which depicts not only the eternal state but the supernatural glory of the Church in history, is exalted above the earth (14:10; Rev 21:10), enjoys perpetual light (14:7; Rev 21:23–25), flows with living water (14:8; Rev 22:1–2, 17), and is imbued with a holiness that permits nothing unclean within (14:20–21; Rev 21:27).

14:1 day of the LORD: A day when the Lord intervenes powerfully in history to judge the wicked and bring salvation to the righteous. See word study: *The Day of the LORD* at Joel 1:15.

14:2 the city shall be taken: A future conquest of Jerusalem reminiscent of its past destruction by the Babylonians in 586 B.C. The Roman conquest of the city in A.D. 70 seems to be in view, as in Dan 9:26. • Zechariah, writing after the return from Babylon, prophesied the Roman siege and subjugation of the Jewish people. The remnant of the people to be saved is a precise reference to the Savior's apostles (Eusebius of Caesarea, *Demonstration of the Gospel* 2, 3).

14:3 the LORD will go forth: As a Divine Warrior who fights for his people and gives them victory (Ex 14:25; 15:3; Josh 10:14; Ps 24:8).

14:4 his feet: An anthropomorphic way of describing the Lord's descent upon the mountain, causing an earthquake (cf. Ex 19:18; Ps 18:7–9; Hab 3:6). **the Mount of Olives:** Rises directly east of Jerusalem and separated from the city by a deep ravine called the Kidron Valley. Splitting the mountain in two provides a path of escape for the people under assault in the city (14:5). The description recalls how the Lord fought for Israel of old by dividing the sea and enabling his people to escape Egypt (Ex 14:16, 21–25; Ps 78:13).

14:5 you shall flee: A remnant of God's people will evacuate the city. **the earthquake:** Also mentioned in Amos 1:1 and estimated to have occurred around 760 B.C. **Uzziah:** Ruled the Southern Kingdom of Judah from 792 to 740 B.C. **God will come:** As the divine King (14:9) and Judge of all nations (14:12–15). **the holy ones:** The heavenly army of angels (Ps 89:5). • The NT describes the glorious return of Christ in the same way, i.e., as the divine Lord who is King and Judge of all nations who is accompanied by an army of holy angels (Mt 16:27; 25:31; 1 Thess 3:13; 2 Thess 1:7; Rev 19:14).

14:6 neither cold nor frost: A time of perpetual summer and harvest. **not day and not night:** A time of perpetual daylight with no more evening or nightfall. As Isaiah describes it, this endless light will come, not from the sun or moon, but from glory of the Lord, who will dwell in the new Jerusalem (Is 60:19–20; cf. Rev 21:23; 22:5).

ᵘ Heb *my.*
ᵛ Gk Syr Vg Tg: Heb *you.*
ʷ Compare Gk Syr Vg Tg: Heb uncertain.

8 On that day living waters shall flow out from Jerusalem, half of them to the eastern sea and half of them to the western sea; it shall continue in summer as in winter.

9 And the LORD will become king over all the earth; on that day the LORD will be one and his name one.

¹⁰The whole land shall be turned into a plain from Ge'ba to Rimmon south of Jerusalem. But Jerusalem shall remain aloft upon its site from the Gate of Benjamin to the place of the former gate, to the Corner Gate, and from the Tower of Hanan'el to the king's wine presses. ¹¹And it shall be inhabited, for there shall be no more curse;ˣ Jerusalem shall dwell in security.

12 And this shall be the plague with which the LORD will strike all the peoples that wage war against Jerusalem: their flesh shall rot while they are still on their feet, their eyes shall rot in their sockets, and their tongues shall rot in their mouths. ¹³And on that day a great panic from the LORD shall

fall on them, so that each will lay hold on the hand of his fellow, and the hand of the one will be raised against the hand of the other; ¹⁴even Judah will fight against Jerusalem. And the wealth of all the nations round about shall be collected, gold, silver, and garments in great abundance. ¹⁵And a plague like this plague shall fall on the horses, the mules, the camels, the donkeys, and whatever beasts may be in those camps.

Survivors of the Nations Will Come to Jerusalem

16 Then every one that survives of all the nations that have come against Jerusalem shall go up year after year to worship the King, the LORD of hosts, and to keep the feast of booths. ¹⁷And if any of the families of the earth do not go up to Jerusalem to worship the King, the LORD of hosts, there will be no rain upon them. ¹⁸And if the family of Egypt do not go up and present themselves, then upon them shallʸ come the plague with which the LORD afflicts

---

14:8: Ezek 47:1–12; Rev 22:1–2. **14:11:** Rev 22:3. **14:18–19:** Is 19; Jer 46; Ezek 29–32.

14:8 living waters: Flow in abundance and perpetuity from the fountain that the Lord will open in Jerusalem (13:1). Ezekiel and Joel witness these life-giving waters gushing out from the Lord's Temple (Ezek 47:1–12; Joel 3:18). • Jesus evokes this prophetic hope when he offers the Samaritan woman the living water of eternal life (Jn 4:7–14) and when he invites worshipers in Jerusalem to drink from this living water that flows from him (Jn 7:38–39) (CCC 694). **the eastern sea:** The Dead Sea. **the western sea:** The Mediterranean. **continue in summer:** Unlike a wadi, a seasonal stream that flowed in the rainy winter months but dried up in the hot summer months. • The law of salvation flows out from Jerusalem to the nations, which are symbolized by the two seas, eastern and western. The living waters are the precepts of Christ that water their hearts continually in summer as in winter (St. Ephrem the Syrian, *Commentary on Zechariah*).

14:9 king over all the earth: The kingship of the Lord, long recognized in Israel (Ps 99:1–5), will be recognized by all nations as well (14:16). It is not explained how this divine kingship fits with the Davidic kingship of the Messiah announced earlier in the book (6:12–13; 9:9–10). • Christian faith sees these expectations converging in the mystery of the Incarnation, in which God exercises his kingship over the world through the Davidic humanity assumed by his eternal Son, Jesus Christ (Lk 1:32–33; Jn 1:49; Acts 2:29–36). **the LORD will be one:** An allusion to Deut 6:4, the monotheistic creed of the OT. It affirms that the Lord alone is God and that he alone is to be served by his covenant people. The coming of the kingdom of God will make this ancient faith, formerly entrusted to Israel, the common faith of all nations who invoke the Lord's name in worship (Is 45:21–24).

14:10 Geba to Rimmon: Towns near the northern and southern boundaries of the land of Judah (Josh 15:32; 2 Kings 23:8). **shall remain aloft:** The future exaltation of Jerusalem, described in poetical and apocalyptic terms to stress its preeminence (as in Is 2:2; Mic 4:1). A change in the physical landscape around the city is not intended. **Gate of Benjamin:** In

the northeast wall. **Corner Gate:** In the northwest wall. **Tower of Hananel:** North of the Temple. **the king's wine presses:** Presumably near the southern limit of the city near the king's garden (Neh 3:15).

14:11 curse: Literally, "ban of utter destruction" (Heb. *ḥērem*). Before becoming Israel's capital, Jerusalem was a Jebusite settlement that was among the cities of Canaan devoted to destruction (Deut 20:16–17). See word study: *Devoted* at Josh 6:17.

14:12–15 A plague from the Lord that strikes down the armies arrayed against Jerusalem, both warriors (14:12) and animals (14:15).

14:13 a great panic: A madness from the Lord that causes the city's attackers to turn against one another (cf. Josh 10:10; 1 Sam 14:20).

14:14 wealth ... collected: Spoils of war will be gathered from the fallen soldiers (Ezek 39:10).

14:16 all the nations: Identified earlier in the book as non-Israelites who will seek the Lord (8:22) and join themselves to him as members of the covenant people (2:11). Rendering the "obedience of faith" (Rom 1:5), they will converge on the new Jerusalem to serve the Lord and honor him as their sovereign **King** (cf. Is 2:2–3; 56:6–8; 60:3–7). **the feast of booths:** A pilgrimage festival held in Jerusalem every autumn. It celebrated the end of the harvest season and commemorated the Lord's care for Israel when the people wandered for forty years in the wilderness (Lev 23:33–43; Deut 16:13–15). It was also known as the feast of ingathering (Ex 23:16) and Tabernacles (Jn 7:2). During the festival, participants prayed for God to bless the next year's harvest by sending abundant rain (14:17). Gentile observance of Tabernacles is a fulfillment of its deepest meaning, showing that God, who called Israel as the first fruits of the nations (Jer 2:3), ultimately desires to gather the full harvest of all nations into his kingdom (Gen 12:3; Jer 3:17). See note on 14:1–21.

14:17 no rain: Rainfall is a blessing of the covenant (Deut 28:12). Drought, by contrast, is one of its curses (Deut 28:24).

14:18 Egypt: Infamous in Scripture as a foreign nation that resists the Lord's demands. However, Egypt's conversion to the one true God is envisioned in Is 19:19–25. **the plague:** The one described in 14:12–15.

ˣ Or *ban of utter destruction.*
ʸ Gk Syr: Heb *shall not.*

the nations that do not go up to keep the feast of booths. [19]This shall be the punishment to Egypt and the punishment to all the nations that do not go up to keep the feast of booths.

20 And on that day there shall be inscribed on the bells of the horses, "Holy to the Lord." And the pots in the house of the Lord shall be as the bowls before the altar; [21]and every pot in Jerusalem and Judah shall be sacred to the Lord of hosts, so that all who sacrifice may come and take of them and boil the flesh of the sacrifice in them. And there shall no longer be a trader in the house of the Lord of hosts on that day. *(Clearing of the Temple)*

14:20–21 The new Jerusalem indwelt by the Lord will be thoroughly sanctified. Decorative **bells** fitted on animal straps and harnesses will be as holy as the high priest's garments, which featured golden bells around the bottom edge of his tunic (Ex 28:33–34) and a golden plate on his turban that bore the inscription: **Holy to the Lord** (Ex 28:36–37). Likewise, every household **pot** in Judah will be as holy as the Temple vessels used to boil the priestly portions of sacrificial animals (Lev 6:28)

14:21 a trader: Literally, "a Canaanite", which the RSV2CE takes to be a merchant. The holiness of the new Jerusalem will not permit anything unclean within (cf. Rev 21:27). Jesus' effort to cleanse the Temple of money changers and animals for purchase may be a prophetic enactment of this verse (Jn 2:13–22).

STUDY QUESTIONS
Zechariah

Chapter 1

For understanding
1. **1:3.** Whom is the Lord addressing, and what are they urged to learn? What does the language of repentance include? With what will the Lord of Hosts return to his people? According to St. Augustine, how are free will and divine grace simultaneously affirmed? What did the Council of Trent cite this passage to affirm and, at the same time, acknowledge?
2. **1:7–17.** In this first vision, what does Zechariah see, and what do they report? What is the message?
3. **1:8.** How is the man riding a red horse identified in 1:11? What is his role, and what presumably are the other three riders? To what does "he was standing" refer? What color is sorrel?
4. **1:12.** As a round number, what period does seventy years approximate? What was happening during this period? How do the seventy years of Zechariah's vision coincide with the "seventy years" of Judah's subjugation to Babylon that Jeremiah prophesied?
5. **1:18–21.** What does the second vision, where Zechariah sees four horns toppled by four smiths, signify? Whom does the prophet have in mind? Of what are horns the symbols in the Bible, and what does the number four signify?

For application
1. **1:3.** While it is possible for the Lord to "return" to a person who does not return to him, what usual condition must be met before the Lord acts? Why must the penitent first return to the Lord?
2. **1:11.** Read the note for this verse. What is the best time to seek the Lord? Is there a time limit on seeking him (cf. Is 55:6) or a time when it is too late?
3. **1:14.** Skip ahead to the note for 8:2 regarding the meaning of God's jealousy. How jealous is he for your salvation? What do you think he will do to ensure it? What is the only thing that could prevent it?
4. **1:18–19.** As symbols of strength, what horns threaten God's people today? How might the prayer to St. Michael serve as an effective intercessory prayer? What does the prayer say that St. Michael's role is, and with what power does he operate?

Chapter 2

For understanding
1. **2:1–5.** In this third vision, what does the man whom Zechariah sees set out to do? What three things, however, does Zechariah learn? What is the message?
2. **2:6–13.** Whom does Zechariah address? What are they urged to do? What will the regathering of exiles to Zion also be for the Gentiles?
3. **2:11.** What does the invitation to the nations to join themselves to the Lord imply? What will the Gentiles become? Although prior to messianic times, only Israel was called the Lord's special people, what did the prophets foresee? What oath will this fulfill? How does Paul picture the Gentiles entering the Lord's covenant? What will fulfillment of the prophecy verify?
4. **2:13.** While silence is an act of reverential awe and adoration, what sense or anticipation can it also indicate? What is the Lord's holy dwelling, and of what is it the unseen counterpart?

For application
1. **2:4–5.** In ancient times, what defenses did a village without walls have? When you face temptation, what defenses do you have? In times of doubt or temptation, how quickly do you remember to take advantage of those defenses?
2. **2:8.** What does this verse imply about how precious you are to the Lord? As for yourself, what does it mean for you to regard the Lord's teaching as the apple of your eye (cf. Prov 7:2)? What is the connection between these two viewpoints?
3. **2:10.** Rev 21:3 says that the dwelling of God is among mankind. In how many ways is God present among his people? What practical difference does it make that God dwells in you?

Chapter 3

For understanding
1. **3:1–10.** In this fourth vision, whom does Zechariah see standing trial in the heavenly court? By whom is he being prosecuted, and by whom defended? Following the removal of his filthy garments, for what does the prophet then call? What does the redressing of the high priest, who represents his people before the Lord, reveal? What does purification from the defilements of the past create?
2. **3:1.** Who is Joshua? Through whom is his priestly line traced? How did early Christians often view him? On whose behalf does the angel of the Lord speak? What does the title Satan mean? What does the heavenly trial scene suggest about him, and what does he appear to be? How does Christian tradition identify this figure? Of what does Satan accuse Joshua? When does the Book of Revelation allude to this vision?
3. **3:4.** What passage does the reclothing of Joshua signify? What is the "clean turban"? According to St. Gregory of Nyssa, how does Zechariah prophesy clearly of Jesus, and what does his prophecy teach us? According to St. Justin Martyr, why was this revelation given to believers in Christ the high priest?
4. **3:8.** For whom is "my servant" an honorary epithet? Who is the Branch, and what will he do? With whom is he often identified? However, why does he not fit the description of a coming one who will rule upon a "throne"? How is Zerubbabel better viewed? How will the Branch be like Solomon?

Study Questions

For application
1. **3:1.** According to Rev 12:10, the "accuser of our brethren" accuses them "day and night before our God". Of what does he accuse them? Of what does he typically accuse you, and how often? How do you resist him?
2. **3:5.** What are some of the vestments that priests wear when celebrating Mass or the Divine Liturgy? How are the vestments worn by a bishop different from those of a priest? Why is the bishop's miter removed when he prays (cf. 1 Cor 11:14) but worn when he preaches?
3. **3:7.** Read the note for this verse. In a modern church building, what does the sanctuary area represent, especially if emphasized by the presence of an iconostasis? During liturgies, who has access to that area? What attitude toward the sanctuary is most appropriate for the rest of the congregation?
4. **3:9.** Why is Jesus called the cornerstone, and of what (cf. Eph 2:20)? According to Rev 21, what forms the foundations of the new Jerusalem? What is written on them, and how are they decorated? What do these metaphors signify about the Church?

Chapter 4

For understanding
1. **4:1–14.** In this fifth vision, what does Zechariah see? What do the lampstand, its supply of oil, and the seven flames represent? With the help of the angel to interpret its meaning, what is the message?
2. **4:3.** What do the two olive trees represent? What work did these two persons oversee years earlier? Because olive oil was used to anoint Israel's kings and priests, what else do the olive trees represent? How does the Book of Revelation use this image of two olive trees?
3. **4:6.** Who was Zerubbabel? Why did Zerubbabel need the source of divine wisdom and strength, the Spirit? When else were the abilities required for building the Tabernacle and its furnishings likewise supplied by "the Spirit of God"?
4. **4:7.** What will God enable Zerubbabel to do? In what way, perhaps, are these challenges to rebuilding pictured? What does the top stone appear to be, and what does it represent?

For application
1. **4:6.** Why cannot a person lift himself from the ground by his own bootstrap? What is the gravity that holds the human race to this life only? What abilities are necessary for grace and salvation to come, and who provides them?
2. **4:9.** Which is harder, to begin a project or to complete it? What did St. Paul mean when he accused the Galatian church of beginning in the Spirit but ending in the flesh (Gal 3:3)? How should one complete the Christian life?
3. **4:10.** Read the note for this verse, particularly the last sentence. How does the eye function as the "lamp of the body" (Mt 6:22)? How does the health of the eye affect how one experiences the world? In other words, how does what comes from within the self illuminate the way one sees reality?

Chapter 5

For understanding
1. **5:1–4.** In this sixth vision, what does the giant flying scroll bring that Zechariah sees? How big is it? What is the scroll? Who are cut off from the land, and what happens to their homes? What is the message for the postexilic community?
2. **5:3.** Of which commandment is theft a violation? How is one cut off? How is taking false oaths a violation of the second commandment? What do the two transgressions noted in this verse stand for?
3. **5:5–11.** In this seventh vision, what does Zechariah see? What does the woman represent? How is she now being sent back to Babylon? Since an ephah is too small to contain a living person, what may the woman be? Again, what is the message?
4. **5:9.** What is the wind? What does the wording seem to recall? What class of animal is the stork?

For application
1. **5:4.** According to the note for vv. 1–4, how does the curse from covenant violations abide in a house and cause its decay? If a family is trained, by example or intent, to steal or lie even under oath, what are the prospects for its members' growth in virtue? Instead, what is more likely to happen?
2. **5:8.** If you had to draw an image of Wickedness, what would it look like? If you had to draw one of Virtue, what would it look like? Which images in Christian art most represent these two figures to you? Why?

Chapter 6

For understanding
1. **6:1–8.** In this eighth vision, what does Zechariah see? How are the chariots drawn, and what directions do they take? Who are the charioteers, and what is the patrolling assignment of the chariot with red horses? What is the message? What parallels do Zechariah's first and last visions, which form a bracket around the rest, exhibit?
2. **6:2–3.** What do the four colors of the horses distinguish, and what is their symbolism? When and how does the Book of Revelation draw from this vision?
3. **6:11.** To what does the term for crown in question refer? On whose head is one crown placed? Where is the other placed, and until when? What crown is Joshua, who already wore a priestly crown on his linen turban, now given? Wearing two crowns, whom does he prefigure? How is this expectation fulfilled in Jesus? How is the link with Joshua strengthened?
4. **6:12.** By whom is the Branch also foreshadowed? When would Zerubbabel, who laid the foundations of the Temple years earlier, complete it? What role would the governorship of Zerubbabel prefigure, and what would his work on the Temple also prefigure?

For application
1. **6:5.** Read the note for this verse. Assuming the four winds, or spirits, are angels, which angels are given most responsibility for human beings? What does the Church teach about "guardian angels" (CCC 336)? What relationship might such angels have with unbelievers?
2. **6:8.** The note for this verse says that the Hebrew word for "spirit" can also mean anger. What is the connection between spirit and anger? What, for example, would make anger turn hot or cold? What would set one's anger at rest?
3. **6:13.** What was the relationship between the civil and the religious authorities in ancient times? What is the relationship between church and state in our country now? What do you think would be the ideal relationship between the two?
4. **6:15.** How is diversity understood in the popular culture? What is the Christian understanding of diversity as it applies to the kingdom of God?

Chapter 7

For understanding
1. **7:3.** Where were the priests being consulted, and in what "house of the Lord" were they located? What is the fifth month of the calendar, and when does it occur? What was significant about this month? Why did surviving Jews establish an annual tradition of fasting in the fifth month? What question is the delegation now asking?
2. **7:5.** What is the seventh month of the calendar, and when does it occur? What did fasting in the seventh month (besides the Day of Atonement) commemorate? Why is fasting in remembrance of Jerusalem's demise criticized, and what was the real problem?
3. **7:8-14.** With what is this oracle concerned? What has the Lord expected of his covenant people, both before the Exile and afterward? What is more important than fasting to commemorate tragic events? What was it that led to the desolation and dispersion of Judah in the first place? According to St. John Chrysostom, if those addressed by the prophet acquired no benefit from fasting without doing other good works or driving evil intentions against their neighbor out of their hearts, what is expected of Christians?
4. **7:11.** What does turning a stubborn shoulder mean?

For application
1. **7:3.** Suppose you once committed yourself to a regimen of self-discipline but now feel disappointed in the results. According to the rules of Ignatian discernment, should you give it up or hold to it? What considerations should go into making a decision?
2. **7:5.** People fast for many reasons. What are some of them? When fasting is done following a religious calendar, what are some selfish motives for keeping to the practice? What are some better motives for fasting, whether according to a calendar or voluntarily?
3. **7:9-10.** How can the actions commanded in this verse equate to a type of fast? As promised in Is 58:6-9, what will be the results?
4. **7:11.** How do small children use body language to signal that they do not want to listen to correction? What about adults? What bodily signals might indicate willingness to receive correction, even if it is not welcome? What bodily movements can signal humility before the Lord?

Chapter 8

For understanding
1. **8:1-23.** Regarding the question about fasting in 7:3, what will become of times of fasting and mourning that memorialize the fall of Jerusalem? How does the Lord plan to reverse this national disaster by doing "good" to Judah and Jerusalem in place of the "evil" he sent in the past? At one level, what does the restoration of Zion signal; and at another, what new chapter does it open?
2. **8:16.** How does the Greek LXX translate this verse? From whom does Zechariah likewise call for truthful speech? Why does Paul cite a Greek translation of this passage? What takes place at the city gates?
3. **8:20-23.** With what is this vision concerned? In an earlier vision, what did Zechariah see Gentiles doing? In a later one, how does he picture them?
4. **8:23.** What are "those days"? What does this oracle envision? What will the nations come to see, and what will it prompt them to do? With what affirmation did Jesus likely have this passage in mind?

For application
1. **8:6.** How often has it seemed impossible to you that the Lord should come into your life? What did you think was the chief obstacle preventing him? If that impossibility has been removed, how did it come about?
2. **8:8.** The note for this verse indicates that the "covenant formula" is repeated often in Scripture. What makes it more than just a formula? How often do you repeat it (or its equivalent) to yourself?
3. **8:9-13.** In your service to the Church, what need of encouragement do you have that your "hands be strong"? What challenges do you face? What resources do you have? How would reflecting on Ps 127:1-2 provide encouragement?
4. **8:23.** Who is your spiritual role model? What inspires you to imitate—or at least spiritually accompany—him? What would inspire others to use you as a spiritual role model?

Chapter 9

For understanding
1. **9:1-8.** With what are these verses concerned? In which direction does the path of conquest move? Within which territory did these cities and nations lie? What allusion do some detect, and how certain is it?

2.   **9:9–10.** With what event is the coming of the Davidic Messiah, who rides into Jerusalem on a young donkey, compared? What does he bring to Israel, and how far does his dominion extend? What hope does it fulfill? What rebirth does this event signal?

3.   **9:9.** Who is the daughter of Zion? To which king does this verse refer? How does the picture of the messianic king mounted on a donkey contrast with that of a typical conqueror? In what do the evangelists Matthew and John both see a fulfillment of this prophecy? According to St. Caesarius of Arles, who are the donkey and its colt?

4.   **9:11.** Who is addressed by the feminine singular pronoun "you" in the oracle? What is the "blood of my covenant"? What reference do some detect? What is "the waterless pit"? By contrast, how is the land of Israel watered? What promise has Christian tradition seen in this verse?

For application

1.   **9:9.** The poet John Donne once complained that he could not remain faithful to God unless God did him violence. How does Jesus normally conquer the human heart? What tactics would he most likely use to ensure its fidelity?

2.   **9:10.** St. Paul proclaimed that Jesus' coming brought peace to "you who were far off" and to those who were near (Eph 2:17). Who is the "you" in that passage, and who are those who were near? What did that peace accomplish? How does it affect you, personally?

3.   **9:11.** What does the blood of the new covenant accomplish? What release does it promise?

Chapter 10

For understanding

1.   **10:1.** When were prayers for abundant rainfall before the next harvest season typically made? What do the rains symbolize here? What does the Lord promise? When did spring rains shower the land?

2.   **10:2.** What are teraphim? Who are the diviners? Who are the dreamers? To what does the want of a shepherd refer? To what need is the prophet pointing? When do the Gospels echo the language of this and similar passages?

3.   **10:3.** Which shepherds are referred to here? During what period did Jeremiah and Ezekiel also pronounce God's judgment on the wicked shepherds of Judah? To what animal does the word "leaders" literally refer?

4.   **10:6—11:3.** What does the Lord pledge to do? To what regions did he scatter the northern and the southern tribes? What will he do with them in the future?

For application

1.   **10:3.** What is a bellwether? Who are the leaders who act as bellwethers for our culture? To what ideals are they leading us? By contrast, who should be the bellwethers for the Christian people? How do the saints fill that role for believers?

2.   **10:5.** In Revelation, Jesus is pictured as a warrior king (Rev 19:11–16). Against what enemy is he leading the fight? If he is a warrior in battle, what are his followers supposed to be? How does the battle affect you?

3.   **10:11.** Why is the Exodus event so often alluded to in psalms, prophecies, and other writings in the OT? To which event is the NT equivalent? What promise does it hold out to mankind?

Chapter 11

For understanding

1.   **11:4–17.** Although this is one of the most difficult sections of Zechariah to interpret, what is the basic storyline? What do the two staffs represent? Although he is a good and reforming shepherd, how do the sheep regard him, and what do the sheep merchants pay him? What does the prophet do with the money? How does he signify that God's blessings have been nullified toward his rebellious people? Finally, whom does the Lord recruit the prophet a second time to prefigure? How do many scholars read the episode?

2.   **11:7.** Given the names of the two staffs, what does each signify? In what may the symbolism be rooted? After the Lord made a covenant of kingship with David (2 Sam 7:12–19), giving him dominion over the tribes of Israel and even over neighboring peoples in the region, what happened?

3.   **11:12.** Of what is thirty shekels of silver the price? What does casting away the coins signify? When does Matthew see a messianic fulfillment of this episode? For the evangelist, how does the prophet prefigure Jesus and foreshadow Judas?

4.   **11:16.** For whom is the shepherd who does not care for the sheep a fitting punishment? What is the identity of this figure? Who do some view him to be?

For application

1.   **11:7–10, 14.** Consider the unity among Christians that Jesus desired for his Church (Jn 17:11). How did it come to be broken? How can reunion come about? When do you think unity will be achieved?

2.   **11:8.** Why are reforming leaders often detested by those whom they lead, even when they recognize that conditions need reform? In the lives of the saints, how many examples can you think of where their efforts at reform were rejected? If a bishop or pope wanted to restore strict adherence to the ascetic disciplines formerly required by Church law, how would you respond?

3.   **11:16.** In the three letters of John in the NT, how often is the Antichrist mentioned? Who did John think the Antichrist is? How would the worthless shepherd in this verse, if active today, qualify as an Antichrist?

Chapter 12

For understanding

1.   **12:1—14:21.** What kind of visions are these? What will be the scope of the kingdom of God? Where will its epicenter be?

2.   **12:2.** With what is the cup of reeling filled? Of what is the drunken stupor that results from drinking it a form? What is envisioned as happening to Jerusalem? According to the Book of Revelation, which draws from this and similar oracles

(especially Ezek 38–39), when will history near its end? What do "the camp of the saints and the beloved city" appear to be?

3. **12:10.** For what do the prophets use the language of pouring out, as of a liquid? What is a "spirit of compassion" or "of grace"? What is a spirit of supplication? Who is the "one whom they have pierced"? Either way, what will happen when the city realizes its mistake? To what did some ancient Jews connect this verse? According to the NT, what messianic fulfillment does the oracle have? What did a first-born son stand to inherit? In the NT, of whom is Jesus the first-born, and what does he inherit? According to St. Augustine, how will those on both the right and the left view Christ's risen body?

4. **12:11.** Where is Hadadrimmon? How did Josiah die, and how was his untimely death lamented? To what do others relate the name Hadadrimmon? What is Megiddo, and of what is it the scene in biblical times?

For application
1. **12:2–3.** When has the Church ever been at peace? Who are some of the major persecutors, and what has their rate of success been in destroying her? Which global forces are now arrayed against her? How should the Church prepare for whatever onslaught is coming?
2. **12:5.** From where does the Church derive her strength? How does she communicate that strength to her members?
3. **12:8.** When David encountered Goliath, by what armor was he protected (1 Sam 17:38–40)? When you encounter the forces of evil in the world, by what armor are you protected? Of the cardinal virtues, which is most needed when you confront spiritual and other enemies?
4. **12:10.** Of the four narratives of Jesus' Passion in the NT, which elicits the greatest response from you? What is the nature of that response? How often does contemplation of a crucifix move you to mourn over sins, especially your own?

Chapter 13

For understanding
1. **13:1.** What is "that day"? What does the opened fountain signify? According to St. Jerome, to what does this fountain refer?
2. **Word Study: Pierce (13:3).** What is the meaning of the Hebrew verb *dāqar*, and how often does it appear in the Hebrew OT? Though in one case it is used metaphorically for a person who is stricken with sharp pangs of hunger, what does it otherwise indicate? What is envisioned when the parents of a false prophet put him to death by piercing him through? What two interpretations are provided for the use of this verb when the Book of Zechariah foresees the inhabitants of Jerusalem mourning a figure "they have pierced"? Which one is followed by the NT?
3. **13:7.** How is the sword personified? How is "my shepherd" often identified, and what weighs against this interpretation? Insofar as kings are regularly portrayed as shepherds in the Bible, what is a better way to view this figure? How will the shepherd-king be struck down, and with what result? With what intent did Jesus cite this passage? While he thus appears to have read this verse as a messianic prophecy, how do some maintain that Jesus invoked the passage as a proverb or maxim?
4. **13:9.** For what are refining fires of trial and suffering intended? What does the variation on the traditional "covenant formula" reaffirm?

For application
1. **13:2–6.** What is the role of a prophet? What kinds of false prophecy arise within the Church? What did Paul recommend regarding the charism of prophecy (1 Cor 14:1–5)? From where does genuine prophecy come (2 Pet 1:21)?
2. **13:7.** What efforts have been made in recent years to undermine faith in the divinity of Jesus? What has caused many who profess Christianity to doubt or even deny Jesus' divinity? How can this shattering of faith be reversed?
3. **13:8–9.** How does persecution of the Church function like a refining process? What should be the outcome? If the Lord allows persecution to refine the faith of the small number of those whose faith stands the test, what hope do those majority have whose faith fails it?

Chapter 14

For understanding
1. **14:1–21.** On which city is this apocalyptic vision of the coming kingdom of God centered? How does the sequence of the prophecy move? What does this vision have to do with Jesus' Olivet Discourse in the Synoptic Gospels? How does its picture of the new Jerusalem also influence John's description of the heavenly Jerusalem in Rev 21–22?
2. **14:2.** Of what event is a future conquest of Jerusalem reminiscent? What conquest of the city seems to be in view? According to Eusebius of Caesarea, what did Zechariah, writing after the return from Babylon, prophesy?
3. **14:6.** What does "neither cold nor frost" promise? What does "not day and not night" mean? As Isaiah describes it, from where will this endless light come?
4. **14:8.** How will living water flow from the fountain that the Lord will open in Jerusalem? Who else witnesses these life-giving waters gushing out from the Lord's Temple? When does Jesus evoke this prophetic hope? What are the eastern and the western seas? Unlike what will the water continue to flow in summer? According to St. Ephrem the Syrian, how does the law of salvation flow, and what are the living waters?
5. **14:16.** How are "all the nations" identified earlier in the book? Rendering the "obedience of faith", what will they do? What is the "feast of booths", and what did it commemorate? How was it also known? During the festival, for what did participants pray? How is Gentile observance of Tabernacles a fulfillment of its deepest meaning?

For application
1. **14:5.** In times of active persecution, Jesus recommended flight, if possible (Mt 10:23). To what parts of the world have refugees from religious persecution, such as Iraqi Christians, fled? Where would you go, if the need of escape arose?
2. **14:8.** Why is desire for God compared to water in the desert (e.g., Ps 63:1)? How is a person like a tree growing near a constantly flowing river (cf. Ps 1:3)? How has your thirst for God been slaked by the Holy Spirit?

Study Questions

3.   **14:6–11.** Here and elsewhere (e.g., Rev 21:10–26), Scripture depicts heaven as a city. If your experience of cities is less than positive, what alternative image would you prefer? What features would make you want to go there? How would the promise of God's immediate presence complete the image?

4.   **14:21.** In Mark's account of the cleansing of the Temple (Mk 11:15–17), after Jesus overturns the tables of the money changers, why does he forbid anyone to carry anything through the Temple area? Applying this text spiritually, what stuff do you tend to carry with you through the house of God? Of what does he want you to let go?

INTRODUCTION TO MALACHI

Author and Date The book presents itself as the sayings of the prophet "Malachi" (1:1). Partly because this name is not attested elsewhere in Scripture and partly because the Greek Septuagint translates the name as a phrase ("his messenger"), some scholars hold that the book is formally anonymous. However, this would make Malachi the only prophetic book in the Bible without the name of a specific individual attached to it. The balance of probability thus favors the traditional view that Malachi is the name of the prophet who delivered the oracles of the book. Unfortunately, he provides readers with no genealogy or background information about himself. On the basis of internal evidence, he can be profiled as a man of character and courage who spoke out boldly against the religious and social ills of his day, but little else can be said. It is unknown whether Malachi was responsible for writing down his oracles and compiling them into a book or whether this was done by a disciple or scribal associate.

There are no historical notations or allusions in the book to enable scholars to date its oracles precisely. That said, most agree that the book comes from the Persian period between the completion of the Jerusalem Temple's construction in 515 B.C. and the reforms of Ezra and Nehemiah beginning in the 450s B.C. The rationale for these outer limits: it is clear that the postexilic Temple was fully operational at the time of writing and that the people of Judah were living under a Persian-appointed governor; at the same time, it is not clear that Ezra and Nehemiah's reforms to correct marital and social abuses in Judah had yet gotten underway. The impression one gets is that Malachi was a forerunner who prepared the way for Ezra and Nehemiah. A date for the book between 500 and 460 B.C. is thus a reasonable estimate.

Title The book is named after Malachi, mentioned in the opening verse. Its Hebrew form, *Mal'ākî*, either means "my messenger" or represents an abbreviation of *Mal'ākyāh*, "messenger of the LORD". The name appears in the Greek Septuagint in the title *Malachias*, while this heading is expanded in the Latin Vulgate to *Malachi Propheta*, "Malachi the Prophet". English titles for the book follow these ancient traditions.

Place in the Canon Malachi has long been revered as a canonical book of Scripture. In the Jewish Bible, or Tanakh, it stands among the Latter Prophets in a sub-collection of writings known as "the Book of the Twelve". In Christian Bibles, these twelve books are called the Minor Prophets, not because they are less important than Isaiah, Jeremiah, Ezekiel, and Daniel, but because they are comparatively shorter. In the Hebrew Bible, Greek Septuagint, and Latin Vulgate, Malachi stands as the last of the Minor Prophets, just as it does in English Bibles.

Structure Malachi displays a unique structure among the prophetic books of Scripture. The body of the book consists of six disputations in which the Lord declares a truth or makes an accusation, the people respond with a question, and the Lord brings forth evidence to demonstrate his position. **(1)** The first disputation defends the claim that God loves Israel (1:1–5); **(2)** the second charges Temple priests with dishonoring the Lord by offering defective sacrifices (1:6—2:9); **(3)** the third rebukes the men of Judah for rejecting God's standards for marriage (2:10–16); **(4)** the fourth counters cynical claims that God fails to hold evildoers accountable for their sin (2:17—3:5); **(5)** the fifth accuses the covenant community of robbing God by failing to bring tithes to the Temple (3:6–12); and **(6)** the sixth defends the justice of God with the assurance that judgment is coming (3:13—4:3). The book ends with a short epilogue that urges obedience to the Mosaic Law and promises that Elijah will be sent before the day of the Lord's judgment (4:4–6).

Historical Background Malachi was active in the postexilic period when Judah was an insignificant province in the vast Persian Empire. Around 538 B.C., a remnant of the Jewish people had returned to the homeland after decades of exile in Babylon, and by 515 B.C., the people finished rebuilding the Jerusalem Temple. As time went by, however, the enthusiasm of the initial restoration began to fade, and a period of spiritual decline set in. Corruption found its way into the priesthood, commitment to living by the Torah eroded away, and carelessness in worship became the norm. The embers of religious devotion were scarcely still burning when the prophet appeared on the scene. The reasons for these deteriorating circumstances were many. Judah, now the Persian province of Yehud, remained a subject state under Gentile rule, although lack of political independence was only part of the problem. More than anything, disappointment prevailed in the Judean community because the people had hoped for a glorious restoration that would bring God's people back to the glory days of prosperity and strength that Israel had enjoyed under David and Solomon. The reality was a far cry from the expectation, however. The Davidic monarchy was gone, much of the infrastructure of the country had to be rebuilt, harassment from local populations was an ongoing issue, and unproductive harvests meant that God's people were barely able to survive. All of this added up to the "weariness" addressed by the prophet (1:13).

The Message of the Prophet The Book of Malachi issues a clarion call to restore proper observance of the covenant. The postexilic community in Judah had become accustomed to living and worshiping in violation of the covenants that God had made with Israel over the centuries. Three specific covenants are singled out for mention: the Levitical covenant, otherwise known as the Lord's "covenant with Levi" (2:4); the Mosaic covenant, which the prophet calls "the covenant of our fathers" (2:10); and the covenant of marriage, which binds a man to the wife of his youth (2:14).

(1) *Covenant with Levi.* The Levitical covenant was a gift of "life and peace" for Israel (2:5) because it provided priestly mediators to lead the community in worship and to bestow God's blessings in return. This was the covenant of ordained ministry established at Mt. Sinai when the tribe of Levi proved its loyalty during the golden calf rebellion (Ex 32:25–29). In view of this national apostasy, the Lord called Aaron and his sons to a hereditary priesthood (Ex 40:12–15) and the rest of the tribe of Levi to serve the priests as Levitical assistants (Num 8:5–19). Malachi was distressed that the priests and Levites of his day had little regard for this holy calling. Priests were despising the Lord's name (1:6) by polluting the Lord's altar with blemished sacrifices (1:7–8) and either misinforming or failing to educate the people about the demands of the Mosaic Law, even causing them to stumble (2:7–8). These were blatant violations of the Levitical covenant, which required priests to teach the people the Torah (Lev 10:11) and to inspect all of their sacrifices to ensure that nothing defective was sacrificed to the Lord (Lev 22:17–25). The prophet, speaking in the Lord's name, warns the priests to repent of these sins lest "the curse" of the covenant fall upon them (2:2).

(2) *Covenant of the Fathers.* The Mosaic covenant was also a gift to Israel that was no longer taken seriously by Malachi's generation. Several sins that found acceptance in the community transgressed the limits of the Mosaic Law. The prophet charges Judah with being "faithless" to the marriage restrictions of the Torah by wedding foreign women who served a "foreign god" (2:11), even though intermarriage with pagan peoples was prohibited for the Israelites as a safeguard against idolatry (Deut 7:1–4). Likewise, Malachi accuses the people of robbing God by failing to obey the Mosaic tithe laws (3:8), which required that a tenth of one's new livestock and harvests be given to the Temple for the support of the priests and Levites who ministered there (Lev 27:30; Num 18:21–32; Deut 14:28–29).

Disobedience in this matter led to agricultural productivity being "cursed" (3:9). Other breaches of the Mosaic covenant mentioned in 3:5 included practicing sorcery (Deut 18:10), committing adultery (Ex 20:14), swearing falsely (Ex 20:7), and withholding wages from hired workers (Deut 24:14–15). These failings prompted Malachi's admonition: "Remember the law of my servant Moses, the statues and ordinances that I commanded him at Horeb for all Israel" (4:4). The Lord even challenges the people to repent and realign themselves with the covenant on the promise that he will pour down his "blessing" from heaven, if only they will obey once again (3:10).

(3) *Covenant of Marriage.* A third problem addressed by Malachi concerns divorce. The Mosaic Law allowed for divorce under restricted circumstances (Deut 24:1–4), but it seems that certain men of Judah put away their Jewish wives, not because of serious friction in the home or spousal unfaithfulness, but because they wanted to marry Gentile women instead (2:11). The prophet thus charges them with being "faithless" to the matrimonial covenant that bound them to their wives, a covenant to which God himself was a "witness" (2:14). Because the Lord desires "godly offspring"—children who are formed by devout parents to be faithful observers of his commandments (2:15)—the breakup of marriages by "divorce" is something he hates (2:16). Malachi's admonition "take heed to yourselves and do not be faithless" is a call for repentance among the men of the community (2:16).

Besides addressing the covenant infidelity that plagued his own generation, Malachi also looks toward the future. This is clearest in his prophetic declarations that a "day" of judgment is coming (3:2; 4:1, 3), "the great and awesome day of the LORD" (4:5). This revelation was prompted by complaints about the prosperity of the wicked compared to the adversity faced by many in Judah (3:15). Some, who wondered why sinners flourished without being punished, asked: "'Where is the God of justice?'" (2:17). Others, concluding that religious fidelity brings no tangible benefits, cynically proclaimed: "'It is vain to serve God'" (3:14). To address these errors, the prophet announces that Israel's God is indeed coming to settle accounts with his people. Preparations for his coming will be made by a "messenger" (3:1), the prophet "Elijah" (4:5), who will urge repentance and reconciliation (4:6). When the Lord himself arrives "suddenly" at an undisclosed moment (3:1), he will purify the priests and Levites like a refiner of precious metals (3:2–4), consume unrepentant evildoers with fire (4:1), and save the faithful remnant in Israel who fear him, making them his "special possession" (3:17). The injustices of the present time will thus be rectified in the eschatological time that Malachi envisions.

Christian Perspective The Book of Malachi is cited several times in the New Testament to shed light on

Christian teachings. Paul, for example, quotes the words of 1:2–3 as they appear in the Greek translation of the book: "Jacob I loved, but Esau I hated" (Rom 9:13). He demonstrates from this passage that God is sovereignly free to choose some and not others to advance his plan of salvation. It is also possible that he alludes to 1:11–12 in connection with Christian worship. For instance, he uses the language of 1:11 when he states that "the name" of the Lord Jesus is invoked "in every place" among the churches of the Gentiles (1 Cor 1:2), and later in the letter he uses the language of 1:12 when he describes the Eucharistic altar of the Church as "the table of the Lord" (1 Cor 10:21). Jesus and the evangelists likewise turn to Malachi to explain the role of John the Baptist, who is both the "messenger" of 3:1 and the "Elijah" of 4:5 (Mt 11:10–14; 17:11–13; Mk 1:2; Lk 1:17; 7:27). Moreover, Malachi's strong insistence that God hates "divorce" in 2:16 anticipates Jesus' teaching that divorce and remarriage, while permitted for a time by the Mosaic Law, is contrary to the Lord's original design for marriage as a permanent, lifelong union (Mt 19:3–9; Mk 10:2–11; Lk 16:18). Beyond the New Testament, early Christian tradition reads the announcement in 1:11 as a prophecy of the Eucharist, which is the "pure offering" that honors the Lord's name throughout the world (e.g., *Didache* 14:1–3).

OUTLINE OF MALACHI

1. The First Disputation (1:1–5)
   A. Superscription (1:1)
   B. The Lord Loves Israel (1:2)
   C. The Lord Judges Edom (1:3–5)

2. The Second Disputation (1:6—2:9)
   A. The Lord's Name Is Despised (1:6)
   B. The Blemished Sacrifices of the Priests (1:7–10)
   C. The Pure Offering among the Nations (1:11)
   D. The Weariness and Scandal of the Priests (1:12—2:9)

3. The Third Disputation (2:10–16)
   A. The Problem of Marrying Foreign Wives (2:10–12)
   B. The Problem of Divorcing Jewish Wives (2:13–16)

4. The Fourth Disputation (2:17—3:5)
   A. The Lord Is Wearied (2:17)
   B. The Lord's Messenger and Judgment (3:1–5)

5. The Fifth Disputation (3:6–12)
   A. Return to the Lord (3:6–7)
   B. Bring Tithes to the Lord (3:8–12)

6. The Sixth Disputation (3:13—4:3)
   A. Why Do Evildoers Prosper? (3:13–15)
   B. The Faithful Will Be Spared (3:16–18)
   C. The Evildoers Will Be Consumed in Fire (4:1–3)

7. Epilogue (4:4–6)
   A. Remember the Law of Moses (4:4)
   B. The Lord Is Sending Elijah (4:5–6)

THE BOOK OF
MALACHI

Israel Preferred to Edom

1 The oracle of the word of the LORD to Israel by Mal'achi.[a]

2 "I have loved you," says the LORD. But you say, "How have you loved us?" "Is not Esau Jacob's brother?" says the LORD. "Yet I have loved Jacob [3]but I have hated Esau; I have laid waste his hill country and left his heritage to jackals of the desert." [4]If E'dom says, "We are shattered but we will rebuild the ruins," the LORD of hosts says, "They may build, but I will tear down, till they are called the wicked country, the people with whom the LORD is angry for ever." [5]Your own eyes shall see this, and you shall say, "Great is the LORD, beyond the border of Israel!"

Corruption of the Priesthood

6 "A son honors his father, and a servant his master. If then I am a father, where is my honor? And if I am a master, where is my fear? says the LORD of hosts to you, O priests, who despise my name. You say, 'How have we despised your name?' [7]By offering polluted food upon my altar. And

---

1:1–3: Rom 9:13   1:2–5: Is 34; 63:1–6; Jer 49:7–22; Ezek 25:12–14; 35; Amos 1:11–12; Obad.

1:1 oracle: The Hebrew term *massā'* is a pronouncement of judgment on those who oppose the Lord. It is here directed against Israel, although it is typically uttered against foreign nations and kingdoms (Is 13:3; 17:1; 19:1; 23:13; Zech 9:1). **the word of the LORD:** Prophetic revelation from God entrusted to a human messenger. See essay: *The Word of the LORD* at Hos 1. **Israel:** The postexilic community living in Judah and Jerusalem (2:11; 3:4). **Malachi:** The Hebrew translates "my messenger" or "my angel". It is most likely the prophet's name but possibly a title (e.g., a priest is designated the Lord's "messenger" in 2:7).

1:2–5 The first disputation: (1) the Lord declares his love for Jacob's descendants, (2) they demand proof of his love, and (3) the Lord contrasts his favor toward Jacob with his judgment of Esau. His divine love was shown in his *choice* of Jacob over Esau before the twins were born (= God chose the younger Jacob to be the stronger brother, Gen 25:21–26) and continues to be shown in his *favor* toward Jacob's family over Esau's in recent history (= God preserved Judah through the Babylonian judgments of the sixth century B.C. and allowed its people to return and rebuild, whereas God denied Edom a full restoration after Babylonian judgment and later permitted Nabatean Arabs to displace the Edomites from their land).

1:2 How have you loved us?: The people of Judah doubt the love of God, partly because they were plagued by hardships after returning from Babylon and partly because hopes of a glorious restoration of Jerusalem have not materialized (see Introduction: *Historical Background*). Questions of "how" are put to the Lord repeatedly in the book (1:6, 7; 2:17; 3:7, 8, 13). **loved Jacob:** Divine love is the basis of God's election of Israel as a chosen people (Deut 7:6–8). • Paul quotes this passage in Rom 9:13 as a witness to God's sovereign freedom. He concludes from Malachi's words that the Lord determines the course of salvation history by calling specific people and nations without regard for their merits.

1:3 hated Esau: A Semitic figure of speech in which "hated" means "loved less" or "not preferred" (see Gen 29:30–31; Lk 14:26). Esau's descendants, the Edomites, were not loved insofar as they were not chosen to serve as mediators of God's blessings to the world as Jacob's descendants were. Love and hate in this context are not primarily related to affection and disdain; indeed, the Israelites themselves were not allowed to abhor their Edomite kin (Deut 23:7). For the history of animosity between Israel and Edom, see Introduction to Obadiah: *Historical Background*. **laid waste:** During a Babylonian incursion about 552 B.C. The Edomites who survived were later driven from their native lands by the Nabateans. **his hill country:** The Edomites lived in the highlands south of the Dead Sea. For prophecies against Edom, see Jer 49:7–22; Ezek 25:12–14; Obad 1–21. • Edom's judgment in history is not a sign of its damnation in eternity. The Catholic Church teaches that God predestines no one to hell because he forces no one to reject him or his offer of salvation. His eternal plan includes each person's free response to his grace (CCC 600, 1037).

1:4 the LORD of hosts: A title for the Lord as commander of the heavenly armies of angels (Josh 5:14) and the military forces of Israel (1 Sam 17:45). This title is used more frequently in Malachi than in any other book of the Bible. **the people ... angry for ever:** What people will say about the Edomites after witnessing the Lord's stern judgment. The statement is about their future reputation, not their divine reprobation.

1:5 Great ... beyond ... Israel: God shows himself the Lord of all nations by judging not just the Israelites but neighboring peoples such as the Edomites.

1:6–2:9 The second disputation: (1) the Lord charges Temple priests with despising his name, (2) the priests ask for proof, and (3) God points to the evidence of their blemished sacrifices and their failure to instruct the people in the commandments of the Torah.

1:6 I am a father: The Lord is a Father to Israel by covenant (Is 64:8; Jer 31:9), and Israel as a nation is his first-born son (Ex 4:22; Sir 36:12) (CCC 238–40). See notes on Wis 14:3 and Is 63:16. **I am a master:** God is a mighty Lord (Heb., *adônîm*) who is worthy of reverent obedience. **my name:** Despised by violations of the covenant. The Lord's holy name should instead be honored as great (1:11), feared (1:14), given glory (2:2), and held in awe (2:5).

1:7 polluted: Unlawful and thus unacceptable. **the Lord's table:** The bronze altar of sacrifice in the Temple courtyard (Ex 38:1–7). Because food portions of grain and meat were burned on the altar hearth and ascended to the Lord, it was called his "table" (1:12; Ezek 41:22). Even so,

---

The name Malachi (Malachias) merely means "my messenger," and the book is probably anonymous. Its contents suggest that the historical context is the period of Ezra and Nehemiah. The theme is the love of God for his people in spite of their backsliding. Both priests and people are guilty of not offering a clean sacrifice—and in 1:11 is the prophecy of the universal sacrifice, relating evidently to Messianic times. The prophet also denounces marriages with Gentiles and the practice of divorce. He goes on to proclaim the "day of the LORD," "great and terrible." Like many prophets, he does not distinguish between the first and second coming.

[a] Or *my messenger.*

Need to offer the best

you say, 'How have we polluted it?'ᵇ By thinking that the LORD's table may be despised. ⁸When you offer blind animals in sacrifice, is that no evil? And when you offer those that are lame or sick, is that no evil? Present that to your governor; will he be pleased with you or show you favor? says the LORD of hosts. ⁹And now entreat the favor of God, that he may be gracious to us. With such a gift from your hand, will he show favor to any of you? says the LORD of hosts. ¹⁰Oh, that there were one among you who would shut the doors, that you might not kindle fire upon my altar in vain! I have no pleasure in you, says the LORD of hosts, and I will not accept an offering from your hand. ¹¹For from the rising of the sun to its setting my name is great among the nations, and in every place incense is offered to my name, and a pure offering; for my name is great among the nations, says the LORD of hosts. ¹²But you profane it when you say that the LORD's table

is polluted, and the food for itᶜ may be despised. ¹³'What a weariness this is,' you say, and you sniff at me,ᵈ says the LORD of hosts. You bring what has been taken by violence or is lame or sick, and this you bring as your offering! Shall I accept that from your hand? says the LORD. ¹⁴Cursed be the cheat who has a male in his flock, and vows it, and yet sacrifices to the Lord what is blemished; for I am a great King, says the LORD of hosts, and my name is feared among the nations.

2 "And now, O priests, this command is for you. ²If you will not listen, if you will not lay it to heart to give glory to my name, says the LORD of hosts, then I will send the curse upon you and I will curse your blessings; indeed I have already cursed them, because you do not lay it to heart. ³Behold, I will rebuke your offspring, and spread dung upon your faces, the dung of your offerings, and I will put you out of my presence.ᵉ ⁴So shall you know that I

Israel was cautioned against thinking that God was hungry or needed food (Ps 50:12–13). • Paul uses this language when he speaks of the Eucharistic altar as "the table of the Lord", indicating that he views the Christian celebration of the Lord's Supper, later called the Mass, not only as a meal but as an act of sacrifice (1 Cor 10:21).

1:8 blind ... lame: The Mosaic Law forbids any animal having a physical defect or disability from being offered as a sacrifice (Lev 22:17–25; Deut 15:21; 17:1). It was the responsibility of the priests to inspect the people's offerings to determine if they were suitable for sacrifice (Lev 10:10). The idea is that God is worthy of our best gifts and presenting him with defective gifts is an offense to him. Withholding our best from the Lord reveals that a sacrilegious attitude of contempt has taken root in our hearts (cf. Gen 4:3–7). **your governor:** A Persian-appointed official in charge of Judah. If an earthly ruler is displeased by his subjects offering damaged goods as tribute, the Lord, who deserves infinitely more reverence, is even more insulted by this.

1:10 shut the doors: The Lord would prefer a closed Temple where no worship takes place to one that dishonors him with blemished sacrifices.

1:11 from the rising ... to its setting: A spatial idiom meaning "from east to west" (Ps 50:1; 113:3; Is 41:25; 45:6; 59:19). It may also have a temporal significance: "from dawn to dusk". **incense:** Or "an oblation". Incense was burned on an altar in front of the Temple's inner-most chamber, the most holy place (Ex 30:1–10). Its billows of fragrant smoke symbolized the prayers of God's people rising before him (Ps 141:2; Rev 8:3–4). **in every place:** An expression used in Deuteronomy to prohibit sacrificial worship outside the precincts of Israel's central sanctuary in Jerusalem (Deut 12:13–14). Malachi, with prophetic foresight, looks beyond the horizons of the Deuteronomic covenant to an expiration of this restriction of sacrifice to one location. He envisions the world of nations beyond Israel praising the **name** of the Lord and sacrificing to him a **pure offering**—the very opposite of the polluted offerings of the prophet's own day (1:7). Gentiles worshiping the God of Israel is a prophetic expectation here and elsewhere in the OT (e.g., Is 2:2–3; 19:19–21; 56:6–7;

66:18–21; Zeph 3:9–10; Zech 8:20–23; 14:16). **is offered:** Or "will be offered". • Christian tradition reads 1:11 as a prophecy of the Eucharistic liturgy, which makes the one perfect sacrifice of Christ present on the Church's altars throughout the world (CCC 1330). Its words thus appear in the Roman Canon of the Mass: "so that from the rising of the sun to its setting a pure sacrifice may be offered to your name" (Eucharistic Prayer III). • Speaking of the sacrifices that we Gentiles offer up to God in every place, that is, the bread and cup of the Eucharist, the prophet affirms that we glorify his name (St. Justin Martyr, *Dialogue with Trypho* 41). With bread and wine, Melchizedek, priest of the Most High God, prefigured Christ, the true arch-priest. This bread, also typified by the bread of the Presence, is clearly the pure and unbloody sacrifice that the Lord said would be offered to him from the sun's rising to its setting (St. John of Damascus, *Orthodox Faith* 4, 13).

1:13 weariness: The service of worship has become a tiresome burden to the priests. **sniff at me:** An unholy attitude of indifference or even disdain.

1:14 Cursed: Subject to the punitive judgments triggered by breaking the Lord's covenant (Deut 28:15–68). **the cheat:** One who publicly vows to sacrifice an unblemished male but secretly switches animals and offers a defective substitute. This insincerity is seen by God, even if it escapes the notice of others. **great King:** Mighty suzerains were addressed by this title in ancient Near Eastern treaty covenants.

2:1–9 A final warning for the Temple priests: they must repent and realign themselves with the covenant or face the curses of the covenant that God sends upon the disobedient.

2:2 I will curse your blessings: The blessings that priests pronounce upon others will be rendered ineffective (Lev 9:22; Num 6:23–27).

2:3 dung: Not only feces but also the contents of an animal's stomach and intestines. This was normally burned as refuse outside the camp of Israel (Ex 29:14; Lev 4:11–12).

2:4 my covenant with Levi: The ministry of sacred worship bestowed as a "blessing" on the tribe of Levi after they put down the golden calf rebellion at Mt. Sinai (Ex 32:29; Deut 33:8–11). It included the gift of a "perpetual priesthood" to Aaron, his sons, and his grandson Phinehas (Ex 40:15; Num 25:13) and the secondary order of Levites to serve as assistants to the Aaronic priests in the sanctuary (Num 8:14–19; 18:1–7). This arrangement of priestly mediation in worship is also called a "covenant" in Neh 13:29; Sir 45:7; Jer 33:21. See essay: *Priesthood in the Old Testament* at Num 18.

ᵇGk: Heb *you.*
ᶜHeb *its fruit, its food.*
ᵈAnother reading is *it.*
ᵉCn Compare Gk Syr: Heb *and he shall bear you to it.*

have sent this command to you, that my covenant with Levi may hold, says the LORD of hosts. [5]My covenant with him was a covenant of life and peace, and I gave them to him, that he might fear; and he feared me, he stood in awe of my name. [6]True instruction[f] was in his mouth, and no wrong was found on his lips. He walked with me in peace and uprightness, and he turned many from iniquity. [7]For the lips of a priest should guard knowledge, and men should seek instruction[f] from his mouth, for he is the messenger of the LORD of hosts. [8]But you have turned aside from the way; you have caused many to stumble by your instruction;[f] you have corrupted the covenant of Levi, says the LORD of hosts, [9]and so I make you despised and abased before all the people, inasmuch as you have not kept my ways but have shown partiality in your instruction."[f]

The Covenant Profaned by Judah

10 Have we not all one father? Has not one God created us? Why then are we faithless to one another, profaning the covenant of our fathers? [11]Judah has been faithless, and abomination has been committed in Israel and in Jerusalem; for Judah has profaned the sanctuary of the LORD, which he loves, and has married the daughter of a foreign god. [12]May the LORD cut off from the tents of Jacob, for the man who does this, any to witness[g] or answer, or to bring an offering to the LORD of hosts!

13 And this again you do. You cover the LORD's altar with tears, with weeping and groaning because he no longer regards the offering or accepts it with favor at your hand. [14]You ask, "Why does he not?" Because the LORD was witness to the covenant between you and the wife of your youth, to whom you have been faithless, though she is your companion and your wife by covenant. [15]Has not the one God made[h] and sustained for us the spirit of life? And what does he desire?[i] Godly offspring. So take heed to yourselves, and let none be faithless to the wife of his youth. [16]"For I hate[j] divorce, says the LORD the God of Israel,

---

2:5 covenant of . . . peace: The covenant of high priesthood granted to Aaron's grandson Phinehas was called a "covenant of peace" (Num 25:12; Sir 45:24). **he feared me:** Levi, whose descendants at the time of the Exodus were zealous for the Lord (Ex 32:25–28; Num 25:11; Deut 33:9).

2:7 instruction from his mouth: Religious instruction in Israel was the responsibility of the Aaronic priests (Lev 10:11; Deut 33:10; Ezra 7:10).

2:8 caused many to stumble: The priests, by setting bad examples and failing to teach others the Lord's commands, were causes of scandal and covenant violation (cf. Ezek 44:12; CCC 2284–87).

2:9 partiality: Favoritism shown for the benefit of some and the detriment of others. Partiality in the administration of justice was forbidden by the Mosaic Law (Lev 19:15; Deut 16:19). God himself is the perfect standard of impartiality (Deut 10:17; Rom 2:11).

2:10–16 The third disputation: (1) Malachi asks why Judah profanes the covenant, **(2)** the people ask why God does not look with favor upon their offerings, and **(3)** the prophet responds that the Lord is displeased with their marital practices. Malachi thus turns from rebuking corrupt priests in 1:6—2:9 to addressing the people of Judah in general.

2:10 one father: By covenant the Lord became the Father of Israel (Deut 32:6) and the Israelites became his sons and daughters (Deut 14:1). See note on 1:6. **God created us:** Israel was fashioned by the Lord as a new vessel is made out of clay (Is 64:8). **covenant of our fathers:** The Mosaic covenant, by which Israel became a holy nation (Ex 19:6) and God's adoptive family through a symbolic blood ceremony (Ex 24:8).

2:11 abomination: Intermarriage with non-Jews. **the daughter of a foreign god:** The people of Judah formed interreligious marriages with women from outside the covenant community who served deities other than the Lord. This was forbidden by the Torah, lest the purity of Israel's faith and life be contaminated with idolatrous influences (Ex 34:15–16; Deut 7:3). Ezra and Nehemiah confronted this same problem in postexilic Judah (Ezra 9–10; Neh 13:23–27). See note on Ezra 9:2. • In the Catholic Church, marriages between baptized believers and followers of other religions (disparity of cult) are not disallowed without exception, but a dispensation is required for the marriage to be valid. The Church does not encourage these unions because of the many challenges they bring into the marital relationship, including the temptation to religious indifference (CCC 1633–35).

2:12 cut off: Severed from the covenant community. See note on Lev 7:20.

2:13 no longer regards the offering: God is displeased with the sacrifices of the people, just as he is displeased with the sacrifices of the priests (1:10).

2:14 the covenant: Marriage is not a civil contract devised by human authorities but a sacred covenant established by God that binds man and woman together for life (Ezek 16:8). Spouses bound together in a matrimonial covenant belong to one another (Song 2:16), forming a "one flesh" union (Gen 2:24) that demands mutual fidelity and excludes intimacy with others as adultery (Ex 20:14; Lev 20:10). In the OT, marriage is a reflection of the covenant between the Lord and Israel (Is 54:5–8; Hos 1–3). In the NT, it is a sacramental sign of Christ's covenant with the Church as his bride (2 Cor 11:2; Eph 5:22–33; Rev 19:7–9) (CCC 1612, 1642). **you have been faithless:** Suggests that men were divorcing their Jewish wives in order to marry Gentile women (2:11). **your companion:** Marriage is a holy partnership between persons of equal dignity who provide mutual help to one another (Gen 2:18).

2:15 Godly offspring: Having and raising children in the fear of the Lord is one of the primary purposes of marriage and a sign of God's blessing (Gen 1:28; Deut 6:6–7; Ps 128:1–4; CCC 1652–54).

2:16 I hate divorce: Literally, "he hates sending away". In Deuteronomic law, marriages were terminated when a husband sent his wife away from his home with a certificate of divorce (Deut 24:1–4; Sir 25:26). Malachi asserts, however, that divorce is directly contrary to God's ideal plan for marriage. • The standard for marriage at creation was lifelong monogamy (Gen 2:24); it was only later, after the people of Israel had fallen repeatedly into sin, that divorce was permitted—and even then it was regulated so that a man could not divorce and remarry the same woman multiple times (Deut 24:1–4). Jesus restored marriage to God's original intent by

---

[f] Or *law.*
[g] Cn Compare Gk: Heb *arouse.*
[h] Or *has he not made one?*
[i] Cn: Heb *and a remnant of spirit was his.*
[j] Cn: Heb *he hates.*

and covering one's garment with violence, says the LORD of hosts. So take heed to yourselves and do not be faithless."

17 You have wearied the LORD with your words. Yet you say, "How have we wearied him?" By saying, "Every one who does evil is good in the sight of the LORD, and he delights in them." Or by asking, "Where is the God of justice?"

The Coming Messenger

3 "Behold, I send my messenger to prepare the way before me, and the Lord whom you seek will suddenly come to his temple; the messenger of the covenant in whom you delight, behold, he is coming, says the LORD of hosts. ²But who can endure the day of his coming, and who can stand when he appears?

"For he is like a refiner's fire and like fullers' soap; ³he will sit as a refiner and purifier of silver, and he will purify the sons of Levi and refine them like gold and silver, till they present right offerings to the LORD. ⁴Then the offering of Judah and Jerusalem

will be pleasing to the LORD as in the days of old and as in former years.

5 "Then I will draw near to you for judgment; I will be a swift witness against the sorcerers, against the adulterers, against those who swear falsely, against those who oppress the hireling in his wages, the widow and the orphan, against those who thrust aside the sojourner, and do not fear me, says the LORD of hosts.

God Must Not Be Robbed

6 "For I the LORD do not change; therefore you, O sons of Jacob, are not consumed. ⁷From the days of your fathers you have turned aside from my statutes and have not kept them. Return to me, and I will return to you, says the LORD of hosts. But you say, 'How shall we return?' ⁸Will man rob God? Yet you are robbing me. But you say, 'How are we robbing you?' In your tithes and offerings. ⁹You are cursed with a curse, for you are robbing me; the whole nation of you. ¹⁰Bring the full tithes

---

3:1: Mt 11:10; Mk 1:2; Lk 1:17, 76; 7:27.   **3:2:** Rev 6:17

---

repealing the Mosaic permission and declaring that divorce and remarriage is adultery (Mk 10:2–12; Lk 16:18). Divorce and remarriage, disallowed under the New Covenant, was only allowed under the Old Covenant as a temporary concession to Israel's "hardness of heart" (Mt 19:8). See essay: *Jesus on Marriage and Divorce* at Mt 19. **violence:** Divorce is equivalent to a husband taking hostile action against his wife.

2:17—3:5 The fourth disputation: **(1)** Malachi charges Judah with wearying the Lord, **(2)** the people ask for proof, **(3)** the prophet quotes cynics who claim that God is unjust in allowing evil to go unpunished, and **(4)** he foretells that, to the contrary, the Lord is coming with justice as a purging fire.

2:17 wearied: The Lord is burdened by the iniquity of his people (Is 43:24). **he delights in them:** The wicked seem to prosper without God's intervention or opposition (3:15). This is a frequent complaint in the Bible (Job 21:7–16; Ps 73:1–14; Jer 5:26–29; Hab 1:4).

3:1 my messenger: Identified in 4:5 as "Elijah", the great prophet who worked miracles and spoke out against religious corruption in northern Israel (1 Kings 18–21). His mission is to make Israel ready for the Lord's coming by returning the people to **covenant** obedience and restoring family unity (4:6). For the sins in Israel in need of correction, see 3:5. • Jesus identifies John the Baptist, his forerunner and herald, as the messenger of Malachi's prophecy (Mt 11:10–14; Lk 7:27). John signals his acceptance of this role by wearing "a garment of camel's hair" with "a leather belt around his waist" (Mt 3:4), just as Elijah wore "a garment of haircloth, with a belt of leather about his loins" (2 Kings 1:8). Jesus' interpretation of the prophecy indicates **(1)** that Malachi foresaw, not the return of Elijah himself, but a figure who comes "in the spirit and power of Elijah" (Lk 1:17), and **(2)** that Jesus is the divine Lord for whom these preparations are made (Phil 2:11). See note on 4:5. **prepare the way:** By the removal of obstacles, as when a road is made smooth to prepare for the visit of a king or dignitary (Is 40:2–3). **the Lord whom you seek:** The "God of justice" (2:17). **his temple:** In Jerusalem.

3:2 the day: A coming day of "judgment" (3:5), known as "the great and awesome day of the LORD" (4:5). See word study: *The Day of the LORD* at Joel 1:15.

3:3 refiner and purifier: A metallurgist who removes impurities from silver and gold by a process of smelting. **the sons of**

Levi: Priests and Levites, who were rebuked by the prophet in 1:6—2:9 for offering blemished sacrifices. **right offerings:** Literally, "an offering in righteousness". This may be a reference to the "pure offering" of 1:11.

3:5 sorcerers: Practitioners of black magic and divination (Deut 18:10). **adulterers:** Adultery was a capital crime in Israel (Lev 20:10). **swear falsely:** A form of taking the Lord's name in vain (Ex 20:7; Ps 24:4). **oppress:** By withholding wages (Deut 24:14–15). **do not fear me:** The problem behind all of the covenant violations listed.

3:6–12 The fifth disputation: **(1)** the Lord promises to bless his people if they repent, **(2)** the people ask how they should repent, and **(3)** the Lord calls for prompt observance of the Mosaic tithing laws.

3:6 I ... do not change: Affirms the immutability of God, whose unchangeable nature and character are manifested historically in his relentless fidelity to the covenant (Ps 89:34). Even when his people are unfaithful, God continues to be faithful because he cannot deny himself (2 Tim 2:13) (CCC 212). • God is entirely immutable. He is pure act without any potentiality, and everything that undergoes change has potentiality. It is therefore impossible for God to be changeable in any way (St. Thomas Aquinas, *Summa Theologiae* I, 9, 1). **therefore you ... are not consumed:** Inasmuch as the Lord is forever merciful, gracious, and forgiving (Ex 34:6–7).

3:7 Return to me ... return to you: Repentance is a condition for the restoration of God's favor (Zech 1:3; Jas 4:8). See word study: *Return* at Jer 3:1.

3:8 rob God? : Failure to give the Lord what he is owed amounts to stealing from him. **tithes:** A tenth of one's income (Gen 28:22). The Mosaic Law decreed that ten percent of one's yearly harvest and livestock belonged to the Lord (Lev 27:30); it was given to support priests and Levites, who had no land inheritance in Israel (Num 18:21–32; Deut 14:28–29).

3:9 You are cursed: Disobedience to the covenant, fueled by a failure to trust in God, resulted in meager food harvests, perhaps owing to pestilence, drought, or locust infestations (Deut 28:18, 22–24, 38–39).

3:10 the storehouse: A storage room in the Temple (2 Chron 31:11–12; Neh 10:38). **put me to the test:** Testing the

into the storehouse, that there may be food in my house; and thereby put me to the test, says the LORD of hosts, if I will not open the windows of heaven for you and pour down for you an overflowing blessing. ¹¹I will rebuke the devourer[k] for you, so that it will not destroy the fruits of your soil; and your vine in the field shall not fail to bear, says the LORD of hosts. ¹²Then all nations will call you blessed, for you will be a land of delight, says the LORD of hosts.

13 "Your words have been stout against me, says the LORD. Yet you say, 'How have we spoken against you?' ¹⁴You have said, 'It is vain to serve God. What is the good of our keeping his charge or of walking as in mourning before the LORD of hosts? ¹⁵Henceforth we deem the arrogant blessed; evildoers not only prosper but when they put God to the test they escape.'"

The Reward of Those Who Fear the Lord

16 Then those who feared the LORD spoke with one another; the LORD heeded and heard them, and a book of remembrance was written before him of those who feared the LORD and thought on his name.

¹⁷"They shall be mine, says the LORD of hosts, my special possession on the day when I act, and I will spare them as a man spares his son who serves him. ¹⁸Then once more you shall distinguish between the righteous and the wicked, between one who serves God and one who does not serve him.

The Great Day of the Lord

4 ¹"For behold, the day comes, burning like an oven, when all the arrogant and all evildoers will be stubble; the day that comes shall burn them up, says the LORD of hosts, so that it will leave them neither root nor branch. ²But for you who fear my name the sun of righteousness shall rise, with healing in its wings. You shall go forth leaping like calves from the stall. ³And you shall tread down the wicked, for they will be ashes under the soles of your feet, on the day when I act, says the LORD of hosts.

4 "Remember the law of my servant Moses, the statutes and ordinances that I commanded him at Horeb for all Israel.

5 "Behold, I will send you Eli'jah the prophet before the great and awesome day of the LORD

4:5: Mt 17:11; Mk 9:12.

Lord is generally forbidden (Deut 6:16) except under special circumstances determined by the Lord or his prophets (as in 1 Kings 18:22–40; Is 7:11). The challenge put to Malachi's generation: be generous with God as the Law commands, and God will show himself generous in return, causing the agriculture of the land to prosper. **overflowing blessing:** Obedience to the covenant unleashes its blessings upon flocks and fields (Deut 28:1–14). **the windows of heaven:** The channels of abundant rainfall according to the cosmic poetry of the Bible (Gen 7:11–12).

3:11 the devourer: Probably a reference to the locust, a voracious menace to field crops, vineyards, and orchards. See note on Joel 1:4.

3:13—4:3 The sixth disputation: (1) the Lord charges people in Judah with speaking against him, (2) the accused demand an example, (3) their complaint that serving God is vain is cited as evidence, and (4) the Lord insists they are wrong—the situation will be resolved when he saves the righteous among them and comes in fiery judgment against arrogant sinners.

3:14 vain: Futile or unprofitable. This claim is disproven by God's promise to save those who fear him from the coming day of judgment (3:16–17).

3:15 evildoers ... prosper: Echoes the thought of 2:17, where cynics complain that the wicked succeed and flourish while God seems uninterested in bringing them to justice. **put God to the test:** Contrary to the warning of Deut 6:16.

3:16 a book of remembrance: The Book of Life, envisioned as a scroll kept in heaven that lists the names of those who fear God and records their praiseworthy deeds (Ps 69:28; Is 4:3; Dan 12:1; Rev 20:12).

3:17 special possession: The Hebrew *segullāh* refers to something owned and cherished. Israel was set apart as the Lord's treasured possession at Sinai in Ex 19:5, but here the promise is narrowed to a faithful remnant of Judah. See word

study: *Possession* at Deut 7:6. **his son:** Israel is the Lord's first-born son (Ex 4:22; Hos 11:1).

4:1–6 The RSV2CE follows the Latin Vulgate in making the book's final six verses into a fourth chapter. In the Hebrew MT and Greek LXX, these are considered the final verses of chapter three (= 3:19–24).

4:1 the day: Mentioned four times in the final chapter (4:1, 3, 5). See note on 3:2. **burning:** A devouring fire that consumes and destroys the wicked, as distinct from the purifying fire that refines and perfects the sons of Levi (3:3). **oven:** A furnace or incinerator. **arrogant ... evildoers:** Those whom the self-deceived considered blessed in 3:15.

4:2 the sun of righteousness: Signals the dawning of a new age. The winged sun is a symbol of life in Near Eastern iconography. • Jesus Christ, in stretching out his hands on the holy tree, unfolded two wings, the right and the left, and called all who believed in him to come to him. By the mouth of Malachi, he says: "For you who fear my name the Sun of righteousness shall arise with healing in his wings" (St. Hippolytus, *The Antichrist* 61). **healing:** From the wounds of sin (Is 53:5). **leaping:** With unbounded joy.

4:3 ashes: What remains after stubble is burned (4:1).

4:4 Remember the law: Malachi calls for faithful adherence to the Torah, which the community in Judah had been violating by offering blemished sacrifices (1:8–13, contrary to Lev 22:20–25), marrying foreign women (2:11, contrary to Deut 7:1–3), and withholding tithes from the Lord (3:8–9, contrary to Num 18:21–32). **Horeb:** Associated with Mt. Sinai, where Moses received the laws of the covenant (Deut 5:2–5). See note on Ex 3:1.

4:5 Elijah the prophet: Identified as the Lord's "messenger" in 3:1. He departed from the world and was taken up into heaven in a chariot of fire (2 Kings 2:11; 1 Mac 2:58), giving rise to the Jewish belief that he would be sent back alive before the coming of the Messiah (Mk 9:11; Babylonian Talmud, *Eruvin* 43b). See note on 3:1. • According to Jesus, the prophecy of Elijah's coming is fulfilled in John the Baptist (Mt 11:13–14), who was aware of not being Elijah in the flesh (Jn 1:21). The angel Gabriel announced that he would come "in the spirit and power of Elijah" (Lk 1:17).

---

[k] Or *devouring locust*.
[l] Ch 4:1–6 are Ch 3:19–24 in the Hebrew.

comes. ⁶And he will turn the hearts of fathers to their
children and the hearts of children to their fathers,
lest I come and strike the land with a curse."ᵐ

4:6: Lk 1:17.

4:6 turn the hearts: As translated, the expression denotes
family reconciliation, i.e., the healing of relationships between
fathers and sons, representing all family members. But if
the preposition "to" is rendered "together with", then the
expression indicates community repentance, i.e., fathers and
sons, representing both older and younger generations, are
turned back to the Lord. Other references to Elijah's mission
appear in Sir 48:10; Lk 1:17. For turning as the language of
repentance, see word study: *Return* at Jer 3:1. **the land:** Judah,
home of the postexilic community. **a curse:** A decree of utter
destruction. See word study: *Devoted* at Josh 6:17.

ᵐOr *ban of utter destruction.*

STUDY QUESTIONS
Malachi

Chapter 1

For understanding
1. **1:2.** Why do the people of Judah doubt the love of God? What is the basis of God's election of Israel as a chosen people? Quoting this passage in Rom 9:13 as a witness to God's sovereign freedom, what does Paul conclude from Malachi's words?
2. **1:3.** As a Semitic figure of speech, what does "hated" mean? How is it possible to say that Esau's descendants, the Edomites, were not loved? In this context, to what are love and hate not primarily related? When was Edom laid waste? Where did the Edomites live? Of what is Edom's judgment in history not regarded as a sign? Why does the Catholic Church teach that God predestines no one to hell?
3. **1:7.** About what polluted food is the Lord speaking? What is the Lord's table? Why was it called his "table"? Even so, what was Israel cautioned against thinking? Speaking of the Eucharistic altar as "the table of the Lord", what does Paul's language indicate?
4. **1:8.** What kind of animal does the Mosaic Law forbid to be used for sacrifice? Who would inspect the people's offerings to determine if they were suitable for sacrifice? Since God is worthy of our best gifts and presenting him with defective gifts is an offense to him, what attitude does withholding our best from the Lord reveal? If an earthly ruler is displeased by his subjects offering damaged goods as tribute, what does that say about the Lord?

For application
1. **1:2–3.** Have you ever questioned God's love for you? For example, how do you respond when you notice that a fellow Catholic has more spiritual gifts than you do? Or when your prayers seem to go unanswered? Or when you sin grievously and feel that you are too wicked to be forgiven? How have you resolved such questions?
2. **1:6a.** How have you showed honor to your biological father? Whether your relationship with your father was excellent or difficult, or even nonexistent, how have those circumstances colored your relationship with persons in authority over you? How do they affect your relationship with God the Father?
3. **1:7b.** In 1 Cor 11:17–22, Paul lists several abuses around the table of the Lord and recommends solutions in vv. 27–34. How would you apply these verses to respect for the Eucharist as practiced in your parish? In your family? Within your own heart? Of what do you need to repent, and how can you model true respect?
4. **1:11.** As stated in the note for this verse, the Mass is a sacrifice. In the Eucharistic sacrifice, what is offered? How is it offered? Who participates in this offering? Who benefits by it (cf. CCC 1362–72)?

Chapter 2

For understanding
1. **2:4.** What is the Lord's covenant with Levi? What gift does it include? Where else is this arrangement of priestly mediation in worship called a "covenant"?
2. **2:9.** What is partiality? In what activity was it forbidden by the Law of Moses? Who is the perfect standard of impartiality?
3. **2:14.** If marriage is not a civil contract devised by human authorities, what is it? What does it mean for spouses to be bound together by a matrimonial covenant? In the OT, of what covenant is marriage a reflection? In the NT, of what is it a sacramental sign? What does the faithlessness of Israelite men suggest? What does the role of the wife as "your companion" suggest about marriage?
4. **2:16.** What is the literal wording of the translation "I hate divorce"? In Deuteronomic law, when were marriages terminated? What does Malachi assert, however? Although the standard for marriage at creation was lifelong monogamy, when was divorce permitted, and how was it regulated? How did Jesus restore marriage to God's original intent? Why was divorce and remarriage, disallowed under the New Covenant, allowed under the Old Covenant? To what is divorce equivalent?

For application
1. **2:5–7.** Whom would you consider your favorite preacher or religious teacher? What impresses you about him? How does that person's instruction build and confirm your faith? What would you like to imitate as you provide instruction?
2. **2:11.** Read the note for this verse. What advice does Paul give to Christians who are married to unbaptized spouses (1 Cor 7:12–14)? What is religious indifference? Why is religious indifference spiritually dangerous within a marriage between baptized and unbaptized persons? In granting a dispensation for such a marriage, what stipulations might a bishop place on the Catholic partner?
3. **2:15.** What does Malachi state as a reason for marital fidelity? According to the *Catechism*, what is the twofold end of marriage (CCC 2363)? Why can these ends not be separated?
4. **2:17.** Who nowadays says that "everyone who does evil is good in the sight of the Lord, and he delights in them"? What possible truth might there be in that assertion? How do you answer a person who says that a loving God would never consign anyone to eternal punishment?

Chapter 3

For understanding
1. **3:1.** With whom is "my messenger" identified? What is his mission? Whom does Jesus identify as the messenger of Malachi's prophecy? How did John signal his acceptance of this role? What does Jesus' interpretation of the prophecy indicate? How does the messenger prepare the way? Who is the "Lord whom you seek"?

2. **3:6.** How is the immutability of God manifested? Even when his people are unfaithful, why does God continue to be faithful? According to St. Thomas Aquinas, why is God entirely immutable? Why are the Israelites not consumed as a result?
3. **3:8.** By what means does one rob God? What is a tithe? What did the Mosaic Law decree about one's yearly harvest and livestock, and for what was it used?
4. **3:10.** What is "the storehouse"? Although testing the Lord is generally forbidden, how might it be allowed? What was the challenge put to Malachi's generation? What does obedience to the covenant unleash? What are the "windows of heaven"?

For application
1. **3:2–3.** What might these verses have to do with the doctrine of Purgatory? What is the purpose of Purgatory? What sin might someone be committing who is content with going to Purgatory rather than preparing in advance for heaven?
2. **3:8.** What are the precepts of the Church (CCC 2041–43)? Why does the Church impose these precepts? Although the Church has no positive stipulation about tithing, what does the fifth precept state Catholics are obliged to do?
3. **3:10.** How much of your annual income do you give to the Church? If you do not tithe a full ten percent, what prevents you? How willing would you be to take up Malachi's wager?
4. **3:14–15.** How do the psalms address the objection of Malachi's audience (e.g., Ps 37)? What solution do they recommend for the devout Christian? Why does Jesus say that those who mourn are blessed (Mt 5:4)?

Chapter 4

For understanding
1. **4:2.** What does the dawning of the sun of righteousness signal? In Near Eastern iconography, of what is the winged sun a symbol? According to St. Hippolytus quoting this verse, how does Jesus act as that sun? What healing is offered? What does the image of calves leaping from the stall suggest?
2. **4:4.** How had the community in Judah been violating the Torah? With what mountain is Horeb associated?
3. **4:5.** With whom is Elijah the prophet identified? To what Jewish belief did his departure from the world and assumption into heaven give rise? According to Jesus, how is the prophecy of Elijah's coming fulfilled? How did the angel Gabriel announce that Elijah would come?
4. **4:6.** As translated, what does the expression "turn the hearts" denote? But if the preposition "to" is rendered "together with", then what does the expression indicate? To what "land" does the text refer?

For application
1. **4:2.** How might the rising of the "sun of righteousness" refer to the action of the Holy Spirit? When people pray for the Spirit to "set their hearts on fire", for what are they praying? What changes should they begin to notice in their lives?
2. **4:4.** What does the word "remember" in this verse call on you to do? Can you list the Ten Commandments from memory? Which of these did Jesus remind the rich young man to keep (Mk 10:19)? Why do you think Jesus did not mention the first three commandments?
3. **4:6.** In our culture, what happens when fathers abandon their children and children despise their fathers? How does the turning of the hearts of fathers and children toward each other signify the beginning of a new creation?

BOOKS OF THE BIBLE

THE OLD TESTAMENT (OT)

Gen	Genesis
Ex	Exodus
Lev	Leviticus
Num	Numbers
Deut	Deuteronomy
Josh	Joshua
Judg	Judges
Ruth	Ruth
1 Sam	1 Samuel
2 Sam	2 Samuel
1 Kings	1 Kings
2 Kings	2 Kings
1 Chron	1 Chronicles
2 Chron	2 Chronicles
Ezra	Ezra
Neh	Nehemiah
Tob	Tobit
Jud	Judith
Esther	Esther
Job	Job
Ps	Psalms
Prov	Proverbs
Eccles	Ecclesiastes
Song	Song of Solomon
Wis	Wisdom
Sir	Sirach (Ecclesiasticus)
Is	Isaiah
Jer	Jeremiah
Lam	Lamentations
Bar	Baruch
Ezek	Ezekiel
Dan	Daniel
Hos	Hosea
Joel	Joel
Amos	Amos
Obad	Obadiah
Jon	Jonah
Mic	Micah
Nahum	Nahum
Hab	Habakkuk
Zeph	Zephaniah
Hag	Haggai
Zech	Zechariah
Mal	Malachi
1 Mac	1 Maccabees
2 Mac	2 Maccabees

THE NEW TESTAMENT (NT)

Mt	Matthew
Mk	Mark
Lk	Luke
Jn	John
Acts	Acts of the Apostles
Rom	Romans
1 Cor	1 Corinthians
2 Cor	2 Corinthians
Gal	Galatians
Eph	Ephesians
Phil	Philippians
Col	Colossians
1 Thess	1 Thessalonians
2 Thess	2 Thessalonians
1 Tim	1 Timothy
2 Tim	2 Timothy
Tit	Titus
Philem	Philemon
Heb	Hebrews
Jas	James
1 Pet	1 Peter
2 Pet	2 Peter
1 Jn	1 John
2 Jn	2 John
3 Jn	3 John
Jude	Jude
Rev	Revelation (Apocalypse)